CLINTON IN EXILE

Also by Carol Felsenthal

CITIZEN NEWHOUSE:
PORTRAIT OF A MEDIA MERCHANT

POWER, PRIVILEGE, AND THE POST:
THE KATHARINE GRAHAM STORY

PRINCESS ALICE:
THE LIFE AND TIMES OF
ALICE ROOSEVELT LONGWORTH

THE SWEETHEART OF THE SILENT MAJORITY:
THE BIOGRAPHY OF PHYLLIS SCHLAFLY

CLINTON IN EXILE

A President Out of the White House

CAROL FELSENTHAL

WILLIAM MORROW

An Imprint of HarperCollinsPublishers

Grateful acknowledgment is made to the following for the photographs appearing in the insert:
Page 1: AP Photo/Sharon Farmer, top; AP Photo/J. Scott Applewhite, bottom. Page 2: Reuters, top; AP Photo/Stephen Chernin, bottom. Page 3: AP Photo/Wilfredo Lee. Page 4: Reprinted through the courtesy of the Editors of Time Magazine © 2008 Time Inc., top; AP Photo/Ron Edmonds, bottom. Page 5: AFP Photo/Timothy A Clary. Page 6: AP Photo/Mike Derer, top; CBS/Landov, bottom. Page 7: AP Photo/Haraz N. Ghanbari. Page 8: Reuters/Chip East, top; Jeff Christensen/Reuters/Landov, bottom. Page 9: Reuters/Tim Shaffer, top; AP Photo/Lawrence Jackson, bottom. Page 10: Reuters/Jonathan Ernst, top; AP Photo/Gerald Herbert, bottom. Page 11: AP Photo/CP, Tom Hanson, top; AP Photo/Steve Lawrence, middle; Hofstra University/Brian Ballweg, bottom. Page 12: Reuters/Ric Feld/Pool/Landov, top; Jason Reed/UPI/Landov, bottom. Page 13: Stephen Hilger/Bloomberg News/Landov, top; Brittney Blair, bottom. Page 14: David Scull/Bloomberg News/Landov, top; Dana Mixer/Bloomberg News/Landov, bottom. Page 15: Reuters/Jim Young, top; Jake A. Herrle/UPI/Landov, middle; Reuters/Chip East, bottom. Page 16: AP Photo/Frank Franklin II.

HarperCollins books may be purchased for educational, business, or sales promotional use. For information please write: Special Markets Department, HarperCollins Publishers, 10 East 53rd Street, New York, NY 10022.

FIRST EDITION

Designed by Lovedog Studio

Library of Congress Cataloging-in-Publication Data has been applied for.

ISBN 978-0-06-123159-9

08 09 10 11 12 WBC/RRD 10 9 8 7 6 5 4 3 2 1

*For my husband, Steve,
and my children, Rebecca, Julia, and Daniel*

CONTENTS

CLINTON IN EXILE

Chapter 1

OH, FOR JUST
ONE MORE TERM

HOURS BEFORE HE WOULD HAND OVER THE WHITE House to George W. Bush, Bill Clinton was pulling an all-nighter. He was known for sleeping only a few hours a night even during the calmest of times, but this evening, he was outdoing himself.

He would most certainly have run for the presidency again—if it weren't for the constitutional ban on third terms—and even after the Monica Lewinsky scandal and the humiliating impeachment, he would have won.[1] He had survived scandal after scandal since late 1991 when he launched his improbable run at the White House, and yet, when his second term ended on January 20, 2001, his approval ratings hit 66 percent.[2] Even Republicans who wondered how such a brilliant, empathetic man could be so lacking in basic morality understood that, as president, William Jefferson Clinton had shown just how good he could be. As president, he had eliminated the deficit, coaxed through welfare reform, and presided over years of peace and prosperity.

Jim Guy Tucker, who had competed with Clinton in Arkansas politics (usually landing on the losing side), succeeded him as governor of the state but ended up in prison, tangled in the Clinton-era Whitewater scandal. Nonetheless, Tucker recognizes that Clinton tops the pyramid of ultragifted politicians. He compares him to all-pro NFL Hall of Famer Lance Allworth, who had played for the University of Arkansas. "These really talented athletes have skills that you and I don't even think about," says Tucker. "Their instincts . . . are just different and I happen to think that there are politicians who have those same unique qualities." Clinton is one of them.[3]

Mark Buell, a wealthy San Francisco businessman and generous supporter of Democrats in general and Bill and Hillary Clinton in particular, remembers the president, then in his second term, giving him and his wife, Susie Tompkins Buell, a Sunday-morning tour of the Oval Office. "I love being president," Clinton said. "I could be president twenty-nine more years."[4]

In 1999, Bill Clinton grew wistful at the prospect of moving on: "I confess that I love the job, even on the worst days." By then, more than a year after the Lewinsky scandal turned the president of the United States into a dirty joke on late-night television, there were plenty of bad days.[5]

"It was very hard for him to let go," says Melanne Verveer, First Lady Hillary Clinton's last chief of staff. "He loved being president. He loved the house. He loved his relationship with the American people. He did not leave easily."[6]

Clinton needed to savor the remaining hours, pride mixed with regret mixed with brooding over the beating his reputation had taken after he admitted that, yes, he did have sex with that woman, Ms. Lewinsky, and not only that, he had it just steps from the Oval Office.[7] He was obsessed with framing the historic impeachment that followed as a badge of honor—the right-wingers tried to force him out of office and he had held his ground and would serve until the last minute of the last day of his last term.

As happens at the close of every administration—Clinton being Clinton it was happening closer to the close of his—he was wrestling with the question of pardons and who should get them.

That afternoon of January 19, Salt Lake City mayor Rocky Anderson was in Washington for the U.S. Conference of Mayors meeting. Anderson was pushing for a commutation of a fifteen-and-a-half-year prison term for Cory Stringfellow of Salt Lake City. A first-time offender convicted of a nonviolent crime—he sold LSD—Stringfellow had served six years and earned a master's degree while in prison. He was a victim, his parents argued tirelessly, of mandatory minimum sentences.[8]

President Clinton met with the mayors, and, during the photo op, as Anderson and Clinton were shaking hands, a hundred mayors behind him waiting for their photograph with the president, "I took that opportunity," Anderson recalls, "to remind President Clinton that we had put in for this pardon and really appreciated his personal attention to it." Anderson knew this was Stringfellow's last chance.[9]

The pardon power, granted to the president in Article II of the Constitution, is subject to no one's review, not the Congress, not the courts. Clinton could have pardoned—or commuted the sentence of—a serial killer if he so chose. The framers recognized that there would be political repercussions for a chief executive who granted pardons that offended public opinion.

Anderson wasn't the only one trying to catch Clinton's attention that last day in the White House.[10] His friend Jack Quinn—until 1997, he was Clinton's White House counsel; before that he was Al Gore's chief of staff—telephoned him to push a pardon for one of his clients, commodities trader Marc Rich, a billionaire fugitive-from-American-justice.[11] Rich had fled to Switzerland in 1983, living there on loot he accumulated by trading arms to Iran. He remained there rather than face charges—brought by then U.S. attorney Rudy Giuliani—of tax evasion, racketeering, and trading with the enemy, the latter also covering illegal oil deals with Iraq.[12]

This was not the first time Jack Quinn had lobbied Clinton. During Clinton's last weeks in office, the lawyer/lobbyist plied the president with entreaties and documents. Recognizing that the window of opportunity was closing, Quinn wrote Clinton a letter dated January 5, 2001.[13] In a final push, Quinn sent two more letters on January 18 and January 19, and, according to Bill and Hillary biographer Sally Bedell Smith, Quinn had a twenty-minute meeting with Clinton early that evening.[14]

Rich had other advocates who were contacting the president, including Clinton's friend, then Israeli prime minister Ehud Barak, who, says Quinn, "had appealed to him on not less than three occasions, probably four, to do this."[15] Clinton also received a plea on Rich's behalf from Ehud Olmert, then mayor of Jerusalem, now prime minister.[16] (Not only did Marc Rich give money to the Israeli government, but at the behest of that government, he gave money to the Palestinians. One friend of Clinton's says that the Israelis asked for a pardon for Jonathan Pollard, a navy analyst convicted of spying for Israel, "many times, a hundred times." According to this man's analysis, Clinton couldn't give them Pollard, so he listened to their pleas for Rich.)[17]

The press had been promised the pardon list, but its release time was repeatedly delayed, beyond the last announced time of 9:15 P.M.[18]

Earlier that last night, at an event in the Indian Treaty Room commemorating all of Clinton's health-care achievements, Senator Ted Kennedy gave the president a hand-autographed first edition of *Profiles in Courage*, by Kennedy's brother and Clinton's hero, John Kennedy. Ted Kennedy "broke down and cried," recalls Chris Jennings, a senior health adviser in the Clinton White House.[19]

The president watched with Hillary part of a David Mamet movie, *State and Main*; he talked to friends on the telephone; he asked one of them, his master money raiser and hand-holder, Terry McAuliffe, to come over for a final White House visit. McAuliffe ended up spending the night, the two talking as Clinton packed his books to be shipped to Chappaqua, his new home in suburban New York. Hollywood producer Harry Thomason, who with his wife, Linda Bloodworth-Thomason, helped the president stage his response to the Lewinsky scandal, also slept over.[20]

With only hours remaining before his administration ended, the list of 140 pardons and commutations was finally released. On it was a pardon for his younger half brother, Roger, who had pleaded guilty in 1985 to conspiring to distribute cocaine.[21]

The president, friends say, was teary eyed that night, by turns anticipating his new life—Hillary would be taking her place as the junior senator from New York and Bill would be moving to Chappaqua—and dreading it. He was, in those final hours, replaying the highs and lows of his tenure, believing one moment that he had been a great president and would be so recognized by historians, but in darker moments understanding that impeachment would always mar his standing.

BILL CLINTON is a hedonist, a risk taker who does not worry much about consequences; one of his friends calls him, with sadness in his voice, "narcissistic and reckless."[22] But as he faced the waning hours of the dream of living in the White House, Clinton, that night, could not get out of his exhausted head the price he and the country were paying for his behavior. He knew that even those who insisted that the Supreme Court had stolen the 2000 election from Al Gore, who won the popular vote—and, they argued, would have won the electoral vote had the counting in Florida been allowed to continue—also blamed Bill Clinton. They knew, as he knew, that had their president made the last three years of his second term—the Lewinsky scandal broke on January 21, 1998—about something more elevated than a semen stain on a blue dress and about whether oral sex is sex, Gore would easily have vanquished the inexperienced, inarticulate George W. Bush, whose drunken driving arrest was revealed a week before the election.[23]

The nightmare was amplified because the relationship between the baby-boomer southerners, Clinton and Gore, had been so complementary. Before Dick Cheney, says Melanne Verveer, "Al Gore had more power and more to do as vice president than any of his predecessors."[24] Gore, who cared about the tiniest details of such issues as the environment and foreign policy, was unusually analytic and Clinton was unusually instinctive; Gore was more intellectual, but Clinton had the interpersonal skills that Gore lacked, and Gore had relationships with people in the Congress—he had served in both the House and the Senate.[25] Clinton was famously indecisive, phoning friends for their views and sometimes seeming to go with the opinion of whomever he last woke up. The vice president would put his wingtip down and force Clinton to decide. During the endless meetings over welfare reform, says one man close to Clinton, the president "asked everybody to leave except for Gore and he said, 'What do you think?' and Gore said, 'I think you should sign it.'"[26]

After Lewinsky, Gore went through the motions of being vice president, but he shifted his attention to running for president, barely mentioning Clinton as he campaigned, and, with very few exceptions, sidelining Clinton.[27] Clinton found Gore's strategy self-defeating and hurtful. Mark Buell remembers an Elton John event for Hillary's run for the Senate about three weeks before the 2000 election. Clinton was there and people at the event started screaming, "Bill, get out there and start speaking for Gore. He needs you." Buell was seated with Clinton and recalls him saying, "Well, we haven't been asked."[28]

So long as Tony Coelho, a close Clinton friend, headed Gore's campaign—Clinton's Commerce secretary, Bill Daley, replaced Coelho in June 2000—he and Clinton, behind the scenes, talked strategy, two or three times a week, sometimes in the White House. Some in the Gore camp, Coelho says, believed Clinton was a saboteur who secretly wanted Bush to win and to serve eight years. Cheney was too unhealthy to run for president; Hillary would win the Senate seat, run for reelection to prove herself, and then run for president in 2008. When Gore lost, Coelho says, these people felt that outcome was Clinton's wish all along. In an interview with Tim Russert, Sally Bedell Smith, author of a book on Bill and Hillary's relationship in the White House, mentioned that early in Bill's first term, the new president mused about eight years of Hillary following his eight years; i.e., he was playing with the notion of Hillary, not Al, as his successor.[29]

With Coelho's exit, those strategy sessions stopped. And they did not restart once Bill Daley took over. That, says Jake Siewert, Clinton's last press secretary, was a mistake. If Clinton on the stump would have turned off swing voters, as Gore's people argued, he could have been used as Coelho used him, as one of the world's greatest political strategists.[30] Clinton held Gore's victory in his hands, says Leon Panetta, Clinton's former chief of staff, if only Gore had let the master campaign in Tennessee, Arkansas, West Virginia, Florida, and New Mexico.[31] Former Democratic National Committee chief Don Fowler calls Gore's benching of Clinton "the worst self-inflicted political wound I can name." He calls Gore "self-righteous" and "the biggest Boy Scout I have ever run into in big-time politics."[32]

"I think there's a morality to Al Gore," says historian and presidential biographer Douglas Brinkley, "and I think that he actually believed in Bill Clinton." Clinton told Gore that nothing had happened between him and Lewinsky, and Gore believed him. "At that point the Gores became disillusioned that this guy wasn't honest, that he had a deep character flaw and that they were all now suffering because of it."[33] Also, says Larry Sabato, University of Virginia political scientist and writer, there were "other relationships . . . that the Gores knew about and . . . whatever you think of the Gores, they're a faithful couple and this was not the image they wanted to project."[34]

Gore's ostracizing Clinton left an enormous hole in Clinton's schedule and his confidence. Clinton was born to campaign, and, says Lynn Cutler, who was Clinton's deputy assistant for intergovernmental affairs, he was "chomping at the bit" to get out on the hustings.[35]

By election day 2000, Clinton had higher approval numbers than either Gore or Bush. Clinton was reduced to comforting himself with that and with the knowledge that Gore, whose father, a U.S. senator from Tennessee, had groomed him from birth to be president, had run a comically inept campaign.

Gore, who appeared wooden, programmed down to the color of his shirt, needed Clinton to make the sale. While crowds of people energized Clinton, they depleted Gore, who would have made a great college professor. "I'll meet Al Gore again for the first time," jokes Howard Tullman, a Clinton friend who gives generously to the Democrats.[36] A top official of the DNC in the Midwest was taking Gore from one campaign event to the next. At the end of the day, Gore tipped him—$2.[37]

Then came the nightmare of the recount, and Clinton's belief that he should have been a key player in Gore's campaign was confirmed; but the recount, which Clinton considered incompetently handled, was painful because nearly everyone in the media raised the "what if"—as in, what if Bill Clinton hadn't had sex with a twenty-one-year-old intern in the White House.

On December 13, 2000, Gore conceded to Bush. Eight days later, the president and vice president met, at Gore's request, in the Oval Office. "I've heard they had a heated discussion about the campaign and got it off their chests," says Tony Coelho.[38] "A screaming match . . . filled with profanity" is how Larry Sabato has heard it described.[39] Gore blamed Clinton for saddling him with a sex scandal and Clinton blamed Gore for not running on their record.[40]

Gore's defeat robbed Clinton of what he wanted most—a "home-run exit," in the words of Chris Jennings, who worked for Clinton for eight years in the White House.[41] Not even Hillary's clear victory for the Senate could make up for it, even though her win "really was quite difficult," says Jake Siewert. She had "to convince New Yorkers that she really was on some level a . . . New Yorker and to take an image that was pretty tarnished in the minds of a lot of swing voters and turn it on its head to become sort of an asset."[42] (A Chicagoan by birth and an Arkansan for most of her adult life, she defined the word *carpetbagger*.)

Contemplating Hillary's victory in her first run for any office made Clinton both happy and sad. Hillary was striding toward the spotlight and the gifted Bill Clinton was, by no desire of his own, moving away from it. "She was really gearing up to take the front stage," says Jake Siewert, "and he was trying to sort out what he would do with his life."[43]

Tony Coelho had faced his own problems in public office; a former House majority whip, he resigned from Congress in 1989 in the wake of controversy over profits from a junk bond deal.[44] Coelho would tell the president in his waning White House days, "You've got to believe in yourself and your abilities. . . . The country will move on and you've got to move on."[45]

The advice was good and the president was poised to take it, but move on to what? Among the suggestions he had fielded had been the presidency of Harvard, but, after Lewinsky, feelers put out for Clinton to become a mere visiting lecturer at the school had not been encouraged. (Clinton's Treasury secretary, Larry Summers, the youngest tenured professor in Harvard history, on the short list to become Harvard's president, was said to be one of those making inquiries.)[46]

There was much talk that Clinton would go to Los Angeles to head a Hollywood studio. Leon Panetta recalls not just studio head jobs being dangled, but also opportunities for Clinton to host radio and television talk shows. Both possibilities were on the table. Panetta says that Clinton did not dismiss them out of hand.[47] But even such a movie and movie-star fan as Clinton—a "star fucker," one important Democrat called him—knew such work was not appropriate.[48]

Others suggested he run to be mayor of New York, a ludicrous idea, even though he once said that the job was the second most important in the world. "I think for a few seconds he considered it," says John Catsimatidis, chief executive of the food and oil conglomerate Red Apple Group and a major financial backer of the Clintons. Catsimatidis stopped by the White House in December 2000 to make the suggestion. "He didn't rule it out as foolish the minute it was mentioned."[49]

AS HE packed the mementos of his presidency, this normally most optimistic of men knew how difficult it would be to figure out what to do next, and to settle on something that would match the good works of another former president, Jimmy Carter. Aside from raising money for his library—in 1998, he had put that task in the always open hands of Terry McAuliffe—and earning money to pay his legal bills and support his family, Clinton had only the most hazy notion of his future. He knew that it had to be something worthy, something serious, that his natural bent toward good times and late nights would have to be curbed.

Friends say that Clinton, that last night in the White House, was full of regret both for the shrunken expectations of where he would go next and for missed opportunities. He had proceeded full force on a Middle East peace plan, meeting with Yasser Arafat in the Oval Office on January 2, publicly endorsing a Palestinian state in a speech in New York on

January 7, but, in the end, he could not close the deal. (Letters he wrote urging each side to continue to push to peace were published in Israeli and Palestinian newspapers on his last day in office.)[50]

That night and into his last morning, Clinton was busy issuing executive actions; releasing funds to help cities, towns, and suburbs hire more police officers; giving Governor's Island off Manhattan national monument status; protecting from logging millions of acres of national forests; regulating ingredients in hot dogs, arsenic in drinking water, and lead in paint; and so on.[51] "We were doing quite a bit on environmental initiatives that could be done by executive order," says Jake Siewert. "There was a whole . . . effort around trying to use the executive order process to cement the legacy."[52] Many of these orders, Clinton predicted correctly, would be undone by Bush as soon as he took office; that, of course, would not have been the case had Al Gore been elected.[53]

ONCE IT was obvious that Al Gore wanted Bill Clinton out of his campaign and out of his life, Clinton had plenty of free time. For the last year or so, the man whose nightly sleep was about the length of most people's afternoon naps had hours to fill. He seemed almost lonely. Sometimes the most powerful man in the world needed a playdate. When Bill Daley was still secretary of commerce late in Clinton's second term, Daley would sometimes receive a call from the president asking him, in effect, to come over and play—to watch a movie or play golf. Daley would have to decline because he was too busy at the office.[54]

Bill Clinton watched himself become almost an afterthought, a onetime powerhouse of serious policy reduced to spending increasing time on ceremonial or social activities. On March 7, 2000, he received in the Oval Office the Clinton chapter of the American Political Items Collectors. The members had been promised fifteen minutes, but Clinton gave them forty-five. "He took us inch by inch through the Oval Office," says Phil Ross, the group's president, "explaining everything there was to explain."[55]

Around the same time, former senator and presidential candidate

George McGovern and his wife, Eleanor, were spending the night at the White House. The president organized an after-dinner game of "Oh, Hell." When one of the other guests, Steven Spielberg, boarded his jet to go home, everyone else went to bed except the McGoverns and the president, who escorted the couple to the Lincoln Bedroom. For the next two and a half hours, Clinton told them the history of the room, the people who had slept in it.[56]

Mike Medavoy, a Hollywood producer and studio head, also spent the night at the White House with his new wife, Irena, and their toddler son. With them was another Hollywood couple, Bud Yorkin—he had executive-produced *All in the Family*—his wife, Cynthia, and their two children. The president got down on his hands and knees and, says Bud Yorkin, "spent the whole night" playing with the children.[57]

In September 2000, Clinton invited Chicago supporters Lou Weisbach and his wife to stay in the Queen's Bedroom. The president kept them up talking until three in the morning. "We had to push him to bed. . . . We said, 'You must be so tired. We could talk all night but we're sure you have something to do tomorrow.'"[58]

Shortly before Clinton left office, he headlined a fund-raiser at Stefani's, Chicago restaurateur Phil Stefani's first restaurant. (Since 1994 Stefani, the son of a baker, had become a close friend of Clinton's: "He has never left one of our locations without taking a picture with every single individual who works here. . . . A dishwasher gets a picture with the president and gets to mail it back to Mexico.") At eleven in the morning, on the day of the fund-raiser, Stefani was summoned to meet the president in his suite at the O'Hare Hilton. Clinton wanted company. As the time approached for the drive into the city, Stefani headed for his car. A presidential aide interceded: "No, he wants you to drive down with him in his car."[59]

Two weeks before his term ended, Clinton invited Stefani and his wife for their first Lincoln Bedroom sleepover. They played a Scrabble-like game called Upwords. Hillary was "in the building," says Stefani, but not playing games. The president got his guests going—Stefani says he's not much of a game player himself but of course would not have refused, and he listened as the president instructed him on the rules. Clinton then announced, "I have to go and call Arafat and I'll be back." At around eleven, he returned. "Oh, you guys are playing this game?" as if it had been their idea. He mentioned that the next morning he had to be out by five to fly to Nebraska, the only state he had not visited during his two terms. "I'd love to play with you, but I've got to go to Nebraska tomorrow morning at five, but, you know, I'll play for a little while." They played until 2:30 in the morning.[60]

On January 9, 2001, en route to Chicago for a speech at an elementary school, he was riding in Marine One with Eric Holder, then acting attorney general. Holder recalls the president as "just kind of musing about the fact that he had not been used as much in the campaign as he thought he should have been. . . . He seemed more hurt . . . by that and almost struggling to figure out why it had happened."[61]

After that speech, he delivered a stem-winder at the Palmer House Hotel. He described the accomplishments of his terms and his desire to be remembered as the "champion of the 'little people.'"[62] He basked in the adoration of what veteran newsman Paul McGrath described as "the great unwashed," crowds of mostly poor people who had been ushered out of the bitter cold into the opulent, rococo lobby of the historic Loop hotel.[63]

"I wanted to come here to say goodbye and say thank you," Clinton said, as some in the crowd booed: "Look, I've got a senator to support. I'm not really saying goodbye. I'm just saying goodbye as president."[64]

From there, he met some two hundred of his friends and supporters at 437, another Stefani restaurant. Big political names—Jesse Jackson, Mayor Daley, Rahm Emanuel, Dick Durbin, Bill Daley, fresh off the Gore fiasco—were waiting. Diet Coke in hand, Clinton, who would never run for anything again, "worked this room as effectively as I've ever seen any politician work anything," said *Chicago Tribune* reporter Rick Kogan.[65]

Clinton talked longest to *Chicago Sun-Times* movie critic Richard Roeper, who later wrote about it. "It just seems like the pacing of these movies is too slow," Clinton told Roeper. "I like a lot of the films from these young directors, but I think they should exercise more discipline when they're editing." He told Roeper that they screened *Chocolat* at the White House and in attendance were the film's director and star. "And I really liked it, but even that could have used a quicker pace."[66]

One week before George W. Bush's inauguration, Bill Clinton greeted friends at Camp David for a final good-bye. Robert Torricelli, then U.S. senator from New Jersey, nicknamed "The Torch" and famous for having dated Bianca Jagger, was among them. "It was a little melancholy," he recalls, "lots of meals, movies."[67] Also there were Terry McAuliffe and his wife, Dorothy; former studio chief Frank Biondi and his wife, Carol; along with Clinton's hugely wealthy LA supporters grocery magnate Ron Burkle and Haim Saban, producer of *Mighty Morphin Power Rangers* and *Teenage Mutant Ninja Turtles*, and Saban's wife, Cheryl.[68]

McAuliffe, Hillary, and Bill excused themselves to talk to Clinton's personal attorney David Kendall, about a settlement that would remove the threat, however unlikely, that Clinton's next home could be a jail cell.

The following Friday, January 19, Clinton's last day in the White House, his lawyers and aides reached a resolution with Robert Ray, the successor to despised Special Prosecutor Kenneth Starr who had pursued the sex charges against the president with what Clinton and his friends saw as a manic, loony, partisan intensity. Until hours before he left office, Clinton had reason to fear that he could be indicted for perjury, for "misleading statements" about Monica Lewinsky in the Paula Jones sexual harassment case. (A clerk working for the state of Arkansas, Jones claimed that Clinton, then governor, summoned her to his hotel room, exposed himself, invited her to "kiss it," and touched her inappropriately. Clinton denied every detail and stated that he did not remember ever meeting her.)

Aides worked overtime to pack the president's and first lady's papers in acid-free boxes, destined for storage in Little Rock until the Clinton Library opened. As Clinton sorted through his books and mementos, stopping to tell stories about almost all of the latter,[69] reporters had been asking the incoming president, George W. Bush, if he might issue a pardon for Bill Clinton.

The deal struck with the new prosecutor was a relief, but it was also a monumental embarrassment. He had to admit, and admit it while still in office, and with no twisting of the English language that he gave "false testimony under oath." In another deal, this one with authorities in Arkansas—where he was building his library—also made just under the wire, he kept his law license, but agreed to a humiliating five-year suspension and a $25,000 fine. "I tried to walk a fine line between acting lawfully and testifying falsely, but I now recognize that I did not fully accomplish this goal and that certain of my responses to questions about Ms. Lewinsky were false."[70]

THE NIGHT of January 19, 2001, the president took a couple of catnaps but never went to sleep.

The centerpiece of the next morning—the Clintons and Gores hosting the Bushes and Cheneys for coffee—was, Clinton knew, going to be difficult. Clinton could have been posing for triumphant photos with his successor, his vice president, the man whose ascension to the Oval Office was to be Bill Clinton's legacy, his redemption, a validation of his service. Instead he would have to endure the bitterness of Al and Tipper Gore and turn over the executive branch to the Republicans.

Chapter 2

THE BEST HOUSE

INAUGURATION MORNING, SATURDAY, JANUARY 20, 2001, the *Washington Post*'s headline announced, "In a Deal, Clinton Avoids Indictment; President Admits False Testimony."[1]

With two hours left, his last weekly Saturday radio address was broadcast to the nation—he had delivered a television farewell from the Oval Office the Thursday night before—he signed off on his pardon and commutation list, strolled in the Children's Garden with Chelsea, and prepared to receive the Bushes, the Cheneys, and the Gores. While awaiting their guests, Hillary and Bill began to "sway" to "Our Love Is Here to Stay," played by the pianist who would provide background music for the coffee.[2]

Press secretary Jake Siewert describes the atmosphere as "awkward," because "Gore and Bush couldn't have felt great about each other."[3] (And then there was the matter of how Gore and Clinton, barely speaking, felt about each other.)

At 11 A.M., Bill and Hillary left the White House for the last time as president and first lady. The Clintons and Bushes climbed into one limousine and the Gores and Cheneys into another for the ride to the Capitol, where, at noon, Bush and Cheney would take the oath of office.[4]

On a cold, drizzly day, President Bush delivered his inaugural address at the West Front of the Capitol. Bill Clinton briefly dozed off, missing some of the words the new president was obviously aiming at his predecessor. "America at its best is a place where personal responsibility is valued and expected" and "Our public interest depends on private character."[5]

In the meantime, back at the temporarily vacant White House, at one second past noon came the jarring scene that signals the change from one administration to the next. The doors were opened, and scores of workers—to Sarah Wilson, a young lawyer who had worked in the Office of the White House Counsel, it seemed like "hundreds," some stationed on the lower level of the Old Executive Office Building (OEOB) with "huge rolls of carpet"—rushed in, like runners out of the starting gate. Wilson, who says she "turn[ed] off the lights" in the White House as the Clinton administration ended, describes the workers as literally "stripping" carpet, wiring, and drywall in the White House, including the Oval Office, redoing the basics and the decor—the carpet and upholstery are replaced to the specifications of the next occupant. They followed the same drill in the OEOB. This "major overhaul," Wilson explains, had to be completed between the time the Clintons left to go to the inauguration and the time the Bushes returned postinaugural to settle into their new home.[6]

With the miserable weather matching the mood of some of the Clinton staffers who, as Sarah Wilson puts it, were "saying good-bye to one of the best jobs they'll ever have in their lives," former president Bill Clinton and his suddenly shrunken entourage had to drive to Andrews Air Force Base, across the Potomac in Maryland, from which the former president would fly to his new home in suburban New York. The weather was too nasty for Clinton, suddenly one among four living ex-presidents, to travel, as planned, by helicopter.[7]

It was striking, says Siewert, who accompanied his boss, how quickly Clinton's change in status affected his routines. He had "already lost . . . the full police escort, what they call intersection controls. . . . It's not completely shut down the way it would be for the president. So a pretty quick comedown; . . . all of a sudden you're in traffic."[8] His armored black limousine was shorn of the presidential seal.[9]

Clinton arrived at the AAB hangar—the same place to which coffins of American soldiers are brought—at about 1:15 P.M. to a full military honor guard, the military band substituting "Ruffles and Flourishes" for "Hail to the Chief." Scores of people who had served in his administration had come to say good-bye. The president's mood was nostalgic. "When you leave the White House you wonder if you'll ever draw a crowd again," he said, in a voice hoarse from exhaustion. In the crowd an admirer held a sign, "Please don't go." Clinton's response, to cheers, was "I left the White House, but I'm still here."[10]

Chuck Robb, who had just lost his Senate seat in Virginia to George Allen, recalls Clinton as "really clearly enjoying his last minutes," although there was no particular focus to his remarks.[11] Siewert calls it "sort of a nonevent. He didn't say anything terribly interesting; it was just a chance to say good-bye."[12]

But in typical Bill Clinton fashion he said nothing for too long, and he was criticized for trying to "steal George W. Bush's thunder" as the new president led his inaugural parade. Siewert calls it the "classic conundrum, the media . . . runs a split screen and then complains that Clinton's trying to get in Bush's face during the parade."[13] *Newsweek's* Jonathan Alter calls Clinton's remarks the "long good-bye" and adds, "People were really, really happy to see him go at that point."[14]

"He's doing more encores than his friend Barbra Streisand," joked the *Washington Post's* television critic Tom Shales. He predicted that Clinton will "pop up on 'Who Wants to Be a Millionaire' or 'Who Wants to Marry an Ex-President' or, appropriately, 'Survivor,' but he'll definitely pop up."[15]

Those gathered in the hangar, recalls Mickey Ibarra, who had worked in the White House as Clinton's director of governmental affairs, had "mixed emotions." There was no escaping Clinton's "squandering of political power that was the result of . . . impeachment . . . and all of the energy that was averted from getting the real work of the nation done to defending our actual completion of our second term. It was very disappointing to people. . . . Some were angry, some simply sad, some disgusted."[16]

Chuck Robb, husband of Lyndon Johnson's older daughter, Lynda, went to AAB to say good-bye because he felt it was his duty. "I knew because of the association with the former presidential family how much it meant to outgoing presidents to have friends go out to Andrews to see them off." Lynda would have gone, he says, but she was in Texas with her mother who had suffered a stroke.

Robb slipped in toward the back of a reserved section in the hangar. When Clinton happened to spot him seated behind several of his now former Cabinet members, whom he had not mentioned by name in his remarks, "he asked me to stand, and, quite unexpectedly, publicly praised me for my service, and then sent somebody to ask me to join his cabinet members when he boarded the plane, as the final good-bye." So Robb left the heated, covered hangar to stand outside at the foot of the ramp in the freezing rain, to shake Clinton's hand as he boarded, not Air Force One, but Special Air Mission 2800.[17]

Former Treasury secretary Larry Summers had not brought his coat. He was wearing a muffler around his neck and shivering as Clinton, still inside in the hangar, took "a very, very long time," says Sarah Wilson, "shook every possible hand . . . on this very long receiving line of former employees."[18]

When the plane carrying the Clintons and some friends and advisers—Terry McAuliffe; Clinton's national security adviser, Sandy Berger; his friend Vernon Jordan Jr.; his secretary, Betty Currie, among them—finally took off at 2:57 P.M., Wilson recalls that although the day was heavily overcast, "You could see the plane going up. . . . It was really a beautiful image and then all of a sudden it was sort of swallowed up by the clouds. It was like a movie screen ending," minus only the words "The End."[19]

MAYOR ROCKY Anderson, a Democrat, sat through the new president's inauguration speech. "It was a dreary, pretty depressing, terrible inauguration speech. The only applause he got the entire time was when he talked about cutting taxes."

Anderson figured that the commutation petition for Cory Stringfellow had been denied, and that added to the mayor's dark mood. He had worked so hard at it, says Mickey Ibarra, who had grown up in Salt Lake City and served as the president's liaison with all the mayors and governors. Ibarra, now a Washington lobbyist, says Anderson "became almost obsessed with this."

Anderson was walking toward Union Station when his cell phone rang. "Mayor, we got it!" shouted Ibarra, who was at Andrews Air Force Base. Ibarra told Anderson that the president had signed the commutation on his way out the White House door. A bit of an exaggeration, but not much.[20]

Others received less happy news.

Stan Brand, a criminal defense lawyer who says that he was on television "a hundred times" defending Bill and Hillary during the two terms, figured his chances were pretty good to get a pardon for his client, former Arkansas governor Jim Guy Tucker. Clinton and Tucker, although both Democrats, were more rivals than friends. A Harvard College graduate, Tucker was a guest at Bill and Hillary's wedding in Fayetteville on October 11, 1975. (Having lost his first race for Congress in 1974, Bill and his Yale Law School girlfriend, Hillary, were teaching law at the University of Arkansas when they married.)

As Brand explains it, "Tucker got sucked into the Whitewater vortex through no fault of his own and became a victim . . . because they saw him as a way station to Clinton." But, says Brand, Ken Starr had the wrong guy. Tucker "took the full brunt of the government and refused to rat out the president on anything." He was convicted of conspiracy and mail fraud related to the complicated real estate deal. He was forced to resign from office in 1996, and he served prison time. To this day, Tucker professes his innocence and says "the clear message I was receiving regularly" from Starr and his people was he could save himself if he would just tell Starr what he wanted to hear.

Brand speculates that Tucker's pardon fell victim to the "mayhem over there at the end, . . . a real sort of chaotic situation and nobody was in charge and nobody was focused."

Brand and his wife had left Washington and were driving to Vermont because they could not bear to be in town for the inauguration. It was then that Brand received a call from the White House counsel saying that Tucker would not be pardoned. "I had to call him and try to explain it to him and I really couldn't." Tucker, expecting the pardon, was shocked. "He had told a number of people that he was going to pardon me," Tucker says.[21]

The other man who was said to be waiting by his telephone for good news that never came was the Clintons' old friend Webster Hubbell, an Arkansan and a partner of Hillary's in the Rose law firm. Hubbell went to Washington with the Clintons after the 1992 election and was installed in the Justice Department as associate attorney general. His downfall came fast. In 1993, he was playing golf on Martha's Vineyard with his buddy Bill, and in 1994, he resigned his position. In 1995, he was in a federal prison serving eighteen months for stealing from his former law partners and clients. During Clinton's second term, he pleaded guilty to mail fraud and tax evasion.[22]

AS BILL CLINTON left office, he did not have a father (he died in a car crash three months before Bill's birth) or a mother (Virginia Kelley died of complications from breast cancer in January 1994). He had not had a settled, comforting place to retreat when things got tough in Washington. He now had the newly purchased house—($1.7 million in 1999) in Chappaqua, in Westchester County—but it was purchased for one reason only, to give Hillary the address she needed to run for the Senate. It was hardly inviting, full of unpacked cartons and unfinished spaces. He and Hillary were headed there together after the event at AAB, but she would soon be decamping for her new life in Washington where she had acquired a house with a name, Whitehaven—it is located on Whitehaven Street—but more commonly called "Hillary's house."

MUCH WOULD be made of the difference in style between Clinton's exit and that of his predecessor, the patrician and dignified George H. W. Bush.

When he and Barbara Bush left the White House to Bill and Hillary and Chelsea on a sunny January 20, 1993, hundreds of Bush supporters gathered at AAB to see them off. Ron Kaufman, who had worked for Bush since 1978, choreographed his run in 1988, and served as his political director in the White House, recalls that Bush wanted no one there, "wanted to downplay the whole thing, . . . felt it was very much 42's [Clinton's] day and wanted it as low key as humanly possible." Kaufman can't remember Bush addressing the crowd, just that the friends traveling back with them to Houston hurried to board the familiar blue and white Boeing 747 bound for Ellington Air Force Base in Houston, the same plane that now carried Clinton and his party. The Bushes' two dogs, Millie and Ranger, were also on board.[23]

On January 20, 2001, Clinton was exhausted. Melanne Verveer describes him as "almost asleep standing up on the plane."[24] When the plane landed at Kennedy International Airport in New York, there was still another rally inside a TWA hangar—at this one Hillary gave a longer, campaign-like speech and Tom Shales described Bill as "gaz[ing] off into the distance as if terribly bored"—and then McAuliffe joined Bill and Hillary in a van for the drive to their house in Chappaqua. "As soon as we got inside the van," McAuliffe wrote, "Clinton's head went down on Hillary's shoulder and he was out, dead asleep." They arrived in Chappaqua at 6 P.M.[25]

That night, McAuliffe hosted a dinner at the historic Kittle House in Chappaqua (circa 1790) for the people who had flown with the Clintons to New York. Sandy Berger, who was there with his wife, calls the dinner "a very poignant and warm exit." Some of those assembled had served Clinton for eight years and some had been in the campaign also, "so it was just the end of a decade."[26] Siewert recalls the mood as "pretty festive." But many of the people on the plane and at dinner were Hillary's staffers because, explains Siewert, she was "getting ready to be a senator so she had her whole team with her." After dinner nearly everyone went back to the city and the Clintons went to their eleven-room century-old Dutch Colonial at 15 Old House Lane on a woodsy cul-de-sac, a guard-house for Secret Service agents at the foot of the driveway.[27]

One woman who has lived in Chappaqua describes it as "a completely beautiful upper-middle-class enclave . . . that has more Democrats than Republicans, . . . not the fanciest part of Westchester which is Bedford and Pound Ridge. Those are where the masters of the universe live. . . . Chappaqua is the land of doctors and lawyers." If she did not know the house was the Clintons', this woman says, she'd guess it belonged to a doctor or a dentist.[28]

Some of the Clintons' friends describe the house as "modest." Howard Tullman describes it as "like a New England ranch. . . . When I think of the people's houses we went to for events, they were ten times the size."[29] The woman quoted above says, "It's a generous-sized suburban house" and not particularly "charming."[30]

LARRY SABATO, who has made a specialty of writing about political scandals, describes Clinton as leaving the White House under a dark cloud and going off to Chappaqua "to lick his wounds."[31] When he slept his first night there as former president, Bill Clinton had no idea how deep those wounds would become.

On Sunday morning, January 21, their first postpresidency morning together in Chappaqua, Hillary sent Bill into town to buy breakfast. According to one newspaper account, "He lingered over coffee at the local deli and made a point of speaking to, or shaking hands with, everyone who had turned out to catch a glimpse of their new neighbor. It took a full 90 minutes, but he seemed unhurried, as if the day had little else in store. Only after he had autographed the last [coffee] cup did he retreat to his new suburban home in Old House Lane with his greaseproof package of egg sandwiches."[32]

That casual outing would be his last for a while.

Clinton's plans included work on his presidential library (i.e., on his legacy) and vague plans to show up the knaves who had hunted him nearly every day of his presidency. He was the first president ordered to give blood so a DNA test could connect his semen to an intern's dress, but he was going figuratively to remove that stain and show how minuscule it was next to his huge successes, including a bombing campaign in Bosnia that shoved a dictator from power and resulted in not a single casualty. It would not take long, he figured, before the pundits and the people saw that he was one of the greats—up there with Abraham Lincoln and Franklin Roosevelt.

That daydream was rudely interrupted.

Mark Buell attributes the stories that broke just as the Clintons were trying to settle into their new home to "the Republicans [who] just couldn't let go of him as a punching bag."[33] And so came reports that made the Clintons look like trailer trash. They were charged with filching furniture and other items from the White House that belonged to the nation, not to them. The allegations leached from the tabloids to the broadsheets to the late-night comics. "There's talk on Capitol Hill of impeaching Clinton again," said Jay Leno. "How do you do this? He's not even president. The first time he got impeached for staining the furniture, now they get him for stealing it!"[34]

Eventually the stories were largely debunked—although the Clintons did return to the White House $28,000 worth of furniture, lamps, and rugs that were from the White House collection—but the damage was done. "To think that he was running around the White House saying, 'I need this couch,'" says Jake Siewert, was simply ridiculous.[35]

Hillary in particular was "really discouraged," says Susie Tompkins Buell. "They took the things that were personally given to them, that every other president and first lady does."[36]

Reports that the Clintons and their friends had stripped the 747 on the swan-song flight back to New York of everything that wasn't nailed down had developed a life of their own, fueled not only by talk radio and cable television, but also by respectable newspapers and magazines. Before those stories could be discredited, which they ultimately were, the Clintons were portrayed as the sort of lowlifes who steal towels from hotels.

Reports of Clinton staffers trashing government offices and equipment on their way out came next. Chris Jennings answered one charge by saying he and other staffers were working so hard until the final hour that they hadn't "the time or creativity" to pull the "W's" off the computer keyboards.[37] "Clinton justifiably got pissed off," says *Newsweek*'s Jonathan Alter, "because the Bush people made up a lot of stories about them. . . . That was when we started to learn that these were not good people who were coming in. . . . Here's Clinton leaving, not president anymore, and they felt like they had to make up stories about it."[38]

Sarah Wilson, who calls those press reports "a load of crap," was assigned as Clinton's term ended to inspect the offices "and make sure that everything was in order and there were no cartoons on the walls or anything like that. . . . I remember taking down one . . . anti-Bush cartoon off a wall." Wilson claims that the Clintons and staffers John Podesta and Bruce Lindsey "wanted to go out and leave for the incoming president . . . memos, guidance, . . . because they remember when they came in that everything was a mess. . . . Staffers were asked to write memos, . . . to leave an orderly, nonpartisan process, help the next team understand."[39]

"There were posters hanging of Bill Clinton with darts through his head," says Lynn Cutler, a former vice chair of the Democratic National Committee, of Clinton's arrival in 1993. "We didn't go and talk about it."[40]

George W. Bush seemed magnanimous when he proclaimed that the Clintons should be left alone and that the country should move on (presumably to a more refined first family).

It hardly matters whether these reports were true, false, or merely exaggerated, says Larry Sabato. "Those last scandalous developments, . . . however true they all were, just underlined some of the worst parts of the Clinton presidency and encouraged people to want to turn the page. And so they did. And they did it by focusing on a new president, which was inevitable."[41]

The trashing stories were nothing compared to details bubbling up about Clinton's pardon of Marc Rich. That pardon exploded into a controversy that had politicians threatening to haul the former president in front of a congressional committee, and editorial-page writers excoriating the president as unethical, unpatriotic, and downright sleazy—the politician from Dogpatch who was an embarrassment to the nation and whose pardon of Rich was par for his crooked course.

Clinton and his close advisers, including his press secretary, Jake Siewert, were dumbfounded. On Clinton's last morning in the White House,
when Siewert announced the pardons, "I didn't get a single person asking
me about Marc Rich. Not one knew who he was. He's not out of that
Washington world; it was a real New York story." Over the next couple of
days that was confirmed when the New York tabloids pounced on it, dig-
ging up gossip and innuendo and collecting reactions. The *New York
Post* had really "ginned" up the story, says Siewert, but then nearly every
news outlet followed the *Post*'s lead. Siewert remembers Clinton as "just
mad. Certainly, no one ever warned him that the Rich thing would be
that big a deal."[42]

Clinton did not know how to respond. He was accustomed to the
elaborate White House press office. In Chappaqua he had six Secret Service agents in the garage; Oscar Flores, a military valet, there to wash his
socks and cook his meals; and Doug Band, a former White House intern
turned presidential coat and water holder and traveling aide, sometimes
called Clinton's "butt boy."[43]

So much thought had been given to Hillary's life after the White
House and so little thought to Bill's that he had not bothered to hire a
postpresidency press secretary or to line up a staff. Jake Siewert had asked
the previous December if the president would require his services post
January 20 and was told "it wasn't necessary."

"It was sort of an unspoken assumption around some of the people
who were planning his life afterwards," says Siewert, "he doesn't need a
communications plan, she needs a communications plan. . . . She is becoming a senator; she's going to be in the spotlight, so a lot of the
focus . . . was really on how do you manage her transition from first lady
to senator."

No one but Siewert, apparently, had considered the obvious: "Sometimes when you don't want press, you still need someone to deal with the
press, because the press writes whatever the hell it wants to write, and you
need someone to put those stories back in the box. . . . At the White
House, he had this extensive . . . communications operation that was
constantly managing stories about him." Siewert estimates that during

that period when Clinton was without a spokesman, "probably fifty percent of what was said about him and Marc Rich; him and the [alleged trashing of the] plane, . . . was just complete fabrication."

Into this category Siewert puts the news reports and gossip that Clinton was going to take a job in Hollywood heading a studio. Siewert calls it an example of "the idiocy that gets printed when you don't have someone to speak on your behalf."

Nobody expected, Siewert adds, that "he should just stay in the basement at Chappaqua while she becomes senator. . . . It was really more like she needs the help and she needs the planning and that's where the resources are going to be, not on his life in Chappaqua. We'll worry about that later. And so when all hell broke loose . . . there was just no one in place to [handle] it."[44]

Five days after Clinton left office, Mary McGrory, the reliably liberal *Washington Post* syndicated columnist, wrote just the sort of column that would ruin a press secretary's day: "President George W. Bush is having a fine first week in office, helped enormously by . . . Bill Clinton. Clinton's departure lent a deafening resonance to the Bush campaign mantra about 'restoring dignity to the White House.' . . . The Clinton exit was . . . a script that would have made 'Saturday Night Live' blush."[45]

For a man with Bill Clinton's insecurities, his situation was dreadful. His idol John Kennedy had sex in the White House much more often than Bill Clinton ever did, but the people Bill Clinton cared about still revered Kennedy. Clinton recognized that in some ways he was in worse shape when he left the White House in the conventional way than Richard Nixon was when he was, in effect, thrown out. "Unlike Nixon," says Larry Sabato, "Clinton had just become a joke. Nixon was roundly condemned and was despised but he was taken seriously. . . . There's never been a president in American history who has been such continuous fodder for the late-night TV show hosts. Even to this day I think there are almost as many jokes about Clinton as there are about Bush, the incumbent. And that's just unheard of."[46]

A small sample follows from just one Jay Leno monologue, the same day as the McGrory column; Leno jokes about Bush's first one hundred hours in office, much of it poking fun at Bush for being dumb, but Clinton is prominently featured:

> HOUR 100: Walked around Oval Office with pants around his ankles saying, "Look, I'm President Clinton!"
>
> LENO: And President Clinton—we still call him president. You keep the title for life. You are always "President." Kind of like how we still refer to him being "married." . . . President George W. Bush has imposed a new dress code at the White House, a little more strict, as opposed to Clinton, where staff members just needed a new dress. . . . An intruder broke through security at Bill Clinton's inauguration. The guy, four years ago, got up and shook Clinton's hand. He was harmless. He was able to do it again this year and shake Bush's hand. Bush said that he wasn't worried about the intruder breaking security, he was more worried about the guy touching Clinton's hand and then touching his. . . . [47]

Jake Siewert had rented a house in Wyoming to ski for a month. But at the end of Clinton's first week as a private citizen, "the press was so bad that he called me up to ask if I'd come up to help him out."[48]

There was the president sitting in Chappaqua, a prisoner in his house—reporters were waiting for him to take his dog Buddy for a walk so they could pounce with questions and cameras—and he had no spokesperson, nightmarish press that portrayed him as being for sale, and, worse, in Clinton's mind, "the President from Dogpatch." Some of his former staffers, like Siewert, were trying to help, but, says Melanne Verveer, "they were also creating their own new lives. They all needed to find jobs."[49]

Clinton was in a bind. Hillary had left after two days to go to Washington; McAuliffe writes in his memoir that "Clinton called me the afternoon Hillary left and seemed down in the dumps. I said I'd fly up to New York the next day and we'd play some cards." He and Clinton walked to lunch on the main street of Chappaqua and passed an ATM: "Clinton looked at the machine . . . and scratched his head. . . . 'It gives you cash?'"[50]

Even if Hillary had wanted him there, which she didn't, with the pardon scandal unfolding, he could not join her in Washington, although there was no reason, legal or otherwise, for him to be in New York. Hillary's advisers wanted her to keep her husband at bay; he could only hurt her. Having him even briefly visit Washington would have been "incredibly distracting" for Hillary, says Siewert. When the Senate went into recess, Bill and Hillary were scheduled to take a vacation together; until then the plan was for him, in Siewert's words, "to stay undercover."[51]

Clinton's only child was in college across the country in California; he had a strained marriage that some said was a charade. Friends say that the former president understood that it was now Hillary's turn; he was to stay quiet, out of the spotlight, and out of trouble and share his political wisdom only when asked. Mark Buell suggests that "it had to be pretty tough" to watch Hillary get all the attention: "I think he was a little lost at times."[52]

SOME OF the pardons Clinton issued as he left the White House were judicious and appropriate, but others seemed Bill Clinton's way of thumbing his nose at his enemies, particularly Special Prosecutor Ken Starr. Friends maintain that Clinton connected the plight of any pardon seeker who could be seen as the victim of an overzealous prosecutor with his own. He would never be able to let go of his anger at Starr, who had turned most of Clinton's second term into a living hell; who had issued "The Starr Report," snickered at by millions around the world, making explicit the most humiliating details of a pathetic tryst with an intern not much older than his beloved Chelsea.[53] She had read the "Report" online at Stanford, a fact that "drove her father to tears," writes Sally Bedell Smith. (Smith also notes that Chelsea used to do her homework in the private study off of the Oval Office where Lewinsky later serviced Chelsea's father.)

And so he had decided yes on a pardon that he had anguished over that last night—for Susan McDougal, an Arkansan and FOB (friend of Bill), who went to prison for eighteen months after being convicted of bank fraud, snared in the Whitewater investigation, because, she claimed, she would not tell Ken Starr what he wanted to hear. McDougal was often seen on national television in her orange jumpsuit. She has never wavered in her refusal to implicate Bill or Hillary.[54]

Clinton also pardoned his former secretary of housing and urban development, Henry Cisneros, convicted of lying to the FBI about how much money he had given to a former mistress. In Clinton's mind, Cisneros too was the victim of an out-of-control special prosecutor. And so was Cisneros's former mistress, whom Clinton also pardoned.[55]

Many later attributed Clinton's decision to pardon Marc Rich to his overtaxed physical and emotional state as he prepared to enter private life. "I don't think he slept for a week," says Melanne Verveer, "and if he slept, he had catnaps." She describes him as "just running on empty."[56]

Newsweek's Jonathan Alter, who has covered Clinton for years, says that the president "was acting . . . very sort of hyper in his last hours and I think that his judgment was impaired. I think he was just doing a lot of things very, very quickly. He was very tired; he was very . . . depressed about leaving the presidency. . . . And he had a kind of 'screw it' attitude. 'They're never going to like me anyway. I'll do what I want.'"[57]

Not even his friends had a kind or even neutral word to say about Clinton's pardon of the billionaire fugitive-from-American-justice accused of trading with the enemy. Massachusetts congressman Barney Frank, a liberal Democrat and the brother of Hillary Clinton aide Ann Lewis, called the Rich pardon "one of the worst things President Clinton has done."[58] Congressman Henry Waxman, an equally liberal Democrat, called Clinton's pardon a "chaotic mess" that should "embarrass every Democrat and every American."[59]

At best his loyalists bitterly accused former White House counsel Jack Quinn, Rich's lawyer—some charged really his lobbyist—of taking cruel advantage of Clinton's vulnerabilities and betraying his former boss/ client, the president of the United States, in order to make a fat fee.

As the details seeped out, things did not look good. Although Rich was not a friend of Clinton's, Rich's ex-wife, Denise, who was pushing for the pardon—in phone calls, notes, and a conversation with the president at a party at the White House on December 20—was; there were even unsubstantiated rumors that the president and the songwriter had been lovers. In 2000, Denise Rich had bestowed more than $1 million on the Democratic Party, $450,000 on Hillary's Senate campaign, and $450,000 on Bill's presidential library. On a smaller scale she gave Bill a new saxophone and Hillary $7,375 worth of furniture.[60]

The pardon stories moved beyond charges that Clinton sold a pardon to Denise Rich's husband in exchange for her hefty contributions and/or because the two were romantically involved, into a scandal that featured Clinton trashing this noble constitutional prerogative. In these stories, Clinton, unlike his predecessors, had reduced the pardon power to cronyism and worse. There were enough irregularities in the Rich pardon to give this story muscular legs.

Over many administrations, by custom, not requirement, the Justice Department's pardon attorney had been part of the process, advising the White House on meritorious pardons and advising against others. In issuing the Rich pardon, Clinton had bypassed the pardon attorney. He simply granted the pardon.

The pardon also drew Eric Holder, who had been number two in Clinton's Justice Department under Attorney General Janet Reno, into the mess and made it look like somehow Holder had manipulated the process in hopes of becoming Al Gore's attorney general. In this scenario, Holder would do Quinn's bidding in exchange for Quinn, not only Vice President Gore's chief of staff but also his friend, pushing Gore to name Holder his attorney general, the first African American in history to have that office.

The press fed on the details. Quinn acquired Marc Rich as a client after a dinner in New York in November 1998 when a public relations man named Gershon Kekst, who represented Marc Rich, chatted with another guest at the dinner, Eric Holder. The two men did not know each other, but, on discovering his position, Kekst allegedly asked Holder who could help get a pardon petition in front of Bill Clinton. Holder, allegedly, pointed to Quinn, whom Kekst already knew. At that point Kekst "pursued me," says Quinn. "He came to me on at least three occasions, urging me to take on this matter."[61] (Holder, now in private law practice, says that "the conversation never concerned Marc Rich's pardon. . . . This guy just asked me general questions about appealing . . . a decision . . . and how does that happen in the Justice Department. There was never a mention of Rich or Jack Quinn.")[62]

In the storm that followed, Holder, who had overall responsibility for pardons, was portrayed as so ambitious to be attorney general in the expected Gore administration that he played ball with Jack Quinn. This plot line had Holder failing to alert prosecutors of the impending pardon and making certain that the Justice Department pardon attorneys would not review the Rich pardon, raise concerns, and recommend to the president against issuing it.

Quinn was then meeting "frequently," he says, with I. Lewis "Scooter" Libby, who was then another of Marc Rich's lawyers and was about to become the top aide to Vice President Richard Cheney. It was Libby who was reportedly the brains behind the analysis Quinn used to advocate for the pardon.[63] Quinn says he was motivated to take the case and persuaded of its merits by Libby's analysis, as well as by the "tax arguments" of still another lawyer employed by Marc Rich—Martin Ginsburg, the husband of Clinton-appointed Supreme Court justice Ruth Bader Ginsburg.

Having himself been White House counsel, Quinn says, "I was well aware of the pardon attorney's guidelines for the matters that came before the pardon attorney and this didn't fall within the parameters of the pardon attorney's authority." So, Quinn says, he went directly to Holder. He says he also discussed his course with Beth Nolan, who was then Clinton's White House counsel. He insists he did not try to sneak in the pardon.[64]

One man who served in the Clinton Justice Department claims that other presidents have issued pardons without Justice Department consultation—naming, for example, the George H. W. Bush pardon of six men, including Caspar W. Weinberger, Ronald Reagan's Defense secretary, involved in the Iran-Contra scandal, which saw money from arms sales to Iran directed to the Contras in Nicaragua.[65] Then there was

Gerald Ford's pardon of Richard Nixon in 1974, granted before Nixon had even been charged with anything, a way to wipe clean the national slate, also done without consulting the Justice Department pardon attorney.[66]

The pardon of Marc Rich proved to be a migraine not only for Bill Clinton and Jack Quinn, but also for Eric Holder whose chances of becoming attorney general in any future Democratic administration are likely over. Like Quinn, Holder was hauled before a televised House Government Reform Committee chaired by Clinton nemesis Dan Burton, Republican of Indiana. Burton called Holder, who testified voluntarily, a "willing participant in the plan to keep the Justice Department from knowing about and opposing" a pardon for Marc Rich.[67] Burton's report also cited an e-mail from Jack Quinn dated November 18, 2000, as they were working on the pardon petition, and sent to members of Rich's team, that seems damning: Quinn wrote that he spoke to "Eric" the night before. "He says go straight to wh. also says timing is good."[68]

Holder adamantly denies there was any secret deal: "There were a whole host of people who expressed their support assuming Gore would win . . . you become attorney general. . . . The notion that someway or other these things were in any way tied is totally, totally wrong."[69]

While Clinton sat in Chappaqua watching his reputation take another beating, those still willing to defend him charged that he was bamboozled by Quinn, that he was relying on Quinn for the facts and details of the case and was too distracted or exhausted to understand its repercussions. "He did it for Jack Quinn" is a charge made by several of Clinton's friends.[70] Quinn "was pushing Marc Rich's pardon and he was pushing and pushing," says John Catsimatidis, "and got to the point where [the president] finally said, 'Okay, I'll do it.'"[71]

Quinn argues to this day that Clinton was as sharp as ever and knew the details of the Rich case cold, as he knew the details of every matter he handled. Clinton gave the pardon, Quinn says, because "he was persuaded on the merits."

In retrospect, Quinn says, "the single biggest regret of my life" was pushing the pardon because it so damaged the reputation of Bill Clinton.

Quinn says that he "miscalculated the political effect of this and the public reaction." He calls himself "one of the people who thinks that [Bill Clinton] is among the very greatest presidents this country has ever had. I . . . wish that I had not had a role in putting him in a difficult situation."

Quinn himself endured a dark period, summoned before a congressional committee, his reputation "damaged in the firestorm of reaction." Quinn describes himself as a victim. After leaving Clinton's employ, he had been a regular on broadcast and cable political shows—especially in the wake of the Lewinsky scandal. Invitations to appear on television dried up. "I believe that no one . . . was on television more than I in defense of Bill Clinton." Furthermore, he says, "When I was out there defending him on the Lewinsky stuff, . . . there was at least one occasion when I said to people in the White House, 'I feel like I'm pretty far out on a limb here and . . . if I am saying things that are not true, that I shouldn't be saying, please pull me back in from that limb,' and no one ever did."[72]

"Who knows?" answers Leon Panetta when asked why Clinton pardoned Marc Rich. "It's one of those things sometimes you think is part of Clinton's cycle in which every time he's doing very well, every time things are going very good, somehow a mistake is made or something happens, that sends you from an up roller coaster to a down roller coaster and I think he was leaving on a high. He was doing very well; people had high regard for him. I think [his approval rating] was in the 60s. . . . To then do what he did at the end, it's very hard to find an explanation for."[73]

During those lonely days in Chappaqua, Bill Clinton was also regretting that he hadn't pardoned Jim Guy Tucker and Webb Hubbell.

Tucker, now a businessman in cable television and software, has let his anger at Clinton go and says he sees the former president every other month or so in Arkansas, sometimes at funerals. A few years ago, in the lobby of the Peabody Hotel in Little Rock, says Tucker, "with tears in his eyes, [Clinton] said he was terribly sorry and [not pardoning me] was one of the worst mistakes he made when he was president. He promptly volunteered his regrets and dismay." Did Tucker ask Clinton why he didn't pardon him? "It's not something that I've ever inquired into in the form of 'Why in the heck didn't you.'"[74]

As for Webb Hubbell, "the president and he were so close," says Jake Siewert, "and their relationship was so deep that I'm sure that he would have preferred to have done that but was convinced by someone that it would just look like he was taking care of a friend. . . . Given all the flack he took for someone he didn't care much about, he probably feels 'If I took all that flack anyway I might as well have taken care of people that I like.'"[75] Today Hubbell, who had been mayor of Little Rock and a justice on the Arkansas Supreme Court, sells life insurance to "responsible marijuana users."[76] (Hubbell refused requests for an interview.)

Clinton writes in his memoir that he "gave in" to his staff's entreaties not to pardon Tucker and Hubbell. One can only wonder why he followed their judgment on those pardons but not on Marc Rich. Two of the president's closest advisers, John Podesta and, especially, Bruce Lindsey, pleaded with their boss not to pardon Rich.[77]

SIEWERT, WHO would join Alcoa the next October as vice president of global communications, drove to Chappaqua on February 1, 2001, which happened to be his birthday. The former president "had barely left the house at that point." An Israeli television journalist and his crew were there to interview Clinton. The idea, says Siewert, was for him to "talk about anything other than Marc Rich or some of the alleged stuff that went on in terms of trashing the White House or trashing the plane." Siewert says that Clinton did the interview as a favor to Prime Minister Ehud Barak.[78] (One might think that Clinton, whose pardon for Marc Rich was supposedly influenced by the Israeli prime minister's appeal, would not have been inclined to grant him another favor so soon.) When the crew left, Clinton insisted on taking Siewert to lunch in town. They were trailed by reporters.[79]

Clinton told Siewert that the press, including New York Times columnist Maureen Dowd, who was part of the cul-de-sac stakeout, had been "pretty rough," and that he hadn't been reading the newspapers, although several days after arriving in Chappaqua, he had managed to escape to Lang's Little Store and Deli to buy them.[80]

In downtown Chappaqua that day, Clinton attempted, for the first time, to use the ATM. He had his card, but he did not know his pin number. He was trying to call Hillary to get it, but he could not reach her. "Look, I'll buy lunch," Siewert said, but Clinton wanted to treat because it was Siewert's birthday. "We were going to some diner in town; he wasn't sure if they took credit cards, so he wanted some cash. . . . We split it. I think he had enough cash to pay about half of it."[81] When they entered the diner, he was treated like a celebrity, and, for a short time, the old Clinton was back.[82]

Clinton's mood at the time was "a roller coaster," says Siewert. "He wasn't sitting around sulking," but he shifted between being "angry with the coverage" and "constructive about trying to work through some of the things." Siewert recalls that Clinton was particularly "furious about the implication that they had . . . stolen furniture." But then he would lose his anger when they went out for lunch and "[we would] have a perfectly pleasant lunch." Clinton, says Siewert, was unusually "reflective," a quality not much noted during his days in the White House. "He was unpacking and he was finding things, as you do when you unpack, . . . that reminded him of little incidents that he had forgotten and was telling some stories about some of those things." He was "very happy" with the house. "It was really the first house they'd owned," says Siewert, "and . . . he was like any person who has moved into their first house, kind of thrilled about that."[83]

On the other hand, "if you got him on the topic, which I didn't try to, . . . of what was in the press, he worked himself up pretty quickly. But if you were just talking about the house and what he was going to do next, and kind of reflecting on his period in office, he was fine." Asked if Clinton expressed regrets over impeachment and Lewinsky, Siewert says, "I wasn't born yesterday. I wasn't going to spoil my day by asking about that."[84]

On February 11, 2001, a *New York Times* editorial cast Clinton as a scoundrel, while praising the new president, George W. Bush, for his "mature insistence on order." The *Times* editorialized against a man who "in the last moments of his presidency [seemed] to plunge further and further beneath the already low expectations of his most cynical critics. . . . We sense a national need to come to grips with the wreckage, both civic and legal, left by former President Clinton."[85]

Appearing on MSNBC on February 16, Jake Siewert described the former president as "bewildered" by all the attention that the Rich pardon generated. "You've got congressmen now who have made a living getting on TV, becoming famous by attacking Bill Clinton. He's gone. He's not president anymore. He's not running for anything anymore. . . . And they're going to have to get used to it and find something new to do . . . with their lives."[86]

As Bill Clinton attempted to plot his next move, he could not accept that his pardons had sparked such outrage. He felt the aggrieved victim. One reporter whom Clinton knew well asked him about the Rich pardon during a wide-ranging interview and Clinton "just took off in a torrent of words." And then he took off after George H. W. Bush, the man who later became his friend but at that time was a former president with whom, in the character and class departments, Bill Clinton was often compared unfavorably. "So I guess you're not going to mention Orlando Bosch, are you?" Clinton asked, referring to an anti-Castro Cuban exile whom Bush had pardoned in 1990 even though the man admitted to participating in the bombing of a Cuban airplane that resulted in the deaths of seventy-three passengers and crew.[87]

Clinton's White House diarist and friend, Janis Kearney, uses the word *depression* to describe the president's mood at that time.[88] The darkness at the end of this long road, says Melanne Verveer, came in "knowing that his presidency was over. He had had this extraordinary opportunity; it would never come around again."[89]

Historian Douglas Brinkley, who has written biographies of Presidents Carter and Ford, and edited the diaries of President Reagan, says that Clinton was not much different from his predecessors. "This happens to all of them; leaving, being stripped of power and going back to being a common citizen is hard to adjust to. . . . You lose your entourage. . . . You find yourself in debt; you're almost obligated to write a memoir and raise money for your presidential library." He calls the period before all those tasks are accomplished "like a purgatory . . . that lasts a couple of years."[90]

Larry Sabato, who has studied presidents in extremis, sees Clinton as almost in the mainstream of this tiny brotherhood. The exceptions are Ronald Reagan who was "quite content, but then he normally was"; also he was returning to a ranch he loved with Nancy at his side. Reagan, it was always clear but made more clear by the publication in 2007 of his diaries, would have been bereft were Nancy not with him. Gerald Ford, says Sabato, took the loss to Jimmy Carter hard, but he too was "happy to just move to the next phase of his life."[91]

Other presidents have experienced misery that came close to Clinton's—Lyndon Johnson, who never adjusted, and, some believe, died from the transition, and Nixon, and certainly Jimmy Carter, who, Sabato says, "has admitted to virtually a depression . . . in the wake of his land-slide defeat, and the nothingness that came afterwards as they returned to Plains, Georgia."[92]

Closest in temperament to Bill Clinton was Theodore Roosevelt, who, unlike Clinton, left the White House with his reputation intact, but who, like Clinton, left filled with regret. Both would have given al-most anything to serve another term and regain the bully pulpit. Like Clinton, Roosevelt was almost freakishly energetic, stuck in a perpetual adolescence—First Lady Edith Kermit Roosevelt used to say that she had seven children, counting her husband. Both dominated any room they were in. When Alice Roosevelt Longworth, his firstborn, said of her father, "He was the bride at every wedding; the corpse at every funeral," she might have been describing Bill Clinton. TR decamped to Oyster Bay, his beloved New York country house, and to the company of a lov-ing marriage to Edith, who longed for private time with him and their children. Those children were solace to TR, who led them on strenuous "romps." Many noted that TR was more rambunctious than any of his boys. He was soon off with one of them on a thirteen-month African safari, followed by another, unsuccessful, race for the White House.[93]

Bill Clinton was accustomed to being the center of attention every single day, even if the attention was negative. "Then suddenly," says Sabato, "there's a nothingness and it was emphasized in his case by those last-minute scandals and the fact that his wife had a completely new career, near the center of the action, while he was on the periphery."[94]

Yes, Hillary had returned with him to the Chappaqua house, which was awaiting renovation, but two days later she was gone. Chelsea was across the country at Stanford University. He was, says one friend, "an empty nester."[95]

Oddly, visitors were few. "He didn't have a steady stream of visitors," says Jake Siewert.[96] The Reverend Anthony Campolo, author, teacher, and an ordained minister in the American Baptist Churches, one of several "pastoral counselors" who helped Clinton after the Lewinsky story broke, visited him in Chappaqua and said he found him "in good spirits. . . . He was exceptionally proud of . . . Hillary and what she was accomplishing politically and was very consumed in advising and helping her in any way he could." (Campolo was not surprised to find Clinton upbeat, recalling sitting with him in the Oval Office on the afternoon of his impeachment. "We talked, we prayed, and he seemed to be totally unshaken by the events that confronted him. He is a very strong personality.")[97]

Mike and Irena Medavoy flew from Los Angeles to visit him, shortly after Hillary left for Washington. "He wanted to show us Chappaqua," says Irena, "and if you're real friends, you don't just go and stay in the Lincoln Bedroom like we were lucky to. . . . You go when he's in Chappaqua, and you go and see his life there. He was so proud of it. . . . He loved his house and he showed us every room." She remembers the dog bed in his bedroom and Clinton telling them that Buddy, his Labrador retriever, slept with him. She noted "this bonding and love" between Bill and Buddy and attributed it to "empty nest syndrome." He also showed them all "his mementos" and notes he had made for his memoir. He seemed eager to start to write, she says.

When they walked around the neighborhood, Buddy at Clinton's side, "he loved it" when people stopped him, Medavoy recalls. "He's a man who wants to be in the fabric of a town. He is a small-town boy at heart."

She describes Chappaqua as "charming, like small-town America," and the house as "a small, little traditional home. . . . It's not imposing."[98] (One woman who lived in Chappaqua says only someone from Hollywood would describe the Clinton home as small.)[99]

When the Medavoys left late that afternoon, Clinton was once again alone, not a comfortable position for someone who, as political consultant Hank Sheinkopf puts it, needs an audience, who is accustomed to drawing "tremendous energy from being in the public spotlight," who prefers not to be alone with his thoughts.[100]

According to a report in *Newsday*, on a Sunday morning soon after Clinton moved into the house, he asked his Secret Service agents to invite a neighbor and his daughters, then fourteen and twelve, over to his house and chatted with them for thirty to forty minutes. He talked to the girls about school, showed their father his carpets, and suggested that one day they could play golf.[101]

After the trashing stories were shown to be "absolute garbage," Siewert was waiting for the next loony story to drop. It didn't take long for stories to appear that Clinton was trying to join a golf club, apparently almost any golf club, and was being rejected. In fact, Siewert says, Clinton doesn't belong to a golf club. Why would he? "He's got plenty of people he can play with." That fact did not stop people from "leaking that they had banned him from the club before he'd even heard of the club. . . . You'd read in the paper that some club had blackballed him and I'd ask him and he'd say, 'I've never heard of that. . . . [S]ounds like someplace I'd like to play.'"[102]

But the tone was set; in fact, it had been set years before as the press covered the most intimate details of Bill Clinton's life and learned that when it came to him, nothing was off-limits. In late February, the *New York Times's* Adam Nagourney described Clinton going to an AIDS fund-raiser at the Apollo Theater in Harlem. Accompanied by Representative Charles Rangel—it was he who recruited Hillary to run for the Senate from New York—singer Roberta Flack, and Secret Service agents, Clinton drew "a flicker of applause and recognition from the audience." Nagourney described him jammed into a center seat for four hours, "occasionally autographing a program that was passed over the seats. Mostly, though, he was a very famous man who was sitting very much alone."

Nagourney also described a distant relationship with Hillary; the planned vacation never happened, and Bill had stayed only one night at her house in Washington. Nagourney reported that Hillary's staffers were still urging her to keep her distance from her husband so that his pardons did not damage her debut.[103]

No matter how chastened Bill Clinton was by recent missteps, he was still Bill Clinton—but without the structure of the presidency.

IN EARLY February 2001, while at loose ends in Chappaqua, Clinton asked Bob Kerrey, former Nebraska governor and senator, and a some-times Clinton rival—they competed in the 1992 primaries for the Democratic nomination—to accompany him to a St. John's–Connecticut basketball game at Madison Square Garden. They followed that with dinner at Babbo, a chic Italian restaurant in Greenwich Village.[104] Clinton, also accompanied by two former aides and one current aide, then behaved like such a boor that he ended up in the gossip columns.

Someone should have warned Clinton that Kerrey, with whom Clinton had a strange and prickly history—Kerrey had advised the president to resign before he could be impeached—might not be his best companion. (Kerrey served in Vietnam, won the Medal of Honor, and left behind part of his foot. Clinton famously dodged the draft and then lied about it.) "Something went really bad between them," says Jonathan Alter. "Kerrey is really quirky and in a way that is off-putting to Clinton on a lot of different levels."[105]

Bob Kerrey's run for the 1992 nomination had been fatally damaged when a microphone captured him telling Clinton a joke about two lesbians and former California governor Jerry Brown. Clinton had responded in kind, but he was not on tape, and his campaign survived while Kerrey's folded. "I was very impressed by how he handled it," says Kerrey. "They didn't catch him; why confirm it?" Kerrey is certain Clinton would not have done what Kerrey did next: "I went to San Francisco the next day, not a great place to go in 1991 after you told a lesbian joke." He soon found himself with "a very large bouquet of microphones sticking in [his] face," and then did something that he figures Clinton would have been way too smart ever to do; he issued an "abject apology, which made matters worse."[106]

During Clinton's first term, they had a profane fight about the budget bill, Clinton warning Kerrey, then a senator, that his no vote would bring down Clinton's presidency. "Fuck you," Kerrey responded, offended at Clinton's suggestion that Kerrey was responsible for the survival of the Clinton presidency.[107] In 1996, Kerrey had called Clinton "an unusually good liar,"* the meaning of which, as is the case with many statements emanating from Bob Kerrey, was not quite what it seemed. Friends of Bill Clinton's say he does not have a particularly good sense of humor, while "one of the things that makes Bob Kerrey very appealing to reporters," says Jonathan Alter, ". . . is that he has that really quirky, ironic sensibility. . . . Clinton's not Mr. Irony."[108]

At Babbo, Clinton was talking too loudly and a nearby diner heard parts of the conversation and called Lloyd Grove, who then presided over "The Reliable Source," the *Washington Post's* gossip column. According to Grove's report, "Clinton regaled the table with, uh, raunchy lesbian jokes. A whole series of them." According to other reports, Clinton confessed that he had indeed told Kerrey a joke about lesbians in 1991. Clinton then loudly retold the joke to those at the table.[110]

One part of the conversation reported later by Elizabeth Kolbert in *The New Yorker* had Clinton mentioning his five least favorite members of his White House team, a list that included George Stephanopoulos, who had been in the Clintons' inner circle and then wrote a critical book

---

*Asked by a reporter, "Why do politicians lie?" Kerrey answered, "All healthy human beings lie to a certain extent. . . . It's true that politicians are prone to tell the truth . . . less often. . . . Take Bill Clinton, he's an unusually good liar. . . . It was right after he had gone to Texas and given that talk to people in which he said that he didn't really want to raise taxes, but . . . Congress made him do it." Kerrey adds, "There's a sense in which I meant it as a compliment. I think a president who is a one-hundred-percent truth teller is not [a person] I want as president."[109]

about them; Louis Freeh, his FBI director who found Clinton too scandal prone and soft on terrorism; Janet Reno, his attorney general, whom Clinton's friends blame for Ken Starr; and Robert Reich, his Labor secretary, who had also written a candidly critical book about Clinton. Kolbert reported that Kerrey, who told her the story, could not remember the name of the fifth person. (Kerrey claims that Clinton never said those names to him, but Kolbert says she stands by her reporting, and Kerrey allows that one of the Clinton aides might have listed the names and Clinton would have nodded his head in assent.)[111]

AT THAT point, Clinton was still without much notion of what he would do next. There was no more talk about his becoming president of Harvard, a job that, according to Kennedy speechwriter Theodore Sorensen, would have interested JFK had he lived to have had a postpresidency.)* [112]

That Clinton's interest in a visiting lectureship at Harvard—he saw it as a buffer, a structure for his immediate postpresidential days and a reason for him to spend time in a politically friendly community—had been met with such silence had, says his friend Howard Tullman, caused the former president to pull back from the idea of teaching. As much as he would have "desperately loved" an appointment, says Tullman, "I think he did not want to subject himself to the prospect of these politically correct idiots . . . rejecting him."[114]

That the rumors of his heading to Hollywood were so persistent and seemed so plausible was, Clinton also understood, a kind of insult. Clinton friend and CNN talk-show host Larry King calls the rumors "logical. . . . If I were a studio I would have hired him, because one of the keys of being a Hollywood studio head is that you're bidding on films, trying to persuade people to come to your studio to do a movie. Who would have been better than Clinton?"[115]

---

*Sorensen says that, postpresidency, Kennedy also would have been interested in being "secretary of state in Robert Kennedy's administration," or publisher of a "major newspaper."[113]

NELSON SHANKS, whom Clinton had selected to paint his portrait for the National Portrait Gallery—he had also painted Katharine Graham, Margaret Thatcher, Pope John Paul II, Princess Diana*—had two or three sessions with Clinton the November before he left the White House. Shanks had delayed work on the Clinton portrait because he felt the commission was left a little "ambiguous." In 2002, officials at the National Portrait Gallery called: "Hey, where is it?" Shanks called Clinton's people and scheduled a couple of sittings at his New York studio, located in an apartment on West Sixty-seventh Street.[116]

Shanks rented the space from an elderly woman who lived there full-time. Before the sittings, Clinton's security people and his "art person" went to the apartment to scout it out. They "were absolutely insistent" that no one not authorized by them be in the apartment. "They were watching like a hawk, who could be there," Shanks recalls, "and my landlady was in her eighties and they refused to allow her to be present." Given that she lived in the apartment, Shanks found it awkward to banish her from her own home. "We thought it a bit unnecessary. I don't know if they were worried about physical security or whether just any female presence could be seen potentially as a problem. . . . It was just strange."

Shanks found the former president "more serious this time"—different from the Clinton he observed during their last meeting in the White House when he had been chatting so energetically and for two hours with the photographer Shanks brought with him. "I think I make him a little bit nervous," Shanks speculates. "I tried to even paint him that way, as looking a little at dis-ease. I think he was a little uncomfortable being examined by me. . . . I've painted so many people and . . . I see him as quite self-conscious, a certain discomfort in his own skin perhaps."[118]

---

*Shanks was promoted for the commission by his patron Beth Dozoretz, a friend of Denise Rich's. Dozoretz was known for her energetic fund-raising for the Democrats, and for pushing Clinton to pardon Marc Rich.[117]

———

AS HE was leaving office, one of his aides told a reporter that Clinton had been reading books about the two postpresidential careers he most admires: that of John Quincy Adams, who was elected to the U.S. House and argued before the Supreme Court for freeing the slaves, and that of Jimmy Carter, "who has monitored elections around the world."[119]

In fact, Bill Clinton found the prospect of looking to Jimmy Carter totally unattractive. On leaving office, Carter was widely reviled as incompetent, plodding, and unstylish, the anti-Kennedy if there ever was one. Yet he had become one of the most admired ex-presidents in history.[120] How galling it was to Clinton to give even a moment's thought to Carter, whom he genuinely disliked—Carter and Clinton had a long, unpleasant history, and the ever-pious Carter made no attempt to keep private his disgust at Clinton's trysts with Monica Lewinsky.

There was no denying that Carter had not only kept his place on the public stage, both nationally and abroad, but that he wrote bestselling books—how would the disorganized, easily distracted Clinton ever pull off his memoir—and that he had won an honor that Clinton coveted: the Nobel Peace Prize.

Yet Clinton knew that he had to move quickly before he became irrelevant; at times lately it seemed to him that his character and his future were being defined by late-night comics, cable talk-show bullies, and right-wing radio ranters.

Melanne Verveer describes the question he was asking himself: "How somebody so young who had had this enormous power . . . How does he take . . . his extraordinary talents and his place in the world and begin to put together a new life that doesn't compete with the current occupant of the presidency?" He knew that if he tried that, he'd be laughed off the world stage, while helping to increase W's stature and watching his own sink even lower—and, as Verveer frames it, he knew too well that "whatever he's going to do next in some ways would be less than what he's done."[121]

At first, as he tried to dig out from under the pardon mess, it seemed that his magic touch and stunning luck were gone.

But then the resilience, the optimism that defines Bill Clinton kicked in. Clinton liked to call himself "Baby Huey," after the cartoon character who keeps getting knocked down and keeps getting back up. John Emerson calls that "Baby Huey" quality key to his friend's "brilliance" and says that Clinton was able to make that "a metaphor for the American people." The "I feel your pain" promise that is so closely linked to the Clinton campaigns—Emerson claims that Clinton never actually said those words—was "very genuine and I think something people responded to because of his ability to take hits and come back, his resilience. Everybody loves that, they love an underdog story, they love a comeback story, and that's this guy's life."[122]

In trying to explain why they knew Clinton would find some way or other to come back after the fiasco of his White House exit, Clinton's friends hark back to 1988 and "the speech." Having decided not to run for president in 1988, but determined to run in 1992, he was delighted to receive the invitation to introduce nominee Michael Dukakis at the 1988 Democratic National Convention in Atlanta. That keynote speech, broadcast in prime time, is intended to highlight future stars—the most recent example, the surge of Barack Obama after he delivered the keynote at the 2004 convention. For Clinton, the speech, which was supposed to be twenty minutes but bloviated to fifty, was a colossal embarrassment. As it was ridiculed that convention week it grew even more tedious; his only applause line was, "In closing."[123]

"Everybody recognized that as a major faux pas," says Don Fowler, who was CEO of that convention. "It was a golden opportunity for him because . . . this was prime time, man, this was big time for a governor of a small state like that and he blew it and he knew it."[124] Pundits and politicians—Walter Mondale for one—wrote Clinton's political obituary. So did Jimmy Carter aide Hamilton Jordan: "It was clear that whatever remote possibility he had of national office was dashed that night."[125]

One Democratic operative recalls that within minutes of delivering the dud, Clinton "has such self-assurance" that he hit all the restaurants where the important politicos were dining. This woman was having dinner with a pollster when Clinton stopped at their table to do what she calls "damage control," trying "to ingratiate himself and do what he does best, which is just to get people to like him. And act as though everything was just fine."[126]

His friends, television writers and producers Linda Bloodworth-Thomason and Harry Thomason—the latter, one of Clinton's sleepover companions his last night in the White House—booked him on the Johnny Carson show. He traded self-deprecatory barbs with Carson— joking that his speech was deliberately crafted to make Dukakis look good—he donned sunglasses, and he played the saxophone with Doc Severinsen and the NBC Orchestra.[127] Remembering that night, Chuck Robb said Clinton "was sort of like kudzu and bamboo. . . . You just can't keep him down. He's going to bounce back."[128]

John Emerson, who first met Bill Clinton when he was governor, and who would run the Clinton/Gore campaign in California, credits Clinton with inventing the shamed politician's appearance on late-night TV. Emerson also points out what he calls "a hallmark of the Clintons"—the hard work that followed. "People minimize that. . . . They think, 'Oh, this guy's very glib and . . . it comes easy.' Man, this guy works his tail off." He "tirelessly covered the country for Dukakis," says Emerson, and was "fully rehabilitated by the end of that '88 campaign."[129]

Jake Siewert, who saw Clinton up close both in the White House and in Chappaqua, says that the most important thing to keep in mind about Clinton is "he wakes up every day and he may grumble a little bit . . . but he's not the kind of guy who pulls up the sheets over his head and says, 'I'm not going to go out today and play.' So people say, 'Oh, he was paralyzed or he was furious.' He may be furious but he's still relatively constructive. . . . I heard a lot of people picture him walking around . . . Chappaqua . . . talking to himself; even in those days when he really didn't have anything to do, he was still . . . fairly constructive in trying to handle the problems that he had caused for himself or had been thrown at him."[130]

Arkansas Democrat-Gazette political editor Bill Simmons echoes Leon Panetta's explanation about why Clinton gave the boneheaded pardons: because things were going too well. Simmons calls Clinton's political history a "Ferris wheel; he's always up and down."[131] To political consultant Hank Sheinkopf, Clinton is "a political Fred Astaire, he knows how to dance." He "finds the moment" to pick himself up "and his timing is excellent."[132]

ALL FORMER presidents have offices paid for by the taxpayers. Clinton was now a suburban householder, husband of the senator from New York, and no one expected him to be anywhere but Manhattan. It wasn't his fault that Manhattan is among the most expensive real estate markets in the country. But again, his famous political instincts seemed to fail him—temporarily.

On February 2, 2001, when the *Washington Post* ran a story that the space Clinton was leasing would cost $600,000 or more a year, "three times the amount authorized by Congress," conservative talk radio had another hot topic.[133] Two weeks later, the *New York Times* reported that the rental would cost even more: $738,700 a year for the fifty-sixth floor at Carnegie Hall Tower, 152 West Fifty-seventh Street.[134] His office neighbors would include Eddie Murphy, Jerry Seinfeld, and Barry Diller.[135]

Representative Ernest J. Istook Jr., Republican from Oklahoma, said that that price was way too steep. And he had a soapbox from which to chastise Clinton because he was chairman of the subcommittee that oversees the General Services Administration (GSA), the agency charged with arranging office space for presidents as they leave office. Istook warned that the taxpayers should not be stuck paying the full cost of "a penthouse" for Bill Clinton[136] and claimed that the Carnegie Hall Tower rent cost "more than the annual rent of all other offices of former presidents combined."[137]

Jay Leno got into the act, with a joke that might seem to the average American to be more commonsensical than funny, although Leno's was a point never raised about any other president. "Here's my question: why does he even need an office? He doesn't have a job. Shouldn't you get a job first and then worry about an office?"[138]

Clinton was saved by African American congressman Charles Rangel, whose district includes Harlem. Rangel telephoned the man whom novelist Toni Morrison had dubbed "the first black president," and suggested that he put his office in Harlem.[139] (Morrison paid Clinton that compliment in 1998, when the Lewinsky scandal threatened to bring down his presidency.)

Jake Siewert calls Rangel's suggestion "a stroke of genius" and credits Clinton with seeing "a way out on that one and [taking] it pretty fast."[140] Bill Clinton, it seemed, was back in his zone. An idea that was not his was credited to his natural inclusiveness and openheartedness. "It was a great foresight for him to establish his office in Harlem," said Vartan Gregorian, president of the Carnegie Corporation, expressing a common sentiment: "I think [he has] done more for Harlem . . . because he broke the line by moving there."[141] That accolade pales in comparison to that of Clinton backer Joe Power, a Chicago trial lawyer: "What he's trying to do symbolically by taking his office and putting it in Harlem . . . [is] look to the future and pick up those who are the poorest among us. . . . I think he's trying to do whatever he can to end world hunger, to end hunger in this country, to provide medical care to everyone who needs it."[142]

As one Clinton friend puts it, "Bill Clinton owes Charlie Rangel bigtime on that move."[143]

A negative story that made him look profligate with the public's purse turned into a public relations bonanza, and, in the end, Bill Clinton got his fourteenth-floor penthouse, with spectacular views of Central Park, Midtown, and the George Washington Bridge, but at 55 West 125th Street, on the neighborhood's busiest shopping street.

Before the deal was closed, he had to battle a political opponent of Hillary's, Mayor Giuliani, whose city agency, the Administration for Children's Services, had already rented the space for a Harlem field office. Although at first cranky about the transaction, Giuliani agreed to take lesser space so Clinton could have the penthouse. "I believe that President Clinton's being in New York, and particularly being in Harlem, is a very good thing," he said at a news conference at City Hall. "I think it is something that will say something very significant about where Harlem is now, not only to the people of New York, but to the rest of the country."[144]

The annual rent was modest at $210,000 as opposed to the rent at the Carnegie Hall Tower, which was finally reported at $811,000.[145]

When Clinton went to look at the space, the New York Times reported, "a crowd of people in the street shouted 'We love you, we love you! . . . Please come to Harlem.'" On one of his first visits, he took a walk, trailed by fans, and he made a beeline for Bayou, a nearby Cajun Creole restaurant, where, according to the Times, he ate "shrimp and okra gumbo."[146] "I used to tell people he's very happy to drink out of fine china but he doesn't mind if his coffee comes in a styrofoam cup," Jake Siewert says. "He's not that kind of a person who's real stuck-up."[147]

The newly renovated building was closer to his house in Chappaqua, and it was not as if he had to take the subway to get to the rapidly gentrifying area. He had a black SUV and a Secret Service agent to drive him.[148] He would go to that office only once a week or so; he thrived on the adulation of his new neighbors, and he appreciated the fact that African Americans had loved him through Monica and impeachment, and, in his opinion, had correctly seen the scandal as manufactured by a bunch of uptight white Republicans.

If Clinton did not exactly deserve the badge of courage bestowed upon him, he did deserve an "attaboy" for putting himself in the center of a spectacularly positive story. His new office was in an economic empowerment zone, which he as president had helped to create from Charlie Rangel–sponsored legislation.[149] And he constructed a centerpiece for his postpresidential work by proclaiming, as the Times reported, that Harlem represented "a lot of what I want to do in my post-presidential years—bringing economic opportunity to people and places who don't have it here at home and around the world, and bringing people of different races and religions and backgrounds together."[150]

He swerved off the believability track when he told the Times reporters that as a Rhodes scholar at Oxford, when he was in his early twenties, he used to come to New York, "and every single time I did, I took the public transportation to 125th Street on the West Side—I mean the East Side—and

I would walk down 125th all the way west. . . . And people—this is back in the 60's now—people would come up to me and say—ask me what I was doing here and I said I don't know, I just liked it; I felt at home."[151]

Not surprisingly, the senator from New York, Hillary Clinton, was all for it. Public relations don't get any sweeter than that.[152]

However, Hillary was also reportedly miffed that her husband's press conference upstaged her first speech—on health care—in the Senate.[153]

Vernon Jordan, an African American civil rights leader turned investment banker, who lives at the Regency Hotel on Park Avenue, liked to tease Clinton, "Did you ever in your wildest dreams imagine that you'd end up in Harlem and I'd end up on Park Avenue?"[154]

"I've got to let it go," Clinton told Jonathan Alter. "Being angry or resentful is totally destructive."[155] Clinton liked to tell the story about when, in 1998, he visited South Africa—he is proud that he made the first trip by an American president to South Africa—he toured, with Nelson Mandela, the jail cell on Robben Island where he had suffered for twenty-seven years. Clinton asked Mandela if, as he walked out of that cell to freedom, he hated his jailers, some of whom he would later invite to his inauguration and place in his government. Mandela said he did, but he recognized that if he didn't let the hatred go, his jailers would "still have me. I wanted to be free and so I let it go." Clinton seemed to equate his political problems, even his pursuit by Ken Starr, to Mandela's battle against apartheid. "Whenever I feel anger and resentment rising inside myself, I try to think of what Mandela said, and follow his example. We'd all be a lot happier if we could do that."[156]

He was also starting to see the outlines of a plan. "You lose your power but not your influence," he said to the *Atlantic Monthly*'s James Fallows. "But the influence must be concentrated in a few areas."[157]

The memoir loomed large, but the actual hard and lonely work of writing was not inviting. Jake Siewert says Clinton saw the project as "his job, . . . in his mind that was what he was going to be doing."[158] But he was not ready to start, and he put off meeting with publishers. He and his Washington agent, lawyer Robert Barnett, were waiting for some of the negative headlines to subside.[159]

The high-rent stories pushed the pardon stories off the front pages for a time, but the pardon controversy was back and there were calls for investigations and even speculation that Clinton might have done something illegal.

He needed something far more dramatic that would catapult him back on the world stage and he found it in an earthquake that had struck the western state of Gujarat in India on January 26, 2001. The quake was described as the most powerful to hit India in more than fifty years, registering a magnitude of 7.9, rendering more than nine hundred villages rubble, killing some nineteen thousand, the actual toll perhaps as high as a hundred thousand.[160]

The former president was already a much-loved figure in India and so the visit he was planning in April and the several million dollars in contributions for earthquake relief that he was trying to raise, much of it from the Indian American community, guaranteed he'd be greeted as a hero. "India was the perfect choice of country," says Richard Feachem, executive director of the Global Fund to Fight AIDS, Tuberculosis and Malaria, and under-secretary-general of the United Nations. "He has a very special status in India, he is a much-loved figure in India because of what he did during his presidency."[161]

Raymond C. Offenheiser Jr., president of Oxfam America, a Boston-based organization dedicated to ending global poverty, was in Bombay when he saw "massive crowds on the streets trying to . . . see [Clinton] go by; there were massive events at the major hotels in the city that turned out everybody who was anybody in Bombay. . . . It was the major [story] in the major Indian newspapers all over the country for that entire week as he traveled through India." While in the United States, Clinton's work raising money preparatory to his trip drew scant notice, pushed out of the headlines by pardon stories, including a *Time* cover story, "The Incredible Shrinking Ex-President: How Can We Miss You If You Never Go Away?; Smelly Pardons, Expensive Gifts, Deluxe Offices—Is This Any Way for a Former President to Behave?" That was not the case in India. "You could just see the energy that was in the air," says Offenheiser.[162]

He would also visit his friend Nelson Mandela in South Africa and he would go to Nigeria to get a close-up look at the AIDs crisis. Mandela was a special pleasure for Clinton, a way to remind himself that there was a world of good feeling for him beyond the ugly carping in New York and Washington. At the height of the impeachment mess in 1998, Mandela had come to the White House—while there he accepted a Congressional Gold Medal—and, during a speech in the East Room, said, "I just don't understand what your country is doing to this great man." Melanne Verveer, who was there, recalls that Mandela "talked about what Bill Clinton represented to him and his country and the world. . . . It was just so personal and so embracing of Bill Clinton in one of his lowest moments."[163]

Verveer, who was part of the large entourage for that Africa trip in 1998, says that Clinton had insisted that the trip not be fancy dinners and toasts, but that he venture into the rural areas and "really mix it up with the people." She recalls a stop in Senegal; "a very poor" villager on the side of the dusty road waved to the president and he ordered the motorcade stopped, bounded out, and hugged the man. "They're still talking about that in Senegal," she says. "Imagine the president of the United States. . . . There were pictures of this all over the paper."[164] After his presidency, Clinton knew that he wanted to revisit that poor village.

The trip to India for earthquake relief was a tonic, and Clinton was happy to travel abroad. He soon learned that foreign hosts were happy to have him.

IN 1990, WHEN he was still governor of Arkansas, Bill Clinton's salary of $35,000 was the lowest among governors of the fifty states. New York's Mario Cuomo made $130,000.[165]

Clinton did much better as president, $200,000 in salary, a $50,000 expense account, and no living expenses, but he left the White House owing approximately $12 million to the lawyers who represented him during the scandals that pockmarked his presidency.[166] As part of his last-day-on-the-job deal with the independent counsel, he had to promise not to seek government reimbursement of his legal bills.[167]

The stories about the Clintons and their lives of public service forgot that Hillary had been a partner in the Rose Law Firm, the most important in Arkansas, and that they would make millions on leaving the presidency. Hillary had already signed an $8 million contract for her memoir, just before her new position as U.S. senator would have made acceptance of the advance illegal, and Bill figured that when he signed for his memoir, his advance would be even higher. His immediate postpresidency staffing needs might not have been sufficiently addressed, but his staffers had signed him, while he was still in the White House, with the Harry Walker Agency, which was busy booking speeches at a minimum of $100,000 each.[168] At that rate, if he gave ninety speeches a year, he would earn $9 million, so there was no doubt that he was poised to become a wealthy man.

But friends say that Clinton was not reassured by his potential; he would feel better about his family's future only when he had money in hand. His financial fears were expressed in his red-faced rage, in late August 1999, when he learned, while on the golf course with Terry McAuliffe, that he would not be approved for the mortgage he needed to buy the house in Chappaqua that would allow Hillary to run for the Senate from New York. McAuliffe remembers Clinton's anguish: "We're going to lose this damn house." In an unusual bit of candor, McAuliffe reveals that Clinton was terrified to tell Hillary that they were being turned down because of the scandal-related legal bills. McAuliffe offered to loan the president $1.34 million and the deal was saved. (Once the news broke of the McAuliffe loan, banks offered the Clintons a conventional mortgage and McAuliffe got his money back. He called it "the shortest $1.35 million loan ever.")[169]

A bright spot for Clinton was his presidential library in Little Rock. His legacy "was so important to him," says Bud Yorkin. When Yorkin and his wife visited Clinton at his Harlem office, "He always had to show you the model—'Look at this. Right down here, they can read every letter I ever wrote.'"[170]

The not-so-bright spot was that he had a stack of bills to pay, a daughter still in college with graduate school in her plans, and two expensive residences to maintain.

At first as Clinton arranged his boxes of books, he wondered, with good reason, if he would be able to make his fortune as a speaker. During his lowest moods, he worried that the business, policy, and nonprofit worlds would reject him out of fear that their members would be offended by his very presence. That fed into his biggest insecurity—that he did not really belong in the elite circles in which he mixed, that he was, after all, just white trash. It hardly seemed to matter that he was one of only forty-two men who had been president of the United States and the only Democrat to be reelected since FDR.

"Initially a lot of people ran scared of him," recalls Jake Siewert. "There was a lot of hesitancy at some of the firms for all the obvious reasons. . . . At the time it was as if you were taking a stand if you asked him to speak to you."[171]

His first postpresidency speech, to Morgan Stanley Dean Witter & Company's Global Leveraged Finance Conference in Boca Raton, Florida, was scheduled for February 5, 2001, for a fee of $125,000. Newspapers reported that the company's chairman, Philip J. Purcell, had e-mailed clients that he thought it a mistake to have invited Clinton. "We should have thought twice before the speaking invitation was extended. Our failure to do so was particularly unfortunate in light of Mr. Clinton's actions in leaving the White House."[172]

Purcell might have fretted that his audience of important customers would be listening to Bill Clinton talk about the accomplishments of his administration or tax policy or globalization but they would not be able to get out of their minds the image of Monica in the president's study, just off the Oval Office, giving the president oral sex while he lobbied a congressman on the telephone.[173]

Robert Torricelli, one of Clinton's confidants, then a U.S. senator from New Jersey, saw this insult to the former president as one more blast from the lunatic Right: "He found his footing. The Far Right . . . is never going to be comfortable with Bill Clinton's success . . . and what he has come to represent to many Americans."[174]

Clinton gave his speech, basked in enthusiastic applause, and the boost to his mood was palpable. Five days later, on February 10, he was warmly received at a synagogue, the Aventura-Turnberry Jewish Center in Aventura, Florida, and paid a fee of $150,000.[175]

The objections voiced at Morgan Stanley Dean Witter did not stop there. "This has happened over and over," says Melanne Verveer. She recalls talking to a businessman who said that "he stuck out his neck at his company and basically made the decision that Bill Clinton would be the keynote speaker, and . . . there were a lot of murmurings that is this really what we want? . . . They weren't die-hard Democrats by any stretch of the imagination. And the long and short of it was he came, he saw, he conquered. They couldn't stop applauding; they thought it was the best speech they ever heard."[176]

The lecture agent, Donald Walker, denied reports that some groups that had invited the former president were canceling. "There has never, ever been a speaker nearly as much in demand as President Clinton on the lecture circuit," Walker told a reporter for the *Boston Globe*. "He is the highest-priced speaker in the history of the lecture circuit."[177] He was soon outearning his nearest competitor, former secretary of state Colin Powell.[178]

To his relief, Clinton found that paying off his debts was easy. He gave essentially the same speech everywhere he went, so there was not much work involved; he got to travel in style, and, before long, he owed no one anything, says Bud Yorkin, "not a dime."[179] He was, says another friend, "surprised" and "enormously" pleased at just how easy it was for him to earn all those hundreds of thousands of dollars.[180] He soon had a net worth in the millions. "He felt a lot better after he got all his bills paid and had a lot of money," says Jonathan Alter. "He wasn't doing it for the money, but the money . . . eased the pain. You know how money is a motive for a lot of people. For him it wasn't a motive; it was more like a treatment for his transition."[181]

Republican strategist/lobbyist Scott Reed watched Bob Dole climb out of debt after a lifetime in public office; and then he watched Clinton do the same by getting "two hundred grand a whack for the speeches." Reed also points to another income source that is often missing from the calculations of Clinton's postpresidential earnings. His billionaire friend Ron Burkle gave Clinton a piece of his Yucaipa Global Opportunities Fund, which has reportedly yielded him millions and will continue to do so. Before long, the speeches were just frosting on a very large cake.[182] The *Wall Street Journal* estimated that the fund would yield Bill Clinton "tens of millions."[183]

The former president would make more than $50 million in speaking fees over seven years, according to newspaper analyses and a review of Senator Hillary Clinton's financial disclosure reports through 2005. He earned an additional $10.2 million in speaking fees in 2006, including $450,000 for one speech in London in September 2006. Hillary's disclosure forms do not reveal how much her spouse collects from Burkle's Yucaipa fund, only that it's more than one thousand dollars. Much more.[184]

Still, it wasn't until he gave his first speech abroad in March 2001 that he realized that he was home free. Audiences loved him; reporters described him ad nauseum as a "rock star." He did not like it that some bluenoses back home thought him an unsavory character, but it was easier to take once he recognized that he was a hit in Europe, Asia, South America, Australia, Canada. Between March 9 and March 14, 2001, he gave speeches in Vancouver, in Maastricht, the Netherlands, in Baden-Baden, Germany, and in Copenhagen, Denmark. (His take was $700,000.)[185]

In Baden-Baden, Clinton watched the awarding of the German Media Prize—which he himself had received in 1999—collected $250,000 for a speech, and, as reported in the *Boston Globe*, "cried after delivering an emotional appeal for rich nations to give more aid to poor countries. Then he walked the mile back to his hotel, mobbed by local residents."[186]

Chicago supporter Mike Cherry and his wife traveled there to be with the former president. Cherry remembers how happy Clinton looked, almost a look of freedom, as if he had been sprung from a prison cell. "A little kid," Cherry recalls, "was running down the street trying to get ahead of this group. We were like a rock star going through, . . . the little boy still running carrying a scruffy piece of paper and a pencil." Clinton gestured him over and, as the cameras clicked, gave him the autograph.[187] He was regaining his touch.

Friends use medical metaphors to describe the joy Clinton felt at the approval he found. "It's like somebody who's anemic who gets a blood transfusion," says Alan Solomont, former national finance chairman of the Democratic National Committee. "He got his footing and as the world came to accept him he stopped feeling sorry for himself."[188] Tony Coelho describes how cheering crowds "juiced up" the deflated former president.[189]

The fees he commanded abroad that first spring out of the White House—$250,000 in Hong Kong—were twice what he was making at home. Between May 14 and June 8, 2001, he delivered speeches in Norway, Sweden, Austria, Poland, Spain, Ireland, England, France, back to England. His total take was $1,599,999. During the last quarter of 2001, Clinton pulled in more than $3,353,000; fifteen of the twenty-three speeches were outside the United States.[190]

"When he stepped down," says Tony Coelho, "he felt that people globally felt the same way that people domestically felt. He found that wasn't true, that people globally loved him." Clinton had many more speaking invitations coming in from abroad than he had available dates. "And when he did travel internationally, the rooms were packed," says Coelho. "He'd go to these . . . conferences where he would be only one part of a conference and the rooms with the other conference speakers were empty and people were demanding to get into his speech. And it gave him all the confidence in the world again. He became a rock star internationally."

At that point, says Coelho, Clinton's luck resurfaced: the domestic press was so busy with the aftermath of the pardons and the presidential election recount that reporters tended not to look too closely at the former president's other activities. If editors thought about the disgraced president, they presumably figured he was hanging out at home. Meanwhile, says Coelho, "they didn't concentrate on the hundreds of thousands of dollars that he was making. . . . They would have written that up front-page and tried to embarrass him on that amount of money."

The coverage from the international media was adoring. "He can charge a group $300,000 for a speech," says Coelho, "and the media would make it look like he was giving that group $300,000."[191]

Rabbi David Saperstein, director of the Religious Action Center of Reformed Judaism—he lobbies for the interests of Reformed Judaism before Congress and the administration—is not surprised that Bill Clinton emerged on top. "I do know that as is so often the case with him, the actual doing of things, the actual engagement with life, took on its own life. . . . No one could draw the crowds, no one could excite the crowds, the way he did, and I'm sure that helped to get the juices flowing again."[192]

Eyebrows were raised over the number of zeros on the checks that foreign entities paid for his services. According to a report in the *Washington Post*, he raked in $600,000 for two speeches to an investment firm in Saudi Arabia; $200,000 for one speech to a real estate development company in China; and $400,000 for one speech to a "political studies center" in Japan.[193] "It's perfectly okay," says Larry Sabato, "he's now a private citizen. But it's not the most admirable thing for an ex-president to do."[194]

Eventually the American press began to notice and to report that Clinton was collecting large fees from poor nonprofits—including modestly endowed public colleges. On March 26, 2001, Clinton spoke in Salem, Massachusetts, to Salem State College. His fee was $125,000. This was Salem State, not Harvard (where he spoke on November 19, 2001) or Yale (October 6, 2001). Both Ivies were presumably pro bono, because they do not appear on Hillary's disclosure forms. Salem State certainly didn't lose money on the event, and Clinton's fee was said to be raised from private sources—the thirty-six hundred tickets, ranging in price from $25 to $125, quickly sold out.[195]

That Clinton was not the first celebrity to speak at the college, which in years past had hosted Presidents Bush, Carter, and Ford, as well as Gloria Steinem and former secretary of state Henry Kissinger,[196] seemed hardly to matter to the *Boston Globe* reporter who lambasted Clinton. "While Clinton would prefer that the public take note of his interest in helping poor nations, the reality is that, for Clinton, much of his time since leaving office has been focused on money."[197]

Three days later, Joe Fitzgerald, writing in the *Boston Herald*, more conservative, working class, and never a fan of Clinton's, asked, ". . . were you, also, a bit appalled watching Nancy Harrington, the matronly president of Salem State College, giddily greet the disgraced Bill Clinton like some goo-goo-eyed adolescent fawning over her favorite rock star? . . . If there's one place this empty vessel ought not to be welcomed, it's a campus populated by coeds, most of whom, presumably, have been taught not to tolerate the kind of workplace exploitation that became Clinton's calling card. . . . And that's to say nothing about pardoning criminals, lying to grand juries, grabbing gifts and looting souvenirs." He branded as disgraceful the "hero's welcome" given "to someone so predatory, so vile, so deep in denial."[198]

At the end of his speech, Clinton was greeted with a standing ovation. Earlier, the *Boston Herald* reported, outside in the bitter cold stood a handful of protesters clutching LIAR, LIAR signs. At a private dinner for Clinton at the Hawthorne Hotel in Salem, protesters carried signs warning COUNT THE TOWELS.[199]

In June 2001, he was a guest at a surprise birthday party for Juanita Jordan given by her then husband, Michael, at a restaurant he owned in Chicago.[200] Film critic Roger Ebert was also there. "Now you've got Michael Jordan in a room and Bill Clinton comes into that room, the center of gravity shifted and in particular I was looking around at all the women. . . . First they were looking at Michael and now they're looking at Clinton."[201] (Clinton played golf with Michael Jordan at Conway Farms Golf Club in Lake Forest, near the Chicago Bears training camp.)[202]

Clinton was starting to have more fun, to revel in the return of his personal magnetism. But he recognized that he had a long way to go.

Chapter 3

GETTING SERIOUS, STUDYING THE LEGACY OF JIMMY CARTER

B ILL CLINTON CAN'T STAND JIMMY CARTER.
"There are a few people who have offended him . . . on whom he
never gives up, he never forgives," says South Carolinian Don Fowler,
who was Democratic National Committee chairman from 1992 to 1996
and is a friend of both Bill Clinton and Jimmy Carter.[1]

Yet Clinton could see what a remarkably productive postpresidency
Carter had built for himself. When Lynn Cutler, who is close to both
former presidents, is asked on whom Clinton modeled his post–White
House life, she immediately replies, "Oh, there's only one who has done
anything—Carter."[2]

Carter's status on leaving the White House was as grim as Clinton's.
After losing to a grade-B movie actor, Carter was dismissed as incompetent, lacking in vision, a micromanager, and the kind of ridiculous figure
who could go out fishing on a pond at his farm in Plains and get threatened by a "killer rabbit." By the time Carter turned the White House over
to Ronald Reagan, he had become almost a cartoon, a man who seemed
to turn everything he touched into failure—the humiliating 444-day

hostage crisis, gas lines, "malaise," 21 percent interest rates, lectures about turning down the thermostat and remembering to wear that grandfatherly cardigan.

"Carter had frogs and boils and every damn thing happening to him," says Bob Kerrey.[3] At the 1980 Democratic Convention, when Carter chased Ted Kennedy around the stage trying to shake his hand, many Americans could understand Kennedy's impulse to dodge the sitting president. (Kennedy had attempted to wrest the presidential nomination away from Carter.) The betting was that Carter would go into a quiet retirement and Americans would at last be free of his lectures and piety.

But Carter defied expectations, and while there are people, like Bill Clinton, who detest him, there are many more who pack audiences at his lectures, make his books bestsellers, and agree with Gore loyalist and Kennedy School lecturer Elaine Kamarck that Carter's is "the gold standard for the postpresidency."[4]

When Clinton turned his attention to righting the world's wrongs, he recognized that. "Clinton had a lot of respect for how Carter had managed to maintain a role in public policy in his postpresidency and certainly saw that as a model," says Jake Siewert. "If you look at what he's done, a lot of it is modeled directly on what Carter has done." Siewert points to, among other things, Carter's skill at "pick[ing] issues."[5]

Mark Updegrove, who has written a book on the American postpresidency and calls the relationship between the two "contentious," says that Clinton, determined to remove the stain of his sexual misdeeds from his legacy, also is drawn to the "redemptive aspects of Carter's postpresidency."[6]

Yet the differences between them prevented a cooperative relationship from taking root. Clinton is motivated both by wanting people to like him, and by making a difference in the world. Carter, free of the need to win votes, does not care if people like him; he simply wants the world to work in the way that he believes is the right way. Clinton's need for approval was also part of the problem, says Jody Powell, a friend of Carter's and his presidential press secretary. "Clinton is one of these people who always tries to leave people with a good feeling and sort of tries to tell them what they want to hear. And President Carter is if anything the opposite extreme, . . . very direct. . . . The couple of . . . occasions that I know about that produced some hard feelings, President Carter thought he understood President Clinton to be saying one thing and then would find out that wasn't what was going to happen."[7]

Clinton sees Carter as a failed president and a surprisingly successful ex-president. He sees himself as an extremely successful president, who might have done even more had the right wing not tried to hound him from office. Clinton recoiled from Carter's schoolmarmish style, his chilly, stubborn morality. Clinton understood his own need for the big stage, the deafening applause, the rock star's entrance.

Yet Clinton also understood that it was Carter's unglamorous crusades against hideous third world diseases that brought him the Nobel Peace Prize, and Clinton wanted to win one, too. Much as he would have liked not to give Jimmy Carter another thought, he was, in a way, stuck with him.

The history between the presidents is downright ugly.

Clinton was in his first term as governor and Carter was finishing his only term as president when, in 1980, Carter dispatched eighteen thousand of the hundred thousand Cuban refugees that Fidel Castro's Mariel boatlift had deposited on beaches in Florida to Fort Chaffee in Arkansas. Some had committed crimes or were mentally ill. In Arkansas, the gubernatorial terms were then only two years, and Clinton was up for reelection. His opponent portrayed him as a Carter crony, a description that hurt when hundreds of the refugees broke out of Fort Chaffee and rioted. Carter promised that Arkansas would get no more refugees but then reneged and dispatched still more to Fort Chaffee. Both men lost in 1980, and Clinton never forgave Carter for the humiliation of that potentially career-killing defeat.[8] Others say that Clinton's naïve decision to raise fees on car tags would have cost him the election anyway.[9] Reporter Bill Simmons, who covered Clinton back then, said the voters reacted negatively to Clinton's plow-ahead manner and his dismissive attitude. "He meant to do so much in such a short period of time and he went at it so aggressively that he irritated a lot of important segments of the Arkansas political power establishment."[10]

The loss sent Clinton into what Carter aide Hamilton Jordan described as "a personal funk. Arkansas acquaintances told me that he was having trouble absorbing his defeat, that he talked about it and relived it endlessly. Clinton found himself suddenly out of office with nothing to do and was recklessly chasing women."[11] According to Simmons, Clinton eventually pulled himself out of the dumps, and "resurrected his political career . . . by going on TV" and making an "abject apology . . . for pressing too hard on things that the people weren't ready for." He paid for the ads himself.[12]

When Clinton became president, the relationship soured even more. Jody Powell recalls that Clinton's young staffers "wanted to make sure that they were in no way to be compared to the Carter administration."[13] Hamilton Jordan saw that for himself when he was invited to Little Rock to meet confidentially (i.e., he was not to tell the press) with Clinton aide George Stephanopolous, who was uninterested in taking any advice from Jordan. Jordan gave it, anyway, warning Stephanopolous: ". . . if you don't do anything else, get rid of the Independent Counsel law. It is a bad law!' . . . It will bite your administration in the ass just like it did our administration and Reagan's and Bush's."[14]

A week before the Clinton inauguration, Carter gave an interview to Alessandra Stanley of the *New York Times* in which he proclaimed himself "very disappointed" that the Clintons had decided to send Chelsea to Sidwell Friends, an exclusive private school in Washington, instead of following the example of the Carters who sent their daughter, Amy, to a D.C. public school. "Amy really enjoyed going to a very low income school with students whose parents were the servants of foreign ambassadors," Carter said.[15]

At his inauguration, the new president and first lady publicly ostracized the Carters, going so far, Jordan wrote, "as to celebrate the Reagans in public ceremonies, while ignoring the Carters, who had enthusiastically supported Clinton in his campaign for president."[16] Clinton praised his predecessors of both parties but never mentioned Carter. "It was rude beyond belief," Rosalynn told Douglas Brinkley. "Not even Reagan would have done a thing like that."[17]

Postinauguration, Carter alienated Clinton with his bull-in-the-China-shop approach to diplomacy. One writer who has covered Carter calls it "reckless freelancing diplomacy." If he believed he was right, off he went, diplomatic niceties be damned. One prominent Democrat attributes Carter's behavior during the Clinton presidency to pique over being ignored by Clinton, who rarely sought his advice and did not effectively brief him, an accommodation routinely afforded former presidents.[18] "President Carter may have had expected to be able to do more and be of more help with a Democratic president," explains Jody Powell.[19]

Carter got Clinton's attention by involving himself—Clinton would have called it "meddling"—in North Korea, where he attempted to negotiate a nuclear-freeze deal with the dictator Kim Il Sung, and in Haiti, where Carter tried to negotiate the removal of the military dictator and the return to democratic rule. What happened in Haiti, says Larry King, resulted from "Carter feeling stiffed." King recounts the story he heard from Colin Powell who was there: "Midnight was the bewitching hour. At ten minutes before midnight, Clinton called Carter and said, 'You better get out because I'm sending in the troops,' and Carter said, 'You can send 'em but I ain't leaving.' I think that embarrassed Clinton; in other words, he didn't listen to the president. . . . It left some scars."[20]

Carter would volunteer for freelance diplomacy, not by calling Clinton or his secretary of state or his national security adviser. He'd simply announce his mission by appearing on CNN. "There were times when we felt Carter was being just sort of intrusive and not adding a lot of value," says Jake Siewert.[21]

And then there was sex.

Jimmy Carter always viewed Clinton as a scandal waiting to happen, says Larry Sabato, who adds that Carter was "well aware of Clinton's problems even before he became president." Carter "did not regard Bill Clinton very highly because of his sexual escapades. . . . That's not Carter's thing at all. He may have lusted in his heart [as he said in his famous *Playboy* interview], but he never followed through on it."[22]

Douglas Brinkley, author of a biography of Carter, says that "Carter let me into his diaries, personal papers, documents," and they are full of reasons why "Carter doesn't like Clinton."[23] Brinkley writes of a visit by Carter to Clinton in the Oval Office a few days after the Lewinsky story broke. For ninety minutes, Brinkley wrote, Clinton told Carter about the right-wing conspiracy.* "As Carter prepared to leave the Oval Office, Clinton asked [him] . . . to pray for him in his hour of darkness. It was the most intimate moment the two men ever shared."[24]

Instead of keeping his thoughts about Lewinsky to himself, Carter said that he had been "deeply embarrassed by what occurred."[26] Eight months later, Carter said that Clinton "had not been truthful in the deposition given in the Paula Jones case or in the interrogation by the grand jury."[27]

Jimmy Carter was close to Al Gore, whom he saw as having a strong moral core. He admired the Gores' close marriage, as well as Al's crusade against global warming and Tipper's crusade for warning labels on rock albums. As couples the Gores and Carters are close.[28]

Clinton's friends call Carter "self-righteous,"[29] "morally priggish,"[30] "finger wagging, judgmental,"[31] and they guffaw over his lust-in-his-heart remark.

Carter continued to show an ugly knack for moralizing about Clinton when he was at his lowest: for instance, Carter, as quoted in the *Arkansas Democrat-Gazette*, called the Marc Rich pardon "disgraceful" and said, with his characteristic honesty, "I don't think there is any doubt that

---

*Clinton called Gerald Ford during the darkest hours of the Monica Lewinsky crisis and asked for, but did not take, his advice: "Bill, you've got to be straightforward with the people on this. Because it's not going to go away." Ford told Mark Updegrove that Clinton had told him that the Lewinsky charges were all a lie. "He's sick—he's got an addiction," Ford told *New York Daily News* Washington Bureau chief Thomas M. DeFrank in 1999, in off-the-record-until-his-death conversations. Betty Ford, who battled addictions to drugs and alcohol, agreed that Clinton was a sex addict but concluded that he would never seek treatment because he was in denial. Ford added that Clinton had "already damaged his presidency beyond repair." In other conversations with DeFrank, Ford, who enjoyed Clinton's company, opined that Clinton's sex addiction "affects his judgment." Ford was particularly troubled by the Marc Rich pardon which he called "unconscionable." Ford reflected on Clinton's character: "He's a very talented guy, but he has no convictions—none whatsoever."[25]

some of the factors in the [Rich] pardon were attributable to his large gifts."[32]

Carter also thought it unseemly that Clinton made millions from his speaking engagements. Carter rarely gives speeches for money, and, when he does, he gives the money to charity or to fund Carter Center programs.[33] Carter, who still lives in his old family house in Plains, makes his money on books[34] and does not sit on boards of directors or accept consulting fees.[35]

Carter also looked askance at Clinton's constant use of other people's private jets. Carter proudly pulls his wheelie bag through airports to commercial flights, although, according to Jody Powell, supporters and some of the companies that support Carter's programs "do provide chartered, private flights for him on occasion." When Jimmy and Rosalynn recently visited Powell and his wife at their house on the eastern shore of Maryland to fish and hunt, "they were on a commercial jet coming out of Atlanta and sat on the tarmac for three hours, the weather was bad, waiting to get into Baltimore."[36]

Carter refrained from building the typical self-glorifying and perpetuating presidential library and instead built the decidedly activist Carter Center, which, among other good works, promotes human rights around the world, and works to eradicate guinea worm and other diseases.[37]

Former *Time* magazine columnist Christopher Ogden calls Carter "a pain in the ass to a lot of administrations."[38] The former president had, for example, sent letters to all members of the United Nations Security Council urging them to vote against President George H. W. Bush's use of force in the first Gulf War and thereby destroy the coalition Bush was building as he took on Saddam Hussein. Bush was furious. "What the hell's the matter with this guy?" Bush raged.[39] According to one person who held a top position on a newsmagazine, Bush considers Carter's actions "tantamount to treason almost."[40]

IN THE summer of 2001, Bill Clinton with his agent, Robert Barnett, decided that the negative headlines had receded sufficiently for the former president to sign a contract to write his memoir. Unlike Hillary, whose book had gone to auction and ended up at Simon & Schuster, Barnett, also Hillary's agent, took Clinton's memoir exclusively to Knopf.

Bill Clinton had frequently mused that he wanted to write a memoir that approached in quality Katharine Graham's *Personal History*, published by Knopf in 1997. That book was edited by Robert Gottlieb, a veteran of decades in book publishing, who had returned to his longtime home at Knopf, after editing *The New Yorker*.[41]

Hillary Clinton had also held up the memoir by Graham, who had died earlier that summer, as a model for her book. Hillary did not hold up Bill's mother's memoir, *Leading with My Heart*, which described Virginia Kelley's first impression of the young Hillary as "No makeup. Coke bottle glasses. Brown hair with no apparent style," and portrayed the young feminist Hillary as lacking in style, but Bill did, telling friends that he hoped to emulate its honesty.[42]

Hillary's advance for her memoir was $8 million.[43] Bill's for his was $12 million, believed to be the largest advance ever for a nonfiction book. He signed the contract in August 2001 with a due date of early 2003.[44]

That Clinton was then seen as a disgraced president obviously did not depress the size of the advance. His tarnished image might have pushed the advance up, in hopes that he would reveal what he was thinking when he had sex with an intern in the White House. Maureen Dowd wrote that Clinton and Barnett promised "a very thorough and candid telling of his life." To Dowd that meant, "hot Oval Office sex scenes with you-know-which highly accommodating intern."[45]

At the deal's announcement, Sonny Mehta, Knopf's president and editor in chief, said that Clinton was obviously capable of writing candidly about all aspects of his life and presidency. "Have you listened to him talk?" Mehta asked a reporter for the *New York Times*. "That is one of the things that convinces you."[46]

Clinton had promised people at Knopf not to discuss the memoir and then goofed by talking to Jonathan Alter, who was writing a piece for

Newsweek about the book deal. During that conversation Clinton said that the book "may not be as mean as some people want it to be. This shouldn't be about settling scores but setting the record straight." He said he was "going to let a lot of stuff go." He told Alter that he did not want a book that is "either turgid and boring or unduly defensive. I want to explain to people who I am and what I tried to do in public life—the good things we did and the mistakes I made. And I want to make it come alive."[47]

Clinton said his model was Ulysses S. Grant, who wrote his memoir while he was dying of throat cancer—he finished it days before his death—and openly admitted that he did it for the money. *Personal Memoirs of U. S. Grant*, published in 1885, is about the Civil War; Grant died before he could write about his presidency. The book, published by Mark Twain, sold 350,000 copies at publication, earned Grant's family $450,000 in royalties, and remains in print. It is considered one of the greatest works of nineteenth-century nonfiction.[48]

"Odds are Clinton's book will be some combination of disappointing and delectable," Alter predicted, "just like the man himself."[49]

The former president told his publisher and editor that he intended to write the book himself. Unlike his wife, busy in the Senate, he would not hire a ghostwriter.[50] Although Clinton likes to think of himself as an accomplished writer—when friends visited him in Chappaqua he showed off the desk where he planned to write his memoir—accomplished talker is more like it. One can imagine that Clinton fantasized that the memoir would become so celebrated that the desk on which he sweated over every word would become a historical treasure, like Lincoln's bed.

Getting started was difficult; the discipline of writing was "not exactly his thing," says one political strategist who is close to him,[51] and the prospect of trying to explain his lapses fueled his penchant for procrastination. His excuse was that his calendar was packed with speeches, which, when bundled, were much more lucrative than the $12 million advance, and much more fun.

———

THE LAST TIME Bill Clinton and Al Gore spoke was on the day of George W. Bush's inauguration. Tipper and Al were not among those who went to dinner in Chappaqua. Both men blamed the other for his plight, and neither reached out to try to made amends.[52]

On September 8, 2001, Bill Clinton was again bundling speeches, on the circuit in Australia, where he addressed a group in Sydney; again in Sydney on the ninth; and on Monday, September 10, he was in Melbourne. He was still there when he learned about the terrorist attacks of September 11. Because of the time difference, it was already eleven at night.

He immediately called AP reporter Ron Fournier, who had covered Governor Clinton for the *Arkansas Democrat*. Fournier moved to the AP as White House correspondent during the Clinton years, and on 9/11 was in the same job covering Bush. Clinton told Fournier that he wanted to make a statement of support to the president and to the country. Fournier quickly filed a story, "Former President Clinton, who led the nation through the 1995 Oklahoma City bombing, urged Americans to rally behind President Bush in the aftermath of Tuesday's terrorist attacks. 'We should not be second-guessing. We should be supporting him.'" Fournier described Clinton as "traveling in Australia."[53]

Clinton also worried, and it was a worry that would consume him going forward, that he and his advisers would be blamed for not doing enough to thwart al Qaeda and kill or capture Osama Bin Laden.

With American airports shut down, George W. Bush sent an air force plane to pick up Clinton, who returned to New York on Thursday, September 13.

Al Gore heard the news of the attacks while he was in Vienna, Austria, also fulfilling a speaking engagement. He took a commercial flight to Toronto, where he and an aide rented a car and crossed into the United States at Buffalo. At around eight that Thursday night, Clinton reached Gore, then just outside Buffalo, and invited him to spend the night in Chappaqua. Gore arrived at 3:30 A.M. Friday, and the two men stayed up until dawn talking.[54] According to friends, there was some closing of the breach between them.[55]

"Of course they knew it was al Qaeda," says Elaine Kamarck, "because as we now know they had been watching al Qaeda; and the Bush administration had not been watching al Qaeda."[56]

After an hour's sleep, Clinton and Gore (and Chelsea) flew to Washington on the air force plane that President Bush had provided. There they attended a memorial service at the National Cathedral. They left together to go to Al Gore's house in Arlington, Virginia, and spent much of the afternoon talking. An account in the *New York Times* described something close to a reconciliation and ended with one unidentified person speculating that Al Gore had to fix his relationship with Clinton if he ever planned to run again for president.[57]

"I don't think that they're exactly bosom buddies," says Jonathan Alter of the impact of those conversations.[58] Tom Downey says they had "a long reconciliation," but adds that when he talks to his friend Al Gore, which he does at least once a month, "we don't talk about Clinton. We spend most of our time talking about Bush. . . . There's probably a distance, but at the end of the day they shared something very important together."[59] The men decided, says Elaine Kamarck, to "let bygones be bygones, and I think they've had a much better relationship since then." She adds, however, that "they're not buddies like they were in the first term of the administration."[60] Others describe a wall of ice between them that shows little sign of thawing.[61]

That was evident four years later when Gore did not even respond to an invitation to attend the Hofstra University conference evaluating Bill Clinton's presidency. He was invited "more than once," says conference coordinator Natalie Datlof. "Maybe he felt that he couldn't handle it because he could have been president."[62]

FRIENDS SAY that in the aftermath of 9/11, Bill Clinton's thoughts often dwelled on how sorry he was that he was not president when those planes hit the Twin Towers and the Pentagon.

Bill Clinton is "a voracious reader of biography," says his friend Steve Grossman, DNC chief in Clinton's second term. "There is not a major

American political figure about whom Clinton hasn't read one or more biographies. I think he has compared and contrasted in his own mind over the years the styles of these leaders during moments of crisis."[63]

For Clinton, the problem was that the "crisis" occurred after he left office. He has told Grossman and others that he would have handled things much differently from the way Bush did, starting with his charge to the American people. He would have recognized 9/11 as a Pearl Harbor kind of moment, says Grossman, that called for "serious and true sacrifice on the part of the American people at a moment when he would have had every American behind him, regardless of political party or ideology." Drawing on JFK and his charge to the American people in 1961, Clinton would have said, "Let's develop a serious energy policy in this country. I am going to ask the American people to take some steps. . . . I'm going to do it in the name of finally doing more than just talking about it." Grossman says that he is not suggesting that Clinton is "the only one who could have done it. I believe Ronald Reagan could have done it as well."[64]

It was not just speeches to the nation from the Oval Office dancing in Clinton's head; it was about his legacy, his desire to be included in the ranks of great American presidents—Washington, Lincoln, FDR—all of whom were president during war or depression or both. The nonsense about Monica and impeachment would have been swept away if only Bill Clinton had had the opportunity to grasp this horrific event and deal with it, if only he had been in charge on September 11.

He had communed with the nation so well in 1995 after the Oklahoma City bombing; but Clinton knew that Timothy McVeigh was child's play compared with Osama Bin Laden—more of a body paragraph than a lede in the history of America in the 1990s and into the new century. (Clinton's deputy attorney general, Eric Holder, calls Oklahoma City "not a first-tier event in the way that 9/11 was.")[65]

Clinton's extraordinary communication skills, his ability, even when addressing millions of people, to make each person feel as if he is talking directly to him or to her, might have, Clinton knew, resulted in one of history's greatest speeches. But where was his power, his platform? What was he doing in Australia collecting his fee for addressing J. T. Campbell and Co. Pty. Ltd., a firm of bankers?

Clinton knew that the old speech that had been yielding him those six-figure fees would have to be rewritten. This was a new world, and he knew he would have to work to keep himself relevant.

Still, for the moment, he could not escape the fact that in a post-9/11 world he had a lot of time to play golf.

LATER THAT September 2001, in Chicago, at the Harborside International Golf Center, Bill Clinton sank his first hole in one; he told Mark Buell that it was the first one he had ever seen.[66] Perhaps because it seemed trivial in the wake of September 11, it was hardly big news, although the gossip column "Washington Whispers" noted that the "infamous links cheat" won "bragging rights" by making it "without cheating."[67]

"He was very excited about it," remembers Cook County assessor Jim Houlihan, who was in Clinton's golf party. Houlihan describes the former president after that feat as having "that Cheshire grin and he was just quite pleased." Houlihan remembers no press there to observe.[68] Had it happened when he was president, it would have made news worldwide; one can imagine it leading every network newscast.

Although Clinton did not want the public to see golf as a staple of his postpresidency, he loved the game and found it hard to turn down invitations to play.

When New Jersey state senator Ray Lesniak heard that real estate developer Charles Kushner had invited the former president to speak on October 17, 2001, at a bank Kushner owned in Livingston, New Jersey, Lesniak, an avid Clinton supporter—New Jersey cochairman of the 1996 Clinton-Gore campaign—started to plan for a golf date. Clinton accepted the invitation, and Lesniak immediately set his sights on the tradition-rich Baltursol, host to PGA and U.S. Open tournaments. Located in Springfield, New Jersey, it's considered one of the top ten golf courses in the country. Lesniak was not a member, so the Monday before

Clinton's Wednesday speech, he called a friend who was. "I asked him if he wants to play golf with President Clinton and me." The friend agreed to make arrangements at Baltursol but soon called back: "We can't play; it's a members-only day." Lesniak was shocked but not surprised. "So they wouldn't let the president of the United States play. . . . This is how stuffy this crowd is. . . . They weren't going to make any exceptions for President Clinton?" Lesniak surmises that the reaction would have been different if George H. W. Bush had wanted to play. "So I took him to my club, the Suburban Golf Club in Union, New Jersey, . . . and I'm so glad that Baltursol turned him down because he was welcomed with such open arms at this club."

Lesniak had been warned that Clinton had landed from Europe that day, and that he would be tired and planned to play only four or five holes. "He played all eighteen," Lesniak says. On the way back to the clubhouse, "some people approached him on the tee and asked him some questions about Northern Ireland, . . . and I tried to signal them off and Clinton just put his hand out and spent ten minutes explaining the situation." He also was not too tired, says Lesniak, to take "pictures with the caddies, with the waitresses, with the greens keepers. . . . Everybody was beaming [whereas] at Baltursol they probably would have been very uppity and not care."[69]

Donna Shalala calls Clinton "a competitive golfer." One of the few women who has played golf with him—at the Army/Navy Club when he was president—Shalala says, "He spends a lot of time teaching. He's a good analyzer of games."[70] Clinton's former national security adviser, Sandy Berger, says Clinton will offer improvement tips even when not wanted. "He's a real student of golf," says Berger, "and understands the mechanics. 'Listen, stand up straighter. Put your hand right here,'" he'd lecture Berger; but "it's goodhearted," Berger adds, "it's not at all judgmental."[71]

Some of Clinton's golfing partners claim that in deference to his position they always let him win. Former Arkansas congressman Beryl Anthony, who volunteers that he is a better golfer than Clinton, says with a chuckle, "You always let the commander in chief win."[72] Others maintain that they would never do that: "I don't think anybody who's a real golfer lets anybody win," says John Emerson. On the other hand, he admits, "Maybe they'll give him a putt that they wouldn't give somebody else."[73] Not always. Mark Buell recalls a game with Clinton when Clinton "got upset with me when I made him putt a short putt and he missed it. . . . 'You're not going to make me putt that, are you?' And I said, 'You bet, Mr. President; we've got a bet going here.'"[74]

Jim Houlihan, who had golfed with the president at the historic Bal-lybunion Golf Club in County Kerry, Ireland, scoffs at the very notion of letting Clinton win. "I won't even let my kids beat me in sports. I'm not someone who's going to play some customer golf. I'd say he probably hits a longer ball farther, but I'd be happy to take him on in a competition, and wager on myself." He says that some years back he and Clinton had the same handicap of about thirteen. Hanging in the air is that Houli-han's is now lower.[75]

Clinton seemed at his happiest when he was on the links. Leon Pa-netta describes him telling great stories and showing off his warm person-ality, chatting with other golfers, bystanders, and people there just to catch a glimpse of him. Those people will usually get more than a glimpse; he'll shake their hands, ask about their families, and if he ever meets them again, chances are he'll remember. When he agreed to lec-ture pro bono at the Panetta Institute (at California State University, Monterey Bay Seaside), in lieu of a fee—Panetta told Clinton he could not afford even a cut rate—Clinton happily accepted Panetta setting up a golf game for them with Clint Eastwood, the actor and onetime mayor of Carmel.[76]

People who don't trust Clinton are given to saying that he cheats at golf and that the man who cheats at golf also cheats at life (and on his wife). Others say that Clinton is no different from most golfers. Yes, he takes "mulligans" (extra shots) and "gimmes" (free putts), Shalala says, and "so does every other golfer I know."[77] Leon Panetta, who calls him-self "a recreational golfer," laughs as he recalls Clinton's tactics, which, he stresses, are fine with him. "He can be very competitive on the golf course to the point that he always wants to hit the ball well and if he doesn't, he'll use another ball." Panetta says he's fine with Clinton's style and seems amused by Clinton's need to post a low score. "I think it's fair to say that he kind of likes a very casual game of golf in which at the end of the day he can post a good score, real or unreal."[78]

Bud Yorkin, who has played golf many times with Clinton, insists that Clinton's scores are accurate. "There were some times when he'd take a shot, it wasn't a great shot, and he'd drop a ball and hit a second one. But he never played the second one. He'd do it just to see why he didn't hit the first one the way it should be."[79] Mark Buell explains that Clinton takes mulligans because he often has the club pro with him "and so if something goes wrong he wants to know what it is and so he'll hit another shot to see if he can correct it, but . . . he always scores off the first ball." Buell blames Republicans in general and Rush Limbaugh, an avid golfer, in particular, for stirring up bogus stories and taking "cheap shots" at the president.[80]

As with most aspects of Clinton's life, there's always a dark side: Robert "Buzz" Patterson, a military aide to Clinton, who often rode in the golf cart behind the president (carrying the nuclear football), portrays him as a downright cheat—"with ball placements and extra shots"—even in "inconsequential" games, because he wanted to be able to boast a good score to the press. He claims that Clinton cheated "pretty much on every hole. . . . If there was a bad shot, he'd drop two or three balls and hit them all and play the best shot. . . . On any given hole he might have seven, eight, nine shots and counted it as a four or five."

When Clinton played golf with Vernon Jordan, Patterson claims, the two of them would tell off-color jokes, and Clinton would point out attractive women and describe them in crude terms.[81] Don Hewitt recalls a *60 Minutes* episode about Jordan when Mike Wallace asked him, "What do you and Bill Clinton talk about on the golf course?" and Jordan answered "Pussy." When people asked Jordan, "How could you say that on the air?" Jordan replied, "If the president of the United States says that, what do you want me to say?"[82]

Clinton would often smoke a cigar while playing, sometimes even an illegal Cuban cigar, some of them compliments of Ray Lesniak. "I didn't tell him they were Cuban, but he could tell from the first puff."[83]

Bill Clinton could have played every day, but he knew he had to resist that temptation or, in the public's mind, he would become a southern-fried Ike or Jerry Ford.

BILL, HILLARY, and Chelsea, along with the Clintons' benefactor, infoUSA chairman Vinod Gupta—he was later pushed aside after a shareholder suit questioned the large sums of money directed to the Clintons from the publicly traded company[84]—were on vacation in Acapulco in January 2002. Gupta flew the Clintons there on his company's jet. While they were away, the president's chocolate Lab, Buddy, died after being hit by a car on a two-lane highway in Chappaqua. He had followed a contractor out of the Clintons' house.

Since his White House debut Buddy had been a loving friend to the president—his master's only comfort and companion in August 1998, sleeping and otherwise, after Clinton admitted he had had sex with Monica Lewinsky. One of the most famous images from that Martha's Vineyard vacation was of the three Clintons walking to Marine One across the White House lawn, Chelsea bravely bridging the divide between her parents by walking between them, holding hands with her father on her right and her mother on her left. In his right hand the president holds a leashed but still rambunctious Buddy, walking with his head turned to the president.[85]

The president was supposed to have had the companionship of his moneyman and golfing buddy, Terry McAuliffe, on that trip, but, after Bill confessed, Hillary told McAuliffe to forget about coming with them. That was one way she could punish her husband to whom she refused to speak for the duration. Buddy was truly his only comfort.[86]

The death of his Chappaqua roommate in 2002 came at a time when Clinton was still treading water, reliving the glories of his presidency without a firm plan in hand for the present, much less the future. He spent time with old friends, such as Mark and Susie Buell, who admired him unreservedly and were important supporters of Hillary's. Much of their conversation focused on the past—a favorite story involved Fidel Castro.

Toward the close of Clinton's second term, the Buells traveled to Cuba and visited in his home the photographer Alberto Corda, who had snapped the iconic photograph of Che Guevara in 1960, sporting a beret and long curly hair.[87] Corda pulled negatives out from under his bed, including one of Castro in 1959 standing in front of the Lincoln Memorial in full fatigues with his hat off, gazing at the statue of Abraham Lincoln. Buell asked Corda to have a copy of it made so he could give it to President Clinton. Corda was "quite impressed" with that, says Buell, and happily inscribed it to the president, "With great honor."

Corda later mentioned that he had called "Fidel last night and I told him that one of his pictures was going to Bill Clinton, and Fidel told me to tell you to tell Bill Clinton that this Monica Lewinsky is the work of his enemies."

Buell gave Clinton the Lewinsky message but held the photograph until after he left office, "because it would have been illegal for him to accept anything from Cuba."

In June 2002, the Buells returned to Cuba, this time with their home state senator, Barbara Boxer. Castro invited Boxer's delegation to the Palace of the Revolution where, at a cocktail reception, they met the Cuban leader, dressed in his "olive greens and looking," says Mark Buell, "somewhat like Clinton. . . . He's very charismatic and makes you feel like you're the only person he's talking to." Buell told Castro that he and Susie were the people who gave Clinton the Corda photo, to which Castro replied, "I met President Clinton once. He wasn't supposed to shake my hand; we backed into each other at a reception at the United Nations and I turned around and extended my hand and President Clinton shook it and we had a very interesting conversation. I'm not at liberty to tell you the nature of that conversation."

The night went on so long that only Bill Clinton would have appreciated it—four hours of meetings until midnight and then a four-hour meal. It would have gone longer except that Senator Boxer was tired. As they were leaving, Castro gave all the women flowers and all the men a box of cigars. "If you give me another box," Buell told Castro, "I'll give one to Bill Clinton."

"And he just lit up and . . . took ten minutes with his interpreter because he wanted to do it right and he put a note on this box of cigars . . . and puts the dates that they had met at the United Nations and some very cordial comments and signs it and dates it."

As he hands the box to Buell, Castro says, "Now I will tell you the conversation we had, and only three people in the world will know it and he will know this box really came from me. You tell the president, the tests we discussed [at the United Nations] have been completed."

Three months later, in September 2002, Clinton was at the Buells' house in San Francisco for a fund-raiser for Congresswoman, now Speaker of the House, Nancy Pelosi. Buell gave Clinton the cigars. "And he reads the message and the first thing he says is, 'Well, he's got the dates wrong by two weeks.' Only Clinton would tell you that. But he did say, 'We did have a very nice time,' and he said, 'I'll cherish this because I have mementos from almost all the world leaders when I was president, but I have nothing from Castro.'" Buell then gave Clinton the secret message, and "Clinton just looked at me. He didn't say anything." (Buell speculates that Clinton and Castro had discussed AIDS in Cuba. Castro was worried that an outbreak of the disease would hurt tourism.)[88]

A MONTH later came some speculation in the press that Bill Clinton might run for senator from New Jersey—the Clintons would have had to buy a third house—in the wake of his friend Robert Torricelli's announcement that he would not run for reelection. Buffeted by ethics investigations, afraid his party would lose the seat to the Republicans, Torricelli announced he'd step aside with a little more than a month to go to election day.[89] Clinton was not interested.

In the midterm elections the next month, Clinton's reputation for being the world's smartest political strategist took a hit. Some candidates wanted nothing to do with him. Those who did accept his help were often sorry. Nearly every race he touched landed in the losers column. Writing in *Vanity Fair*, Robert Sam Anson had Democrats greeting "his offer of assistance like a sleepover with Typhoid Mary."[90]

George W. Bush, instead of suffering the typical midterm losses, gained seats in Congress. The Bush victory had meaning beyond control of Congress. Complaints that the 2000 election had been stolen from Gore lost their resonance. Kennedy School of Government lecturer Elaine Kamarck, who had been a senior adviser to Al Gore, saw Clinton as radioactive: "Look at every marginal race in the 2002 election, Bill Clinton was not asked to campaign." And, she adds, in close gubernatorial and Senate races that year, he was in "zero" commercials.[91]

Janet Reno, Clinton's attorney general for eight years, running in Florida for the Democratic nomination for governor, wanted Clinton nowhere near her, going so far, according to Robert Sam Anson, as to omit any mention of Clinton in her Web biography.[92] Today, Reno heaps praise on Clinton—"one of the smartest people I've ever met"—adding that "he made one terrible mistake," but that she did not try to distance herself from him. She admits, however, that she never asked him to campaign for her.[93]

Robert Torricelli, who blames Reno for Clinton's woes—it was Reno who gave Ken Starr the go-ahead at crucial junctures—recalls that in the 2002 Florida gubernatorial primary he was raising money for Democrats, with the exception of Reno. "I used to call across Florida, raising money," says Torricelli, "and during my conversation I would ask people not to contribute to Janet Reno."[94]

Reno lost in the primary in an upset to Tampa lawyer Bill McBride,[95] whom Clinton campaigned for in the general election against Jeb Bush, a particularly important target for the Democrats who were eager to pay him back for his alleged help in giving Florida and thus the presidency to his older brother. In an enthusiastic reception for Clinton at a McBride rally in Fort Lauderdale the Saturday before the election, the *Washington Post* reported, "a woman lofted a sign that said, 'Remember when the president was smart?'" Jeb Bush won easily.[96]

In North Carolina, Clinton's old friend and former chief of staff, Erskine Bowles, asked the former president not to campaign for him in the race for the U.S. Senate. (He lost anyway to Elizabeth Dole.)[97] And so it went, all over the country. One bright spot was Rahm Emanuel's win for a congressional seat in Chicago.

After that election, Bill Clinton gave a speech to the centrist Democratic Leadership Council blaming weak candidates who couldn't persuade voters that they'd be strong on security. Ridiculing Clinton's anemic performance in the midterms, a *New York Post* gossip columnist referred to Clinton as "the former horndog in chief." Playing off Toni Morrison's tribute to Clinton as the "first black president," the paper quoted the Reverend Al Sharpton as calling Clinton "the first beige president."[98]

IN DECEMBER 2001, gold shovel in hand, Clinton turned the dirt for his library. Construction began in earnest six months later.[99]

President Clinton directly sought money from friends and closed the deal with, to name several, Denise Rich, Vinod Gupta, David Geffen, Steven Spielberg, John Catsimatidis, Ron Burkle, John Emerson, Barbra Streisand, and Howard Tullman. Early on, Clinton met with Carnegie Corporation head Vartan Gregorian for library fund-raising tips. Gregorian put Clinton "in touch with the Annenbergs, and the Annenberg Foundation gave a million dollars to the Clinton Library." (Gregorian also primed the pump with Scottish philanthropist Tom Hunter, who later traveled with Clinton to Africa and committed $100 million to the Clinton Global Initiative.) Another donor, according to a recent investigation by reporters for the *New York Times*, was Bernard L. Schwartz, then CEO of Loral Space and Communications, at that time under a cloud of suspicion involving allegations of provision of satellite technology to China. It was later reported in the *Washington Post* that 10 percent of the money for Clinton's library came from foreign sources, a huge chunk from Saudi Arabia.[100]

Although there are limits on donations to presidential campaigns, there are no limits on donations that individuals can give to presidential libraries; some legislation is in the works, however, that would require quarterly disclosure of the source of any donation over $200. The bill, whose sponsors include Democrats Barack Obama, Rahm Emanuel, and Henry Waxman, would change the law just in time to hurt fund-raising for the George W. Bush Library.[101]

In his memoir, McAuliffe writes about his library fund-raising efforts as if they were essential to the future of the Republic. "We knew these same cowards would keep attacking the President and trying to smear his good name long after he left the White House, and that was why it became my central focus to work toward establishing a forum for a factual, accurate account of the Clinton years that Americans and people all over the world could visit to learn more about the Clinton years and why they were the best eight years of our lives. The Bill Clinton Presidential Library was going to be our vehicle to establish his legacy."[102]

FRIENDS WHO hoped Clinton would keep a more conventional schedule once out of the White House noted that he seemed just as undisciplined—like an undergraduate out from under his parents' supervision for the first time. Leon Panetta describes his former boss's schedule as "haphazard." He can tell when Clinton has pulled a string of three-hours-of-sleep nights. "It begins to take a toll on his voice."[103]

His admirers attribute his habits to his insatiable intelligence. "I think he has . . . a ravenous appetite for information," says Donna Shalala, "and . . . he reads more than any politician I've ever known."[104]

One prominent political strategist recalls visiting Clinton in the White House: "I went up with him to the residence and he's carrying a full armload of books, having just finished a group and got a new group to read."[105] Conrad Black wrote a 1,200-plus-page biography of FDR, published in 2003, and sent a copy of it to Bill Clinton, who responded by letter with "specific questions about Roosevelt. It was clear that he did read the book."[106] John Emerson pegs Clinton as reading "faster than the speed of light." He recalls the daily White House press clips that were "almost an inch thick" and Clinton noting a negative comment from an economist in California that was on the jump page of a Los Angeles Times business story eighty pages into the briefing.[107]

The premonition that he will not live a long life, friends say, fuels this disinclination to waste time sleeping. And then there is his freakishly gregarious nature. Whether it's demons or some holdover from a dysfunctional childhood, he cannot stand to be alone.

One person who has observed him closely describes Clinton as more likely to be playing cards with his traveling companion Doug Band until 4:00 or 5:00 A.M. than reading. "He never sleeps. He's an insomniac, very restless mind and body. He doesn't need sleep. He's just metabolically a freak." This person also notes that given the number of Diet Cokes he consumes—"more Diet Coke than you can imagine a person can drink, starting in the morning"—it's surprising he sleeps at all.[108]

Clinton's friends insist that he has a photographic memory; almost all seem to have a story about his remembering the name of someone's aunt having met her for thirty seconds five years before. "See if you can find somebody whose name he has forgotten," challenges David Schulte, who was at Yale Law School with Bill and Hillary.[109] The *Chicago Tribune's* Rick Kogan calls Clinton's recall "some kind of Asperger's syndrome; [he's like an] idiot savant about things and people."[110]

"Ask him a question and he answers with a prolonged response, carefully and logically structured, supported by a myriad of facts and figures," says Anson M. Beard Jr., a retired Morgan Stanley executive who supports Clinton's postpresidential causes. "It is an incredible mind and reminds me of my great-grandfather who purportedly could read an engineering book and remember what the third paragraph on page 62 was all about."[111]

But one Washington political consultant says Clinton's mind is more than merely photographic. "He is a synthetic thinker; he brings together disparate ideas and material and recombines [them] to get fundamentally new and different thoughts."[112] People who have worked with him often mention his ability to absorb information, select the most salient pieces, weave them into a coherent message, assemble it all in his head, rather than using a computer to cut and paste, and deliver it as a cohesive, persuasive speech.[113]

ALL THOSE BRAINS; all that energy. Bill Clinton knew he needed to stop treading water. How could he project an image of a statesman, a player on the world stage? How could he shed the "Boy Clinton" moniker slapped on him by *American Spectator* editor in chief R. Emmett Tyrrell, who portrayed Clinton as undisciplined, dishonest, and frightfully immature; a man in his fifties who reminded some of their adolescent sons?[114]

He continued to ask himself the question, as framed by his friend, Mark Buell: "How am I going to get back to a place where I can pursue the things that interest me . . . while being very careful of Hillary's career; not to try to upstage her or to be controversial on issues where people could celebrate a split in the family over politics."[115]

For the most part, each year out of the White House has been better than the one before, his gradual ascent attributable to Bush's grievous misjudgments in the prosecution of the war in Iraq and to the realization that Bush's embarrassing inarticulateness might reflect mediocre intelligence more than regular-guy plain talk.

Friends have often said that Bill Clinton would have made a mesmerizing preacher. He seemed to be tapping into that as, in combination with his speaking schedule, he began, in a sense, to preach to the converted, lecturing at the elite conferences where opinion makers gather to network. At the World Economic Forum in Davos, he became increasingly in demand. "He's so available," says Mark Buell. "He makes himself available to . . . Davos where he is the rock star; he is the guy everybody wants to listen to."[116]

He also began to gravitate to an issue that would come to define his postpresidency work.

In late 2000, as Clinton was trying to figure out what to do with his postpresidency, Tony Coelho advised him to focus on "the poor and AIDS"; bring to it "a moral indignation." Coelho reminded him that he was "the first black president."[117]

Clinton first began to look at the HIV/AIDS epidemic in Africa in 2001, but the seeds were planted in the final months of his presidency when he took his second trip to Africa and was struck by the virulence of the epidemic and by the recognition of how little he had done as president. Melanne Verveer, who was on that trip, calls the charge that Clinton did not do enough "an understatement" and describes him as trying "to make up for lost time in those remaining months of his presidency."[118]

By visiting Africa, talking about Africa, and taking Africa seriously, says Richard Marlink, a physician, professor at the Harvard School of Public Health, and scientific director at the Elizabeth Glaser Pediatric

AIDS Foundation, Clinton began to try to alleviate the problem, but it was too late in his administration. Time ran out on him.[119]

Clinton's record had not been good. In 1997, he said there would be a vaccine for AIDS within a decade. AIDS activists were skeptical because he put no money behind that prediction.[120] (The previous prediction came in 1984 from then secretary of health and human services [HHS] Margaret Heckler, who forecast a vaccine within two years.)[121] Clinton's own Advisory Council on HIV/AIDS threatened to resign en masse and approve a no-confidence vote in the administration's ability to halt the spread of HIV because the Clinton administration would not approve federal funds to pay for clean needles for drug addicts.[122]

Kevin De Cock, the director of the Department of HIV/AIDS in the World Health Organization, calls the Clinton years "a fairly dry time in AIDS scientifically and from a public health perspective." As president, Clinton and the Congress allocated only $150 million to the African AIDS crisis.[123] When Richard Marlink, who spends six months of every year in Africa, suggested to Clinton postpresidency that he could have done more, he blamed not himself, but the Republican Congress: "We tried to increase funding and it always would get voted down or taken out of the bill."[124] Clinton's HHS secretary, Donna Shalala, not surprisingly, supports Clinton, rejecting the notion that the administration was wanting in its response to a disease that was first identified in 1981, at the start of the Reagan administration. "He basically saved thousands of Americans," she claims. "We couldn't get Congress to focus on the international pieces."[125]

Others who worked for Clinton also defend him. His national security adviser during his first term, Tony Lake, gives his former boss credit for having an "extraordinary impact when he said for the first time that HIV/AIDS is a national security problem."[126] Lake's successor, Sandy Berger, agrees that the linkage was important, but admits, "I think we didn't do enough and so I think . . . that may motivate him."[127]

Clinton was also moved by criticism from his own daughter. Eric Goosby, director of the Pangaea Global AIDS Foundation, who had directed AIDS policy in the Clinton White House and at HHS, recalls that the first time he heard the president express "any kind of regret" was when Chelsea, doing graduate work at Oxford, wrote her thesis on HIV/ AIDS. Goosby was asked to help the first daughter find websites that would provide the data she needed. Her paper, recalls Goosby, was "pretty critical of her father's track record, not so much with prevention but with treatment. And he verbalized at that time, just kind of in the hallway, 'Yeah, you know, she's right, I really should have done more.'"[128] He has, postpresidency, admitted that for too long he defended patents of the big pharmaceutical companies and so contributed to blocking poor people worldwide from access to cheaper generics.[129]

Once out of office, having established the Clinton Foundation but not yet certain what to do with it, Bill Clinton came to understand what was wrong with U.S. policy toward the spread of HIV in Africa and how to fix it. He was helped along by Ira Magaziner, on whom he bestowed the title chairman of the Clinton Foundation HIV/AIDS Initiative. He and Magaziner, sixty-one, had a long relationship stretching back to Oxford where they were both Rhodes scholars. Later, Magaziner, then a management consultant, came to work at Clinton's White House, managing Hillary's failed universal health-care plan. After that fiasco, Magaziner stayed on and, in 1996, took on the additional role as Clinton's chief Internet adviser, making sure that the Internet did not get carved up like radio frequencies and that it remained a global free-trade zone.[130]

Magaziner first contacted Eric Goosby in 2001 to ask if Clinton should focus on treatment as opposed to prevention.[131] Once Magaziner was satisfied that the answer was treatment, he started to recruit. At the Barcelona International AIDS Conference in 2002, Magaziner asked Marlink to volunteer and to advise him who else would be interested in the treatment aspect of HIV/AIDS in Africa.[132]

The next year, Magaziner contacted Richard Feachem. The question at what Feachem calls a "brainstorming dinner" was what role the Clinton Foundation should play. The answer, says Feachem, was a shift of focus from prevention (i.e., abstinence and condoms) to helping those who were already HIV positive or who would pass the virus to their spouses during sex or to their babies during childbirth or breast-feeding.[133]

The antiretroviral drugs (ARVs) that HIV-positive people in the United States were taking as a matter of course and that were turning a death sentence into a chronic, manageable illness, but that were priced out of the reach of most third-world people, had to be made available in Africa. And so Clinton focused on bringing down the number of deaths by getting ARVs to Africans who were infected, sick, and dying.

"I think Clinton saw this as an inescapable moral issue of our time," says Richard Marlink. "If we're going to take Africa . . . seriously, this epidemic is going to threaten countries' very existences, and he saw that . . . we're essentially denying, like the Tuskegee syphilis experiment where you're denying treatment that existed to people. . . . And so it was an epiphany for Clinton. . . . When it's doable to . . . treat people, it's not acceptable to say, 'We're going to spend money on prevention,' that treating Africans is 'a bottomless pit.'"[134]

Bill Bicknell, a professor at the Boston University School of Public Health and director of the Lesotho Boston Health Alliance, lays out the cold hard facts of treating or not treating HIV/AIDS. "When you get infected with HIV, if you do nothing you're essentially pretty healthy for . . . four, seven, eight years. So after infection you don't need treatment for maybe five, six, seven years. Then you need treatment, and if you don't get treatment . . . you die in two years. If you do get treatment, you live a long while. Nobody knows how long, but there have been people who started treatment in the early '90s who are doing fine just now." He compares it to diabetes, which, before insulin, "killed you in a few years. Now, 'Oh, I'm a diabetic. I'm an old man or an old woman.'"[135]

Clinton started to use his voice, his influence, his access to world leaders, and his ability to travel the world and raise the subject of HIV/AIDS. Almost from the start, says Richard Feachem, he made a difference.[136] Still, Richard Marlink feared that Clinton, struggling to establish his legacy, would treat the AIDS fight as a political campaign, show bursts of energy followed by loss of interest. Marlink confronted the former president when they first met in 2002 and he delivered his "conditions of service." Clinton was not accustomed to being talked to in that tone and of having his commitment questioned. Marlink recalls Clinton getting "red in the face. 'You don't think I'm telling the truth?'" When he got beyond his pique, says Marlink, the former president said, "'I hear your . . . concerns,' and then he kept reassuring, 'You need me, I'll be there. . . . If you need me to make phone calls, . . . that's my job and Ira [Magaziner] will organize it.'" Marlink recalls the president as adamant: "This is not just for this year, and not just for next year. This is something I'm going to do from now on until it's solved."

Still Marlink worried that Clinton's involvement would become one giant photo op. "When we met in the Harlem offices we insisted as a group of volunteers that there not be public announcements or press releases [or] . . . photo ops unless there was something substantial to announce or unless it helped the . . . local government move forward their AIDS agenda." Marlink could not get over the fear that Bill Clinton was and remained too much the showman.[137]

Chapter 4

NOT QUITE READY FOR PRIME TIME

IN JANUARY 2003, DON HEWITT, THE CREATOR OF CBS's *60 Minutes* and then its executive producer, went to Chappaqua to see Bill Clinton. Hewitt had an idea—an update on the James Kilpatrick/Shana Alexander "Point/Counterpoint," a popular feature during the program's early days in the 1970s. He wanted Bill Clinton to be the new liberal voice, and Hewitt thought it best to propose it in person.

Clinton seemed happy for the company, Hewitt recalls, and the two men chatted for four hours. The former president showed the veteran producer all his "great souvenirs of all his trips: 'Let me show you this. I got this from an Indian tribe in God knows where.'" Hewitt was "awed by the guy."[1] Clinton was interested, contingent on whom Hewitt selected to be the conservative voice.

A television pioneer who had started with CBS News in 1948, crafted programs for Edward R. Murrow and Walter Cronkite, produced the 1960 Nixon/Kennedy debates, and launched *60 Minutes* in 1968, Hewitt, then eighty, knew in his bones who Clinton's sparring partner should be—Bill O'Reilly, host of Fox News's *The O'Reilly Factor*. That matchup would make great television because O'Reilly had strong, loud opinions and refused to back down. That would be a "stunner," Hewitt says, "but Clinton's advisers thought that was beneath him and you're always dealing with the ex-president of the United States and protocol and this nonsense. . . . [Clinton] wouldn't do it." That did not stop Hewitt from continuing to push the matchup: "Just think where the world would be if in the famous Scopes trial, Clarence Darrow had said 'It's beneath my dignity to do it with William Jennings Bryant.' . . . Sometimes you've got to take on guys like that."[2]

Hewitt could have saved his arguments, says Larry King. "Clinton wouldn't sit down with Bill O'Reilly in a million years. He has no respect for O'Reilly. O'Reilly is a prankster, a huckster."[3]

Hewitt also understood that the O'Reilly gambit was dead on arrival for another reason—the unpredictability of how it would affect Hillary's run for the White House. "You never know when you're dealing with Bill Clinton how much he has on his mind 'Is this good or bad for Hillary's candidacy?'"[4]

So Hewitt was stuck. He wanted Clinton badly enough to take the sparring partner Clinton's people wanted—Bob Dole, Clinton's opponent in the 1996 presidential race. Clinton's staffers warmed to the selection of Dole because they wanted someone of great stature to face off against the former president, and Dole, war hero and former Senate majority leader, had stature to spare. And he was not a shouter; he was the reasonable man.

The matchmaker was the Democratic power broker Lloyd Cutler, an old Washington hand who had served in both the Carter and Clinton White Houses. The agent was Robert Barnett, the Washington lawyer/literary agent who already represented both Clintons and Dole (and scores of other big political names of both parties). Barnett negotiated a hefty fee for the tryout period of ten weeks—for a weekly forty-five-second commentary and fifteen-second rebuttal, each man would be paid $100,000, a million dollars total. *Newsweek* calculated the take at $1,667 per second per man.[5]

Hewitt was not optimistic. He knew he needed to pair Clinton with someone with whom he "violently disagreed." That didn't describe Dole at all. Clinton liked and respected Dole and Dole reciprocated. Their 1996 contest brought them closer. "I think the president always felt that if he talked to Bob Dole that Bob Dole usually stuck by his word," says Leon Panetta. "That's worth a lot in politics."[6] Shana Alexander and James Kilpatrick's verbal sparring worked, Hewitt says, because they "had no use for each other's opinions."[7]

From the start, there were no sparks. As Larry King analyzed it, "a former president and a former majority leader of the Senate will tend to always be respectful. . . . They're not going to say, 'You're an idiot.' If you're going to do point/counterpoint, you have to say, 'You're an idiot.'"[8]

Tony Coelho, a longtime friend of both Clinton and Dole—he and Dole worked together on the Americans with Disabilities Act in which they both had a personal stake; Coelho has epilepsy and Dole crippling war injuries—describes the relationship between the men as warm and emotional. During Clinton's first term, Dole celebrated the twenty-fifth anniversary of his first Senate speech—about disabilities. Coelho arranged for President Clinton to make a surprise visit at a luncheon in Dole's office. "Dole was absolutely shocked and started crying," Coelho recalls. Clinton had read Dole's speech from twenty-five years before in the car on the way over to the Senate, and, without having it in front of him, "he quoted in effect the whole speech verbatim." Tears rolled down Dole's cheeks as the president spoke, and Dole often told Coelho that it was "a moment he would never forget."[9]

Even after the 1996 election, in which Dole never came close, their relationship thrived. Scott Reed, Dole's campaign manager, recalls a White House East Room gathering just after Clinton's reelection at which he bestowed on Dole the Presidential Medal of Freedom. "Dole wiped away a tear, and then, according to an account in the *Baltimore Sun*, said, 'I, Robert J. Dole—do solemnly swear—sorry, wrong speech. But I had a dream that I would be here this historic week receiving something from the President—but I thought it would be the front door key.'"[10]

After 9/11, Clinton and Dole worked together to raise $105 million to pay college tuition for children, unborn children, and spouses of 9/11 victims.[11]

As Hewitt had predicted, Dole's impressive sense of humor was way too dry for television. It's often said that the camera loves Bill Clinton; it doesn't love Bob Dole. "I didn't think it was the greatest forum for Senator Dole," says Scott Reed. "Clinton is a guy that charms the birds right out of the trees every day. They land right on his arm. . . . He really knew how to seduce the camera and it worked, and so to be put in a position where you're in a contrast to that is very difficult for nine out of ten politicians."[12]

The nightmarish logistics added to the looming failure. On the prowl for big fees, Clinton had "speaking engagements everywhere," Hewitt recalls. "He was constantly on airplanes going to places, some of which I never heard of." Because of Clinton's schedule, only once were the two men ever in the same studio at the same time.[13] There was none of the chemistry generated when Shana Alexander and James Kilpatrick sat glaring at each other across a table.

After two weeks, not just Hewitt but the viewing audience lost interest. "There was no sizzle to it," says Tony Coelho.[14]

The Alexander/Kilpatrick exchanges had such attitude that *Saturday Night Live* parodied it with actors Jane Curtin and Dan Aykroyd. "Jane, you ignorant slut" became a line so famous it has long outlived its origins.[15] "*Variety* actually said I took it off the air because *Saturday Night Live* was doing a parody of it," Hewitt recalls. "And I said, 'You stupid bastard, that's why I kept it on the air. That was flattering to me.'"[16]

In retrospect, Hewitt regrets that he did not suggest former Speaker of the House Newt Gingrich as Clinton's sparring partner. "I think he would have gone with Newt Gingrich. He respects Gingrich."

Hewitt had only to call Bob Barnett to kill it. "I don't think it's doing either one of them any good," Hewitt told him, "and it's not doing me any good." Nobody, including Clinton, objected, Hewitt says, because "it was a dud. . . . It wasn't being talked about or written about; it wasn't making a splash and I think he lost interest, as we all did."[17]

IN JUNE 2003, just as his television gig got canceled, Bill Clinton was out at night—as usual, without Hillary—in Manhattan at a book party at

Tina Brown's Upper East Side apartment. The event was for journalist-turned-Clinton-aide-and-booster Sidney Blumenthal. His book in fulsome defense of the Clintons, *The Clinton Wars*, had just been published.

Brown, the former editor of *Vanity Fair* and *The New Yorker*, asked one of her guests, David Carr, the media reporter for the *New York Times*, if he'd like to meet the president. "Yeah, I'd like to shake his hand," Carr replied.

"Clinton heard my last name was *New York Times* and he launched into what I would characterize . . . as either a tirade or a filibuster on the *New York Times*." He accused the paper, or rather Carr, whom he apparently saw as the *Times* incarnate, of "willful ignorance of the failings of the Bush administration. . . . 'These people understand power and they've got you'—meaning the *New York Times*—'totally cowed.'" Carr found the blast, sprinkled with profanities, both alarming and "hilarious" because he considers himself hardly an insider at the paper; and, in any case, he covers media and culture and business, not politics. "I'm the definition of a middle guy at the *New York Times*."

Clinton was just getting going: "Then he launched into a recitation of his history with the paper beginning with Whitewater and through numerous and countless transgressions, beautifully argued, comprehensively remembered, . . . and people began to gather as he got more and more worked up." Inevitably he got to Lewinsky. "By the time he got done talking," Carr recalls, "I was just covered in flop sweat; giant guy yelling at me and he circled back to the fact that we cuddle up to the administration and won't give the Democrats a chance to break through with their message. . . . When I finally got a chance to talk, I said, 'With all due respect, Mr. President . . . I must tell you that I heard more effective rhetoric in a five-minute speech out of you tonight at an Upper East Side cocktail party than I've heard out of your party in the last two years and I think part of the reason that's true is because of how you left the presidency.' He stopped at that moment and he came back and said, 'You got me; okay, you got me.'"

At that point, says Carr, Clinton was "very good-natured about it" and, he recalls, "had a smile on his face most of the time. . . . But his big, meaty hands were gesturing fairly close to me."

His lambasting by Clinton, says Carr, was "spontaneous," and, oddly, "charming. . . . He was analyzing the relationship of the nation's leading newspaper with the current administration and doing a masterful off-the-cuff deconstruction of it. . . . I would have enjoyed it if I wasn't the one standing in front of him."[18]

One student of the newspaper says that Clinton's ire was probably mostly aimed at then executive editor Howell Raines, whose tenure as the paper's editorial page editor coincided almost exactly with Clinton's tenure as president. Editorials had often been unkind to Clinton and, he thought, unfair. Post-Lewinsky, the *New York Times'* editorial writers, for example, bemoaned the president's "documentably dysfunctional personality."[19] Clinton had been heard to say that the disharmony between him and Raines was "a southern thing"—Raines was born, reared, and educated in Alabama. "You'd have to read all of Faulkner to understand what was going on there."[20]

THAT SAME month, June 2003, Hillary's ghost-written memoir, *Living History,* was published. Hillary made her deadline, but Bill missed his early 2003 deadline, no surprise to anyone who knew him.

Some of Clinton's more melodramatically inclined friends pushed the notion that Clinton sat alone in his house, his valet Oscar Flores bringing him steaming cups of coffee, writing and by so doing cleansing his soul. "You could see that it weighed heavily on his mind," says Irena Medavoy. "He has a very strong survival instinct and I think the book was cathartic for him. I think that book saved his life at that point. It gave him such focus, such direction. If there's one thing we know about him, it's that he is meticulous in memory and meticulous in writing things down. What I saw was a man who really wanted to throw himself into that book."[21] His spiritual counselor and friend Tony Campolo writes that "the time immediately after he left office was spent on writing his book and reviewing his life in writing."[22]

Sounds good, but not true. Clinton found it difficult to get to work until his deadline was imminent. The final preparations and the actual publication of Hillary's memoir had spurred the former president to action, of sorts. Much of the work was done in 2003, and into the spring of 2004. Knopf hoped to publish that June. Working around his speaking schedule, he typically devoted one to two days a week to the book, usually working at home in Chappaqua.

Leon Panetta describes his former boss as "one of these kids we all knew in school who didn't do a lot of studying and then the night before crams and gets an A."[23] In other words, Clinton procrastinated. He reportedly often called friends to read them anecdotes and passages, sometimes entire chapters that he particularly liked.[24]

Friends say he did have some help with the writing. He hired Ted Widmer, a historian (author of books on Martin van Buren and on Jacksonian democracy) and a speechwriter for Clinton in the White House, although Widmer, now director of the John Carter Brown Library at Brown University, was called a researcher or an interviewer. By interviewing Clinton about his own life, Widmer helped the former president gather his thoughts about his prepresidency years. For reasons unclear, Widmer did not work on the second part.[25] (Contacted for an interview, Widmer said he'd talk only with Clinton's permission, which was not forthcoming.)

People around Clinton at that time report that they saw pages written by him in longhand—he claims to have filled twenty notebooks—which he then handed off to a staffer who typed them into the computer.[26]

CLINTON WAS distracted from writing as much by his glittering social life as by his speaking schedule.

"Do the Clintons have any friends who aren't really rich?" asked *New Republic* editor Martin Peretz, a question that many of the Clintons' old friends also ask, just not for publication.[27]

They complain that they find it much more difficult to reach him. "I could always call Doug [Band] for years and get to the president," says Lou Weisbach. "Now, and I've heard it from everybody, he's becoming less reachable."[28]

In Hollywood, even, some of the older FOBs don't talk to him much these days. "I haven't talked to the president in a long time," says Bud Yorkin, one of those credited with introducing the young Bill Clinton to Hollywood's deep pockets. (Yorkin and his wife gave a dinner for Clinton in 1992 when, Yorkin recalls, "All of show business was for [Bob] Kerrey." Nobody wanted to meet the Arkansas governor, but Yorkin talked David Geffen and Sidney Pollack into coming and ended up with eighty to ninety people for a sit-down dinner, almost all of whom, says Yorkin, were hugely impressed.[29] The Yorkins later raised $250,000 for the Clintons' legal defense fund.[30])

One hears that complaint in the voice of Stanley Sheinbaum, an old Hollywood activist and friend. Sheinbaum claims, along with several others, to be the man who persuaded Bill Clinton to run in 1992 and raised six figures to help him do that.

In 1981, after he lost his bid for reelection as governor, Bill and Hillary stayed with the Sheinbaums in the same Brentwood house in which Stanley now convalesces in a hospital bed. By any conventional standard he is wealthy—he's married to Betty Warner, daughter of studio magnate Harry Warner; he has an impressive art collection and a staff—and in the 1970s, 1980s, and even the 1990s he was at the center of the Hollywood Left.[31] As late as 2003, *The Hotline* called Sheinbaum a "Democratic kingmaker,"[32] and the *Los Angeles Times* described him in 2001 as host of "a legendary salon of powerful and famous liberals for more than 20 years."[33]

Stanley and Betty were guests in the Lincoln Bedroom during the Clinton years. They supported the president through impeachment. Sheinbaum complains that now Clinton has time only for "the bigger man, Ron Burkle."[34]

"Clinton leads a totally different life, different friends," says Betty Sheinbaum.[35]

Sheinbaum, a pauper next to Clinton's new LA friends, is now old, ill, and hard of hearing, and his memory appears to be fading.

When asked about the former president, he replies, "Who's Bill Clinton?" and that question is dripping with sarcasm and unrelated to any possible memory loss. He complains that since Clinton left the White House he has not seen him for "more than two minutes," that he has been "cut off," that he wrote to him soon after he left the White House but Clinton never responded.[36]

The new FOBs do have several attributes in common that Stanley Sheinbaum never had—they're billionaires, they're younger than Bill, they're mostly divorced or single, they're players on the dating and power circuits, they're flashy, and they own at least one private plane, which they happily lend to Bill Clinton—sometimes to do good work, sometimes for pleasure, sometimes to get to Europe or some other continent to give a high-priced speech.

They also know what the former president has been up to and who knows how that knowledge might be used. As one woman who knows Clinton well puts it, "He has this problem with women, which I find appalling. . . . When you do things like that and then you're trying to cover things up, you could become beholden to people you really don't want to become beholden to."[37]

One friend who describes Clinton as the smartest, most interesting man he has ever met—"He's off the charts; he's almost a different species"—also calls Clinton "the most narcissistic human being I've ever met." This man complains that Clinton "doesn't discriminate very well in the people he allows to surround him. . . . Presidents are surrounded by sycophants and fans and groupies. . . . Sometimes you . . . wonder, 'What's he doing with that guy?'"[38]

In describing Clinton's circle these days, Don Hewitt says simply, "He sees the money guys."[39] To Dick Morris, Clinton's current circle "represents the triumph of materialism in a man who had once only wanted power and recognition."[40] (Morris was forced to resign as a Clinton adviser during the 1996 Democratic National Convention in Chicago when news broke of his cavorting with a prostitute who indulged his taste for having his toes sucked.)[41]

"What's wrong with him traveling on the private plane of Ron Burkle?" asks Hank Sheinkopf. "He's a private citizen and . . . thanks to Clinton a lot of people made a lot of money and became very rich very fast during the Clinton years. . . . He's reaping the benefits of what he did."[42]

How many people in Clinton's position would turn down the offer of a plane? Friends claim that people are falling over one another to offer him their planes. Think about the mileage, so to speak, some chieftain gets out of casually mentioning on the golf course or at a dinner party in the Hamptons, "I lent Bill Clinton my plane because he had to be in Johannesburg to celebrate Nelson Mandela's birthday."

In Bill Clinton's case, sometimes a private plane is not just a plane. One insider explains that it's a matter of logistics; for moving around the world, "there's no better friend to have than a guy with a private plane." But then comes further grist for the rumor mill: "I've been told that there are women on the plane."[43]

For a speech Clinton gave in a major city, he arrived and departed on the plane of one of his billionaire buddies. The executive who invited the former president expected him to join him and other business leaders at a four-star restaurant for dinner. Clinton declined. The executive believes that Clinton was with a woman. The situation, says this man, is "dangerous, and there's more than one."[44]

CLINTON'S BEST FRIEND—even closer than Terry McAuliffe, friends say—is Ronald Wayne Burkle. He is fifty-four, and divorced; he made his billions—*Forbes* estimates his worth at about $2.5 billion—buying, merging, and selling supermarket chains. (In the 1990s, for example, he bought Ralphs and Fred Meyer and then sold them to Kroger for $8 billion.) He is chairman of Yucaipa Companies, a private equity firm that owns such grocery chains as Jurgensen's, Falley's, and Alpha Beta. He founded the company in 1986, naming it after the small California town in which he was then living.[45] Burkle boasts that he spends five hundred hours a year with Clinton. And he keeps an office in Clinton's Harlem headquarters.[46]

Clinton met Burkle in 1992, the same year Burkle separated from his wife.[47]

The myth of how Bill and Ron met had a sweet, progressive ring to it, but it was entirely made up. The *New York Times* reported that, in 1992, in the wake of the Rodney King riots in Los Angeles, candidate Clinton was touring poor neighborhoods, seeing destruction all around him except for some grocery stores that were left relatively undamaged. When Clinton asked why those stores were spared, he was told that they were owned by Burkle who, the *Times* reported, "treated his customers and employees fairly." (Not all of Burkle's stores were spared and the *Times* ran a correction.) Clinton asked to meet him. Burkle, a registered Republican, was so impressed that he cast his first vote for a Democrat that fall when he voted for Bill Clinton.[48]

In fact, says Darius Anderson, once head of Burkle's government relations, now a lobbyist in Sacramento, the person who brought the two men together was Bob Burkett, a political consultant who had been raising money for Bob Kerrey in the 1992 primary.[49] The Bill/Ron meeting had nothing to do with Burkle's treatment of employees and everything to do with the Beverly Hills house that Burkle had recently purchased—the forty-four-room, twenty-six-bath Green Acres, one of the largest and most lavish private homes in Los Angeles. Originally the home of the silent screen star Harold Lloyd, it was later owned by movie producer Ted Field, an heir to the Chicago department store and newspaper fortune. Field was politically active and he refurbished the house specifically to accommodate huge fund-raising events.[50]

Burkle immediately began to throw the biggest fund-raisers in town. "There are very few houses in LA where you can do that type of event," explains Anderson, "and so when Ron bought it, it sort of put him on the map overnight and everybody started calling." Green Acres, says Anderson, was "one of these houses that . . . was like an extension of the DNC on the West Coast. Instead of having events at the Sheraton, you'd have them at Ron Burkle's house."

The night Clinton and Burkle met, Burkle had offered up Green Acres for a DNC fund-raiser for the Democratic nominee for president, Bill Clinton. Burkle, says Anderson, had never "played at the presidential level before. . . . This was sort of his first move into the national scene." The event was spectacular. "Barbra Streisand performed . . . the who's who of Hollywood, business, and industry . . . a total of about three thousand people were there."

On Clinton's arrival, Burkle, whom Darius Anderson describes as "painfully shy," led Clinton to his library and the two chatted. "The great thing about Governor Clinton at the time that made him so effective was his ability to connect and to make you feel special. Ron was very impressed with him. . . . The reason they got along so well over the years is that they have a similar story in essence. They came from tough backgrounds, self-made." (Burkle's father, "a supermarket guy," says Anderson, worked his way to be regional manager for one of the big chains and eventually became president of the company, but he had a humble start.[51] Even as a young boy, Ron spent evenings and weekends stocking shelves, in part so he could be with his father. He started as a box boy, tried college—his father wanted him to be a dentist—but dropped out and never earned a college degree.)[52]

For Burkle, Clinton was the perfect partner. Burkle hated being the center of attention as much as Clinton loved it.[53]

In the late 1990s, Burkle bought a luxuriously appointed Boeing 757, complete with what a former employee describes as "two massive sleeping cabins, . . . beautiful living room and full galley and crews' quarters."[54] (The plane carries the numbers 770BB, or Box Boy Local 770, the union to which Burkle belonged when he started in the grocery business as a box boy.) Clinton has dubbed it "Air Force Two" or "Ron Air."[55]

Owning a commercial-sized plane that can fly anywhere in the world is extremely unusual, explains Anderson. "There are very few in private hands. . . . Most of the time when you get to that level you . . . do Gulfstream or business Boeing jets; that's what the Spielbergs and Geffens of the world have." Most of the time the huge cabin holds Burkle and a few friends and perhaps a staffer or two. "He doesn't take thirty people with him," says Anderson. Because the 757 is too large to land some places where Burkle wishes to fly, he now has a second, smaller plane for local jaunts.[56]

Postpresidency, in April 2002, Burkle hired Clinton as "senior adviser" to two Yucaipa Companies investment funds.[57]

Burkle did not respond to requests for an interview made directly to him, to people in his company, and to an outside PR man and gatekeeper, but he did tell Matthew Miller of *Forbes* that when he was trying to do a deal with McDonald's, he asked Clinton to call the company's chairman, who was so eager for things to go well with Clinton that he gave Burkle his home and cell phone numbers. Burkle volunteers that CEOs who would never take his calls jump at the chance to take Clinton's.[58] The deals have not always seemed appropriate for a former president. When Burkle used Clinton to open the door to the Teamsters and Teamster president James Hoffa Jr., Clinton's name was soon drawn into an ugly battle, complete with lawsuits and charges by truck drivers that the bottom line would be lower wages for them.[59]

Both Bill Clinton and the Reverend Jesse Jackson sit on Burkle's board. Jackson's former girlfriend, Karin Stanford—also mother of his child—was given a $10,000-a-month retainer for a time by Yucaipa Companies. An even bigger beneficiary of the Burkle/Clinton tie has been Jackson's son, thirty-seven-year-old Yusef.

In 1998, Yusef, a lawyer, was sold a majority ownership of a lucrative Anheuser-Busch beer distributorship covering Chicago's North and Northwest Sides. (In the early 1980s, his father had called for a boycott of the beer company because of a lack of minority distributors.) Yusef Jackson met August A. Busch IV, a close friend of Burkle's and son of Anheuser-Busch chairman August III, at a party at Burkle's mansion in 1996. Seated next to each other, the two discussed the ups and downs of life with name-brand fathers, and the deal was put in the works after Burkle vouched for Yusef.[60] With Burkle's financial backing, Yusef would later invest in magazines, including *Radar*.[61]

When he's in Los Angeles, Clinton almost always stays in a private wing at Green Acres that contains a guest suite.[62] Irena Medavoy calls it Clinton's "refuge . . . because in Green Acres he could be protected. . . . There's no one coming in and out." She says that Bill and Ron "will stay up until three or four in the morning and discuss everything."[63]

As Clinton suffered the humiliation of the Lewinsky scandal, he found Green Acres to be a "safe harbor," says Medavoy, who recalls being with the president at "a very small dinner" at Burkle's house during those dark days. Also there was Jesse Jackson, just back from Belgrade, where he helped to negotiate with Slobodan Milosevic, the Serbian president of Yugoslavia, the release of three American POWs.

That dinner at Burkle's mansion, Medavoy says, allowed Clinton to relax, to find solace and people who were not going to sit in judgment. "He could be himself," she says, "and . . . no one here betrayed him." At that dinner, Medavoy recalls, they talked about the success of the hostage release, about other "hot spots" around the world, and how issues such as ethnic cleansing in Bosnia were all shunted aside so the world could focus on Bill Clinton getting "a blow job."[64]

Located above the Beverly Hills Hotel, Green Acres shares a common border with the property of another erstwhile Clinton billionaire supporter, David Geffen. Geffen joined the billionaire ranks in 1992 when he sold his record company to MCA; later he became a founding partner with Steven Spielberg and Jeffrey Katzenberg of Dreamworks. When Geffen, in an interview with the New York Times' Maureen Dowd, called the Clintons liars and the former president "a reckless guy" who "gave his enemies a lot of ammunition to hurt him and to distract the country," and said he would not support Hillary for the Democratic nomination in 2008, many saw behind it jealousy on Geffen's part that Clinton liked Burkle's mansion better than Geffen's.[65]

According to a report in the New York Times, while Clinton was president, "Geffen insisted that Clinton stay at his home even on nights when Geffen was out of town. Clinton spent much of the evening at an event at Burkle's . . . mansion . . . , but then dutifully went around the block to neighbor Geffen's estate."[66]

The story became a tasteless, silly spat over whose compound is bigger and whose Clinton liked better. Geffen's, filled with expensive contemporary art, is on 9.4 acres and was once owned by movie mogul Jack Warner; Burkle's acreage is smaller, reported variously as five to eight. Whatever the precise size, their lots are the first and second biggest in Los Angeles.[67]

Burkle carries an air of mystery, a Gatsbyesque mix of riches, eccentricity, and striving that provides endless fodder for the gossip pages—one described Green Acres as "one of Southern California's best-known party houses"—and even the *New York Times* has more than once put stories featuring Burkle on its front page. For a man who is so often described as shy he seems to invite publicity. A fund-raiser at Green Acres will include the most gorgeous stars and celebrities, a far cry from a political fund-raiser in the grand ballroom of a Chicago hotel, where celebrity might mean a politician or a trial lawyer.[68]

Burkle favors a uniform of Levi's, a black polo shirt, and blue Converse sneakers. He is friends with rapper Sean "Puffy" Combs, and Burkle reportedly invested $100 million in the "Sean John" line. He shares a New York City pied-à-terre with actor Leonardo DiCaprio.[69]

Today, Burkle is all over the place. He tried to buy twelve Knight Ridder newspapers when the company was broken up; he tried to buy the Tribune Company and then the *Los Angles Times* and then proposed a plan to buy the *Wall Street Journal*. With Yusef Jackson, he tried to buy the *Chicago Sun-Times*.[70]

Since 1999 Burkle has been part owner of the Pittsburgh Penguins and has floated the idea of moving the team to Las Vegas. He attempted to bring an NFL team to Los Angeles. With Yusef Jackson and others, he bid $450 million but failed in 2006 to buy the Washington Nationals.[71]

He serves on the board of Yahoo! and is in business with Vice President Al Gore; he has a stake in Gore's cable channel. The college dropout is also the money behind the Burkle Center for International Relations at UCLA and the Claremont Graduate University business school.

Some say that Burkle and Clinton are also partners in philandering. Burkle is said to like much younger women, especially models. The *New York Times* used suggestive language in describing their friendship; the word *zipping* was much remarked upon: "Mr. Clinton is rarely without company in public, yet the company he keeps rarely includes his wife. Nights out find him zipping around Los Angeles with his bachelor buddy, Ronald W. Burkle."[72]

One Hollywood woman who knows Burkle well raves about him, describing him as shy, brilliant, loyal in a way rarely seen anymore, an honest businessman, "the one who hardly ever says anything, so when he does, it's always of value. . . . If you have Ron Burkle as a friend, you're a lucky person." But this woman seemed to hint that Burkle and Clinton spend time together doing things that Hillary would not want made public.[73]

"That's the word around Hollywood," says one major star, "that it has to do with women, like the friendship he had with Vernon Jordan, supposedly all about women."[74] Darius Anderson says he never witnessed any philandering "firsthand," but specifies that he left Burkle's employ in 1998 just as he acquired the plane, "so I wasn't there for the whole jet-setting around the world thing. . . . I'd hear the same things; some people like to spread rumors. I'm sure there's some truth to [it]; where there's smoke there's usually fire." One Washington journalist who has written extensively about the Clintons says that, in private, Burkle refers to his plane as "Fuck Jet."[75]

The most cynical of Clinton watchers say that Hillary would look the other way if her husband and Burkle were chasing women. Burkle is a key player in Hillary's political future.[76]

One well-known journalist says that Burkle "creeps me out," and he mentions Burkle's attempt to expose Jared Paul Stern, a freelance gossip reporter for "Page Six" of the New York Post, a paper that Burkle detests because of its suggestive and, Burkle claims, false coverage of his private life. This journalist, while stressing that he carries no brief for Stern, calls Burkle "fucking crazy" and says he reminds him of former Miramax head Harvey Weinstein, "another Bill [Clinton] familiar who [has a] . . . prurient interest in manipulating and jacking around the press."[77] (Clinton is so close to Weinstein that he was with the president on election night 2000.)[78]

The Jared Paul Stern "Page Six" fight with Ron Burkle was sparked by Burkle's anger over an unbylined item in May 2002 about his buying a modeling agency, Elite Models, in part so former president Bill Clinton could run it. The item also described Burkle as flying models around on his private jet.[79] On March 22, 2006, Stern and Burkle met; the meeting's purpose, allegedly, was for Stern to advise Burkle on steps he could take so no more modeling agency–type stories would appear in the New York Post. Burkle, unbeknownst to Stern, made video recordings. The

New York Daily News obtained a transcript that had Jared Paul Stern saying, "I wouldn't be asking you for this kind of money if I didn't think I could help you when it is needed." (The amounts were reportedly $100,000 up front and a $10,000 monthly stipend.)[80]

It appeared that Stern was trying to extort money from Burkle, and a federal investigation ensued. Stern, who was fired from his freelancing job, claimed that he was merely attempting to persuade Burkle to invest in Stern's clothing company, Skull & Bones. Months later, someone from the U.S. Attorney's office advised Stern's lawyer, "They are not proceeding with any case against Mr. Stern."[81]

Unhappy about losing his freelance work, Stern filed suit against Burkle, the *New York Daily News*, Burkle's PR man, and Bill and Hillary Clinton. The affidavit describes Burkle as a billionaire who "carries on sexual liaisons with fashion models, some of whom are under the age of consent." In November 2007, Stern predicted, "Burkle will do anything to keep us from taking Clinton's deposition."[82]

Another important FOB (and FOH)—one of Hillary Clinton's biggest financial supporters in her bid for the White House—is Haim Saban. When Mike Medavoy is asked if Bill Clinton has lobbied him to support Hillary for the presidential nomination in 2008, he says, no, but "Haim asked me."[83]

Saban, who did not respond to a request for an interview, was one of the extreme loyalists who never wavered in his support for Clinton during the worst of the Lewinsky days. At a fund-raiser for Democrats at his house in September 1998, attended by a cast of two hundred, including Burkle, Madonna, and Rob Reiner, Saban, according to a report in the *Washington Post*, assured the beleaguered president, "Our prayers are with you and our support is absolutely unwavering." The take for the party that night in his neo-French château in North Beverly Park, a gated community, was $1.5 million.[84]

Saban, sixty-three, an Egyptian-born Israeli who left Israel for France in 1975 and moved to Los Angeles in 1983, made his fortune producing the children's cartoons *Mighty Morphin Power Rangers* and *Teenage Mutant Ninja Turtles*. In 2001, then chairman and CEO of Fox Family Worldwide

Inc., he increased his wealth by $1.5 billion when he sold his share.[85] In the approach to the 2002 midterm elections, he donated $7 million to help the DNC build a state-of-the-art Washington headquarters.[86]

Former DNC national finance chairman Alan Solomont calls Saban "a classic Israeli, kind of gruff exterior, tough guy." Saban founded the Saban Center on Middle East Policy at the Brookings Institution and gave "a bunch of money" to Tel Aviv University to establish the Saban Institute for the Study of the American Political System. He arranged for Bill Clinton to receive an honorary doctorate from the university in January 2002.[87]

Instead of flying to Israel with Saban on his G-7, Clinton flew with Burkle on his 757. "I've noticed that for very wealthy men," says Solomont, "planes take on a life of one of their organs; it's like whose dick is bigger. And at that particular moment Burkle's was."[88]

Corky Hale, a musician and Hollywood activist, calls Saban, whom she says is second in his generosity to Democrats after George Soros, "very close to Clinton, after Burkle maybe, because anybody who's extremely, extremely rich . . ."[89] She leaves the thought unfinished, but its meaning is obvious. Saban's *Who's Who in America* entry notes under "Awards" that he was "Named one of *Forbes'* Richest Americans, 2006."

Another man whose friendship with Bill Clinton has flourished post-presidency is New Yorker Jeffrey Epstein, fifty-three, a billionaire money manager, president of J. Epstein & Co. in Manhattan. Epstein, who limits his clients to those who have a billion dollars or more, started life in Coney Island, the son of a Parks Department worker. He was teaching calculus and physics in the 1970s at the Dalton School in Manhattan when the father of a student arranged for him to meet Alan "Ace" Greenberg at Bear Stearns. Epstein rose quickly at the firm before moving on.[90]

Epstein, who did not respond to a request for an interview, lives in a forty-five-thousand-square-foot house on East Seventy-first Street on the Upper East Side that, according to one published report, he describes as "the largest private residence in the city." He also owns a fifty-one-thousand-square-foot castle in Santa Fe, reportedly the largest house in the state, a villa in Palm Beach, and a hundred-acre private island off St. Thomas in the U.S. Virgin Islands.[91]

Epstein's fleet consists of a Boeing 727, a Gulfstream, a Cessna 421, and a helicopter to carry him from his private Caribbean island to St. Thomas.[92]

In 2002, Clinton traveled to Africa with Epstein on the 727—also along were Epstein's (and Clinton's) friends Kevin Spacey and Chris Tucker. The trip, which was dismissed as "The Three Amigos' Most Excellent African Adventure," put Epstein in the spotlight; and New York magazine soon assigned a writer, Landon Thomas Jr., to profile him. In describing the Africa trip, Thomas breathlessly portrayed Epstein's crush on Clinton. "While Epstein got an intellectual kick out of engaging African finance ministers in theoretical chitchat about economic development, the real payoff for him was observing Clinton in his métier: talking HIV/AIDS policy with African leaders and soaking up the love from Cape Town to Lagos."

Thomas's portrayal had Epstein loving beautiful women, but being so much deeper. "As some collect butterflies, he collects beautiful minds. 'I invest in people—be it politics or science. It's what I do,' he has said to friends. And his latest prize addition is the former president. In his eyes, Clinton as a species represents the highest evolutionary form of the political animal. To be up close to him, as he was during the African journey, is akin to seeing the rarest of beasts on a safari."

Thomas also quoted Donald Trump: "I've known Jeffrey for 15 years. Terrific guy. He's a lot of fun to be with. It is even said that he likes beautiful women as much as I do, and many of them are on the younger side." Unlike the others quoted in the profile, including Bill Clinton paying tribute to Epstein, Trump turned out to be right on the money.[93]

In 2006, while at his Palm Beach villa, Epstein, according to reports in the Palm Beach Post, was jailed for two hours before posting bond, for activities involving underaged naked girls, one reportedly fourteen years old, a naked Epstein, massages, and a reported request for "a happy ending." (The official charge was soliciting a prostitute.)[94]

That year, New York magazine took another look at Epstein, this one, by Vanessa Grigoriadis, not quite so starry-eyed: "Epstein was known to be a womanizer: He usually travels with three women, who are 'strictly not of our class, darling,' says a friend. They serve his guests dinner on his private 727, and are also there for touching. But it seems that he was also interested in younger women: Over the past few years, a then-17-year-old Olive Garden waitress . . . brought at least five high-school girls between the ages of 14 and 16 over to Epstein's house in Palm Beach to 'massage' him, which meant watching him masturbate and even allegedly having sex."[95] (The case is expected to go to trial; Epstein claims that he did not know the girls were underage and he passed a lie detector test in which he asserts that he thought the girls were eighteen.)

One well-known New York journalist says of Epstein, "He's truly a brilliant autodidact, but sort of crippled in a personal sense and who does that remind you of?"[96]

Philip Levine, forty-five, a Miami businessman—he made his fortune on cruise-ship concessions—and bachelor, a mere multimillionaire, became friendly with President Clinton the usual way; he gave a lot of money to the party. Levine cohosted a star-studded fund-raiser in Beverly Hills for the DNC and another in Miami Beach, both with Clinton in attendance. He was quoted as saying that he has "contributed more than $100,000 to the party and its candidates."[97]

Levine, who did not respond to a request for an interview, described President Clinton as a combination of Elvis and JFK and explained their friendship as one "self-made guy" enjoying another. Levine has had overnights at the White House, entertained Clinton at his house, and traveled with Clinton postpresidency. Robert Sam Anson in *Vanity Fair* quotes Hillary as saying, "I need to start coming on those trips." Levine also keeps an apartment in Manhattan.[98]

One longtime (and disapproving) friend of Clinton's describes Levine as "a single guy who likes to party." He ponders why Clinton wants to spend his time with Levine, comparing him unfavorably to close Clinton advisers Ira Magaziner, Sandy Berger, and the late Eli Segal: "There's this dissynchrony in the kind of people around Bill Clinton. . . . He does love to be around those folks who will throw themselves at his feet and worship him and do his bidding and pay his bills."[99]

And then there's movie producer (*The Polar Express, Beowulf*) Stephen Bing, heir to his grandfather's real estate fortune of nearly $1 billion, owner of a Boeing jet, often in the gossip columns, most famously in 2001 after Elizabeth Hurley claimed Bing fathered her son. A DNA test backed up Hurley's charge. Paternity tests also showed Bing as the father of a daughter born to Kirk Kerkorian's former wife, Lisa.[100]

A recent *Wall Street Journal* article described Bing as competing with Burkle and Saban to see whose haul for Hillary is bigger.[101] Before that he was a reliably ultragenerous supporter of Bill and the party. He wrote a check for a million dollars to help fund the 2000 Democratic National Convention.[102]

According to one journalist who has written about Clinton, "Stephen Bing epitomizes that crowd. Clinton's still very much a skirt chaser and these guys in Hollywood are movers and shakers. Stephen Bing [is a] rich, young guy on the loose with power and . . . who is bedding every broad. . . . That really appeals to Clinton. . . . He has done some things that are wildly inappropriate, even after Monica Lewinsky, even after he's trying to become this venerable sage of American politics, he still does it. He's just fundamentally flawed. And these guys, . . . he likes being around them. . . . He likes the beautiful women . . . and he likes the power they wield and likes the fact that they'll cut him fat checks . . . and help to enhance his lifestyle by offering him their private planes and the other things they have available to them."[103]

Irena Medavoy, who briefly dated Bing, describes the attraction between the two men as "everything, because Bill Clinton's also a guy who likes to laugh and he likes to have fun. . . . He was a young president . . . and I think being around young people makes him happy. . . . I think Steve for him was . . . an outlet."[104]

There are still others, substantially lighter in the wallet and even lighter in the gravitas department, who, with some reason, consider themselves FOBs. Some members of Clinton's staff were said to be appalled that the former president would keep company with the likes of

Jason Binn, twelve years Clinton's junior, CEO of Niche Media, publisher of high-end glossy magazines for the ultrarich in New York, Los Angeles, Washington, Boston, the Hamptons, and Aspen.

"To the consternation of legacy protectors," Robert Sam Anson wrote, "Binn also puppy-dogs with Clinton, and Clinton appears pleased to have him at his heels. It can't be for the chat. . . . One undertaking at which Binn incontestably shines is entree with models."[105]

Binn refused a request for an interview.

Terry McAuliffe is described by one Clinton friend and supporter as "probably Bill Clinton's best friend." Still, this man wonders why Clinton would want to spend so much time with a man who may be shrewd but seems limited intellectually and whose adoration for Bill and Hillary is creepy. McAuliffe appears to have devoted his life to raising money for the Clintons and bailing them out of embarrassing situations. "Terry's . . . the world's greatest salesman," says this man. "In a sense I can kind of see they're kind of kindred spirits in their energy and even their charisma, but Bill Clinton's a fucking genius, it's just . . . an odd best friend, to be honest."[106]

Former DNC head Don Fowler, who tangled with McAuliffe, says of his relationship with Clinton, "He [McAuliffe] lives off of that."[107]

As Bill Clinton was leaving the White House, and, more important, after Hillary was elected senator, Oscar de la Renta began to invite them for Easter week trips to his house in the Dominican Republic.[108]

On de la Renta's end, says Conrad Black, the Canadian media mogul recently convicted of mail fraud and obstruction of justice, this was all about business—designing for Hillary should she become president. De la Renta designed her second inaugural gown and the dress she wore on the cover of the December 1998 issue of *Vogue*, at the height of the Lewinsky scandal, that made her appear, as Robin Givhan, the *Washington Post* fashion critic, wrote, "glamorous, regal and defiant."[109]

The famous designer, a Dominican native, continued to invite them even though, Black adds, de la Renta's genuinely close friend and Connecticut neighbor Henry Kissinger disapproved. "Kissinger purports to regard Clinton as a very shabby character and a very second-rate president."[110]

Too much is made of Clinton's befriending people with private jets and then being shameless in mooching a seat (and a bed), says David Schulte: "Once you've flown Air Force One for eight years, you think you want to fly United? . . . You'd have to be brain-dead to prefer commercial aviation." He adds that Clinton's yen for billionaire-style travel is "peanuts, compared to the Marc Rich pardon."[111]

One New York journalist says he understands why Clinton is attracted to the staggeringly rich, illustrating it with a reference to the *New Yorker* cartoon, "I've been rich and I've been superrich and superrich is better." He says of the "superrich guys," with whom Clinton consorts these days, "They can help him on what he cares about: his issues. It isn't just about the jets. . . . When he's trying to get into their pockets, a lot of times it's cause oriented."[112]

Besides, says another journalist who has covered Clinton since his gubernatorial days in Little Rock, "he came a long way and as soon as he got out of lower-middle-class lifestyle, there was no looking back."[113]

POST–WHITE HOUSE, Bill Clinton dresses like the rich man he has become.

In 1996, the AP writer Ron Fournier described a Bill Clinton who no longer exists. "The president gently unwraps presents so the paper can be reused. He used to buy his shoes at a discount self-serve store in Arkansas—one black pair, one brown pair. 'That's all anyone needs,' he'd say."[114]

As governor, he proudly wore a Timex watch—the Ironman LCD, not a bad idea for any Arkansas politician because the company had manufacturing facilities there, was one of the state's big employers, and made the first wristwatch affordable to the workingman.

Today Bill Clinton collects high-end mechanical watches and wears a Rolex, or a Patek Philippe or a Cartier or an Audemars Piguet or a watch by the young German watchmaker Michael Kobold. These are watches that cost thousands of dollars; some reach to six figures. Clinton has about fifty watches in his collection.[115]

In 2004, when Michael Kobold, German born and only twenty-seven, first met Clinton at a small private party, the former president was wearing an Audemars Piguet skeleton watch that was worth well over a hundred thousand dollars. Kobold's designs—advertised as the preferred watch "for polar explorers, NASA test pilots, NSA and CIA operatives"—range in price from $2,500 to $25,000. Kobold gave the former president the Kobold off his wrist to try on. Clinton took off the Audemars Piguet, and Kobold, needing to adjust the presidential cuff, put the watch in his suit jacket pocket. "We got talking and I told him that's actually Jim Gandolfini's [aka Tony Soprano's] personal prototype watch because Jim and I had worked on that particular watch together. So he said, 'Well, I love Jim, and I love this watch.'"

Kobold left Clinton with the watch and was some distance away when he realized he still had the president's Audemars Piguet in his pocket. He rushed back to return it.

Kobold calls Clinton "a charmer," who told the watchmaker specific reasons why he loved his watches. Kobold receives regular letters from "Bill," who expressly asked Kobold to call him by his first name. (Mostly everyone else calls him "Mr. President.")

Kobold ended up lending Clinton three watches, and James Gandolfini gave Clinton one as a gift. Kobold is delighted when Clinton wears his watch at some "high-profile event." He wore a Kobold on *Larry King Live* and also when he was photographed for the cover of *Ladies' Home Journal.* "He has given my watch a lot of wrist time."

Kobold describes the former president as having hands that are "very powerful; they are not too sleek but also not a farmer's hands, refined looking." His nails, says Kobold, are manicured. His clothes are "incredibly well finished." Kobold makes watches for Secret Service agents and has befriended some who were on Clinton's detail, "and they say that he is sort of known in endear[ing] terms as a clotheshorse; impeccable taste and always likes to get dressed very nicely."

Clinton also told Kobold that he "really enjoyed watches with a second time zone indicator, so I'm actually in the midst of designing one anyway, so I told him . . . 'I'll send you a picture of one and see if you like it.'" If he does, says Kobold, he'll send him one to wear.

Another president, George W. Bush, also wears a Kobold. One of Bush's assistants ordered it, the president paid for it, and that was that.[116]

SENATOR JOHN KERRY of Massachusetts, in a battle for the Democratic nomination for president, had begun to wonder at some of the Clintons' activities early in 2004. They were not so subtly supporting General Wesley Clark—the retired NATO supreme allied commander, an Arkansas-reared late entry in the race for the Democratic nomination. Some of the more Machiavellian-minded believed that the Clintons were using the politically naïve general as a stalking horse. He couldn't possibly win and that would leave the field open for Hillary to run in 2008. If Kerry won in 2004, he would presumably be the hands-down favorite for reelection in 2008.

Mark Buell laughs as he recalls sitting beside Hillary at a dinner at her house. "She knew that we announced early that we were supporting Kerry, and she said to me, . . . 'Do you think that General Clark would be viable?'" The Clintons were definitely supporting Clark, says Buell.[117] Kerry's finance chairman, Lou Susman, had come to the same conclusion: "We were sure that the Clinton crowd had put Wesley Clark in the race." The "Clinton crowd," Susman adds, included Terry McAuliffe, whom Clinton, as noted in the *Boston Globe* and other papers, had installed as head of the DNC in order to protect his and Hillary's interests. McAuliffe, Susman explains, would not have pushed Clark into the race without approval from the Clintons. The Clintons' close friend, the late Eli Segal, moved to Little Rock where he became the Clark campaign's chairman.[118]

Clinton was on the phone often with Clark, a fellow Rhodes scholar, with Segal, and, most important, with potential donors. But Clark was inept. He cheerfully admitted having voted for Reagan in 1980 and George H. W. Bush in 1988. Clark told reporters that Kerry would soon "implode" over an "intern problem." Kerry's daughter Vanessa said she almost died laughing when she read about the rumor, which quickly died, as did the Clark campaign.[119]

Strategist Hank Sheinkopf chuckles at the notion of backroom maneu-vers by the Clintons. "Most of what happens in politics is the same thing that happens in the media; it's called 'the Confederacy of Dunces,' a lot happens by accident." Sheinkopf suggests that Clinton might have felt grateful to Clark, who had "served him well. . . . The management of the Bosnian conflict is something the president can look back on with some pride."[120]

Bill Clinton, missing the political arena, was talking to many of the candidates because that's what he likes to do. "I remember being with John Edwards [in 2004]," says Lou Weisbach, "and Edwards said, 'It's amazing, Bill Clinton calls me all the time and asks me what my plans are and gives me advice,' and then you talk to another candidate and hear the same thing."[121]

THE MONTH before his presidency ended, Bill Clinton had met with another portrait painter, Simmie Knox, who would become the first Afri-can American to be commissioned to paint the official White House portrait of a president.[122] The son of a sharecropper,[123] Knox grew up in Alabama on a plantation/farm and attended segregated schools.[124] He had painted Justice Thurgood Marshall, which led to a commission to paint Justice Ruth Bader Ginsburg who recommended Knox to Clinton.

Hillary Clinton, impressed with Knox's study showing the president in five different poses, asked him to paint her as well.[125] The senator sat for him in her house in Washington; she also looked at the portrait of her husband and asked Knox to make his beard area a little pinker, "put a little color in it" so it matched his cheeks. "I agreed with her; she was right about that," Knox says.

Knox had recommended the blue necktie, one that would bring out the blue in the former president's eyes. Although famous for having avoided the draft, Bill Clinton wanted military medallions in his portrait and the former first lady wanted her book, *It Takes a Village: And Other Lessons Children Teach Us.* "I asked them if there are things that they feel that helped to shape them and make them the person that they are."[126]

In June 2004, in the East Room at the Bush White House, Knox unveiled the portraits of Bill and Hillary. President Bush won over the Clintons with his greeting, "Welcome home," and reminded the assembled that he and his father call each other "41" and "43." Turning to Clinton, he said, "We're glad you're here, 42." It was the start of a thaw that would soon produce a genuine friendship between "41" and "42" and a fragile cordiality between "42" and "43."

"Over eight years it was clear that Bill Clinton loved the job of the presidency," Bush said, striking just the right note and bringing his predecessor to tears at the mention of his late mother. "I am certain that Virginia Kelley would be filled with incredible pride this morning." President Bush also evoked laughter and his Texas roots when he said, "People in Bill Clinton's life have always expected him to succeed, and more than that, they wanted him to succeed. And meeting those expectations took more than charm and intellect. It took hard work and drive and determination and optimism. I mean, after all, you got to be optimistic to give six months of your life running the McGovern campaign in Texas." [127]*

Larry King took note of the reception that "W" gave his predecessor. "Bush was glowingly praising of him; I mean really overglowingly. So the next time I saw Bush, I said, 'Why were you so . . . ?' and he looked at me and he said, 'Are you kidding? . . . How could you not like Bill Clinton?'"[129]

THAT SAME MONTH, June 2004, Bill Clinton's memoir, *My Life*, was published.

*In late spring 1972, Bill Clinton went to Washington to be interviewed by George McGovern's campaign manager, Gary Hart. The Yale Law student wanted to work for McGovern in his race for the presidency. Hart called George McGovern, who recalls the conversation: "There's a young guy who wants to work for you and he says he could organize Arkansas for us, but he's so smart and resourceful . . . I think we should send him to a bigger state." They decided on Texas, which McGovern lost, along with every other state except Massachusetts and the District of Columbia.[128]

Democratic leaders were not happy; they wanted the book out earlier or later, but nowhere near election day. They feared that Bill Clinton would not only steal the spotlight but that he would also remind swing voters why not to vote for John Kerry for president.

Among presidential memoirs, Clinton's does not rank high. One might expect it to be self-serving, but it's also boring, and, especially in the second half, more a laundry list of events and people and legislation than an insightful look back at two turbulent terms.

What he wrote himself continues to be murky. The far better first half was said to benefit from Ted Widmer's handiwork. "I don't know why they only let Widmer go for the early years but that's what he did," says Douglas Brinkley. "He did interviews with President Clinton . . . and they would transcribe them. They were like long oral histories. . . . President Clinton would work off of the transcript. . . . Maybe Ted would craft them up a little bit from what Clinton said. . . . I think that collaboration between Widmer and Clinton bore great fruit because that's clearly the most gripping part of the memoir."[130]

For the book's second half, Clinton relied heavily on White House diaries kept by Janis Kearney, an Arkansas native and old friend. It was the first time a president had hired a diarist, she explains, "and so we kind of structured what it was as we went along." Kearney recorded Clinton's daily activities, assembled relevant documents. She called herself his "shadow," and as much as she could while still affording the president privacy, she recorded everything that transpired in the business part of a day—events, meetings, who was there, who said what, and so on. She took notes in pigeon shorthand and then typed them up at the end of each day. As part of the Oval Office staff, "I could hang out there whenever I felt that I needed to." She says there was no taping system in the Clinton White House. "We knew all the things that had gone down before."[131]

The "fly on the wall" nature of her relationship with Clinton meant that she had to endure an appearance before the Lewinsky grand jury. She got stuck in that nightmare because she kept records of who entered and exited the Oval Office.

Clinton's editor, Robert Gottlieb, was considered first-rate—among his authors were Toni Morrison, Robert Caro, Joseph Heller, Jessica Mitford, John le Carré—but his skills were not apparent here. "I was very surprised that an editor of that skill let it go," says former *Time* magazine columnist and biographer Christopher Ogden, "but I think it was a financial decision."[132]

Rushed to publication, the 957-page hardcover of *My Life* was a mess. In this writer's copy, the cover is on upside down and backward. The index is unreliable.[133] In the last two lines of the book, in the "Acknowledgments," he thanks a long list of people, and then concludes on what was meant to be an earnest, high-minded note: "None of them are responsible for the failure of my life, but for whatever good has come out of it they deserve much of the credit." Although certainly the innocent mistake of a rushed copy editor or proofreader, still, says Jonathan Alter, Clinton was "furious."[134]

While acknowledging that Widmer was "heavily involved" in the writing, Alter argues that the book sounds too much like Clinton to believe that he didn't do "most of it, himself." To Alter, the book has that "kind of all-over-the-map, up-until-four-A.M. Clinton thing." He adds, "If it had been a lot better, I would have been awfully suspicious about whether he wrote it or not." The laundry-list aspect of it, Alter explains, "that's just him sitting there with his legal pads."[135]

Donna Shalala is typical of his friends in saying she "loved" the first part and then trailing off when talking about the rest.[136] A surprising number of people didn't read it; they read the reviews and just couldn't muster the enthusiasm. Leon Panetta says he "brushed" through it, that he read enough "to get a feel for it." While the first half perhaps merits an "A," the rest, says Panetta, is a failure. When he got to the presidency, the deadline noose was tightening and he "just kind of ran through his schedules."[137] One friend calls it "a brain dump."[138]

In 2003, Panetta had advised Clinton to write two books: one to take the reader through his governorship and then a second volume on the presidency.[139] Other friends have expressed hope that he'll have the confidence to admit that the hundreds of pages on his presidency are largely without insight or subtlety—"boilerplate and unimaginative," says Douglas

Brinkley—and that he'll write another book.[140] One of those is Jake Siewert, who pronounces *My Life* "rushed" and says "he'll probably have to go back and do that section again, but I wouldn't expect that any time before the next couple of elections" (i.e., until after Hillary finishes her second term).[141] "I think he has to write another one," says Vartan Gregorian, who found the second half suffered from the fact that "time dictates content." He wrote Clinton after publication but says he was "polite as you have to be with a president. He's not your pal."[142]

Clinton was disappointed by the reviews. (Kay Graham's memoir won the Pulitzer; Clinton's did not.) Douglas Brinkley reviewed it for the *Financial Times* and was surprised to hear that Clinton thought the review "snarky." "I was very hard on the whole impeachment problem and I got wind back from Camp Clinton that there was some unhappiness at my analysis." Given that Brinkley wrote essentially a positive review, Clinton's displeasure results from Brinkley's "refusing to allow him to claim impeachment as a badge of honor. . . . They're determined to wash it away, . . . to turn it into a minor event, and it wasn't minor. As a historian you have to recognize that that consumed a great deal of his energy."[143]

Sensing, friends say, that people whose opinion he valued, whether they read it or not, were belittling the memoir irritated Clinton most of all. "I'm told that it reminded some people of that famous speech down in Atlanta in 1988," says Theodore Sorensen, JFK's speechwriter (and, some say, author of Kennedy's Pulitzer Prize–winning *Profiles in Courage*, which Sorensen adamantly denies).[144] Larry Sabato calls it "one of the most boring [presidential memoirs] I've ever taken a look at."[145] Christopher Ogden liked the first two hundred pages "because it was fresh and then it became a diary dumper, and so disappointing because he could have done a good one," but then, Ogden adds, Clinton's "such an undisciplined guy" and the book is "an undisciplined effort."[146]

To Elaine Kamarck, the memoir is "a total mess . . . nothing really of intrinsic interest there."[147]

"I would never claim to have read his memoir," says Paul Greenberg, "except perhaps as a sleep aid."[148] When Greenberg's then deputy, Kane Webb, is asked if he read the memoir, he answers, "No, life is short."[149]

Knopf claimed that the book broke opening-day records for a nonfiction title, selling more than 400,000 copies.[150] The publisher had estimated that it needed to sell 1.8 million hardcovers in order to cover the president's advance. It ended up selling 2.2 million in hardcover and 500,000 in paperback in the United States alone. Knopf reportedly reaped at least $6 million from publishing rights to *My Life* sold to foreign publishers.[151]

Bill did end up selling more books than Hillary, whose *Living History* sold 1.7 million hardcover copies.[152]

The publicity buildup to the book's release was huge—interviews on *60 Minutes*, *Oprah*, and *Larry King Live*, a cover story in *Time*, and thousands of people waiting in line whenever Clinton made an appearance to sign books. When he appeared at a Borders in New York City on release day, the store sold more than two thousand copies.[153]

Mike and Irena Medavoy stood in an impossibly long line outside Brentano's in Century City. "He just started laughing when he saw us," Irena recalls. "You did not!" he said in surprise as he motioned them over to his table. They sat there chatting with him until the store closed, and he headed off to spend the night at Ron Burkle's house before awakening early the next day for another signing.[154]

ONCE JOHN KERRY won the nomination, Clinton reportedly pushed him to take General Clark or Hillary as his running mate and was ignored.[155] Clinton continued to call Kerry with advice[156] and warnings. People who had worked on the Clinton campaigns—Joe Lockhart, Mike McCurry—went over to help Kerry. "There are people who believe that that effort was helpful and there are people who believe it wasn't helpful," says Lou Susman, seeming to indicate that he believes the latter. Susman says he is not conspiratorially minded but does comment that Clinton's advice resulted in "two camps . . . people who were more loyal to Clinton than they were to Kerry as opposed to the Kerry people who had been there from the beginning."[157]

That summer, the Medavoys hosted a dinner at their home in support of the Burkle Center for International Relations at UCLA. (Mike Medavoy is cochair of the Burkle Center.) Senator John Kerry, by then the Democrats' nominee for the presidency, was to be the guest of honor, discussing foreign policy with a Harvard professor, a former foreign minister of Australia, along with movie stars—Barbra Streisand and Annette Bening—and an audience of Hollywood players. Her husband's hope, says Irena Medavoy, was that this group would do for Kerry what it had done for Clinton in 1992. The day before, Kerry called to cancel. The Medavoys panicked. "We've got this full house coming," recalls Irena. "Mike picked up the phone and called Clinton. 'I'm in China, but I'll stop by on the way back.'"

Kerry made no friends that night, but Clinton was "mesmerizing." Clinton was "a bigger draw" anyway, says Irena Medavoy.

Despite his nonstop, worldwide book tour, Clinton, coming off that plane from China, was full of energy and wisdom about foreign affairs, including the main topic of conversation, the war in Iraq. He left the Medavoys' house at two or three in the morning.[158]

Mike Medavoy reportedly told someone who was there that night, "Kerry will not win. He doesn't get it."[159]

WHEN BILL CLINTON signed his book contract three years earlier, Jonathan Alter had pointed out that Clinton was probably worth the record advance: ". . . [U]nlike the ailing Ronald Reagan or the pope, who received huge but not as huge advances, Clinton can hawk the hell out of his book on everything from 'Oprah' to 'Good Morning Bangladesh.' Knowing Clinton, he'll probably do the 6 A.M. early news in Topeka, too."[160]

Not to mention Peoria, but publicity plans for My Life were scuttled in late August 2004, when Bill Clinton could no longer ignore tightness in his chest that persisted even when he was standing still.

He would later tell a reporter who accompanied him on a trip to Africa in 2005 that he had felt symptoms of what turned out to be severe coronary artery disease as early as 2001. When New York's Jennifer Senior asked him what the symptoms were, he hesitated and then said, "The one I feel comfortable mentioning is that although I lost a bunch of weight in 2001, I couldn't run a mile without stopping and walking. It didn't make any sense." He did not say which symptoms he was not comfortable mentioning.[161]

Friends did notice that Bill Clinton seemed tired that summer of 2004 and attributed it to his book tour.

In Ireland the last week of August, he signed one thousand copies of his memoir at Eason's, a Dublin bookstore, and then went straight to the Royal Dublin Golf Club, before dinner with Prime Minister Bertie Ahern. According to a report in the *Irish Independent*, "Asked if he was tired after the morning's hard work, Mr. Clinton said that it was tough trying to sign for everyone that had turned up. 'I normally like to do it standing up, but after so many you get tired and need to sit down.'"[162]

That same week Robert Torricelli ran into former Clinton aide Doug Sosnik, a regular traveling companion of Clinton's during the White House years. Sosnik told Torricelli that he had seen Clinton on television and was concerned about how he looked.[163]

By Thursday, September 2, 2004, at home in Chappaqua, he felt a definite clenching sensation in his chest as well as shortness of breath. His Secret Service detail drove him to the hospital closest to his home, Northern Westchester Hospital in Mount Kisco, New York.[164] Detecting nothing unusual, doctors sent him home, but, apparently worried about that decision, they called him back early the next morning and suggested that he go to Westchester Medical Center, in Valhalla, New York, for more tests, including an angiogram, which found that several of his arteries were "well over 90 percent" blocked.

A stent would not solve the problem; he needed major, invasive surgery. He was taken by ambulance to the Columbia Presbyterian Center of New York–Presbyterian Hospital, above Harlem, in Washington Heights, scheduled for surgery the next Monday, and monitored in the hospital until then. Doctors feared that he could have a "substantial heart attack in the near future," and did not want to risk sending him home.[165]

When the news broke that Clinton had been scheduled for quadruple bypass surgery on Labor Day, September 6, 2004, many of his friends were surprised and said that they had not noticed any symptoms at all. "We were all in a state of shock," says Melanne Verveer, "because he was so vigorous, he jogged, he wasn't a couch potato by any stretch."[166] Jake Siewert points out that his life was healthier after he left the White House—less stress, better diet, more exercise.[167]

The year before, he had finally found a diet that worked—the low-carbohydrate, low-fat South Beach plan—and he had lost twenty pounds.[168]

Terry McAuliffe wrote in his memoir that the night before Clinton went to the hospital they talked on the telephone for nearly an hour, and "he sounded great and we joked around a lot."[169]

Leon Panetta was not surprised to hear the news because while Clinton, aware of a family history of heart disease and early death, tried to regulate his diet and his exercise—he had installed a home gym in Chappaqua and hired a personal trainer—he would often "stray" from good habits. That, Panetta says, combined with the stress of the "pretty hard decompression period leaving the presidency," might have triggered or exacerbated his condition. Panetta describes the former president as "trying to make up for [the stress related to becoming a private citizen] and running around doing speeches . . . just kind of getting careless in terms of his lifestyle." He liked to talk about his healthy diet and give advice to others about theirs, but he was a serious backslider, still a binger of unhealthy foods. In 2000, during his last physical as president, he had elevated cholesterol levels and was taking a statin drug to bring it down.[170]

When his friend Tom Kean had a heart attack, Clinton called him in the hospital and told Kean that he had seen his [step]father suffer a heart attack in front of him and then started to give Kean, just out of the operating room, still woozy and sweating, detailed advice about diet. Later Kean visited Clinton in the White House and the president called to order lunch. The two men had decided on heart-healthy veggie burgers, a first for the president. A uniformed worker came in to take the order, Kean remembers. "Can we have a couple of veggie burgers?" The man was almost out the door when Clinton added, "Just one second, and lots of French fries."[171]

Clinton seemed remarkably at ease as he approached the first serious medical procedure of his life. He played Boggle with Hillary and Chelsea. Tony Campolo talked to him in "a pastoral role just before . . . his surgery."[172] Talk-show host Larry King, himself a veteran of bypass surgery, talked to the president the night before. "He was very, very courageous," King recalls. "I was scared to death the night before I had it. . . . If they didn't give me sedation, . . . I might have walked. You know what they're going to do to you."

King notes that Clinton was totally unlike another bypass veteran, Vice President Dick Cheney, who had his open-heart surgery in August 1988. King recalls spending time with Cheney at the Republican National Convention just before Cheney's operation. "We sat on the back steps of the New Orleans Superdome; Cheney wanted to know everything that happened to me. 'What they do to your chest, . . . what was it like when you woke up?' Clinton, on the other hand, was like, 'I'll face it. I've got faith in these doctors.'"[173]

His Arkansas friend Vic Fleming, the father of Chelsea's best friend before moving to the White House, hoping to get Clinton's mind off the bypass, wrote a crossword puzzle for Clinton to work as he recovered. Fleming sent the puzzle to Chelsea so she could hand-deliver it, and Fleming says that Clinton got word to him that he had received it and worked it and liked it. The theme was "the Clinton Family." He made the clues "pretty hard," says Fleming, who has written puzzles for the *New York Times*, "knowing that he wouldn't much enjoy it if it were a real no-brainer."[174]

One of Clinton's most fervent fans, Phil Ross, the collector of Clinton memorabilia, blamed the Republicans for Clinton's condition. "The Republicans beat the shit out of him for how many years? He had to go through an impeachment based on the most embarrassing stuff. . . . I was not surprised when he came up with an almost totally blocked heart. A lot of stuff like that takes its toll, not immediately, but if you tend to internalize it, which he always has had a knack for. . . . I really to this day think that if he had not been demonized by the Republicans and if he had been more careful in his own private life, he might not have had such a problem."[175]

The four-hour surgery, performed by a team of twelve—including the lead surgeon, Craig Smith, who had contributed that year to Bush's re-election campaign—was routine and successful. (Sections of arteries and veins from Clinton's chest and leg were harvested to bypass the blockages.) It was necessary to stop the heart at one point in the surgery, and he was placed on a heart/lung machine.[176]

Bypass surgery patients, especially those who are being kept alive by a machine, sometimes feel a bit less sharp after the surgery, and the condition, known colloquially as "pump head," sometimes lasts indefinitely. People who know Clinton say he's still the smartest guy in the room.

After his surgery, Will Shortz, the crossword puzzle editor of the *New York Times*, sent Clinton an advance copy of a puzzle, titled "From the Presidential Record Books." That puzzle was published in the *Times* magazine on December 5, 2004. The following week, in place of the usual completed answer grid, readers found a facsimile of Clinton's hand-written (in ink) completed puzzle, signed and dated October 29, 2004. Next to it was the note: "Another recent rainy-day activity for President Clinton: solving last week's puzzle. He says that it took him less than an hour."[177]

A year later, in an interview with CNN's Sanjay Gupta, Clinton did admit to some memory loss. "I have seen two or three examples where I couldn't remember the name of someone that I had known quite well. . . . But it eventually came to me. And so far, there's nothing permanent that I can recall."[178]

His recovery was difficult, and friends were shocked by how frail he appeared.[179] "The first time I saw him I was really upset," says Susie Tompkins Buell. "He looked like a cadaver."[180] Former Arkansas governor Jim Guy Tucker says that Clinton "looked bad; I thought his condition appeared to be very poor and I suspected that he might be really considerably more ill than had been suggested. . . . He looked very, very drawn and weak."[181]

Although his spokesmen and his doctors said he was doing great, people who were accustomed to being around him saw he was not. "I think that it took him a long time to recover," says Donna Shalala.[182] Jonathan Alter said that Clinton "complained of being tired. We compared notes." (Alter was then battling lymphoma.)[183]

George McGovern, whose late wife had bypass surgery, said that when he saw Clinton he looked so ill that "at first I thought maybe the operation had failed."[184]

FROM HIS hospital bed as he awaited surgery, Labor Day weekend, 2004, Clinton called John Kerry to give him advice—they spoke for ninety minutes, with Clinton doing most of the talking—and to warn him about the problems in his campaign.[185]

Bill Clinton was still in the hospital when he received a call from George W. Bush: "The Kerry campaign is the most inept group I have ever seen in politics," Bush told him. "Don't let them ruin your reputation."[186]

As it turned out, President Clinton did not have to worry because John Kerry did not call much on Bill, or Hillary, for that matter. Clinton was sidelined by his surgery, but Susie Tompkins Buell insists that before that and after, neither Bill nor Hillary Clinton was asked to help the Kerry campaign, until close to the end, when, Buell says, it was too late.

Susie Buell recalls Hillary calling her to complain, "I'm really worried. . . . They [Kerry and his team] haven't called us to help them."[187]

Bill Clinton and John Kerry had never been close. One man who is close to the Clintons, and who calls Clinton "the best people person I've ever met," describes Kerry's people skills as weaker even than Al Gore's. This man recalls a dinner at which a prominent woman sat next to Kerry. Three weeks later they were at another dinner, and "he had no idea who she was."[188] Corky Hale was invited in 2004 to mix with John Kerry at Ron Burkle's house. With her was her husband, the songwriter Mike Stoller. (With his partner, Jerry Leiber, Stoller wrote "Hound Dog," "Jailhouse Rock," and other songs for Elvis, all of the Coasters' hits, and songs for the Beatles and the Rolling Stones.) Stoller approached Kerry and told him that he and his partner wanted to donate to his campaign their song "Stand By Me." Kerry was delighted. "What a great idea, get back to you tomorrow." They heard nothing more—no recognition that Kerry had been offered such a unique gift.[189]

Looking back at the campaign, strategists disagree about whether Clinton was welcomed to campaign for Kerry or stiff-armed as he was by Gore four years before. Kerry's top adviser, Bob Shrum, was no friend of Clinton's. "John relied on Shrum more than anybody," says Lou Susman. Clinton is known to deeply dislike Shrum, to wonder out loud why anyone would hire him—he has lost every presidential race, including Al Gore's in 2000, with which he'd been involved. Shrum is said to have advised Gore not to use Clinton in 2000 and Kerry not to use Clinton much in 2004. One fund-raiser for the Democrats says of Shrum, "He could screw up a one-car parade; he's just so arrogant and out of touch."[190] (According to Noam Scheiber, writing in The New Republic, John Kerry's aides "fumed" when the hospital-bed telephone conversation between Clinton and Kerry the Saturday night before Clinton's surgery ended up on the front page of the New York Times the following Monday. Those aides, presumably, thought that Clinton and his people had leaked it to the paper. In the Times account, Scheiber writes, Clinton carries "a Yoda-like glow," while Kerry comes off as a "cipher.")

On October 25, in downtown Philadelphia, Bill Clinton, seven weeks postsurgery, stood next to John Kerry to address a lunch-break rally of some eighty thousand people. With the crowd shouting, "We love you, Bill," Clinton, looking painfully thin, his wedding band slipping down his finger, replied, "If this isn't good for my heart, I don't know what is." Pennsylvania went narrowly for Kerry, although the other states in which Clinton campaigned just before election day—Nevada, New Mexico, Arkansas—went to Bush.[191]

That Philadelphia appearance, says Elaine Kamarck, put Arkansas in the Bush column. Until Clinton's appearance, she says, Arkansas seemed to be leaning blue. "People have told me that internal campaign polls in Arkansas saw . . . Kerry close to Bush in Arkansas, and then somebody decided to bring Clinton into Philadelphia to campaign—national news, you don't keep anything secret—and Kerry lost Arkansas by nine points. And they say that Arkansas just bled when Clinton got on the stage in Philadelphia."[192]

Tony Coelho argues that had Clinton kept his health, "the political community" would have demanded Bill Clinton's participation. Kerry would have had no choice. "I think the political community came to the realization that Gore made a huge mistake not using Clinton in 2000, so it didn't make any difference what Shrum or even Kerry thought. . . . If Kerry hadn't used Clinton he would have been booed offstage in effect. He had to use him." And, Coelho argues, Clinton's appearance on Kerry's behalf all through September and October in two or three key states could have won Kerry the election.[193]

"Kerry would have lost anyway," maintains Stan Brand. "His candidacy was flawed. . . . I don't think they were tough enough in striking back on the Swift Boat thing, and I don't know that Bill Clinton could have bailed him out."[194]

Not even Bill Clinton could have reversed Kerry's biggest problem—his elitism, his grossly expensive bicycle, his spandex bike shorts, his windsurfing gear, his exotic wife, and his many estates. "No poor person in America thought for a minute that John Kerry knew anything about their lives and their struggles," says one prominent Democrat.[195]

The day after the 2004 election, Bill Clinton was one of the people who received a personal call from John Kerry informing him that he was going to concede to Bush.[196]

Chapter 5

CLINTON OPENS
HIS LIBRARY IN
A DOWNPOUR

O N NOVEMBER 18, 2004, A BIT MORE THAN TWO WEEKS
after the Kerry defeat—with some Democrats insisting that they
were still paying for Bill Clinton's sexual indiscretions—the William J.
Clinton Presidential Library and Museum opened in Little Rock on a
miserably cold day, rain falling in sheets.

Bill Clinton, a bit more than two months out of bypass surgery,
looked gaunt, his hair wet and flat against his head. His signature springy
bouffant was replaced by what looked like Ross Perot's $2 cut on a bad-
hair day.

Perhaps figuring that such a downpour couldn't last long, someone
had made the bad decision to keep the festivities, which went on for two
and a half hours, outdoors. "I've never been that wet with my clothes on,"
says Lynn Cutler.[1]

Clinton "had no business being there," says Phil Stefani. "He was not
ready to be there."[2]

"Oh, it rained, and he got sick again after that," says Janis Kearney, "and
I'm saying, my God, the man was sick when he came to the library. . . . He

was sitting out in the rain. . . . A lot of people thought he wouldn't be there, but of course he wouldn't have missed that."[3]

President Clinton had selected the New York architects Jim Polshek and Richard Olcott of Polshek Partnership Architects. They designed in an industrial section of Little Rock on twenty-six acres a stark rectangular structure suspended over the Arkansas River, intended to reflect the nearby bridge and railroad trestles. Some compared it to a mobile home and others thought it beautifully fulfilled the bridge-to-the-twenty-first-century idea, so central to Bill Clinton's rhetoric.[4]

Kane Webb, then writing editorials for the *Arkansas Democrat-Gazette*, is in the former group—describing it as "like a trailer on stilts" or like "an old-fashioned telephone booth put on its side." But on the inside, Webb says, "it is gorgeous because there's just light everywhere."[5]

While still president in 2000, Clinton had persuaded Little Rock mayor Jim Dailey to run for another term so he'd be in the mayor's chair when the library was dedicated. Dailey remembers the exchange: "'I don't want another mayor here when I open my presidential library.' And I went, 'Yes sir, Mr. President.'"[6]

Dailey's political skills were needed because not all the locals wanted the library. Shortly before he left the White House, Clinton had invited the mayor and his wife to stay in the Lincoln Bedroom. The Daileys would not get much sleep that night, but it was nothing compared with the sleepless nights the mayor endured because of blasts at Clinton in the *Arkansas Democrat-Gazette*. Dailey worried that the paper's harsh coverage of the library plans would so offend the president that he would scrap plans to put his library in Little Rock and instead take it up to Fayetteville, home of the University of Arkansas, or take it to New York or Washington. "We always had that fear that something like that might happen and they would take it out from under us."

And Dailey fretted particularly about Clinton's most relentless critic in the local paper, Paul Greenberg, the *Democrat-Gazette*'s Pulitzer Prize–winning columnist and editorial page editor, who had belittled Clinton for thirty years and who had coined the phrase that Clinton is said to hate most: "Slick Willie."

Greenberg and his deputy, Kane Webb, took off after Dailey for his decision to provide public land for the library.[7] Webb, who has since left the newspaper, says he and Greenberg "did not endorse the way that the city bought the twenty-six acres . . . , using money from fees from the parks and the zoo without a public vote." Webb called it "a shell game" that was "rammed down people's throats." The editors wanted a referendum, but, Webb claims, Dailey feared the vote would be about Bill Clinton. "This was the period of time . . . around the Monica Lewinsky scandal. . . . Bill's a polarizing figure here in Arkansas and I think they were worried, 'Oh, my God! What if we had this vote on the Clinton library land and it was voted down.'"[8]

That afternoon at the White House, the Daileys briefly saw Clinton. He told them he had meetings, but "you-all just hang tight and I'll drop by and see you later on." He wanted to show the Daileys the architects' drawings. That night, they were desperate to go to sleep—and joked about putting a note on the Lincoln Bedroom door telling him they had "hit the sack," when the president, in jeans and a casual shirt, finally knocked at 11:00 or 11:30. "He has these . . . architectural renderings and floor plans. . . . He just plopped down on the edge of the bed, spread all this stuff out, and started talking about various parts of the library and his vision and how excited he was."[9]

The day before the dedication had seen glorious late-fall weather. On dedication day, Leon Panetta recalls, the morning "began with the steadiest rain I've ever seen." He says that Clinton's sad demeanor, much remarked on, was because he was "depressed by the day. You have an event like that once in your lifetime . . . and you've got all these people coming and all of the celebrities that are going to be there and suddenly it's raining like hell. I'm sure it must have really pissed him off."[10]

Susie Tompkins Buell recalls Clinton looking "really sad" on "the last really big occasion before his funeral."[11] Sarah Wilson had the same impression: "One of the first things he said was 'I can't see the faces because of all the umbrellas.'"[12]

An indication of just how "miserable" the day was, says Kane Webb, was that "I left in the middle of U2 playing; that takes a lot for me to do. I couldn't take anymore."[13] Bono sang "The Hands That Built America." Lawrence Hamilton, a native Arkansan who sang on Broadway, also performed. (Hollywood celebrities in attendance included Barbra Streisand, Ted Danson, Robin Williams, Kevin Spacey, and Morgan Freeman.)

For the Clinton loyalists this was a reunion—a plane was chartered to take former White House staffers from Washington to Little Rock—a chance to see people they might have last seen on inauguration day 2001. John Emerson calls it "our version of an inauguration party."[14]

Plenty of Republicans were there, including the most hated, Karl Rove, still riding high after being hailed by Bush as "the architect" of his victory over Kerry. Some Democrats, Susie Tompkins Buell, for example, thought that the Republicans were "showing off. . . . It was like gloating to come down like that so close after the election."[15]

Besides Clinton, two other former presidents, Jimmy Carter and George H. W. Bush, were in attendance. (Carter offered a belated apology to Clinton for contributing to his gubernatorial defeat in 1980 by sending those Cuban refugees to Fort Chaffee in Arkansas.)[16]

His friends were relieved to see that when Clinton rose to speak, the spark and some of the color returned. Mickey Ibarra, who was there with his mother, describes the former president as "undaunted." Clinton led with a nod to his mother: "I'm thinking of my mother, Virginia Kelley, right now. She used to say rain is just liquid sunshine."[17]

Clinton seemed to catch a second wind and attended one party after another over the next couple of nights. Susie and Mark Buell hosted one at a bar, but left at ten. Clinton showed up at 10:30 "raring to go," says Mark Buell.[18] Lynn Cutler says the event was "hard on him," because even when feeling ill, "it's not like he's a guy who's going to leave the party early."[19]

He was delighted with his first-rate, cut-no-corners library. Jimmy Carter's center cost $26 million to build, Ronald Reagan's library cost $57 million, and George H. W. Bush's cost $83 million. Bill Clinton's cost $165 million and includes offices for his foundation and a luxurious apartment for him at the top of the building—decorated to the nines by

Little Rock resident and Clinton friend Kaki Hockersmith*—complete with an ecologically correct roof garden.[20]

Clinton was also delighted with the museum's exhibits. Paul Greenberg offers the other side of the assessment: "The Monica Lewinsky affair is almost hidden at the Clinton library; it's portrayed as just a right-wing conspiracy because of Bill Clinton's great accomplishments. The Clinton library overdoes the praise of Clinton even for a presidential library." He does give the library its due "as a great place to listen to chamber music."[22]

It was also great—an "economic engine"—for the down-at-the-heels warehouse and rail yards district in which it was built. Kane Webb credits it for "opening up that end of the city . . . that used to be kind of a wasteland." Webb also calls it "a huge attraction for tourists"—according to the library's own count, 279,278 in 2006. (Only the Reagan library gets more visitors.)[23]

As soon as ground was broken, says Jim Dailey, "that was when we started to see things just absolutely take off"—loft apartments; a major international organization considering a move to Chicago, which stayed and built on twenty-five acres next to the Clinton library; more conventions attracted to Little Rock because of the library; and speakers such as Bill Gates Sr., Ted Turner, Michael Bloomberg, who, as Dailey puts it, "get to see that we're not just, as some politician said years ago, barefoot and pregnant; we have a city with high-rise buildings and obviously a city that's on the move." Dailey estimates that since the announcement of the library, "just in the downtown area alone public and private investment [is] probably pushing a billion and a half to two billion dollars."[24]

*Hockersmith had decorated the Governor's Mansion for the Clintons, and they later hired her to decorate the Oval Office, the Treaty Room, the Family Dining Room, and other White House spaces. She also decorated the president's cabin and the dining hall and lodge at Camp David, worked on the re-creations of the Oval Office and the cabinet room in the Clinton library, and decorated the house in Chappaqua—but not Hillary's house in Washington. That work went to fancy Georgetown decorators. Maureen Dowd described Hockersmith's decoration of the Lincoln Sitting Room as so garish "that even Belle Watling might feel at home."[21]

As long as Clinton remains involved nationally and internationally, says Dailey, as long as he is strongly identified with Arkansas—even though he has become the proverbial citizen of the world—his library will "pay dividends." Clinton visits about once a month, sometimes staying overnight in his apartment, sometimes staying with friends, and sometimes not staying over at all but flying to his next destination here or abroad.[25]

Kane Webb says he knows when Clinton is in Little Rock because there's usually a story in the paper. "Bill's definitely an Arkansas boy. I think he has a true love of the state, but there's not much here for him anymore. His life is elsewhere." The locals, Webb adds, "were soon disabused of the notion that when he put his library in Little Rock that . . . somehow it would be like it was when he was governor and he'd be in and out of the McDonald's on Broadway."[26]

THAT DAY of the library dedication produced something of lasting value—the roots of a friendship between Bill Clinton and George H. W. Bush, the man Clinton beat in the 1992 election. H. W. Bush aide Ron Kaufman recalls "this strange" relationship started when the former president Bush—his son George W. Bush was also present—rose to speak; he ended up paying tribute to his successor and, Kaufman says, had the audience of mostly Clinton fans in tears.[27]

"Bill Clinton showed himself to be more than a good politician," former president Bush said. "In the White House, the whole nation witnessed his brilliance. . . . The president was not the kind to give up a fight. His staffers were known to say that if Clinton were the *Titanic*, the iceberg would sink.

"Trust me," Bush 41 continued, "I learned this the hard way. Here in Arkansas you might say he learned how to be the Sam Walton of retail politics."

Bush evoked much laughter when he added, "In the spirit of being kinder and gentler, I've long since forgiven him. After you leave the White House, a number of things happen to you. First of all, the crowds of protesters get smaller—disappointing, really. One-time political adversaries have a tendency to become friends. There is an inescapable bond that binds together all who live in the White House."[28]

Kaufman credits Clinton with most of the work of transforming the relationship: "Bill Clinton worked the relationship hard." After the event, the first President Bush would tell Kaufman that "Clinton was exceptionally warm and gracious and that he was received exceptionally well by everyone down there."[29]

The two former presidents, says John Emerson, spent time during the dedication days "talking to all hours" and "hanging out at the library."[30] Kane Webb attributes the friendship to H. W. Bush having reached a stage in his life "where he just didn't seem to give a damn anymore what people thought of him."[31]

EVEN THOSE watching the opening of Bill Clinton's library on C-SPAN could see that something was wrong with the former president. That Thankgiving, 2004, Hillary invited Terry McAuliffe and his family to join her and Bill at Punta Cana in the Dominican Republic, where the Clintons had been offered the use of Julio Iglesias's oceanfront estate. In his memoir, McAuliffe describes "Oscar," as in Oscar de la Renta, driving over for a visit in his golf cart and the Clintons and McAuliffes visiting Mikhail Baryshnikov in his beach villa. McAuliffe knew that something was wrong with his friend when he quit after twelve holes of golf to take a nap and got winded and chilled from a walk on the beach.[32]

WHEN GEORGE W. BUSH spoke at the dedication of the Clinton library, he had paid joking tribute to his predecessor, a month younger than he, as "the elder statesman." Bush also noted that Clinton's "service to America has not ended."[33]

On December 26, 2004, a tsunami, a giant tidal wave in the Indian Ocean, struck parts of Asia and Africa, battering sections of twelve countries, exacerbated by the most powerful earthquake to strike that region in forty years. President George W. Bush asked his father and Bill Clinton to lead a fund-raising campaign to help the victims—275,000 people dead and another 1,000,000 homeless.[34] The two presidents were to proselytize for the NGOs—nongovernmental organizations such as the Red Cross—that were working on the ground in the awful devastation left behind.

Hillary insisted that Bill see his doctors before he agreed to go. They found impairment in the lower half of his left lung. His friend John Emerson said that Clinton told him that the problem was "fluid buildup the size of his fist . . . near the heart and the lungs that needed to be released."[35] His bypass surgeon described Clinton's condition as "a trapped lung encased in inflammatory scar tissue." It sounded alarming, but Clinton wanted to take on this assignment with former president Bush, and his doctors agreed that he could postpone the surgery until his return.[36]

Clinton, feeling tired, and the older Bush, healthy and energetic, but eighty years old, went to the White House to meet with the current president, and then Bush and Clinton went together to the embassies of the affected countries to sign their condolence books and express their hopes for the future.

Next, on a grueling two-and-one-half-day tour, they assessed the damage firsthand. In Thailand they spent the night at a resort in Phuket—to boost Thai tourism, a booming industry devastated by the tsunami. Then they went to Indonesia, where they visited the province of Aceh and its hard-hit port city of Banda Aceh, with a stop to meet the Indonesian president; then to Sri Lanka, with a stop in Colombo; and finally to the Maldives.[37]

Their technical adviser and traveling companion was Mark Ward, a senior career officer at USAID (United States Agency for International Development)—a lawyer who gave up a Washington practice to join the Foreign Service. Ward, ten years younger than Clinton, speaks of the experience of guiding the former presidents as the highlight of his twenty years in public service.[38]

Also along were Ward's counterpart at the State Department, a couple of journalists, and each former president's own set of aides. Clinton brought along his friend Ron Burkle and his own photographer.[39]

They met in the airport in Burbank, California, where a White House jet—one used by the vice president—was waiting. It was "very comfortable," says Ward, "but it's not as big as Air Force One. . . . So it only has one bed and apparently there had been some discussion between the two presidents about who was going to get the bed and President Bush won. Knowing the two of them I'm sure they both offered it to the other one."

Clinton, just five months out of major surgery, and knowing he would face more surgery on his return, would have had to make do with the equivalent of a reclining business-class seat on the long trip—two fuel stops—between Burbank and Phuket, Thailand. But Bush brought an air mattress—one of his friends is a mattress retailer in Houston—so that President Clinton could lie down. Ward was making his way to the restroom on the first night when he was startled by a Secret Service agent blocking his path, and then he saw the reason: President Clinton sprawled out on the air mattress trying to find a comfortable position.

Ward briefed the two men but spent more time with Bush than with Clinton. "Clinton just seemed to be more familiar with the stops." On the other hand, says Ward, "what impressed me more than anything else about these guys was, unlike other people in high office in government, they had a lot of questions and knew how to listen and they would seek guidance. . . . They were both out of office. They were not getting daily briefs on what was going on in the world."

The scenes of utter wreckage were heart wrenching; the travel, says Ward, was "very brutal." After each stop on the ground, the weather extremely hot, sunny, and humid, everyone would board the plane and, recalls Ward, "kind of collapse and sleep and just rest."

But before he got lost in a conversation or a game of hearts, often with Jean Becker, President Bush's chief of staff, Bill Clinton would always call Hillary; it was the first thing he did when he returned to the plane. "God knows what time it was he was calling her," says Ward. "We were halfway around the world."

Everyone on the plane heard Clinton's end of these conversations. "I guess you could have [had a private conversation]," says Ward, "but he didn't care. . . . He was so emotional the way he described it. 'Hillary, you wouldn't believe it; it's much worse when you're there in person.'"

Ward would express his emotions in a more private manner in letters to his wife. "I knew I'd beat the letters home or I wouldn't even have a chance to mail them." It hardly mattered, just so long as the shock of the sights could be shared with someone.

"I had been out there a couple of times so I kind of knew what to expect," says Ward. But Bush and Clinton were like Ward when he went to inspect the tsunami damage the first time with then deputy secretary of defense Paul Wolfowitz—"Everyone was in tears everywhere we went, including . . . Wolfowitz."

In Phuket, off the coast of Thailand, they visited a village where USAID was helping fishermen secure financing to buy new fishing boats so they could start making money again. Ward worried about Bush and Clinton after a long night of travel; he made certain that they were getting enough water. Clinton refused entreaties to wear a hat; Bush was happy to wear one.

They were met by the banner "Welcome President Clinton"—Ward wondered what President Bush thought when he saw it—and American college students who had volunteered to help the fishermen rebuild their boats. President Clinton "spent a bunch of time with [the students]," says Ward, "just talking about where they were from, what they were doing." That evening, still in Phuket, they attended a dinner hosted by the president of Thailand and stayed in one of the island's resorts.[40]

It was on that stop that Bush mused to a reporter for his local paper, the *Houston Chronicle*, about Clinton, "Maybe I'm the father he never had."[41]

Early the next morning, they flew from Phuket to Madan, the capital of North Sumatra in Indonesia, where Bush and Clinton met with the president of Indonesia, and then took a flight from Madan to the severely damaged Banda Aceh.

The vista from Banda Aceh was disturbing. "You get down on your haunches," says Ward, "and you look at the horizon and you can see the horizon because everything's gone; there's nothing but foundations, except the mosque." He describes the Indonesians as "still in shock, and you saw it in their eyes; they didn't know what to do next. Who would?" Bush and Clinton had to check their emotions because the victims were watching, and, via the international press that followed the presidents' entourage, so was the world. "These guys have seen disasters before," says Ward, "and they were going to see more later with Katrina coming. I think they both had a lot of inner strength to deal with it. They knew that at least in the public eye they had to project a very strong image that things are going to get better."

Next they flew from Banda Aceh to Colombo in Sri Lanka where they had dinner with Sri Lankan president Chandrika Bandaranaike Kumaratunga. She had made the seating plan herself, and the Americans were wondering why the president would tend to such a trivial task, until she gave her opening remarks. "It means so much to me that the two of you who were political rivals in the U.S. . . . . can rise above that to come and help us in this our hour of greatest need, and I'd like to think I can do that too, and that's why the gentleman sitting . . . right across from you is the head of the opposition and the former prime minister."

The next morning, they were aboard helicopters to southern Sri Lanka and the city of Matara, which, Ward says, Bush and Clinton found particularly affecting because they were able to interact with children, most of them orphaned and all of them getting some "very simple counseling to get over what had happened, . . . to express it mostly through artwork."

The presidents had been counseled about what not to say. "Don't ask these kids about the flood, talk about the future. . . . Are you looking forward to getting back to school?" (Ward says he learned never to ask, "Where is your family?" when one man at the scene of the Pakistan earthquake responded, "You're standing on them.")

The children's artwork was set up outdoors, and it had progressed from the drawings they had done just after the tsunami hit—"all very dark," says Ward, "lots of storm and rain and clouds and pictures of their families floating in water, . . . and then slowly, over time, you see the progression, the same kids, . . . starting to see color, starting to see flowers, starting to see rainbows, starting to see houses that aren't damaged."

The presidents sat in a semicircle on the ground with the children, and, Ward says, "my impression was [Bush and Clinton] didn't want to leave. The kids sang to them, did dances, brought pictures to them; and after all the devastation we had seen, particularly the day before in Aceh, we all needed this . . . because you could see that we were making progress with these kids."

Damage in Sri Lanka was less severe than in Indonesia because, although the little Sri Lankan communities on the beach were largely washed away by the tidal wave, unlike Indonesia, Sri Lanka did not first endure an earthquake. The bond between Clinton and Bush was strengthened by neither one of them wanting to disengage from this half circle of hope and friendship. "To this day," says Ward, "they both have in their offices some of the artwork those kids gave them."

President Clinton seemed to care a lot about Sri Lanka, says Ward. "I know he has been very disappointed that, unlike Aceh, where the tsunami and the world's reaction to it contributed to peace, it hasn't worked out in Sri Lanka. And . . . every time I've seen him since, he has pulled me aside and whispered to me how disappointed he is that hostilities are back."[42] (Pre-tsunami there was an insurrection in Aceh and there was civil war in Sri Lanka, making relief efforts far more complicated. A peace accord holds in Aceh, but Sri Lanka continues at war.)[43]

Later that day, the two presidents met the helicopters at a town called Galle on the southwestern tip of Sri Lanka. To Ward's surprise, the British singer and bassist Sting (aka Gordon Matthew Thomas Sumner) was there. Sting knew both presidents, Ward says, but knew Clinton better. "They had a nice little chat."

Their last stop was in the Maldives, a group of twenty-six atolls in the Indian Ocean. The Bush/Clinton group flew to the capital, Male. The islands lost a small number of people, about ninety, but the number is large relative to its population, and its main industry, tourism, suffered a big hit. To show the world that the country was ready to receive tourists, Bush and Clinton visited a resort, where they met the country's president.

Clinton was then met by a friend's private plane and he flew on to China to promote his memoir. George H. W. Bush flew home to Texas.

As they approached Manila in the Philippines, where Mark Ward was leaving the plane to attend to USAID business, President Bush pulled him aside: "I've got some friends who want to give some money, about half a million bucks. . . . You clearly know what's going on on the ground. . . . What do you think they should do?"

Bush's friends took Ward's advice and gave a donation to an organization in Indonesia. And so Ward became involved with what became known as the Bush-Clinton Houston Tsunami Fund and continued to work with the two men.

After Bill Clinton returned from China, he and Bush met in Washington to give President George W. Bush a report on their trip. That report, written by staff but approved by the presidents, described how at every stop they saw USAID and NGOs working hard, in dangerous and uncomfortable situations. "There was this line in there," Ward says, "about, seeing them, we've never been so proud to be Americans." Those words made Ward a fan for life of Bush and Clinton. "We don't often get that kind of recognition."[44]

The two presidents pushed hard for people to give to the NGOs working on the ground. Ray Offenheiser, president of Oxfam America, credits this bipartisan approach with inspiring "unprecedented levels of philanthropy . . . on the scale of which most of us have never seen before. . . . Many of the private humanitarian organizations like ours and CARE and . . . Save the Children . . . and certainly the American Red Cross broke every conceivable record for contribution."[45]

Americans donated $1.2 billion for tsunami relief.[46] Most had never heard of these places, much less visited them. Ward attributes the success of the fund-raising effort to "the magic" of the two men appearing together. He cites an interview he gave to *Time* in which he used the example of his own mother who, he says, "doesn't have that much money, but my mom says, 'If those two guys could work together, I'll find a hundred dollars.' My mom called me after that and complained, 'It was actually $500; you make me sound cheap.'"[47]

Soon after they returned, golfer Greg Norman, a friend of both presidents, recruited them for a tsunami relief golf tournament. With Bush representing the Red Cross and Clinton representing UNICEF, they raised $2.1 million.[48]

The two presidents also quietly worked the fund that had at its foundation Bush's wealthy Houston friends. It wasn't until an event at a tennis stadium in Houston in May 2005 that they announced their grants, all the while continuing to encourage people outside their circles to go to USAID's website and give to the NGOs.[49]

Eventually they raised some $12–$13 million. They gave some of it to the communities they had visited—$1 million to Phuket to rebuild fishing boats; $500,000 to Lampunk to repair the water system and to rebuild a school, a health clinic, a women's center, and a market; $1 million to Sri Lankan coastal districts to build children's playgrounds. Later the Bush-Clinton Houston Tsunami Fund contributed approximately $1 million to the United Nations' "adopt-an-island" program in the Maldives. The money went to the island of Dhiggaru and was used to help repair its homes, harbor, and water and sanitation systems.[50]

Ward suggested that money be spent on scholarships in Indonesia. "Let's get some future leaders of Aceh into some of the best schools in the United States." Playing to his audience, he sold the idea to the initially skeptical presidents by suggesting Texas A & M and the University of Arkansas as host schools. They decided to target women who have fewer opportunities in that Islamic country. The program, funded with $4–$5 million from the presidents' fund, is ongoing, managed by the Fulbright Foundation, and brings seventy to seventy-five young Indonesians to pursue advanced degrees in majors important to reconstruction, such as engineering, agriculture, and city planning.[51]

Ward's affection continues for Bill Clinton and George H. W. Bush, whom he sees as bringing out the best in each other and as a model for young people, including his own teenage sons, for what public service and politics can mean.[52]

IF CLINTON was worried about his second surgery, performed on March 10, 2005, he did not show it and did not complain about his health. USAID's Mark Ward marveled at "that spring in his step. I don't know where the energy came from. . . . People would ask him about [his health] on the trip and he would say he's feeling great."[53]

The procedure, called *decortication* and performed in the same hospital—New York–Presbyterian Hospital/Columbia University Medical Center—as the bypass, is necessary in a small fraction of 1 percent of patients who have heart bypass surgery. It is done to cure a condition called *pleural effusion* by removing scar tissue, which, in Clinton's case, formed on the surface of his lung, as well as fluid, which squeezed the lower section of the left lung and reduced his breathing capacity by more than 25 percent. He remained in the hospital for four days and returned to Chappaqua to recover.[54]

The late-night comics pounced. Craig Ferguson, host of CBS's *The Late Late Show*, quipped a few days after Clinton's surgery, "When he was asked to describe his symptoms he said, 'It felt like there were two interns on his chest.' Maybe it's just one big one." Ferguson also listed "Top Ten Things Overheard During Bill Clinton's Hospital Stay," among them, "A nurse is coming; put him in the restraints. . . . For some reason he always forgets the surgical gown opens in the back. . . . Al Gore! When did you start working as an orderly? . . . Hillary wants to know if you would neuter him."[55]

CLINTON HAD committed to give the opening speech in spring 2005 for a lecture series at Drew University in New Jersey, named in honor of Tom Kean, then about to retire as the university's president.

Although their relationship would be tested in 2006 over Kean's role as adviser to a television miniseries, *The Path to 9/11*—Clinton thought it unfairly blamed his administration for 9/11—there were years of friendship and affection between these two former governors. They were from different parties—Kean a liberal Republican—but they shared a commitment to progressive social policy and a particular interest in improving education.

It would be Clinton's first speech after his second surgery and his doctors had advised him to cancel. His staffers told Kean that Clinton would have to bow out, "and then I guess he got to them," Kean says, "and said, 'We're friends, I'd like to do it.'"

They came back with a bill of restrictions. He'd speak for fifteen to twenty minutes, would take only three questions, and his staff wanted to know in advance what the questions were. Kean asked professors in the political science department to compose the questions, which Kean assumed were passed on to the former president.

When Clinton arrived, Kean was shocked. "I thought he looked awful. He was pale, thin." He opened his shirt to show Kean his surgical scars. "I was worried about him; I was thinking to myself, 'Maybe I shouldn't have pressed this.'"

In passing, Kean mentioned, "We've got the three questions." "What?" Clinton responded, obviously annoyed. He called a member of his staff and let him have it. "I have told you never, ever to do that and I never want to hear that again." He turned to Kean and said, "Of course any questions you want to ask are fine."

Kean introduced the former president to a sold-out crowd that greeted him with a standing ovation. "You could see the color come back into his face," Kean recalls. "It was almost like somebody had done something for him medically. He started to look like the old Bill Clinton. And he talked for fifty minutes. . . . And then he started taking questions and he didn't want to stop taking questions." Then, says Kean, he worked the rope line; students had papers and programs they wanted him to sign, and many had his book. "He didn't want to leave until every kid had been satisfied. . . . I got him back where the car was. . . . There's a . . . hill above [it] and . . . these people were clapping for him on the hill. . . . 'Oh, come on down.' . . . [He] shook all their hands, autographed whatever they had."[56]

That night reminded Kean of another time when Bill Clinton was laid low—by the Lewinsky scandal. Kean was at the White House for a meeting at which Clinton was to receive the report of a panel he had appointed to study the question of race. It happened to be the same day that Ken Starr presented his findings to Congress.[57] Kean, John Hope Franklin, and the other panel members were sitting with Clinton in the Oval Office. Kean could see that the president was "obviously distracted," uncharacteristically unfocused. The panel gave its report to Clinton and then walked over with him so he could present it to a group of about 250 civil rights leaders, including Jesse Jackson and Rosa Parks. As Clinton entered the room, "they gave him a standing ovation and the same darn thing happened," Kean recalls. He got his color back, he focused, "he gave one of those speeches that only Bill Clinton can give, interrupted about six times by applause; another standing ovation when he finished . . . and he looked great. He needs that, he needs the affirmation. And he needs people to understand where he's going and to be with him and supportive of him. . . . That's the medicine he needs. And that's better than any doctor for him."[58]

IN MAY 2005, Bush and Clinton came to Washington, at the invitation of Richard C. Holbrooke, a former U.S. ambassador to the United Nations, for a tsunami-related event in the same building where USAID has its offices. Ward asked them if they would stop by before and thank his people, who, he says, are often dismissed as bureaucrats but were "the folks that were making this tremendous American response possible." Not only did they come, says Ward, "they just worked the crowd and they completely botched up Holbrooke's schedule downstairs." Ward speculates that "people probably decided that day not to retire because it was worth hanging in there to do what we do."

Ward is often asked if the relationship between Bush and Clinton is sincere. He legitimately claims an insider's view and has many examples to offer of their easy camaraderie. They loved to talk sports, to revisit the 1992 campaign—including nitty-gritty, precinct-level analysis of that race—to discuss foreign policy as expressed in recollections of major figures "and how they interacted with that person when they were president;

always in the most respectful terms. . . . There was so much they had in common . . . that they would never run out of positive things they could talk about. They never had to get into anything that they disagreed about."

Before the Houston event when they announced the recipients of the grants from their private fund, they met at Bush's office. "Of course, President Clinton was late," says Ward. ". . . They couldn't be more different in that regard. . . . President Bush is either right on time or early. And they just kidded each other unmercifully about that." During their tsunami tour, Clinton was always late, says Ward, because "he was working a crowd." When President Bush's glance at his watch in 1992 during a debate with Clinton and H. Ross Perot generated harsh criticism, he was simply doing what comes naturally to him. "President Bush is always looking at his watch," says Ward.[59]

At that event, Barbara Bush made the introductions and referred to her long-lost son Bill. "All's forgiven. Welcome home." Clinton stood up and turned to her: "Thanks, Mom." Clinton then suggested that the Bush family would do anything to get another Bush into the White House—so if he's the long-lost son and Hillary wins the White House in 2008, she would be a Bush by marriage.[60]

Ron Kaufman, the former aide to the first president Bush, says that when he characterizes their relationship as "a love affair," he puts it in quotes; while they're not best friends, the relationship is "real and warm," and, he adds, "I would venture to say that Bill Clinton feels a lot closer to George H. W. than he does to President Carter." Kaufman says that 41 likes to joke, "The great thing about me and 42 is I say hello and that's all I have to say, and 42 will carry the conversation from there on. At my age, that's good."[61]

Politicians, all Democrats, who are close to Bill Clinton—Tom Downey, Bob Torricelli, Beryl Anthony, Tim Wirth, Bill White, the mayor of Houston who spearheaded Clinton's campaign in Houston in 1992—say that the first president Bush, like President Clinton, is a nice guy, an intelligent guy with deep experience, easygoing, decent, idealistic, optimistic, and a reasonable, moderate man. The two presidents also share a sentimental nature and the tendency to tear up or even sob in public.

"Look," says the retired Morgan Stanley executive Anson Beard, "no one can help but like Bill Clinton and you can't help but like George H. W. Bush, so why wouldn't they get along well? Two great American leaders out of office."[62]

MARK WARD noticed that when Bill Clinton is in the company of H. W. Bush he usually had something nice to say about George W. Bush, often about something the president had done that had just been in the news. The older Bush would often remark later to Ward, "That really meant a lot to me. He doesn't have to do that."[63]

Clinton's hands-off stance toward his successor took some discipline. "He's really tried to stay out of his hair," says Jake Siewert, "and he probably doesn't agree with 95 percent of what the guy's doing. . . . For a guy who likes to talk as much as he . . . does, . . . he's done a pretty good job of keeping it buttoned up."[64]

Clinton's behavior does seem remarkably gracious, given that George W. Bush had run for president as the anti-Clinton who would restore clean living and fidelity to the White House. When, in 2006, Clinton spoke to a group of left-of-center editors of alternative newspapers, he told them to be open to opposing views and to the people who hold them. He urged them not to turn public figures into "cartoons." He acknowledged that he disagreed with much of what the current Bush has done as president but he credited him with "an intuitive intelligence." When the audience erupted in laughter, he appealed again to these editors to "oppose what he is doing rather than ridicule him." ("I loved it when the Right Wing ridiculed me," he said. "When you ridicule someone, you underestimate them.")[65]

TODAY, WHEN George W. Bush is mired in low ratings and expectations, it is easy to forget that the political skills that brought him to that victory are ones that Bill Clinton admires. Friends say Clinton often mentions how talented, how canny a politician "W" is.[66]

Not everyone admires Clinton's kid-glove treatment of George W. Bush, and some of Clinton's stalwarts in the 1990s wish he would stop being so respectful. And every once in a while, in an unguarded moment, Clinton's real feelings toward W come to the fore, as they did in 2003 when he unleashed his anger at what he saw as the New York Times' "willful ignorance of the failings of the Bush administration." But that tirade was unleashed at a private event, and Clinton's friends fretted that he would remain above the fray until he had to go to battle to help Hillary win the White House.

Bush the father told Mark Updegrove that his friendship with Clinton would "hit a rocky patch when . . . Hillary runs for president," but that in the long run their friendship will survive. (Campaigning in Iowa in November 2007, Hillary said, "As someone said the other day, there seems to be a pattern. It takes a Clinton to clean up after a Bush." A month later, campaigning in South Carolina, Bill added to the insult, promising that on Hillary's first day as president she would send him and George H. W. Bush around the world to say that the U.S. is "open for business" and, in effect, that they, 41 and 42, would clean up the mess made by 43. Jean Becker quickly issued a statement that former President Bush would make no such mission, that he "wholeheartedly supports" his son "and his foreign policy. . . . He is proud of the role America continues to play . . . as the beacon for freedom and democracy.")[67]

Friends knew the relationship was serious when Bush invited Clinton to the family vacation home at Kennebunkport for golf and boating. (Clinton had been there once before, in 1983, when then vice president Bush hosted a governors' conference and Governor Clinton, with three-year-old Chelsea in tow, attended. When Clinton introduced his daughter to the vice president and his "wonderful home," Chelsea was not impressed. "I have to go to the bathroom," she said, and the vice president took her hand and led her there. "It really impressed me," Clinton told a Houston Chronicle reporter.)[68]

Once when Bush's flight was delayed out of New York and he had some hours to kill, his staffer called Clinton's staffer at the Harlem office and asked if President Bush and his entourage could stop by. They were told that President Clinton was not in the office that day but come along anyway. According to a report in *Time*, Bush sat in Clinton's chair, put his feet up on Clinton's desk, called Clinton on his cell phone, and said, "Bill! It's George. Nice view! Nice desk!"[69]

IN 2005, both former presidents accepted special envoy roles, Bush as an envoy to the Pakistan earthquake and Clinton as Kofi Annan's UN envoy for the tsunami—a role Clinton handled in an admirably hands-on fashion.

The first meeting with CEOs of NGOs on the ground in the tsunami-ravaged areas was at Clinton's office in Harlem. Ray Offenheiser was there and remembers that the former president was still visibly recovering from his surgery. "He lost weight, he was a different-looking guy than he appeared in his final days in the presidency."

Offenheiser was impressed, as was every other CEO "to a person." Clinton was able to understand and enumerate "the core problems," and to describe them "in considerable detail, right from the hip without any notes, and basically said to us, 'Have I got this right?' And everyone around the table said, 'You've got it absolutely right, and if this is the agenda we can work on, we're with you.'" Erskine Bowles was there, Clinton having asked him, says Offenheiser, to "come in to help him get this thing jump-started."[70]

As Bill Clinton took off on his UN envoy role, George H. W. Bush was vitally interested in his friend's latest assessments of the area they had visited together, and Clinton eagerly shared his observations. Bush's chief of staff Jean Becker called Ward from time to time to report, "42 just called us with another trip report today." Ward was once at Kennebunkport meeting with Bush, when Clinton called: "President Bush put it on the speaker and we all heard the report because President Clinton had just gotten back from one of the countries in the tsunami area."

"And President Bush just loves it," Ward says, "because he feels like he's still part of it." Realizing that, Clinton seldom missed calling his predecessor first thing: "I know that Bill's coming back," Bush would say. "I know he's going to call me."[71]

Chris Stamos, a partner in the money management firm Sterling Stamos and president of the firm's philanthropy arm—he is involved with Bill Clinton in his work in Africa—witnessed the calls going in the other direction. He was at a reception with Clinton when his cell phone rang and it was Bush. "They'd be talking about something they could work together on, real friendship."[72] On occasion, says Clinton friend John Emerson, Bush takes on a paternal role, asking Clinton if he's doing his exercise and watching his diet.[73]

As for the more caustic Barbara Bush, "I think she genuinely likes Bill," says Mark Updegrove. "He's a charming, albeit rakish character, and it's not hard to be charmed by Bill Clinton."[74] No one claims that she started out liking him, but, as Larry King assesses it, "I think Barbara ruefully likes him."[75] When, in 2005, King asked her directly on air, "Are you fond of him?" she stumbled. "Yes. All right. Yes, no, I like him."[76]

It was Barbara who borrowed a phrase to describe them: "the odd couple."[77]

Some argue that Barbara is irritated with her eldest son, George, for not giving his father more to do, and that she's grateful that George and Bill have found common ground and have taken their show on the road. As Tony Coelho puts it, "W doesn't deal much with Papa Bush, and so Papa Bush and his team enjoy Papa Bush being onstage, so it's a marriage of convenience for Papa Bush . . . a very good thing for Papa Bush and for Clinton to be out there." From Barbara's perspective, Coelho speculates, "George deserves it."[78]

Mark Ward once asked Barbara if she was tempted to join her husband on the tsunami travel, "and she said absolutely not. That was the right thing for the two presidents to do."[79]

Tom Kean, a close personal friend of the Bushes, suggests not getting carried away by testimonials to Barbara's warm feelings for Bill; she is not likely to forget the past or ignore the brickbats that will emerge from a Hillary run for the White House. "I know Barbara very well, and her feeling isn't always as charitable as the president's to a lot of people. . . . He can be very charitable and she isn't, as far as people who criticize the Bushes."[80] Republican strategist Scott Reed says of Barbara, "She's a rememberer; 41 is more of a forgiver."[81] "Spouses tend to hold a grudge," says Ron Kaufman. On the other hand, Kaufman adds, Clinton does not need a "food taster" when he visits Kennebunkport.[82]

Bush publicly recalled a political cartoon depicting his son, the president, opposing gay marriage and then walking into a room and finding his father on a sofa with Clinton's arm around him, prompting him to shout, "Dad! What are you doing?"

Clinton clipped it and sent it to Bush: "Don't you think we ought to cool it, George?"[83] In an interview with ABC anchor Charles Gibson in late September 2007, Clinton said of Bush, "I truly love him."[84]

It also would be a mistake, argues Tom Kean, to buy into the idea that Bush has become closer to Clinton than to his own son. "Knowing the Bush family, that's just not true." He calls them "a very, very close family. . . . He feels very, very strongly about his son and wants to support him in every way he can. I just don't think he likes people to criticize his son."[85]

WHEN HURRICANE Katrina struck in August 2005, George W. Bush asked his father and Bill Clinton to go to work again.

On September 4, 2005, six days after Katrina laid waste to New Orleans and parts of the Gulf Coast, Bill Clinton was chatting in his backyard in Chappaqua with Paul Orfalea (aka Kinko because of his once full head of kinky hair), the brilliantly intuitive businessman who had built Kinko's from one sidewalk copier at the University of California in Santa Barbara to a powerhouse chain and then reaped his fortune by selling it to Federal Express. Clinton had targeted Orfalea as a contributor to his foundation and to the upcoming Clinton Global Initiative and had invited him to Chappaqua that Labor Day weekend. Hillary wasn't there. Orfalea, who had his teenaged son with him, was told that the meeting with the former president would last about fifteen to twenty minutes; they ended up talking for two to three hours.[86]

The next day, Labor Day, Bill and Hillary arrived before dawn at the airport in Westchester County to board a plane loaned to them by John Catsimatidis for a flight to Houston and the Astrodome where many of Katrina's victims had been evacuated—in the weeks following the hurricane, there were more than 250,000 evacuees in Houston. Clinton met his friend George H. W. Bush there and they announced a campaign to raise money for the victims of Katrina.[87] They would ultimately raise more than $130 million.[88]

For their work on the tsunami, the former presidents reaped nothing but praise; on Katrina, because it hit at home, President Clinton caught some criticism. Douglas Brinkley, who wrote a book about Katrina in which he graphically described what he considered a colossally incompetent response by the Bush administration, faults Clinton for providing a "fig leaf" for the administration; for "sugarcoating the failed government response." While agreeing that the "bipartisan spirit" is nice and that "the Bush/Clinton road show is constantly raising money for good causes," Brinkley argues that Clinton needed to "come out of the box and talk straight about . . . the utterly disastrous . . . handling of Katrina." When Clinton and Bush again grabbed center stage, and Clinton said that "'this isn't the time to place blame,'" he was, says Brinkley, "actually aiding and abetting the spin of the Bush White House."[89]

The tsunami work was winding down, as the media spotlight turned to Katrina, and Mark Ward's exposure to the two presidents lessened significantly. But Ward wasn't finished with them yet. Learning that the pair was going to deliver a joint commencement address in May 2006 at Tulane University, which had been closed after the hurricane struck, Ward asked Clinton if he could grab fifteen minutes of their time and the last piece of money in the Bush/Clinton tsunami fund. Would they meet with six or seven young Sri Lankan American professionals, in their twenties and thirties, who were trying to build a pediatric hospital in their home country?

Clinton and Bush agreed to give the money and to meet with the group in New Orleans before the speech. The Sri Lankans, all well educated and working in good jobs, all American citizens, flew to New Orleans and met with the presidents in a room in a downtown hotel. They met privately, no press coverage. Ward had promised them, "You're not going to forget these guys. Some are Tamil and some Sinhalese. They've put all that behind them and they're working together to build this hospital." They had blueprints with them, and, Ward says, the presidents were studying them and talking to the young people and did not want to leave. "And the Secret Service just kept grabbing them—'We're late, we're late.' They didn't want to go."

President Bush was not feeling well that day but seemed to gain strength from the young people and their project and started to ask specific questions. He also said to Clinton, "Let's go back, Bill; let's go back." Clinton was advising them on fund-raising strategies: "Let me tell you about this guy; let me tell you about this guy," giving them names.

The Sri Lankan Americans followed up on Clinton's leads and soon will be breaking ground on the hospital in Matara, the city in which the two presidents had met with the children. "My hope," says Ward, "and I think this will happen, is that one or both of the presidents will be able to go someday and say, 'That's the hospital we got off the ground.'"[90]

George H. W. Bush would later tell Houston mayor Bill White how much fun it was to give the Tulane commencement speech with "Bubba," as he sometimes calls Bill Clinton, and how much he enjoyed going with his friend, on the spur of the moment, to a restaurant in the French Quarter.[91] A client of Ron Kaufman's provided a plane and they flew back together, Bush to Maine and Clinton to Boston.[92]

CLINTON WENT directly to a Boston hotel to appear at the Heart Ball—seeing his appearance as an important way to boost fund-raising and also to get out his message about fighting childhood obesity, which would become one of the major domestic planks of the Clinton Foundation. Steve Grossman, who persuaded Clinton to be there, says that the former president is a perfect spokesman because he has admitted his own unhealthy eating habits, as a boy and as a man.[93]

Clinton's foundation, set up on leaving the White House, featured two issues on the domestic side: global warming, specifically a green buildings initiative, and an initiative to reduce the incidence of childhood obesity.

Many were making their names on global warming, most notably Al Gore, who had become the rock star of that issue; Clinton knew he'd never be able to compete. But the childhood obesity issue was one that he could make his own. "It's such a horrible problem," Clinton said in a speech. "Adult-onset diabetes type two showing up in kids for the first time, . . . is going to shorten too many kids' lives." Childhood obesity, he added, "scares me every single day." Clinton, who volunteered that he had been fat as a boy,[94] knew that taking on that cause would not make his legacy and certainly not win him the Nobel Peace Prize, not when third world children were dying from malnutrition. Childhood obesity took lives but only after years of bad habits; it lacked urgency; it did not move people.

Bill Clinton had been out of the White House for more than four years. Although he had some accomplishments—the tsunami work, for example—he had not yet figured out his legacy. He knew that people whose good opinion he craved were still waiting. "I was concerned at first that the postpresidency was going to consist of very little other than going around and making speeches in all parts of the world for very fat fees," says Ted Sorensen.[95]

Clinton's latest surgery reminded him that if he was to be placed in the top ranks of American presidents, he'd better get going on some major, media-attracting good works. Some historians and journalists argued that he had wasted three-quarters of his second term on a sex scandal, and that he would be lucky if his presidency was judged much more than middling.

At the same time, his unusual circumstances—his marriage to a woman who was intent on becoming president, and even his valuable friendship with H. W. Bush—meant that his work had to be mostly outside the United States. One journalist who knows him well says Bill Clinton "is now in some ways a man without a country."[96] Others would more accurately call him a "citizen of the world."

It was precisely the latter—"elevate yourself above American politics"—that Tony Coelho had urged on Clinton when he was still in the White House. On the practical side, Coelho reminded Clinton that people internationally "didn't really give a damn about the Monica issue and they felt it was idiotic the way it was played up here."[97]

In early 2005, Clinton and a group of his wealthy, politically connected friends invited Jim Wallis—editor in chief of the liberal Christian magazine *Sojourners* and author of the bestseller *God's Politics: Why the*

Right Gets It Wrong and the Left Doesn't Get It—to dinner at the Manhattan home of investment banker Roger Altman, undersecretary of the treasury in the Clinton administration. Wallis, a progressive clergyman, who knew the Clintons from Renaissance Weekends—fashionable New Year's retreats for progressives in government, business, the arts—was invited so that the assembled insiders could, as Wallis puts it, "pick my brain . . . about how Democrats should . . . take back the faith . . . from the religious right." Among those present were Clinton's Treasury secretary, Robert Rubin, Congressman Harold Ford Jr. of Tennessee, Terry McAuliffe, James Carville, the late Texas governor Ann Richards, and John Podesta.[98]

No one mentioned Wallis's harsh criticism of President Clinton over welfare reform or his even harsher criticism of Clinton over Lewinsky. On the latter, Wallis publicly made the connection "between personal and public integrity."[99] He was quoted in the *New York Times* as saying, "Clinton's completely out of the game"; he no longer had the moral podium from which to address such issues as race and poverty.[100]

Wallis had changed his mind about Clinton, whom he told, privately, after dinner, "You could provide a significant leadership role around some of the biggest issues the world faces that politics is failing to deal with." Wallis likely won no points with Clinton when he held up Jimmy Carter as a model by describing him as a "much more effective ex-president than president." Was Clinton offended at the comparison of his presidency with Carter's? "Bill Clinton knows as well as anybody else," Wallis says, "that his presidency was very mixed, great highs and great lows and . . . opportunities that were met and others that were missed."

Clinton told Wallis that night that he was "wrestling" with an idea for an annual meeting whose participants would identify and find the money to help solve some of the world's most intractable problems. Wallis stops short of claiming that he planted the idea in the former president's head for what became the Clinton Global Initiative (CGI). "I didn't lay out his plan for CGI, . . . but I was . . . encouraging him in the role. And when . . . I saw the initiative emerging, I thought, 'Boy, that's exactly what I hoped he would do.'"[101]

Clinton knew that his foundation was tiny compared with the Gates Foundation and many others; it was doing one thing here and one thing there, but there was no particular theme and it wasn't attracting much media attention.[102] It could not be the base on which he built his lasting legacy. But this concept that he had been discussing with people close to him that depended on his supremely charismatic personality to raise money and inspire good works sounded right. Vartan Gregorian, who describes Clinton as having a personality so potent that he "sucks all the oxygen out of the room," says that 99 percent of CGI depends on Clinton's personality, on the response he generates when he strides onstage to greet and exhort the assembled.[103]

Clinton knew that he had what his friends call "convening power." As Jake Siewert puts it, "It made sense for him to kind of figure out how to leverage his convening power."[104] But Clinton also knew that if he tried to present another all-talk, little-action venue like Davos, which carries the airy subtitle "committed to improving the state of the world"—but in certain circles is ridiculed as bloviating on the Swiss ski slopes—it would move him no closer to achieving his legacy.

He quickly nailed down the details of CGI. It would be a three-day conference every September in New York organized around four big issues—energy and climate change, global health, poverty alleviation, and mitigating religious and ethnic conflict. CGI would have the same elite feel as Davos; but, instead of the Davos style of a floating agenda, the buffet of discussion groups on which to nibble and then not think much about until Davos rolled around again a year later, Clinton's CGI would be limited to those four tracks and they would remain constant year to year. Participants would have to pledge money or time or programs and if they didn't make good on those pledges, they would not be invited back the next year. At the first session on the first day of the second CGI in September 2006, Clinton announced that there were about twenty people from the last conference who didn't meet their commitments so they were not invited back.[105]

The guest roster—domestic big names such as Colin Powell; foreign leaders such as Tony Blair and Pakistani president Pervez Musharraf—did not happen by accident. Clinton deliberately scheduled CGI to coincide with the opening of the United Nations General Assembly, so that there are always heads of state for him to invite to sit on his panels and mix with his guests.[106]

To Tim Wirth, president of the United Nations Foundation and Better World Fund and a regular at CGI, the timing is "brilliant." "What would you rather do if you're a diplomat or a head of state; you go and do your cameo that's necessary at the UN and then what is more fun than to go over and see Bill Clinton right across town?"[107]

While there would be scores of the superrich business leaders who frequent Davos, Clinton would bring in heads of NGOs and scholars and mayors and activists and for them he would waive the $15,000 registration fee. The "brilliant strategy," says Susan Davis, chairperson of Grameen Foundation USA, is Clinton's idea to pair people who want to make money commitments with people who do the work and are looking for partners.[108] Chris Jennings, who was Clinton's senior health adviser in the White House, and who now heads a health-care consulting firm, helped to shape CGI's health-care programs and calls CGI "a cause, not a conference." He attributes CGI's remarkable and almost instant success—it took only one, maybe two CGIs for it to have the feel of an institution, and a reserved place on the calendars of the connected—to "the number of . . . the speakers, who are on-the-ground people, people who actually know what they're doing and are delivering care, and have successful programs." It is not, he adds, "a highlighting problems conference; this is a highlighting innovative solutions conference. . . . People who come have to make commitments to address the challenges that are raised."[109]

An invitation from the Bill Clinton of 2001 might have been buried at the bottom of the pile or declined, but the Bill Clinton of 2005 had morphed into the rock star president. Clinton loved that designation, but he wanted to be the rock star with gravitas; a kind of Bono in a business suit, who could attract the kings, the former presidents, the secretaries of state, the foreign ministers, and the billionaire businesspeople and extract money from them to bring his programs to fruition.

So far Clinton has been omnipresent, running on all cylinders. When he climbs the stage at a CGI event, says Carnegie Corporation president Vartan Gregorian, and asks the assembled billionaires to stand up and make a pledge, he is like a revivalist at a tent meeting. Instead of "Do this for Jesus," it's do this for the good of the world, and, left unsaid, for the good of the legacy of the star onstage.[110]

Like a United Jewish Appeals annual dinner at which attendees give public pledges that are sometimes upped by the desire to appear to have the most money or the biggest heart at the table, the CGI is designed to help its attendees find religion (i.e., make pledges, sometimes seven-figure pledges). As Richard Feachem, head of the Global Fund, puts it, "And people come forward and make these major commitments in a very public way. . . . And [they] can't just make the commitment and then quietly forget about it."[111]

Every donor is assigned to a Clinton staffer who keeps in touch, to make certain that the pledge is fulfilled and that the donor knows precisely how his or her money is being spent. Melanne Verveer, chairman of the board of the Vital Voices Global Partnership, a nonprofit that supports emerging women leaders around the world, says the staff is obsessive about keeping on top of commitments both financial and program-related. "There has been almost a religious zeal in following up."[112]

Susan Davis marvels at Clinton's ability to touch or put the touch on the very wealthy. He understands, she explains, that people who have made or inherited big sums can be moved by the right words to wonder, "'What is it that I want to do that has real meaning in life now that I have ten houses and private planes and yachts?' There usually is hollowness and all of these billionaires get to that place and that's where I think Bill Clinton's fundamental . . . belief in the goodness of people . . . comes into play. I really see the guy as a preacher; what he's doing is trying to help raise awareness among the richest in the world on behalf of the poorest."[113]

Sandy Berger, who has become a CGI adviser, describes Clinton's "dazzling," seemingly unscripted closing summaries. He assembles the panels with a showman's eye for drama. Desmond Tutu and King Abdullah discussing peace and reconciliation was "electric," says Berger.[114] Susan Davis remembers an 8 A.M. session featuring Jordanian queen Rania Al-Abdullah, Afghan president Hamid Karzai, and South African archbishop Desmond Tutu. About the latter she says, "He literally put goosebumps on everybody and brought us all to our feet and half the room was crying."[115]

For those who are serious about their philanthropy and their networking, such as Chris Stamos, CGI is a feast: not only is there "the most impressive lineup of speakers on the planet," but also, "you turn to your left and your right and if you're lucky enough to talk to that person, you'll discover . . . they started an NGO or they discovered something that's helping the world."[116]

While at CGI, Stamos was sitting with Tom Hunter, the Scottish philanthropist who had been directed to CGI by Vartan Gregorian. "Bill Clinton came over and . . . put his arm around us and spent a good ten minutes chatting with us about what's going on."[117] The Nobel laureate Joseph Stiglitz, who attends CGI, does not get that kind of attention, and he's completely clear-eyed about why. This is business, and, Stiglitz says, Clinton is "spending his time with the people who are giving money."[118]

Given the nature of the speakers and those in attendance there are plenty of security guards, but, says Georgette Bennett, who heads the Tanenbaum Center for Interreligious Understanding and is an active participant in the "mitigating religious and ethnic conflict" track of CGI, there's a feeling of openness at the meetings, no divide between someone who won the Nobel Peace Prize or is the president of a country, such as Ellen Johnson-Sirleaf of Liberia, and someone who runs a struggling nonprofit. "You can get to any of the speakers." When the panel that included the president of Liberia was over, "people could come up to her, speak to her. She wasn't immediately surrounded by security people."[119]

The heaviest hitters are invited onstage with Clinton, and his performance is generally flawless. He thanked Rupert Murdoch and Barbra Streisand for their commitment to his climate change plank. "This is probably the only thing that Barbra Streisand and Rupert Murdoch agree on," Clinton quipped. Streisand whispered in Clinton's ear that Murdoch is much richer than she is and yet she gave twice as much—$1 million. But Clinton forgot to call up Anson Beard, an equal partner in giving but not a name recognized beyond Wall Street. (Beard was not in the least offended at being overlooked; he seemed to find it amusing.)[120]

As the CGI has caught the attention of the media and as it has restored and raised Clinton's reputation, members or would-be members of the elite are more determined to take part, and if they want to continue to receive their invitations, they have to make good on their pledges. The CGI is so prestigious that, like the Truman Capote Black and White Ball, it is enormously humiliating to be left off the invite list. "Everybody aspires to that invitation," says Steve Grossman.[121] It's a lovely circle that Clinton has created. There have been three so far, in September 2005, 2006, and 2007, and Clinton intends for them to continue every September indefinitely.

Julian H. Robertson Jr., the founder, chairman, and chief executive officer of the hedge fund Tiger Management, says that "probably most of the people there were confirmed Democrats, . . . an alumni meeting of sorts."[122] But there is just enough bipartisan flavor to the event to make it seem above petty politics. Invitees include Condoleezza Rice, Laura Bush, former Senate majority leader Bill Frist.

This nod to making nice with the Republicans does not win unanimous praise, although participants understand its motive. Susan Davis, for example, speculates that were Hillary not running for the Democratic nomination for president, Bill would be a stronger critic of the Bush administration, but he doesn't want to "burn bridges" that she might need. Davis says his "natural instinct is to accommodate and . . . hope everybody gets along and build this big center. That's his personal style. . . . So while this country's engaged in war, . . . he's looking at the systemic underpinnings of peace, on religious understanding and tolerance. He's not having panels [on] should we be in Iraq."[123]

Before writing his check, Anson Beard and his sons went up to Harlem and met with the former president, who kept them waiting for twenty minutes. That's Bill Clinton, Beard says, recalling that he was twenty-five minutes late the first time he met him in 1992 after the New York presidential primary. Then, not now. To the surprise of many, programs and panels start and end on time. "Somebody introduces the forty-second president of the United States, William Jefferson Clinton; he walks out at 8:00 point 000." Beard calls CGI "the best conference I've ever attended . . . not sizzle, it was all steak."[124]

Although CGI '05 was covered with breathless superlatives, CGI '06 was proclaimed an improvement on an extremely successful debut. The panel members were even more impressive, the panels more focused—what works as opposed to some theoretical discussion of poverty. The bottom line on money raised in 2005 was $2.5 billion; in 2006 it was $7.5 billion; in 2007, $10 billion.[125]

Republican Scott Reed is impressed. "The type of money he gets. It's the biggest thing in the world."[126]

One of Clinton's pastoral counselors, Tony Campolo, pronounces CGI to be Clinton's "primary legacy."[127] Georgette Bennett sees CGI as Clinton's third term;[128] Leon Panetta sees the former president as leading "almost a government in exile being created by people like Bill Clinton and billionaires who have basically decided that it's their responsibility to try to deal with the problems of the world." Among the billionaires Panetta has in mind are Bill Gates and Warren Buffett, both of whom have attended CGI.[129]

Clinton told a *Chicago Tribune* reporter that he expects that CGI will have some project going in "virtually every country in the world" and that CGI will have touched a billion people.[130] He told Larry King, himself a CGI regular, that he plans to lead CGI for "at least a decade," and by then, he should have produced "a global network of citizen public servants that will go on and keep growing and growing and growing, whatever happens to me and whatever I do. I just hope I can sustain this for a decade."[131]

By most benchmarks the 2007 meeting was the most successful yet, but its luster was marred by a Ron Burkle deal gone sour. Served up on the front page of the *Wall Street Journal* on CGI's opening day were spicy details about Raffaello Follieri, a young Italian businessman; his

$40,000-a-month penthouse; private jet; five-star lifestyle; executive chef; his girlfriend, actress Anne Hathaway; the Catholic Church and the Vatican; and his public embrace by former president Bill Clinton. That latest installment of the saga also included details about Doug Band, including an alleged $400,000 finder's fee paid to Band for introducing Follieri to a major backer of Clinton's philanthropic causes. Clinton's spokesman claimed that Band, who earned a law degree while working for Clinton and traded the personal aide title for the loftier title of counsel, did not keep the fee. There were also details of Band's salary boosted by indirect payments from Burkle, of Follieri promising to help Hillary with Catholic voters, of Follieri donating funds that might not have been his to donate to Clinton's causes, of Follieri allegedly using his ties to Clinton and his causes to meet with Clinton-connected high officials and billionaire businessmen, including one businessman and Clinton contributor who traveled with the former president through Africa.[132]

Chapter 6

BILL CLINTON FIXES AFRICA

WHEN ASKED WHAT HAS BEEN HIS MOST IMPORTANT work since leaving the presidency, Bill Clinton answers eradicating AIDS in Africa. "It gives me a chance to save more lives quicker," he told a *Chicago Tribune* reporter.[1]

Many of the physicians who have worked with Clinton agree that he is a player in this fight, but not as important a player as he thinks he is, and certainly not as important as his underling Ira Magaziner. Richard Feachem credits Clinton with getting medicines to some of the people who needed them by "driving down prices. . . . He has . . . already had a substantial impact on the price of first-line antiretroviral (ARV) drugs . . . through negotiating special deals with selected manufacturers." The drop in price is substantial—around $140 per patient per year, from a high of between $15,000 and $20,000 per patient per year.

Feachem adds, however, that Clinton has the tendency to take too much credit, that those prices depend on the Clinton Foundation doing the negotiations, but as much or more on the huge purchasing power of the Global Fund. "So it's our money and his negotiation that complete the triangle." The Global Fund and George W. Bush's PEPFAR

(President's Emergency Plan for AIDS Relief),* argues Feachem, "are paying for 80 percent of the treatment that is happening in Africa."[3]

Still, Feachem adds, Clinton's team of negotiators came in "on the back of that trend and [drove] it down further and faster than would otherwise have occurred, by doing some very hard negotiation not only with the drugmakers but with the people who make the components of the drugs, going way back upstream and focusing also on the key ingredients that go into the final pill. . . . I'm not sure the prices would have ever got that low without the . . . Clinton negotiation. I'm sure they wouldn't have got there at that speed."[4]

Kevin De Cock of the World Health Organization calls Clinton's impact "real but limited. . . . They are players and they're taken seriously, but I think it is modest global impact, but scaling up."[5]

Some of these on-the-ground-in-Africa physicians wish that the former president would quit using the word *I* so much. They don't doubt his ability to open doors, but still they wince when he seems to want to don a Superman cape and put himself at the center of every rescue.[6] And, to a man, these doctors, while expressing admiration for Clinton and his foundation and his CGI, say that the word *I* should be replaced by the name "Ira Magaziner."

It was not Bill Clinton, they say, who sat at that table and negotiated those prices. It is often said that the workhorse behind the show horse is Ira Magaziner. Sandy Berger calls Magaziner "the instrument of his commitment."[7] "Ira never stops working," says Melanne Verveer. "He's been single-minded in helping the president do this."[8] Describing Bill Clinton as "a mobilizer," but also as all over the place, giving speeches, and "working on his wife's campaigns," Richard Marlink of the Elizabeth

*Pushing funding through Congress to fight AIDS in Africa was difficult for a Democratic president in a way that it was not as difficult for a Republican. To the surprise of many, George W. Bush has delivered the money. After announcing his plan in his 2003 State of the Union, Bush pushed through Congress a landmark $15 billion, five-year funding bill. He budgeted three times more money for eradicating AIDS than did Clinton. Kevin De Cock calls Bush's increase in AIDS funding "massive" and says he has "helped change the landscape."[2]

Glaser Pediatric AIDS Foundation gives most credit to Magaziner and to his staff at the Clinton Foundation as "the believers" who do the real work.[9]

In a self-celebratory essay in *Vanity Fair*'s July 2007 Africa issue, Clinton never mentions Magaziner.[10] Alan Solomont, who knows both men well, says Magaziner is "always in the background." He refers to an annual report from the Clinton Foundation in which "there are all these pictures of Clinton with [Nelson] Mandela and this and that. Magaziner is always with him . . . but [you never see him]."[11]

Others say that's just the way Magaziner wants it, and he wouldn't get anywhere within camera range unless shoved. But they also say that if there is a Nobel Peace Prize in the future for Clinton's work in Africa, the recipient ought to be Magaziner, not Clinton. Magaziner's work has had "an enormous impact," says Eric Goosby of the Pangaea Global AIDS Foundation, "and [lowering drug prices] may be the most significant thing that they did. And Ira did conceive of that and pull it off."

On the drug negotiation front, says Goosby, it's all Magaziner all the time: "Ira certainly was the person who came up with the strategy and did all of the negotiations with the drug companies, both the generic as well as the branded. . . . His intent was to create a market-driven drop in the cost of these drugs." Magaziner's "brainstorm," says Goosby, was knowing "from the very beginning that in order for it to work he needed to create a competitive market within each of the countries that move into generic drugs. So he very strategically would not identify one generic drug company making the drug. He'd identify two at a minimum, preferably four, . . . so they kept a competitive edge on the pricing, long after the Clinton Foundation has left the dialogue. In terms of the significance of that, that's what brought many of these drugs available to countries where the per capita income is less than $100 a year."[12]

The personalities of Clinton and Magaziner are at opposite ends of the spectrum. Chris Stamos, who accompanied the former president on an eight-country, ten-day tour of Africa in the summer of 2005, describes Bill Clinton as "incredibly polished and just unbelievably likable." Magaziner doesn't spend time thinking about whether or not he's likable, adds

Stamos. "He spends all his time just getting stuff done." Stamos says that if there's anyone's health he worries about, it's Magaziner's. "He's always on a plane, flying somewhere to negotiate a deal."[13]

One journalist who knows Magaziner says that he's one of the few people who can correct Bill Clinton, that Magaziner is the only one whom Clinton considers "an actual peer." She describes him as a man with "a real social conscience, . . . eccentric and kind of poignant and cranky and crotchety. . . . He speaks only when spoken to. He's impossibly smart, once you engage him."[14]

Bill Bicknell, director of the Lesotho Boston Health Alliance, who spends four to five months a year in Lesotho, the second or third most affected country in the world in terms of percentage of population with AIDS—almost a third of the adult population is infected—was talking to the minister of health, who said that he heard that Clinton was working in Africa and wondered if Lesotho could get in on the drug price cuts. Bicknell called Clinton's office in New York and even tried Arkansas, but then discovered that Magaziner was running Clinton's HIV/AIDS program out of a small apartment in a low-income district of Quincy, Massachusetts, that Bicknell drove by every day but had never noticed. Three weeks later the minister of health "signed an agreement with the Clinton Foundation."[15]

On the other hand, where would Magaziner be without Clinton? It's only because of Clinton that Magaziner can engage with the ministries of health. "And that's a big contribution to this effort," says Eric Goosby. "In fact, it's the critical contribution. Having that personal interaction with the head of state, . . . aligns the Clinton Foundation's activities as being . . . in the tent from the very beginning."[16]

Clinton's moral authority outside the United States is impressive; his huge personality was the moving force, for example, in persuading South African government leaders of the viral nature of AIDS and of the efficacy of ARVs. This was not an easy sale. In August 2006, at the International Aids Conference in Toronto, Manto Tshabalala-Msimang, the country's health minister, suggested "that a diet of beetroot, lemon and garlic, and African potatoes was the most effective cure for AIDS."[17]

Clinton went right to the country's president, Thabo Mbeki. "Our ability to engage and partner with the [South African] Ministry of Health," says Goosby, "was facilitated by President Clinton meeting with President Mbeki," who had "a level of trust" with Clinton that dates to 1994 when Mbeki made his first country visit to the United States and Clinton gave him a state dinner. "We were given the nod; we were brought in by order of the president." So Eric Goosby and his people went to South Africa and spent about three months partnering with the South African Ministry of Health and developing their ARV rollout plan.[18]

There is no denying the power of Clinton's presence in Africa. Ira Magaziner could walk into a room and no one would notice; when Clinton walks into a room, everyone notices. When in Africa with Clinton, Chris Stamos heard him give "ten to fifteen speeches, and I think I was moved to tears or near tears every time. It was almost like being in a Baptist church."

When they arrived in a country, Stamos recalls, "the streets would be lined with just throngs of people singing, 'We love you Bill Clinton.'" Stamos says that the former president drove his Secret Service agents crazy. He would "stop the motorcade and get out, shake their hands, hug them, pose for pictures, sign things as if he were running for the president of that country."

Decades younger than Clinton, Stamos observed him up close because they spent some nights together on the 727 that belonged to Issam M. Fares, the businessman and deputy prime minister of Lebanon. Stamos was amazed by Clinton's stamina. "Say we were flying from Lesotho to South Africa; we're on the plane and we're talking. We land; he might have taken a five-minute nap. . . . He slept about three hours a night; the rest of the time we were up talking . . . and then he'd get off the plane, walk to the microphone and just give an incredible speech." He had no notes, Stamos says; it was all in his head and each speech was different from the one before. When they stayed in hotels, Stamos recalls, "we would land in a country, meet the president, visit a few clinics, get to the hotel after dinner; then he'd invite us to his room." Clinton would often have the television tuned to some golf tournament—in Mozambique,

Stamos remembers watching Tiger Woods—"and he'd be talking about golf but in between saying very deep things about global health or anecdotes from his presidency." It took him "a good month," Stamos says, to recover from that trip.[19]

ALTHOUGH IT will be less a factor going forward, Bill Clinton's love affair with Nelson Mandela, whose son, Makgatho, died of AIDS in 2005, is central to understanding Clinton's work in South Africa.[20]

Clinton visits Mandela every July on his birthday. For Chris Stamos one of the high points of his trip to Africa was an afternoon private visit to Mandela's house in Johannesburg. Sitting in Mandela's living room watching the two former presidents, Stamos was awed: "The love between them. . . . They hug each other. And you can tell that Mandela loves this man."

"Tired but still a force," says Stamos of Mandela. "The . . . minute he walks into a room, . . . it's almost like a giraffe walked into a room, not because of his height, but because of his grace. There's something otherworldly about him. You just feel a kind of gentleness, almost like the Dalai Lama. . . . His moral authority is still there, unwavering. . . . But he's getting old."[21]

The men both regret that they didn't do more while they held the bully pulpit of their presidencies. Richard Feachem calls Mandela "perhaps the most respected and the most sincere voice in the global HIV/AIDS struggle. . . . And when Clinton and Mandela joined forces . . . that's pretty unbeatable in terms of advocacy."[22]

When Stamos listened to Clinton and Nelson Mandela talk, there was a theme in their conversation: "Africa really needs a success." Stamos came away thinking that Rwanda could be that success story, "which is why I'm actually interested in investing in Rwanda as well." He hopes to join forces with Scottish philanthropist Tom Hunter who is already contributing there.[23]

Bill Clinton also has enormous clout with leaders of other countries—with the Irish prime minister whose government pledged

$13 million for Lesotho, for example.[24] At a children's hospital in India, Clinton announced that he had worked out a deal for $35 million coming from a group of nations led by France, and including Brazil, Britain, Norway, and Chile, that would halve the price—less than $60 a year per child—for pediatric ARVs.[25]

In that sphere, Clinton, especially over the last couple of years, is making a difference. In 2006, in some African countries, the percentage of children getting ARVs was 2 or 3 percent of all those treated.[26] Clinton stepped into this "gap," says Kevin De Cock, because "they saw a role for themselves. . . . They're looking for a niche and here there is one. . . . It's a very specific area, it's a deserving and visible area, it isn't that huge and it was where they could make a contribution and claim some territory."[27]

Richard Marlink appreciates this shift in Clinton's focus to pediatric AIDS and he's happy to work with Clinton's people. However, Marlink says, they're just "scratching the surface." He expresses his frustration and would like to tell President Clinton, but hasn't yet: "We need more bodies, nurses, pharmacists." The Clinton Foundation, Marlink says, hasn't the funding to accomplish that—not yet anyway, but there's always another CGI to bring Clinton closer.[28]

Will Clinton stick with the AIDS work? Some of the doctors who work in Africa fear that he will lose interest, find some sexier, easier-to-solve issue to capture his imagination—and the headlines.

Early on, says Richard Marlink, Clinton stuck to his promise not to overcommit himself to "a lot of different countries." But Marlink detects some backsliding and worries about it. "Of late, I think that they're back to still just announcing things when it seems like it could get press." Already in the hopper, says Marlink, were Tanzania, Mozambique, South Africa, and Rwanda. "With those four, we said, 'That's enough. . . . We're volunteers here. We need to make commitments and then it's going to be a long-term commitment to a few places, so that things can get accomplished. It's not going to be every country you visit, not going to be making commitments you don't have anything to back it up with. . . . This is not going to be solved in the next few years, if in our lifetime. . . . He agreed, . . . Ira agreed, everybody agreed."[29]

But Clinton could not help himself. His foundation, which has a presence now in twenty-five countries, is, worries Kevin De Cock, spreading itself too thin.[30] Moving beyond Africa, Clinton has expanded his scope to China, India, and Cambodia. The donor in Cambodia is Chris Stamos and his family. That came about after Ira Magaziner came to Stamos's office and sold him on the idea, which appealed to Stamos because "there was very little work being done in getting people ARVs . . . and so for a commitment of $500,000 a year for three years, we could be their donor in Cambodia and get kids and adults on ARVs right away." Stamos is happy with the result: "I have a hospital in Cambodia, . . . it treats 70,000 kids; it trains a thousand doctors and nurses for $800,000. I couldn't stay [for that] in a hospital in New York for two weeks."[31]

A spur to action in China came after Bill Clinton visited the country and publicly embraced an HIV-positive citizen. The country's premier and vice premier followed suit and the next month shook hands with AIDS sufferers. China, the world's most populous nation, has an estimated 650,000 people infected with HIV, although in a country in which the infected are shunned, the numbers are surely much bigger. Nearly 80 percent of HIV-positive Chinese do not know they are infected.[32]

Bill Bicknell does not endorse Clinton's new focus on China and India because both countries have relatively strong economies. "Yes, they've got a problem, but if they choose to they can substantially handle it themselves." Bicknell wants Clinton's support to go to countries like Swaziland and Lesotho and Zambia, which "have very weak economies. . . . The support is now being spread without regard to national income and the strength of national economies, so countries like Lesotho . . . are getting screwed."[33] Richard Marlink agrees and would rather see Clinton stay focused on Africa. "To focus on places that are going to be the economic superpowers of tomorrow even with AIDS is not equitable."[34]

Others, such as Eric Goosby, Kevin De Cock, and Richard Feachem, say that paying attention in China and India and also Russia is crucial. "Although the rates of infection in places like India and China may be low," says De Cock, "a low rate of infection in these huge-population countries can amount to a lot of people."[35] Feachem calls it "a major mistake" to stick to Africa. "HIV/AIDS is a global problem. It's not an African problem. The country with the most HIV-positive people today [in absolute numbers] is not an African country at all, it's India, and growing rapidly." He calls India, China, and Russia "the three time bombs, and if we lose the battle [there] . . . the world has lost."[36]

Richard Marlink explains that he is not one of those people who are in awe of Bill Clinton. "I don't want to be near him. I'm impressed by him but I don't need to be enamored."

When Clinton had a thank-you reception for volunteers in Harlem, Marlink introduced him to his wife who, in 1992, had booked Bill Clinton on the *Arsenio Hall Show*. The candidate donned sunglasses and played "Heartbreak Hotel" on the saxophone. "Clinton's smooth as silk in terms of charming people," Marlink says. Clinton did not neglect the husband. "I know what you're doing," and he named the countries in which Marlink was working and said, "Thank you for doing it." Then he turned his attention back to the wife and started to reminisce. "They were having a great time," so good a time that "I told him to step back and not get so close to her. He was laughing."[37]

"I would hope that he does not kind of butterfly on to another issue," says Eric Goosby. "He needs to hold this issue for the rest of his foundation's life, and support it. . . . I'm a doctor who just lives and breathes this stuff, so I get annoyed . . . when he puts his attention to another activity that I know could have been framed with an HIV frame on it . . . CGI raising . . . billions of dollars for activities that range from anything to everything."[38]

Kevin De Cock worries that Clinton might not have really found himself in this work, that his restless mind might be looking for something else. The evidence he cites is Clinton's "dabbling in so many things. Partly because I don't think he's got the traction. . . . He hasn't got the traction that he had hoped."[39]

ONE COUNTRY to which Clinton is, by all accounts, unreservedly committed is Rwanda. The biggest regret of his presidency, Clinton has said, is not responding to the 1994 Rwandan genocide.[40]

Chris Stamos accompanied Clinton to the genocide museum in Kigali, Rwanda, on Clinton's third visit. "I know I was crying, . . . and the president was definitely moved by what he was seeing there and from there we went to the clinic." At the clinic a local reporter asked, "We know you're dedicated to AIDS everywhere, but is there a particular dedication to Rwanda given what happened under your administration?"

"It didn't happen under my administration," Clinton replied. "It happened under me. I was the administration. . . . We could have done more. And I regret that we didn't."

The group then spent some time with Rwandan president Paul Kagame and Clinton also apologized to him.

According to Stamos, who has become friends with the Rwandan president, "Kagame loves President Clinton; he would have liked history to have been different. . . . The UN and the French take a lot more blame in Kagame's mind. . . . On several occasions he has said . . . he loves Bill Clinton, he feels . . . that Clinton listens to the Rwandans, unlike some NGOs that come in and tell people what to do, or say 'This is what we're going to do in your country.' Bill Clinton's very respectful."[41]

"It's true that he has guilt feelings about Rwanda," says Richard Marlink. "He talked to me when we first started the volunteer group. He wanted it to be the first place that had a public announcement that he was going to partner with the government there."[42]

"Ira and I are here to help you," Clinton says to Kagame. "What do you need? How can we help?" Kagame replies, "We've learned the hard way that if things don't go well, the foreigners get on the plane and they leave and we're left to deal with the consequences."[43]

CLINTON'S WORK in Africa would polish his current image, but it would not cover lapses during the two terms noted by historians as they deconstructed his presidency. A reminder came in October 2005, when Bill and Hillary went to the Roosevelt estate in Hyde Park, New York, so he could receive one of the Four Freedom Awards from the Franklin and

Eleanor Roosevelt Institute. Tom Kean received one, as did former NBC News anchor Tom Brokaw and Cornel West, professor of religion at Princeton.[44]

"I think frankly all of us were reasonably good," says Tom Kean. "West's a preacher so he's particularly articulate. . . . Brokaw was terrific." But, says Kean, Bill Clinton got up and stole the show. He was "just head and shoulders above the rest of us."[45]

Over wine and cheese, the former president chatted with historian Douglas Brinkley, who serves on the board of the institute. Brinkley mentioned the upcoming—not quite three weeks away—Hofstra Conference devoted to assessing the Clinton presidency, for which Brinkley was the endowed scholar. "Clearly at that juncture he hadn't focused on it. . . . It was just another date on his . . . massively busy schedule. So I think he looked at the program and said, 'Whoa, whoa, what am I walking into here?'"[46]

Clinton had been busy with his first CGI conference the month before, but he did have in the back of his mind the fast-approaching conference, titled "William Jefferson Clinton: The 'New Democrat' from Hope." Clinton was determined that the public record of the gathering, which over the years had become a respected early evaluation of the American presidency, show his tenure at its best.

The three-day conference, November 10–12, 2005, at Hofstra University, a liberal arts school on Long Island, featured fifty panels covering specific domestic and foreign policy aspects of his presidency. Clinton was to speak on the first day.

Hofstra was obviously not Harvard or Aspen in terms of prestige, but the Hofstra conferences had developed a certain cachet since the first one was held in 1982 to evaluate Franklin Roosevelt. (More recently, they have been held five years after the man leaves office.) Clinton knew he could not allow the conference participants to confirm the increasingly common perception that he had been distracted from the nation's business during the final three years of his term because of Monica Lewinksy and impeachment.

Eric Schmertz, a former dean of the Hofstra Law School who had directed four conferences starting with Eisenhower, and would direct Clinton's as well, had been working on the Clinton event for three years, starting with a call for papers.[47] He and his Hofstra colleagues had consulted with Clinton staffers to determine the makeup of the panels. Carolyn Eisenberg, a professor of American foreign policy, who had been involved with planning for the conferences on Carter, Reagan, and Bush, thought the Hofstra group was working too closely with Clinton's people. "In my experience, this was the most tightly controlled conference that we've ever had."

Eisenberg, named liaison between the faculty and Hofstra's Cultural Center, which runs the university's conferences, was a critic of Clinton's from the Left, judging him as too much the centrist. She complains that the faculty recommendations on panel makeup were "not really very welcome. . . . We wanted this to be a serious academic conference. . . . That didn't happen." She blames both representatives of Hofstra and of the Clinton Foundation, although especially the latter.

In the last week or so, Eisenberg says, Clinton's people focused most intensely on the conference and did not like what they saw.[48] And they were not bashful about saying so. When the Clinton team "comes at you," says Douglas Brinkley, "it's like the Johnstown flood."[49] Eisenberg claims that Clinton's team presented "a whole list of people that they wanted to be invited at the last minute and put on the program. . . . The program was changed very drastically." An example, she says, was the addition of Bruce Reed, head of the centrist Democratic Leadership Council, from whose ranks came both Clinton and Gore. Al From, who founded the group, was given a bigger role. "All the plenaries were filled up with Clinton people. . . . I did talk with someone at the [Clinton] Foundation who said that they were pretty amazed at how they were able to get the Hofstra officials to give in to all of their last-minute demands."[50]

Eric Schmertz denies vehemently that Hofstra was bulldozed. Still, he describes quite a bit of back-and-forth. Clinton's staffers told Schmertz that "the president took [the conference program] into his office . . . and was able to memorize the entire program, all of the topics . . . and who was participating." It was then that Schmertz started to receive calls.

"We're troubled by such and such a panel. . . . The president thinks it's out of balance."

Schmertz claims he replied, "I'm sorry. You tell the president that we think it's all right. . . . We think so-and-so on the panel, whom he might dislike, from our standpoint has to stay on the panel." On the other hand, Schmertz adds, "Here and there we might add somebody to the panel that they suggested because to us it made sense; we had missed somebody of significance." Schmertz insists that "very few of those Clinton requests" were accepted and only "if we decided it produced a better . . . balance." He also insists that not once was a person removed from a panel at Clinton's request.[51]

Natalie Datlof, executive director of the Hofstra Cultural Center, who has been at Hofstra for every presidential conference, says flatly, "We didn't do anything unusual that we hadn't done for any of the others."[52]

Slade Gorton, former Republican senator from Washington, served on the panel on impeachment—he had been in the Senate when it voted to acquit—and he describes the panel as strongly biased in Clinton's favor. Overall, he complains, "I was probably one of three Republicans in the entire program anywhere." Gorton calls the conference "a reunion" for Clinton people; interestingly the same word that Elaine Kamarck uses in describing her experience in serving on a panel. "It was very nice, it was kind of a reunion."[53]

Hofstra conferences "generally create an upward revision for the presidents," says Douglas Brinkley, "because mostly it's people from their administration coming." But Brinkley, a former professor at Hofstra, seemed to worry that this one, under pressure from Bill Clinton—whose request to see conference papers was granted—was going a little too far to the celebratory. "We had four-fifths of the papers very positive about President Clinton. If we didn't have some papers that were dissenting, it would have been a salute Bill Clinton party."[54]

Clinton was especially irritated that the schedule included two panels on his impeachment. According to Natalie Datlof, "We told him up front that there would be panels on the impeachment and they understood that. We showed them who the scholars were; we gave them printouts."[55]

Still, says Brinkley, "Hofstra started getting some pressure to drop [the two impeachment panels]." Brinkley confirms that the pressure was coming "directly from the Clinton camp." Clinton's people proposed that the impeachment panels be "knocked off" and a session featuring Clinton's White House counsel, Lanny Davis, take its place. "You can't replace scholars with your own lawyer," Brinkley says. "It just became childish in my view."[56] (Davis at first agreed to be interviewed for this book but later changed his mind.) Stanislao Pugliese, a Hofstra professor of modern European history, describes what Clinton was trying to do as "an attempt at a kind of coup d'état."[57]

Brinkley was prepared to go to battle. "I wanted people to realize that we weren't whitewashing. . . . I had to defend that academic process when the pressure was to get rid of that panel and have Lanny Davis talk about impeachment." To the university's credit, says Brinkley, it never came to that. "There was never a second of consideration" that the impeachment panels would be quashed. "We would rather he not show up than to have canceled these professors who had written serious, academic papers on impeachment."

Brinkley stresses that he is not "anti-Clinton . . . and I'm not a conservative at all. . . . But I don't think you can whitewash the fact that he had lied to the American people and it gave his opponents the huge opportunity to derail his agenda. How do you talk about the Clinton years and not deal with Ken Starr and Monica Lewinsky and impeachment?"[58]

The other complaint about Bill Clinton was that he rushed in and out of the conference, giving no time to students. Carolyn Eisenberg was especially disappointed because, in conjunction with the conference, she was teaching a semester course on Clinton's foreign policy. She organized a student debate, a project, she says, that they worked on for months. No one from the Clinton administration, much less the president himself, showed up. "That was really kind of sad."[59]

Some presidents whose administrations are being evaluated meet with students and even attend some of the panels—Jimmy Carter and George H. W. Bush both attended with their wives and were a real presence, gracious and accessible; both Carter and Bush met with students. Clinton helicoptered to the Long Island campus from a speech at the Pierre Hotel in New York—for which he was paid $250,000—and then, hours later, helicoptered to JFK airport to board a private plane for a trip to the Czech Republic.

There was a "ridiculous lack of availability to students," complains Eisenberg, who adds, "He was uninterested in . . . spending some time in our community which was in fact honoring him. Just didn't care, wasn't that interested in the give-and-take."[60]

Hillary Clinton was invited but did not attend, nor did Chelsea, although presidents' children have attended previous conferences.

Eight hundred people bought tickets to a lunch, preceding Clinton's speech, keynoted by Clinton's Treasury secretary, Robert Rubin. When Clinton arrived, late, as dessert and coffee were being served, Natalie Datlof describes the room as "just electrified." As he walked to an adjoining room for a receiving line and photos with people who had backed the conference financially or had played a role in organizing it, "the crowd just rushed him," says Datlof.[61]

Stanislao Pugliese, who had served as exhibition curator, was one of those in line to greet Clinton. He might not have bothered, he said—"I'm underwhelmed by Clinton"—but he belonged to a faculty group called Long Island Teachers for Human Rights. Its members had drafted a letter asking both President Clinton and Senator Clinton to speak out against the war in Iraq, "so I got on line to deliver the letter."

Pugliese was watching Clinton as the line moved. "He was very gracious with everybody, smiling, shaking hands, posing for the photographs. After I said hello and I introduced myself . . . and I shook his hand and the official photographer took a photograph, I pulled the letter out of my jacket breast pocket and I gave it to him and said, 'Mr. President, on behalf of some of my colleagues . . . I'd like to present you with this letter,' and his demeanor immediately changed. He didn't say anything, but the smile was gone and he silently handed off the letter to a Secret Service agent. . . . I was ushered out." As he left the room, Pugliese turned back to look at Clinton. "He returned immediately to his public persona, smiling, 'Hello, how are you?'"

The students' outpouring of adoration had everything to do with Clinton's rock star status and his perceived liberalism, says Pugliese. "They were interested, electrified by Clinton's charisma. If you had asked them to name five specific policies, I'm not sure they would have been able to do that." He judges the conference as a "love fest, . . . a lot of people from the administration and . . . not enough people I think who were critical."[62]

Neither Clinton responded to the letter.[63]

The scene in the university's basketball stadium where people were awaiting Clinton's speech—a capacity crowd of nearly five thousand—was total adoration. Students were "hanging over their seats," says Datlof, "trying to reach out and touch him."[64]

A Clinton aide approached Douglas Brinkley and ushered him over to talk to the former president. Clinton had seen an article in that day's *Newsday*, in which Brinkley was quoted as saying, "I think the gorilla in the room is his impeachment problem," which Brinkley called a "great curse on the Clinton legacy. . . . There is an argument to be made if you didn't have the whole impeachment problem, Bill Clinton would go down as a great president." The problem, adds Brinkley, is "We did have the impeachment."[65]

"Clinton . . . put his arm around my shoulder," Brinkley recalls. "'I just want to tell you something. I'm going to both really praise you but also challenge you today. . . . I just wanted to let you know in advance.'"[66]

After an introduction by his secretary of state, Madeleine Albright, Clinton spoke, without notes—although he had bullet points written on a small pad—for a full hour. From his perspective onstage, university president Stuart Rabinowitz judged Clinton to have "the audience in his pocket. . . . People love him or hate him and in this room they all loved him."[67]

When Clinton got to the subject of impeachment, says Brinkley, "his praise was saying that I was one of the historians he most admired . . . and then came the challenge, 'but I disagree that the impeachment was a black mark on my tenure.' . . . He went off to claim that it should be seen as an historic accomplishment because he warded off the right-wing conspiracy, and if he didn't challenge them and beat them back it would have been an horrific thing for our democracy." He called impeachment "an egregious abuse of the Constitution and the law and history of this country, and I should get credit for standing up to it." Clinton also denied that he was distracted from his presidential responsibilities because of the Lewinsky affair and proceeded to list the things he accomplished while the impeachment was pending.

His speech might have wowed the students, but it did not persuade Brinkley, who maintains, "What is stopping him from hitting that rare category of great presidents—of Lincoln, Washington, FDR, TR, Harry Truman—is that impeachment problem. . . . No matter what happens, President Clinton will be living with that. It's almost like a scarlet letter. It's like a big *I* on his chest for impeachment, and he'll always be remembered for all of that, and that's one part of his legacy."

If that speech was a window into Clinton's mind, says Brinkley, it shows "how wounded he still is," how tired he is of "impeachment constantly rear[ing] its ugly face, and he has to bat it back." Clinton recognizes, Brinkley says, "that if he's going to try to rebuild his legacy, he's going to somehow have to sell this notion that impeachment was a badge of honor."

Brinkley left the stadium with veteran presidential adviser David Gergen, who, Brinkley recalls, shook his head in dismay and observed that Clinton acted like "a used car salesman trying to convince you that his impeachment was a badge of honor." Brinkley agreed, "We're not an audience of fools; people aren't going to go, 'Oh, my God, yeah, it was a badge of honor.'"[68]

While the audience greeted the speech as if it were the Gettysburg Address, those who knew Clinton did not think it was one of his better efforts. "When he got into the impeachment stuff," says Leon Panetta, "[he] tried his best to put the best spin on that but it was obvious he was being defensive about it."[69]

Elaine Kamarck calls the speech "very odd, particularly his contorted defense of his own behavior." She said that she found his argument with

Douglas Brinkley "kind of embarrassing and he shouldn't have even tried."[70]

One woman who knows Clinton well describes the speech as "Clinton's somewhat desperate attempt to create for himself a legacy that overshadows his second term and his big mistake. That's what motivates the guy; that's what eats at him; that's what makes him furious. . . . [The Hofstra speech] is quite revealing in how he's attempting to argue away his misbehavior. . . . Clinton doesn't want to admit that it was basically he that lost the 2000 election for Al Gore." She calls Clinton's postpresidency complicated, "because part of it is trying to say, 'I was great in spite of it.'"[71]

The speech, delivered to "true believers," was "typical Clinton . . . engaging and witty and occasionally flirted with the truth," says Slade Gorton, "and when he was talking about impeachment, he said at one point, 'Well, I understand there's someone here at this conference who voted guilty on one count and not guilty on the other count and I've never figured it out and I'd really like to know.' . . . So I'm sitting back there in the audience saying to myself, 'Well, all you have to do is come to my panel and ask the question and I'll answer it for you.' But of course he was long gone by the time we met in the evening." (Gorton, along with ten other senators, cast a no for perjury and a yes for obstruction of justice; he was defeated for reelection in 2000.)[72]

Michael Barone, a senior writer for *U.S. News & World Report*, figures that behind Clinton's attitude is, "You know what? They would have gotten rid of any other president, but I am so good they could not get rid of me. Any other president had done that, they would have been screwed."[73]

Carolyn Eisenberg certainly disagrees with those who want to examine Clinton's sex life under the microscope, but she found his speech insulting, given the university audience—too much like a political stump speech. "I think it was sort of boilerplate."[74]

With the audience already surging forward, Clinton, in his business suit, received an honorary degree in humane letters. "He completed his speech," Eric Schmertz recalls. "We rushed up and gave him an honorary degree and we all got out of there."[75] (Typically a cap and gown is required, but not this time.)[76]

Stuart Rabinowitz recalls that the crowd rushing up after the speech "scared the heck out of me. . . . It was like a campaign event because they were just reaching out trying to touch him and shake his hand. . . . He appeared to love it. In his usual style, he paid no attention to the Secret Service or our people and just waded into the crowd and shook hands and signed things."

Rabinowitz, who was delighted with the attention the conference brought to Hofstra and the handwritten letter and telephone call of thanks he received from Bill Clinton, has already told Hillary Clinton to mark her calendar for 2021 when the conference evaluating her two-term presidency will be held. Rabinowitz has a relationship with Hillary as his home state senator. "I make two trips a year down to Washington, frankly looking for federal dollars for our program. And Senator Clinton has been very helpful to Hofstra in many different ways."[77]

The more cynical among the Hofstra faculty might have wondered if, in the end, the rather gentle treatment Bill Clinton received from Hofstra had any connection to top administrators wanting to make certain that Hillary Clinton, while she was still senator from New York, continued to look kindly on Hofstra.

President Clinton on his last morning in the Oval Office with his chief of staff, John Podesta. "It was very hard for him to let go," says Melanne Verveer, Hillary's last chief of staff as First Lady. "He loved being president. He loved the house. He loved his relationship with the American people. He did not leave easily."

The Clintons and the Bushes on the North Portico of the White House before leaving for Bush's inauguration. Clinton knew that many Democrats blamed him for the fact that it was not Al Gore who was about to be inaugurated.

Inside an Andrews Air Force Base hangar, Clinton, no longer president, reviewed a full military honor guard, the military band substituting "Ruffles and Flourishes" for "Hail to the Chief." Scores of people who had served in his administration had come to say goodbye. "When you leave the White House you wonder if you'll ever draw a crowd again," he said, in a voice hoarse from exhaustion.

On January 22, 2001, two days after leaving the White House, Bill and Hillary leave their house in Chappaqua to take Bill's dog, Buddy, for a walk. Hillary, just elected to the Senate, would soon leave for Washington and the former president, isolated, lonely, and deluged with criticism over scandals that erupted as he exited the White House, would once again have to depend on Buddy for companionship. A year later, while the Clintons vacationed in Acapulco, Buddy died after escaping from the house and running into traffic on a nearby highway.

Bill Clinton, a couple of weeks out of the White House on February 6, 2001, plays golf with Hillary's brother, Hugh Rodham. Clinton was in Florida to make his first paid speech—to Morgan Stanley Dean Witter & Company's Global Leveraged Finance Conference for a fee of $125,000, modest by comparison to later fees. It was marred by misgivings from the company's chairman that the scandal-scarred former president was perhaps not worthy of the invitation. His speech was a success, as was one given four days later in a Florida synagogue for $150,000.

Typical of the awful press Bill Clinton garnered in the months after he left the White House was this *Time* cover story of February 26, 2001, "The Incredible Shrinking Ex-President: How Can We Miss You If You Never Go Away?; Smelly pardons, expensive gifts, deluxe offices—is this any way for a former President to behave?"

Testifying before a congressional committee about the Marc Rich pardon is Jack Quinn (far left), a former White House counsel to Clinton who pushed him to grant the pardon. Also testifying were three close Clinton aides, two of whom advised strongly against the pardon, which blew up into a scandal so virulent that the *New York Times* editorialized, "We sense a national need to come to grips with the wreckage, both civic and legal, left by former President Clinton."

ARLEM WELCOMES
RESIDENT CLINTON

The former president accepts greetings as he moves into his postpresidential offices in Harlem. Clinton managed to turn a damaging story about high-rent offices in midtown Manhattan—the bill footed by the taxpayers—into a positive story about reasonably priced rent on 125th Street in Harlem.

Former Senator Robert Torricelli, pictured here in 2002, remains a close friend of Bill Clinton's. In the lead-up to the Clinton impeachment, Torricelli would often receive calls from an agitated and forlorn president.

In 2003, President Clinton and former senator Bob Dole—Clinton's opponent in the 1996 presidential race—flank Don Hewitt, the creator of CBS's *60 Minutes*. Hewitt, who proposed an update on the James Kilpatrick/Shana Alexander "Point/ Counterpoint," wanted Bill O'Reilly or Newt Gingrich as Clinton's sparring partner and was correct in his hunch that the exchanges between Clinton and Dole, political opponents but personal friends, would create few sparks. Hewitt cancelled the face-off after ten weeks.

Bill Clinton admires his portrait as it is unveiled at the National Portrait Gallery in April 2006. Reporters quickly noticed that the painter, Nelson Shanks, had inadvertently painted Clinton without his wedding band. A *New York Post* reporter turned the innocent omission into a laugh line: "The artist who painted Bill Clinton's . . . portrait managed to do what Monica Lewinsky could not: make Bubba's wedding ring disappear."

Looking older than his memoir cover photo, Bill Clinton signs books in Manhattan. The reviews were mixed at best, but sales were good— breaking opening-day records for a nonfiction book by selling 400,000 copies. His publicity tour was cut short when chest pains and shortness of breath resulted in quadruple bypass surgery less than three months later.

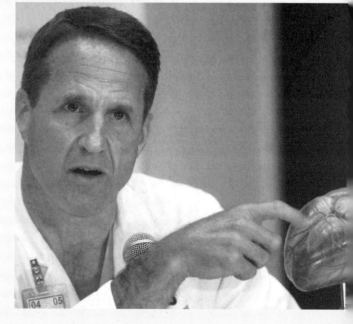

Dr. Craig Smith of Columbia-Presbyterian Medical Center on Labor Day 2004, talking to reporters after performing quadruple bypass surgery on Bill Clinton. Days before, tests revealed more than 90 percent blockage in several arteries. Reporters quickly discovered that Smith, the lead surgeon on a twelve-member team, had contributed that year to the reelection campaign of George W. Bush.

Seven weeks after his bypass surgery, an emaciated Bill Clinton campaigns with John Kerry in downtown Philadelphia. During the lunch-break rally of some 80,000 people, the crowd shouted, "We love you, Bill!" "If this isn't good for my heart, I don't know what is," Clinton responded.

The rain never stopped during the dedication of Clinton's presidential library in Little Rock in November 2004. That sodden day produced the roots of a friendship between Clinton and George H. W. Bush, who said of the man who beat him in the 1992 election: "Bill Clinton showed himself to be more than a good politician. In the White House, the whole nation witnessed his brilliance. . . . The president was not the kind to give up a fight. His staffers were known to say that if Clinton were the *Titanic*, the iceberg would sink."

Bill Clinton and Terry McAuliffe, his fund-raiser, golfing buddy, vacation companion, political operative, and nonstop booster. McAuliffe appears to have devoted his adult life to raising money for the Clintons and bailing them out of embarrassing situations. He is currently serving as chairman of Hillary's campaign.

The former presidents traveled together to countries in Asia and Africa hit by the tsunami. In Sri Lanka on February 21, 2005, they talked to children, many of whom had lost their families and homes. Inspired by the erstwhile rivals working together, Americans donated $1.2 billion to tsunami relief.

Belinda Stronach is twenty years younger than Bill Clinton, a Canadian MP, and the daughter of a billionaire auto parts merchant. When a tabloid ran a photo of Bill and Belinda leaving a midtown New York restaurant, Clinton supporters grew worried. "Bubba's Got a Brand New Blonde," blared one headline. Her biographer notes, "She's not the kind you'd want to ask for her favorite muffin recipe." If there ever was a relationship, it is said to be over.

Bill Clinton and his friend Nelson Mandela at Mandela's home in Johannesburg in July 2005. Clinton visits the former South African president every year on his birthday. During the worst of the Monica Lewinsky scandal, Mandela said, "I just don't understand what your country is doing to this great man."

In November 2005, at the Hofstra Conference assessing his presidency, Bill Clinton accepts an honorary degree from university president Stuart Rabinowitz. Former secretary of state Madeleine Albright, who introduced him to the capacity crowd of nearly 5,000, is at his left.

At the funeral of Coretta Scott King on February 7, 2006, Jimmy Carter takes the microphone as Bill and Hillary applaud. The Clintons' decades-long relationship with Carter was frosty. He won no points with either Clinton when he publicly castigated Bill over his affair with Monica Lewinsky and his pardon of fugitive from American justice Marc Rich.

Hillary speaks at Coretta Scott King's funeral in February 2006 as Bill looks on. His euphoric, pulsating eulogy compared to her stiff, off-key effort became the headline. "When you look at a 150-watt bulb right in your face," said one supporter of Hillary's, "it looks really bright; put it next to the sun, it doesn't look so bright anymore."

Bill Clinton with two of his closest friends and biggest financial supporters, movie producer Stephen Bing, left, and businessman Ron Burkle, at the Clinton Global Initiative meeting in September 2006. Both men are known as playboys, and Clinton often travels with them on their private jets. One journalist who has written about Clinton says, "He likes being around them. . . . He likes the beautiful women . . . and he likes . . . the fact that they'll cut him fat checks . . . and help to enhance his lifestyle. . . ."

A red-faced Bill Clinton jabs his finger at *Fox News Sunday*'s Chris Wallace in September 2006, after Wallace suggested that Clinton was distracted and did not do enough to fight terrorism during his presidency, making him partly responsible for 9/11. "So you did Fox's bidding on this show," Clinton hissed at the nonplussed Wallace. "You did your nice little conservative hit job on me." Some people who are close Clinton observers say he went loaded for bear to the Wallace interview, that he had rehearsed his rant. "It was clear that he had been waiting for that question for a long time," says Leon Panetta.

Bill Clinton holds an orphan girl in Phnom Penh, Cambodia, in 2006. The former president's efforts to tackle the AIDS epidemic in third-world countries define his postpresidency work.

Fearing that Bill would overshadow Hillary as she fought for the democratic nomination for president, her managers kept the former president at bay. When Barack Obama threatened her lock on the nomination, Bill was strutted out in March 2007 to join Hillary in Selma, Alabama, to mark the anniversary of "Bloody Sunday." Here they march across the Edmund Pettus Bridge where, forty-two years before, state troopers had attacked peaceful demonstrators. The Reverend Al Sharpton, whose endorsement both Obama and Hillary sought, is on the far right, next to local activist Rose Sanders. Congressman John Lewis, on the left, later threw his support to Obama.

Sitting off to the side of a stage at a fund-raiser in Washington in March 2007, Bill Clinton watches his wife attempt to reach a crowd.

Bill Clinton on one of his frequent appearances on *Larry King Live*—this one on April 19, 2007. The talk-show host, who admits to loving the former president, says that despite Clinton's lapses in office, "History will be very good to Bill Clinton."

Relations between Al Gore and Bill Clinton have been strained since Gore lost the 2000 election. He blames Clinton and the scandals surrounding Monica Lewinsky for his defeat. Currently a crusader against global warming, he participates in the Clinton Global Initiatives. In 2007, Gore was awarded an honor that Clinton covets—the Nobel Peace Prize.

Bill and Chelsea celebrate Hillary's birthday in October 2007. Chelsea lives in New York and earns a high income working for a hedge fund run by financial supporters of her parents. The father/daughter relationship was strained by the Lewinsky scandal, but the two are said to be close.

Chapter 7

THE PATH TO 9/11

BILL CLINTON WAS SO EAGER TO TESTIFY BEFORE the 9/11 Commission (officially the National Commission on Terrorist Attacks Upon the United States) that as soon as it was appointed in the fall of 2002, but before it started its work, he called his friend Tom Kean, just named the commission's chairman, and invited him to dinner at an Italian restaurant in Harlem.[1]

Kean recalls that Clinton, who was accompanied by then New Jersey senator, now governor, Jon Corzine, "was interested in just how we were pursuing it. . . . I think it was a little legacy protecting. He wanted to make sure that we weren't going to go off on some tangent that was . . . going to be destructive as far as [his] legacy went."[2]

Clinton often felt the need to "blow off steam," says Sandy Berger, especially when it came to interpretation of his foreign policy. Clinton would call him every few weeks, Berger says. "It ranges from 'Do you want to play golf?' . . . to him reading something in the newspaper about the Clinton years that irritates him and he wants to . . . remember the facts and set the record straight."

One of the areas that continues to plague Clinton is the galaxy of issues surrounding 9/11, especially, says Berger, the "effort on the part of the White House in the early days after 9/11 to shift responsibility backwards to the Clinton administration when the fact is that we actually were doing . . . a great deal before we left and they really dropped the ball." The oft-asked question that continues to rankle his former boss is, Did Clinton have a chance to kill or capture Bin Laden in 1996? "The answer is no," insists Berger. "There was never an offer . . . to give us Bin Laden. . . . We hit Afghanistan in '98, targeting Bin Laden, so why in the world would we not take him if we had a chance?"

Berger dismisses the "wag the dog" stories of August 1998, when Clinton took a break from Martha's Vineyard to announce that bombing, as ridiculous. "We erected an absolute Chinese wall between foreign policy and what was happening in the Congress." He bristles at the allegation that he or Secretary of State Madeleine Albright or Secretary of Defense William Cohen were "in the tank for Clinton, were creating the pretext for war on a false basis." Not surprisingly, Berger says that he never saw Clinton distracted during the impeachment mess, "and I was with him every day."[3]

Berger's endorsement aside, Clinton must have recognized that anyone with any common sense at all knew that he had to have been distracted. Former Democratic National Committee chief Don Fowler describes Clinton as spending half to two-thirds of every day dealing with the scandal.[4] Larry King, who has talked extensively with Clinton on air and off, says there's no way that Lewinsky didn't distract him, any more than Vietnam didn't distract Lyndon Johnson or Iraq George W. Bush. "It would be abnormal if he wasn't distracted."[5]

"I saw the president just in rages during that time," recalls Mickey Ibarra. "A couple of times it actually concerned me." Ibarra worried not that Clinton would have a heart attack, but "that it was a distraction, when you're dealing with that much anger and hurt and pain." Asked how the president expressed those emotions, Ibarra says, "I'd say a rant was pretty close to it. When I saw it, it was just the two of us—in the Oval Office, in the limo, once in the bathroom." Clinton's profanity-laden complaint was that Ken Starr and his staff were "attempting to overturn the will of the American people, they're attempting to take me out of

office." The object of his most intense wrath was Ken Starr: "Oh, my God, did he hate that guy."[6]

Robert Torricelli was receiving middle-of-the-night phone calls from Bill Clinton during the worst of the impeachment travails, even when the former New Jersey senator was on vacation in Scotland. Clinton's calls would often awaken Torricelli. "He was in enormous personal pain and I think he was trying to reconcile the mistakes he had made. . . . I think this was just Bill Clinton needing to talk to friends when he was trying to reconcile what had happened and repair his life."[7] Clinton was also calling Senators Chris Dodd and Tom Daschle, as well as his fund-raiser Terry McAuliffe, who writes in his memoir that "night after night the President was calling me around midnight for long talks."[8]

WITH SANDY BERGER at his side, Clinton made an impressive witness, says 9/11 Commission member Bob Kerrey, offering "a brilliant insight" that Americans were "so busy celebrating the end of the Cold War that we didn't make a good inventory of problems that we were going to be facing. . . . And one of the most important ones that we missed was the rise of . . . the capacity of radical Islam with relatively small actions to do a great deal of damage to us."

Kerrey did not buy a key part of Clinton's testimony—that he was "unaffected by impeachment. . . . It's impossible for it not to have affected him. I think it affected him greatly. . . . I wasn't being impeached and I was distracted by it. . . . He was under investigation by the House. The special prosecutor had [Hillary] go down and appear twice before a grand jury. . . . I think his interpretation of the impact of the impeachment on the capacity to carry out effective foreign policy is different than mine."

Kerrey is specific about instances in which he believes the Clinton administration dropped the ball; he cites the attack on the embassies in Nairobi, Kenya, and Dar es Salaam, Tanzania. "We knew that Bin Laden organized that. . . . It was pretty shockingly successful. . . . There was no follow-up attack on Bin Laden's camps and we knew where he was . . . and identified him on the ground and we didn't pull the trigger. . . . It's

true that 9/11 was the first successful attack inside the United States, but it was the eleventh or twelfth attempt at a successful attack against the United States"—he gives as examples Somalia, USS *Cole*, Khobar Towers, the embassies.[9]

Tom Kean rates Clinton the witness as "terrific. He answered every question. . . . His memory was very, very detailed as far as the events we were asking about. . . . I think he was putting his administration's . . . best foot forward as far as what they had done, but I don't think he was particularly defensive."

Kean agrees with his Democratic colleague Bob Kerrey: "You have to be distracted. If someone's being impeached, . . . you're not distracted?" Kean, however, gives Clinton more credit for superhuman concentration than does Bob Kerrey. "Now the question is was he distracted away from the really important things, such as Osama Bin Laden, and I don't think so. . . . He's one of the few people I've ever met in my life with that kind of a mind who can compartmentalize things."[10]

Another commissioner, Republican Slade Gorton, calls Clinton "a wonderful private witness. . . . He was loquacious and he was open." He said that the commission did not ask Clinton all that many questions, but he was there a long time anyway. (More than four hours.) "You can ask Bill Clinton a one-sentence question and get a fifteen-minute answer."[11]

Clinton's testimony was also impressive, Bob Kerrey says, because "these guys were being called back in, they didn't have any staff, they had uneven access to the documents. . . . It wasn't easy to prepare."[12]

In helping Bill Clinton to prepare to testify, Sandy Berger ended up embarrassing his former boss, and permanently damaging his reputation. Berger went to the National Archives, with Bill Clinton's authorization, to examine documents. While there, Berger stole documents from the Archives, hid them in his pants and in his socks, hid some at a construction trailer to be retrieved later, took some home, destroyed some—and lied about it all. (In an agreement, he pled guilty to a misdemeanor charge of unauthorized removal and retention of classified material. He was let off with a $50,000 fine and with community service—picking up trash in a Virginia park—and having his security clearance canceled for three years.)

The more conspiratorially minded thought that Berger had stolen and possibly destroyed original, uncopied, uncatalogued, and highly classified terrorism documents, some of them containing handwritten notes or edits. Berger's motive, they charged, was to keep from the commissioners documents that showed holes in Clinton's record on fighting terrorism.[13]

Steve Emerson, a well-known terrorism expert, speculates that Berger "was trying to clean up, . . . to change history. . . . It was obvious that he was trying to excise material [that] was unflattering."[14] *U.S. News & World Report* senior editor Michael Barone went further: "I have known Berger more than 30 years and find it unlikely that he would have done something like this on his own. Did Bill Clinton ask him to destroy documents that would make him look bad in history? I get a sick feeling in the pit of my stomach when I ask that question. But this or something very much like it seems to be the only explanation that makes sense."[15]

Lanny Breuer, who worked for Clinton as his counsel during impeachment and also represents Sandy Berger, calls that charge "ludicrous. . . . The president had absolutely nothing to do with it. Sandy Berger made a mistake, he has publicly said that. . . . I'll leave it to others to decide whether at times when he's busy he's less than the most organized person, or forgetful."[16]

Slade Gorton terms Berger's behavior "bizarre" and says there's no way to answer the question of whether Berger was acting on Clinton's orders. Members of the commission and its staff, he adds, had determined that Berger's destruction of documents "had no impact on us; that we had seen and had available everything."[17] Tom Kean calls Berger's actions "puzzling," because "it makes no sense that someone of that eminence, that experience with national security, would be violating the law to that extent." Like Gorton he believes the commissioners "saw all the documents including some of the ones he made off with, since there were copies." Asked about a claim that documents went through renditions as editing was done, and that commissioners never saw those documents, he says, "Well, that's possible," but he adds that he does not consider it possible that Berger was acting on Clinton's orders. "I don't believe Bill Clinton would do that."[18]

Berger was fired as an adviser to presidential candidate John Kerry; he is currently, quietly, advising Hillary Clinton, even though the canceling of his security clearance is in effect until September 2008. That did not go unnoticed. Writer Andrew Sullivan blogged at Atlantic.com: "A thief and liar is hired by Clinton. But his thievery is less important to Clinton than his loyalty. After all, his theft was an attempt to keep President Clinton's failures with respect to al Qaeda under wraps."[19]

THE FIVE-HOUR ABC miniseries that so angered Clinton aired, commercial free, on September 10 and September 11, 2006. It opens on September 11, 2001, with Mohamed Atta and coterrorists boarding the planes that they would crash into the World Trade Center towers, into the Pentagon, and in Shanksville, Pennsylvania. From there it travels back to the quasi-thwarted terrorist attacks on the World Trade Center in 1993. The star of the miniseries is FBI agent John O'Neill, an expert on al Qaeda and Osama Bin Laden, played by Harvey Keitel.[20]

Cyrus Nowrasteh, the miniseries' screenwriter and one of its producers, attributes the angry reaction by Clinton and his people to Clinton trying to "control history, control his legacy."[21]

The miniseries seemed to be on no one's radar until ABC arranged a screening at the National Press Club in Washington on August 23, 2006. The network expected seventy-five people; three hundred showed up. "People from all political stripes were there," Nowrasteh claims. Hundreds of DVDs had been sent out to critics, journalists, radio and television talk-show hosts.[22]

Because of his position as chairman of the 9/11 Commission, Tom Kean had been hired as a senior consultant to the film, and ABC executives asked him to suggest names for the invitation list. Kean suggested 9/11 commissioner Richard Ben-Veniste, a lawyer with decades-long ties to the Democrats. (He did not respond to requests for an interview.)

ABC executives could not show all five hours at a single screening, so they decided to show all of night one, which focused on the Clinton years. That, Nowrasteh now says, was a mistake.[23]

Michael Barone was there and he remembers how angry Ben-Veniste and the people at his table appeared as the lights came up.[24]

Nowrasteh, expecting praise, took to the microphone to receive reaction and questions. Ben-Veniste and Warren Bass, a former 9/11 Commission staffer, now an editor at the *Washington Post Book World*, practically jumped out of their seats. Ben-Veniste charged that the movie was fiction and that the scenes that cast Sandy Berger and Madeleine Albright in a negative light had never happened.

Nowrasteh was taken aback and grateful to have Tom Kean try, with humor, to deflect Ben-Veniste. But he would not be deflected. Warren Bass was so "irate," Nowrasteh recalls, "he was practically shouting in my face."

Nowrasteh urged them to watch night two; everyone was given a DVD. "Night two shows the failures of the other side (i.e., Bush). . . . This is an even presentation. . . . Watch the entire thing before you attack it."

Michael Barone, whom Nowrasteh had met during the cocktail hour, invited him to dinner, and warned him, "You have angered some very powerful people . . . and I believe they are going to launch a preemptive strike against your movie and you better be prepared for it."[25]

Nowrasteh claims that Ben-Veniste and others "walked out of there, rallied Bill Clinton and his people, the bloggers, and set out to destroy this movie. It was pure politics and pure spin."[26] Tom Kean says of his commission colleague Ben-Veniste: "He's the one who made all the calls."[27]

One of the people alerted was Sandy Berger, who was not at the screening. "I got calls from people saying, 'This is a hatchet job.'" When he called Clinton, Berger discovered that the president already knew about it. "We decided we were simply not going to tolerate it," says Berger, "and we were going to fight back. . . . We launched a fairly aggressive effort to get ABC to either substantially edit or withdraw the film. . . . At the very least they needed to take out the scenes that were total fabrications."[28]

Not surprisingly, Bill Clinton went right to the top, calling Robert Iger, president and CEO of Disney, which owns ABC. Clinton told Iger that it was inaccurate and distorted and he shouldn't allow it to air.[29] Bruce Lindsey, who heads Clinton's foundation, also talked to Iger. Bill Clinton then called former senate majority leader George Mitchell, chairman of the board of the Walt Disney Company, who, at Clinton's behest, also called Iger. (Mitchell, who had been interviewed earlier for this book, declined to talk about the miniseries.)

Sandy Berger and Madeleine Albright likewise called Iger, but he did not return their calls. Clinton's lawyers sent letters to Iger and so did Sandy Berger's. Nowrasteh later complained that Senator Harry Reid and five other senators sent a letter to Iger "threatening revocation of their station licenses if they didn't pull or recut the movie."[30]

Iger was in a stomach-churning spot; he was not particularly familiar with the miniseries, which had cost more than $40 million to make and had never attracted a sponsor. Iger and others had come to think of The Path to 9/11, a huge money loser for the network, as being a kind of public service, something that would bring them kudos, not barbs. Mike Medavoy, who had already spoken to Clinton about the miniseries, ran into Iger, whom Medavoy describes as "caught in a box. I don't think he could do anything," certainly not cancel the miniseries.[31]

"Bob Iger didn't know crap about this movie," says John Ziegler, a conservative radio talk-show host on KFI in Los Angeles. "All he knows is Clinton's calling him and 'Oh, my gosh, . . . he's [Iger] a friend of Barbra Streisand's. He's got all these liberal buddies and he has to make sure that he doesn't piss them off. . . . So that's why he ended up . . . giving Clinton whatever he wanted."[32]

Not quite. Iger didn't cancel the movie, and he ordered some but not all cuts—about three minutes' worth—made in an attempt to placate Clinton and Berger.[33]

Iger did nothing for Madeleine Albright. The scene involving her shows the Pakistanis being warned that the Americans are about to launch fifty cruise missiles at Bin Laden in Afghanistan. Berger calls the scene "false and defamatory,"[34] but it conforms to his own account of what happened. "We sent General Joe Ralston . . . to Pakistan. He was having dinner with . . . the head of the Pakistani military and at the moment the cruise missiles were basically entering Pakistani airspace, just minutes away from their target, Joe told [the head of the Pakistani military] that we were attacking an Afghan site." A warning had to be issued, Berger says, "because missiles coming over Pakistani airspace, they might think that they're being attacked by the Indians and we could have a nuclear war. So we had to give them some notice."[35]

Clinton got some of what he wanted but not all: an archival clip of the president saying "I did not have sex with that woman, Ms. Lewinsky" was left intact. (It angered the former president because, he felt, the filmmakers' sole purpose was to depict him as too distracted to pay attention to fighting terrorism.)[36] Other references to Lewinsky were removed—for example, a clip of Clinton with his definition of the word *is* testimony.[37]

The Sandy Berger scene, in which he hangs up on a CIA officer who is seeking permission to launch a military operation to get Bin Laden, was cut. Nowrasteh admitted that the scene had been improvised; in real life, Berger did not slam down the phone on the CIA officer.[38] "They never had Bin Laden in their sights," says Berger, "[and] the incident they're referring to . . . was killed at the CIA because it was determined to be not reliable."[39]

There were other changes that Clinton and his supporters forced: ABC had to pull back the claim that the miniseries was based on the 9/11 Commission report. ABC also had to warn viewers repeatedly that they were seeing a docudrama, not a documentary.[40]

Bill Clinton and his people pounced on Nowrasteh, an Iranian American whose parents left Iran after the fall of the shah. Sandy Berger dismissed Nowrasteh as a tool of the Right. "It was a movie that was put together by a group of very hard right conservatives in California who a year or so before decided they were going to produce a film to try to cast blame on the Clinton administration. The writer of the film is a close friend of Rush Limbaugh and is very tied in with various right-wing groups."[41]

Much of the establishment media followed suit: the *New Yorker*'s Jane Mayer described Nowrasteh as "a hard-core conservative" and the son of "a deposed adviser to the Shah of Iran."[42] Maureen Dowd described Nowrasteh as "the Republican and Limbaugh pal."[43]

In touting the miniseries on the air, radio talk-show host Rush Limbaugh had called Nowrasteh "a friend." Nowrasteh claims he met Limbaugh twice, both times briefly and through their mutual friend Joel Surnow, the cocreator and then executive producer of 24. Limbaugh is a fan of that show and talks it up on the air. Surnow made certain that advanced closed-captioned DVDs were sent to Limbaugh, who has significant hearing loss. Nowrasteh saw that Limbaugh received the captioned DVD, along with a note in which Nowrasteh described what had happened at the National Press Club. "Any self-promoting or self-respecting writer," says Nowrasteh, "is going to try to get Rush Limbaugh interested in their show. . . . He's got twenty million listeners. . . . He has had a huge impact on 24's ratings."[44]

John Ziegler says that Limbaugh's calling Nowrasteh a friend "doomed the movie."[45]

Doomed was not too strong a word. Scholastic, the New York publisher, quickly canceled the teachers' guide that was to be released with the DVD and used in classrooms. The DVD, which should have been released early in 2007, will likely never be released.[46] Tom Kean says he guesses that Disney, which owns the DVD distribution rights, will eventually release it, but "not while Hillary's running."[47] Nowrasteh complains that ABC did nothing to promote the miniseries for the Emmys, but after it scored nominations in seven minor, technical categories, he called Robert Iger to ask him when the DVD would be released. Iger would not take his call. Nowrasteh claims he was told by an ABC vice president, "If Hillary wasn't running it wouldn't be an issue."[48]

Although the miniseries controversy involved a former president and so was certainly newsworthy, it was definitely the bloggers who kept the angry conversation going. "The way we found out about it is that the publicists were distributing tapes," says one, "only to the right-wing blogs and refusing to give tapes to anybody else. . . . It's when we couldn't get tapes that it started to become a story." When asked, "You mean you called the publicity people at ABC and they said, 'What's your political leaning?'" this man says he's not sure.[49] Blogger Jane Hamsher makes similar connections: "The fact that Rush Limbaugh had seen it and they wouldn't let Bill Clinton see it was something that was like waving a red flag." She adds, "They gave it out to six hundred right-wing bloggers and then wouldn't let Sandy Berger, Bill Clinton [see it]."[50]

Nowrasteh responds that more than nine hundred DVDs were sent out—and they were distributed, he says, across the political spectrum. "Were copies sent to Bill Clinton, Sandy Berger, and Madeleine Albright? No. They weren't sent to George W. Bush, Dick Cheney, or Condi Rice, either."[51]

When Disney went into closed quarters to determine whether to make any cuts, Nowrasteh claims, "promotions people were ordered to *send no more copies out*. They didn't want the uncut version to keep going out while they were determining what to cut. This is about the time when Sandy Berger and Madeleine Albright and Bill Clinton were doing their media spin condemning a movie they hadn't seen. They asked for copies but Disney was sending no more out to *anyone*."[52]

Nowrasteh would later charge—and said he was talking to lawyers about taking action—that Clinton's press secretary, Jay Carson, "made calls to people employing me" to suggest that they rethink their plans. Nowrasteh claims that Carson called Oliver Stone, with whom Nowrasteh had worked previously, and the president of Paramount, Brad Weston. (Although the project now seems stalled, Nowrasteh was working with Stone on *Jawbreaker*, for Paramount, about the first people to enter Afghanistan after 9/11.)[53]

"The Clintons think they own this town," Nowrasteh complains. He also blasts blogger Max Blumenthal—the son of Clinton friend and aide Sidney Blumenthal—for "heavy-handed, clumsy, McCarthyite tactics," claiming that he had heard from Oliver Stone that Blumenthal was pushing the line that "a Christian Right conspiracy" had hired Nowrasteh and "we had hoodwinked ABC into doing the movie."[54] Nowrasteh calls what happened to him "a witch hunt," "a book burning," and a reinstatement of the "Blacklist in Hollywood." (Blumenthal, who denies calling Stone or anyone else, says that Stone must have gotten his information from

Blumenthal's blog. Carson, now Hillary's traveling press secretary, did not return a call and an e-mail seeking a response to the allegation.)[55]

In explaining the miniseries' origins, Nowrasteh, who claims to have no strong political leanings, says that the idea was developed "in-house at ABC. . . . They came to me." He mentions that his work has won praise from PEN, that he had written the script and directed Showtime's *The Day Reagan Was Shot*. (Oliver Stone was the executive producer, the star was Richard Dreyfuss as Alexander Haig.) He also wrote for Showtime *10,000 Black Men Named George*, about A. Philip Randolph, "an African American Communist" who led the Pullman strike in the 1930s. "If I'm a right-wing ideologue, what am I doing a movie like that for?"[56]

Tom Kean says he did not see Nowrasteh as being of one particular political persuasion or another,[57] but Nowrasteh served the bloggers all the red meat they could have wished for. His miniseries received a rapturously positive review at Libertas, a right-leaning site that is connected to the conservative Liberty Film Festival.[58] A Liberty Film Festival person put Nowrasteh in touch with radio talker Ziegler, and Ziegler, in early or mid-August, was also sent a copy. "I loved it. I thought it was tremendous. . . . I went on the air that night and I said, . . . 'There's no way Clinton is going to allow this to air; no way, not because it was inaccurate, but because the essence of it is so truthful and Clinton is just not used to being treated like everybody else."[59]

Nowrasteh also gave an interview to frontpagemag.com, which is connected to David Horowitz, the same conservative for whom Robert Patterson now works. Patterson, during the height of the controversy, when it was not clear whether ABC would kill the miniseries, watched it, at Nowrasteh's request—the two did not know each other until then—and Patterson called Quinn Taylor, an ABC executive, the man who had put the miniseries in motion in 2004 and had hired Nowrasteh. Patterson vouched for its merits and accuracy.[60]

"We haven't heard a peep," says Nowrasteh, from the Bush administration.[61] That, to Democrats, is all the evidence needed that the miniseries was slanted.

Terrorism expert Steve Emerson calls Nowrasteh's work "overall . . . an accurate portrayal to the extent that docudramas can be accurate. Not all scenes correlated with what happened in history," he admits. But he adds that it did capture the Clinton administration's "not being ahead of the curve on al Qaeda." He says of Clinton, "He just didn't take the initiative," but Emerson does not give George W. Bush a pass: "For all intents and purposes, [he] didn't do anything for the first nine months."[62]

Among the casualties of this controversy, besides Nowrasteh and his colleagues, was Tom Kean, whose until then sterling reputation was tarnished. "Kean is an honorable man," says Sandy Berger, "but I think he got totally bamboozled by this film. . . . Had he been rigorous about his responsibility here, he would have been exercised about the way in which the movie distorted the 9/11 Commission report. I think he got used."[63]

Kean was portrayed as a partisan hack who either went along with the filmmakers' distortion or just collected his fee and paid no attention. According to a report in the *New York Times*, Bruce Lindsey wrote Kean that he was "shocked" by the former New Jersey governor's role, saying: "Your defense of the outright lies in this film is destroying the bipartisan aura of the 9/11 Commission and tarnishing the hard work of your fellow commissioners."[64]

In fact, Kean says, "I read the script. I went and saw one shooting. I talked to the writer from time to time and made suggestions, not all of which were taken but that's the normal role of a consultant. I didn't have any final approval or anything."[65] Nowrasteh says that sometimes he took Kean's suggestions and sometimes, "for budgetary as well as dramatic reasons," he didn't.[66]

Kean's long friendship with Bill Clinton was definitely hurt. Clinton's anger about the miniseries "caught me totally by surprise," Kean says, adding that he never heard from Clinton and "I was sort of surprised by that because we've been friends for a long, long time. . . . I hope we still are."

One of the more interesting aspects of this controversy is how many people proclaimed it a hit job and a failure as a piece of art without watching it. Most said that they had read about the controversy surrounding the miniseries, but it sounded so boring, why watch it? Berger and

Albright and Clinton were all complaining so loudly, says Kean, but "none of them had seen it. . . . I used to tell people, 'You know, I'd like to talk to you better after you've seen it.'"[67]

In fact, Berger says he watched the first night but not the second. "I got a full report on the second night from people who watched it."[68] Barbara Bodine, who blasted the miniseries in an op-ed in the *Los Angeles Times*—as ambassador to Yemen at the time of the bombing of the USS *Cole* in October 2000, she was portrayed as a hysterically angry, unprofessional woman refusing to cooperate with American officials—admits that she never saw it. "I'm a little like Madeleine Albright. I had enough people describe it to me. It was fairly clear what the style and the message was."[69]

The miniseries makers "left a substantial amount of misleading and incorrect information," says Sandy Berger, "but I think by the time the show aired we had done a fairly effective job of getting the media to focus on this and discrediting the movie."[70] But twenty-eight million people did watch it. It was bested by NFL football on the first night, but finished first in the ratings on the second.

Chapter 8

A LUDDITE MEETS THE BLOGGERS

WHEN BILL CLINTON MOVED INTO THE WHITE House in 1993, there were approximately fifty websites; by the time he moved out, there were more than fifty million.[1] In speeches and conversations during that period, the president often ruminated on the Internet and its impact on the nation and the world. His friend Howard Tullman remembers that as far back as the late 1980s and into the early 1990s "he was very much interested in the power of the computer for education." In a speech Clinton gave to a DNC fund-raiser the night before the Monica story exploded in January 1998, he correctly described the Internet as "the fastest growing means of communication in human history."[2]

In a recent speech in which Clinton credited bloggers with fundamentally changing the accountability of governments around the world, Clinton showed, says New Democratic Network president Simon Rosenberg, a "deeply sophisticated" understanding of the power of the Internet. Clinton pointed out that, in the old China, if a SARS epidemic had broken out, the government might have hidden it and a global pandemic might have resulted. In the new China, activists, using cell phones and the Internet, reported on the outbreak and forced the government to act.

"Clinton said some of the most . . . remarkable things about this global phenomenon that I've ever heard. . . . He understands it better than most of the people I work with here."[3]

Clinton has said that the Internet is a more important advance than the telephone, but unlike his friend George H. W. Bush who is constantly fiddling with his BlackBerry, Clinton is a Luddite, a complete computer klutz. For him, the high-tech challenge was figuring out, postpresidency, how to use his cell phone.

His newfound interest in blogs was piqued by Chelsea, by his insatiable appetite for political news, and by his wife's likely run for president, at a time when YouTube was changing the way the game was played. He reads blogs the old-fashioned way; his assistants print them out for him.[4]

Hillary put an actual blogger on her staff before she announced her decision to seek the nomination. Peter Daou, whose title is Head of Internet Outreach, was obviously focused on Bill as well as Hillary, when he invited a group of fourteen bloggers to Harlem to meet with the former president over lunch on September 13, 2006.[5]

The bloggers had one thing in common; all were left of center—they call themselves, says one, "the progressive bloggers"—and not one of them saw anything of value in *The Path to 9/11*. They came from around the country; Clinton, they said, covered their expenses.[6]

Clinton knew how important the "netroots" (the Internet grassroots, mostly from the Left) were in the upcoming 2006 midterms, and he knew that the people sitting around the table with him were supporting the same candidates he was. If Bill Clinton had his way, by the end of their two-hour lunch, they would leave sufficiently impressed by him to support Hillary, or, at least, to go a bit easier on her when she ran for the nomination for president. Jane Hamsher, a movie producer who traveled to New York from Mill Valley, California, and claims 60,000–80,000 people a day visit her blog (firedoglake), suggested, ". . . while Hillary Clinton may never be the bloggers' darling, opening . . . a channel for communications might . . . blunt a lot of the more overt criticism [from] the liberal blogosphere."[7]

From all accounts, these bloggers fell in love with the triangulatorin-chief. One of them remarked on the "overwhelming earnestness of this guy. He's so smart."[8] Jeralyn Merritt (talkleft) talks as if she believes that Clinton has outgrown his centrist streak: "We're so energized and . . . he's so with it. He gets it. . . . We could tell his values . . . were our values." They talked about everything from Iraq to Iran to criminal justice—Merritt, a criminal defense attorney in Denver, was one of the principal trial lawyers for Timothy McVeigh, the Oklahoma City bomber—to health care.[9]

The conversation started with Clinton talking, but then he turned it into a lively discussion. It was difficult, at first, says one blogger, to interrupt the former president, "but after a while we just all got into it."[10] All of them, women and men, seemed charmed. "When he was responding to one of us," says Merritt, "he totally would turn his body to face that person. He always engaged in direct eye contact. He was very animated with his hands. And it was like being at a family dinner."

Merritt was impressed that Clinton seemed to know everybody in the room, and their blogs, and knew that many had day jobs and what they did for a living. They wore no name tags.[11]

Much of the conversation, says Jane Hamsher, was about how the opposition to *The Path to 9/11* bubbled up out of the blogosphere. "So a lot of the meeting was spent discussing taking action and working together." It was an exciting prospect, Hamsher says, because "it was the first time a major politician had come together with bloggers. . . . We really pushed back [against *The Path to 9/11*], and frequently our issues don't get echoed by major politicians. I think that kind of really emboldened President Clinton to step out and push back against it."

A week after the Harlem meeting, Hamsher, who freely admits she never watched the miniseries—"it sounds like an endurance contest"— appeared on Keith Olbermann's *Countdown* on MSNBC and described what sounded like a close working relationship between the bloggers and the former president. "We worked with him very effectively over the course of the last couple of weeks in order to get the message out about . . . *The Path to 9/11*. . . ."[12]

Fans of the miniseries, such as Los Angeles radio talk-show host John Ziegler, credit the bloggers for spooking Disney, the parent company of

ABC, and for spooking the New York publisher Scholastic into dropping the study guide.[13] "We were really hitting Scholastic hard," agrees Jane Hamsher.[14]

Clinton, wearing a suit and tie, looked fine, although older. "He's great looking," says Jeralyn Merritt. "He looks thinner. . . . There are more lines on his face. . . . He . . . looks like somebody who was probably sick at one time."[15] Jane Hamsher offers a rosier prognosis: "He looked healthy, robust, rested; he seemed like a happy fellow."[16]

Lunch was intended to be healthy. Catered by a neighborhood restaurant, the chicken was baked and so were the sweet potato "fries." While the bloggers drank sweet tea, Clinton stuck with Diet Coke. Jeralyn Merritt was somewhat surprised to note that he ate the large sweet potato slices with his fingers. He did not eat his vegetables.[17]

At the end of the lunch, they decided that they'd meet again soon, but the bloggers expect that next time he'll invite a different group.

Before the bloggers left, several encouraged the former president to try his hand at blogging and suggested that he could do so under a screen name. Merritt says when she urged Clinton to contribute to her site, he told her he might take her up on it, but he has not so far.[18] Another participant says that Clinton does not use a computer or send e-mail, and he certainly has never blogged. Kinko's founder, Paul Orfalea, says both he and Clinton have their e-mails printed out for them.[19]

Bill Clinton will likely continue to have blogs printed out and handed to him. Friends say he does not seem inclined to learn to use a computer or e-mail. When he was president, his diarist Janis Kearney recalls, he had made a stab at it. "I've got this really great photo of us standing in the Oval Office as he learned to order something . . . online." (He was ordering Christmas gifts.)[20]

Al Gore may not have invented the Internet, but he did use it while vice president. "Gore used to make fun of Clinton all the time for not knowing how to turn on his computer," says Elaine Kamarck, "and not using e-mail."[21] Leon Panetta explains that Clinton simply "prefers the telephone."[22] When friends, such as John Emerson, want to reach the former president, they "typically e-mail Doug Band who travels with him all the time . . . [Clinton's] a guy who picks up the phone and talks to people. He operates on the cell phone a lot."[23]

LATER THAT MONTH, Bill Clinton's new blogger friends took some credit for his enraged response—"pushback," they called it—to *Fox News Sunday*'s Chris Wallace. When Wallace suggested that Clinton was distracted and did not do enough to fight terrorism during his presidency, making him partly responsible for 9/11, the raw anger, the refusal to back down, the avalanche of words, made him sound, they said, just like a blogger.

"When we announced that you were going to be on *Fox News Sunday*," Wallace said, "I got a lot of e-mail from viewers. And I've got to say, I was surprised. Most of them wanted me to ask you this question: Why didn't you do more to put Bin Laden and Al-Qaeda out of business when you were president? There's a new book out I suspect you've already read, called *The Looming Towers*. And it talks about how the fact that when you pulled troops out of Somalia in 1993, Bin Laden said, 'I have seen the frailty and the weakness and the cowardice of U.S. troops.' Then there was the bombing of the embassies in Africa and the attack on the *Cole*. . . . And after the attack, the book says that Bin Laden separated his leaders, spread them around, because he expected an attack, and then there was no response. I understand that hindsight is 20/20."

That's when Clinton exploded: "So you did Fox's bidding on this show. You did your nice little conservative hit job on me. . . . At least I tried. That's the difference between me and . . . all of the right wingers who are attacking me now. They ridicule me for trying. They had eight months to try. They did not try. I tried. So I tried and failed." He also got personal, telling the mild-mannered and surprised Wallace, "And you've got that little smirk on your face and you think you're so clever."[24]

"My reaction," says one of the bloggers, "is this guy has clearly been reading blogs. . . . I have a feeling that his reading the blogs got him to the point where he said, 'That's enough.'" This blogger says that the fact that Wallace works for Fox News would send any lefty blogger into the sort of red-faced, finger-wagging tirade that viewers saw.[25]

Some people who are close Clinton observers say he went loaded for bear to the Wallace interview, that he had rehearsed his rant. "It was clear that he had been waiting for that question for a long time," says Leon Panetta.[26]

Others say that he was genuinely offended by the question, that he had been promised that the interview, taped just as the CGI conference was concluding, would focus on the highly successful—$7.5 billion was raised—meeting, and that he felt sandbagged by Wallace's question, which, says Sandy Berger, was not even a question but "a speech, basically, saying, 'Why did you fail?' . . . He just decided that he was not going to sit back and take that."[27]

Clinton had grown unaccustomed to harsh treatment from mainstream broadcast and even cable hosts. For the last couple of years, since his bypass surgery, he was more likely to be tossed softball questions, as if a tough one might cause a spike in his blood pressure and spark a coronary or a stroke. Clinton had come to expect star treatment, obsequious interviewers—that same day MSNBC's Keith Olbermann led off the interview by handing Clinton a check: "Here's eight more schools in Kenya from me."[28]

Conservative commentators tried to use the exchange to take Clinton down a notch. John Podhoretz called it "the Bubba blowup . . . a full-bore tantrum on the small screen,"[29] and others pointed out that the last time Clinton wagged his finger on national television, he was lying about his relationship with Monica Lewinsky. Slade Gorton attributes Clinton's fury to his habit of reacting "very unfavorably to any kind of criticism."[30]

Yet the exchange was certainly more of a positive than a negative. It boosted the spirits of friends and colleagues—Robert Torricelli says, "It gave the first shot of adrenaline through the ranks of the Democratic Party in a year," bucking up the base for the midterms then less than seven weeks away.[31] Republican strategist Scott Reed argues that it was a major factor in the Democrats taking back both the House and Senate the next November. "This was a scripted, set-up event. . . . Clinton needed to get the Democrats off their asses."[32]

To Elaine Kamarck it was about time that Clinton punched back. "My only criticism was he should have been doing it all along; instead of making kissy-face with George Bush Sr., he should have been letting them have it between the eyeballs."[33]

Many people on both sides agreed that the two men were unevenly matched. Conrad Black compares Wallace versus Clinton to "sending a chipmunk to deal with my Siamese cat."[34]

To Tom Kean, Clinton's anger was all about the thing most important to him now—more important even than Hillary becoming president, although that is tied to it—and that's his legacy. "He's got a very hot button these days and I think it is his legacy. . . . He doesn't like to hear Monica mentioned at all."[35]

"HE'S LIKE an old fire horse; he hears that bell and he's just gotta go running in there," Paul Greenberg says about Bill Clinton and almost any election.[36]

As the 2006 midterm election approached, Clinton seemed to be in demand almost everywhere. He left the liabilities of 2002—bad reputation—and 2004—bad reputation and health—behind. One consultant says happily that Bill Clinton campaigned for several of his candidates in 2006 and they all won.[37]

Clinton was taking his marching orders that year from his buddy Congressman Rahm Emanuel, who aspires to be Speaker of the House or president of the United States, but for the time being was representing his district in Illinois and running the Democratic Congressional Campaign Committee. Not everyone believed the frenetic, cocky Emanuel when he said the Democrats could win the fifteen seats they'd need to take back the House, but Clinton believed in him. Emanuel says he talks to Clinton every day, and when asked whom Clinton is closest to in the House, he names himself.[38] Constantly on the telephone cajoling candidates to run, promising that Clinton would campaign for them and delivering Clinton, Emanuel was relentless. He was a student of the game of politics who, like Clinton, digested the most minute details of precinct politics, and, being smarter than most of his adversaries, often defeated them.[39]

Elaine Kamarck, the Kennedy School professor who was a senior adviser to Al Gore, continues to insist that Clinton remained a turnoff to a certain kind of Democrat and had to be handled carefully. She claims that Clinton might have been seen at a lot of fund-raisers with fat entrance fees, but he was still not seen in tight races at open rallies, covered by the national press. "The reason is . . . that he is still not universally loved among the swing voters. He is universally loved among the Democratic base, but you don't win . . . elections just with the base."

When it's pointed out to Kamarck that Clinton did campaign for candidates whom she specifically mentions as trying to distance themselves from him, she argues that he was not doing television commercials for those candidates and that "he remains almost as toxic as Dick Cheney. . . . He drives away our swing voters."[40]

That might be almost wishful thinking on the part of Kamarck, who still blames Clinton for eight years of George W. Bush. In an analysis in the *New York Times* during the height of the campaign season, reporters John Broder and Anne Kornblut wrote, "Bubba's back. . . . He remains in perpetual campaign mode." Beyond recognizing that Clinton's tirade at Chris Wallace did buck up the Democrats, Broder and Kornblut describe Clinton as "serving as an overarching strategist and spokesman." Writing with just a bit more than a month to go before election day, they had him making forty political appearances in sixteen states.[41]

That November Clinton, like his new friends, the bloggers, supported Ned Lamont for the Senate in Connecticut. The antiwar Democrat had bested the state's veteran, hawkish senator, Joe Lieberman, in the Democratic primary. Lieberman remained in the race as an independent and was Lamont's major rival in November. But in the primary, Clinton, in close consultation with Hillary, and in opposition to the progressives, bloggers and otherwise, had supported Lieberman.

Clinton's friendship with Lieberman dates back to his Yale Law days, when he supported Lieberman in one of his early runs for the Connecticut state senate. Yet Lieberman had taken to the Senate floor in September 1998 to condemn Clinton for his behavior with Monica Lewinsky.

Some saw Lieberman, an Orthodox Jew, as "the conscience of the Senate"; others saw him as a posturing scold.[42]

Bob Kerrey, then in the Senate, credits Lieberman's sermon/speech with saving Clinton from impeachment by suggesting that the proper punishment for the president was a resolution of censure. "The president himself," says Kerrey, "when he offered his apology to all of us said things approximately the same as Joe Lieberman did."[43] Still, former DNC chief Steve Grossman is one of many Clinton friends who says that the president was "deeply hurt" by the public rebuke.[44]

In the heated primary battle, Lieberman, recognizing that he was in trouble, approached Hillary on the Senate floor to ask if she would ask Bill to come in and campaign for him. Speculation as to why Clinton said yes mostly focused on what was best for Hillary. Clinton realized, says Jonathan Alter, "that it was in Hillary's interest for Lieberman to win because the forces that have been unleashed against Lieberman could swallow Hillary, too."[45] Clinton really doesn't much like Lieberman anymore, says one friend, but he needs to keep that door open because Clinton does not want to offend Jewish and pro-Israel voters and moderate voters—again because Hillary will need them.[46]

As model Democrats, the Clintons explained, they would support the incumbent, Lieberman, in the primary, but they both made clear that whoever won the primary would get their support in the general election. The real story is that Bill Clinton made it possible for Lieberman to win in November by preventing a blowout in the primary. With Clinton's help, Lieberman went from down ten points to barely losing, giving him the legitimacy he needed to run and win as an independent. Lieberman can't "bitch at Clinton," says Tony Coelho, because "Clinton went there and helped him and obviously closed the gap and gave him the capability to run again."[47] (In late 2007, Lieberman endorsed John McCain as he battled to win the Republican nomination.)

CAMPAIGNING FOR Lieberman in that primary and later campaigning in the general election for Jim Webb in his race for the Senate in

Virginia highlighted a Bill Clinton character trait: when it comes to politics and, in Clinton's case, that's like saying when it comes to life, Clinton is pragmatic. He does not hold grudges. "It's all part of his picking himself up off the floor," says one friend. "Not in his interest to look vindictive."[48] Another friend depicts Clinton as a man who "makes love to his enemies."[49]

Rod Blagojevich, now governor of Illinois, formerly a congressman, remembers being at the White House for a meeting with Clinton postimpeachment. Republican congressman James Rogan, one of the managers during the impeachment trial, was also there. Blagojevich describes being in a "little holding room and . . . [Clinton] comes in and spends a little time with you." He recalls Clinton and Rogan chatting amiably. Blagojevich was fascinated by the fact that here is one of the "chief architects" planning Clinton's destruction, but "unlike Nixon, he didn't obsess about his enemies and hold these grudges to the extent that they destroyed him."[50] (Rogan was defeated in the next election.)

Clinton laughingly told a reporter, "It was said of me when I was governor that I'd never remember who I'm supposed to hate one day to the next."[51]

The Senate race in Virginia—Republican incumbent George Allen against Democrat Jim Webb, a decorated Marine veteran of Vietnam—is an even more striking example of Bill Clinton's pragmatism. Webb, a prickly former Republican, did not care much about Clinton's sexual history, but he could not forgive Clinton's lies about the draft. Joe Lieberman's criticism of Clinton was said out of sorrow for an old friend who went astray. Jim Webb's blasts at Bill Clinton were said out of genuine disdain.

"I cannot conjure up an ounce of respect for Bill Clinton when it comes to the military," Webb said. "Every time I see him salute a Marine, it infuriates me. I don't think Bill Clinton cares one iota about what happens in a military unit." Webb called Clinton's presidency "the most corrupt in modern memory."[52]

In 2000, Webb, secretary of the navy in the Reagan administration, had first promised to endorse Democratic incumbent Chuck Robb, but then had switched to George Allen, because, says Robb, who lost to Allen that year, "he was absolutely fit to be tied because he thought Bill Clinton had completely ruined his [Webb's] military. . . . Because I hadn't somehow stopped him from ruining his beloved military, that was all he seemed to care about at the time."[53] Webb supported Bush over Gore in 2000.

Cynics say that Bill Clinton would do anything—even support a man who had been so blunt in his criticism—to see that there was a Democratic Senate because that would help Hillary. Others, such as former Clinton counsel Lanny Breuer, see this as Clinton at his best. "I think he cared a lot about policy and I think [he thought] Jim Webb . . . would be better for the country than George Allen. He takes a deep breath and does what many people wouldn't do, which is to support someone who said pretty mean things about him."[54]

"If I only supported people who never criticized me, I'd have no one to support," Clinton said, according to the *Newport News Daily Press,* while campaigning for Webb.

That Webb ended up winning the Senate race and that the Democrats ended up taking the Senate, as well as the House, may have more to do with George Allen calling a young Indian American at a campaign rally by the slur "macaca," but, in 2006 in Virginia, having Bill Clinton at his side didn't hurt.

He was in top form that election season at a fund-raiser for Jim Webb at the Virginia home of Chuck and Lynda Robb. He spoke to a sold-out group of about 450 people and had the audience "absolutely spellbound," says Chuck Robb.

If there was one problem with Clinton's talk, says Robb, for all "his usual rhetorical magic," it was that he did not even mention Webb during the first ten minutes. Robb was beginning to worry. During a pause, he whispered, "'You've got to say something nice about Jim,' at which point," Robb says, "[Clinton] started weaving his story around Webb and all of his accomplishments. It was masterful."

The star of the show was definitely Bill Clinton; Jim Webb, whom Robb calls extremely bright and very passionate about his beliefs, but "a little bit aloof on occasion, not anything like as gifted or nimble a speaker," did not seem to mind. "He did his pitch and said, 'I know who you're here for,'" and while Clinton spoke, "you could have heard a pin drop."

When it was over, Robb could not get Bill Clinton to leave. "I expected him to be arriving late; what I didn't expect him to do is stick around more than an hour after the party was supposed to be over. He wanted to sign every picture that people had brought. I tried to get him to go," Robb says, "because his motorcade was blocking our driveway and other guests couldn't get out." Before leaving, Clinton wanted to talk to Robb, a member of the bipartisan Iraq Study Group, about the war. The two old friends stood on the porch, and, says Robb, "in his usual thoughtful, comprehensive way, [Clinton] went through the whole Middle East. . . . He had a fully thought-out vision for what he thought should be done. . . . This was a tour de force recap of all the key players in the entire Middle East with all the nuances and the internal dynamics."[55]

BILL CLINTON'S pragmatism also, on occasion, extended to journalists.

"The thing about him," says Jonathan Alter, "is that he's not really a grudge holder unless you seem like you're an implacable enemy." Alter had landed squarely on Clinton's enemies list in the fall of 1999 in the presidential limousine: "I asked him if he was seeking psychiatric counseling and he got very pissed off. . . . 'I can't believe you asked me that question.'" Clinton exited the limousine without saying good-bye.

Alter, who obviously likes Clinton, hated to see a relationship, which stretched back to 1984 and the Gary Hart campaign, end. At the last Clinton White House Christmas party in 2000, Alter recalls, "I saw Jake Siewert. . . . 'You know every magazine from *Toenail Illustrated* on down has gotten an exit interview with Clinton. Why can't I get in to see him?'"

"After that 'Are you crazy, Mr. President?' question?"

In the fall of 2001, as Clinton's star continued to dim, he relented a bit. Alter interviewed him for a column about Clinton's plans for his memoir. His agent, Robert Barnett, "went crazy," Alter recalls. "Clinton was under contract not to talk about it and he talked about it with me by mistake. . . . Sort of as a favor to them, I didn't mislead the reader, but I didn't make it seem as if I had talked to him when I had." That helped Alter land the interview for *Newsweek*'s cover story.

When Alter was undergoing chemotherapy, Clinton wrote him a note; and when Clinton had his bypass, they commiserated. In March 2006, "I was standing in Kmart . . . and he called on my cell phone and told me that he liked the piece I had written about Eli Segal—the architect of AmeriCorps—who died the month before."[56]

BILL CLINTON also gets his entertainment the old-fashioned way, with a pen and the dead-tree edition of the *New York Times*. He is not a tournament-level crossword solver, but he's way above average, and he might have been a contender if he had not had other responsibilities.

His love of puzzles and his longtime ties to puzzle aficionados were the impetus behind his agreeing to appear in the movie *Wordplay*—that his friend Harvey Weinstein was the money behind the movie helped also—a small but well-received documentary about the people who love the puzzle. The brainchild of director, cameraman, editor Patrick Creadon and his wife, Christine O'Malley, who produced it, the film focuses on Will Shortz, the puzzle editor of the *New York Times* and a regular guest on NPR's *Weekend Edition, Sunday*.

In March 2005, when Creadon was filming at the annual American Crossword Puzzle Tournament, Shortz, who directs the tournament, provided Creadon and O'Malley with a list of famous people who are crossword aficionados. Bill Clinton was at the top of Shortz's list. Also on it was Jon Stewart, whom the young filmmakers wanted almost as much.

One of the tournament competitors in 2005 was Clinton's friend, from Little Rock, Judge Victor Fleming. He had already agreed to appear in the movie and persuaded Clinton to do likewise. For the first-time documentary filmmakers, landing the interview with Clinton made their movie. "Having President Clinton in our film," says Creadon, "elevated the entire project. It suddenly became much more than the story of a man [Will Shortz] who is sort of a cult figure."

Creadon and O'Malley had an appointment to interview Clinton in early July 2005 in his Harlem office. (It was postponed until mid-July when Clinton spent an extra day with George H. W. Bush at his home in Kennebunkport.) That, says Creadon, opened the door to Jon Stewart. "We really weren't getting anywhere with his people. . . . Once the Bill Clinton interview was on the books, and we were flying to New York, we called Jon Stewart's people one final time. 'Bill Clinton's going to do an interview? OK, we'll call you back in a few minutes,' and they called us back and said, 'Jon would love to do the interview.'"

The Clinton interview was scheduled for July 14 at 6:30 P.M., but they arrived three hours early just to be sure everything was flawlessly set up.

A Clinton aide warned the increasingly anxious Creadon, "He's had an extremely full day; there's a good chance he might be running a little bit late." By 8 P.M. Creadon was seriously worried. At 8:15, he recalls, "someone in the room says, 'OK, they're walking, they're walking down'; suddenly everyone in the room . . . just practically stood at attention. . . . A moment later, two Secret Service men walk into the room. . . . They didn't say a word to us. . . . They looked around the room, looked through our gear real quickly and then stood there very quietly with their arms folded, and then someone else said, 'OK, they're in the hallway.' . . . The door opens up and eight more people walk in the room and they have books and clipboards and . . . Palm Pilots . . . and the last person to walk in is President Clinton."

Creadon handed Clinton the section of the *New York Times* that contained the puzzle, which was created by Merl Reagle, syndicated crossword puzzle constructor, and edited by Will Shortz, and had run in the *Times* on Tuesday, May 31. (The day of the week is important because Monday is easiest and it becomes harder as the week progresses; the Tuesday puzzle is not nearly as challenging as the Saturday puzzle.) The puzzle's theme was "Wordplay," the title of the film.

How did they know that Clinton hadn't already solved it when it appeared in the newspaper? "He typically only solves the Friday and Saturday puzzles," Creadon explains, "and maybe the Sunday puzzle. He doesn't do the beginning of the week because the beginning-of-the-week puzzles are really pretty easy."

"I'd like you to . . . almost pretend that we're not here and just open up the paper and solve the puzzle like you normally do," Creadon told Clinton. Clinton "starts solving the puzzle and doing the interview at the same time. He's doing it in pen." As he was working, Clinton told them that he recently read in a medical journal that crossword puzzles can fend off Alzheimer's and dementia. "You know, I'm not getting any younger and so I feel like I've reached the point in my life where I need to do everything I can to ward off that sort of condition."

Creadon estimates that it took Clinton six or seven minutes to finish it—they didn't time him—no mistakes, although he did change one letter while solving it. "And he looked at it when it was done and said, 'Yeah, that was fun.'"

Camera off, Clinton shook hands with everyone. "Would it be okay if we took a very quick picture?" Creadon asked. "Come on in." Clinton answered. "He stood there with his arms outstretched like a big mother eagle and we all kind of climbed in under his arms and he pulled us all tightly to him and we took a picture."

Clinton continued to support the young filmmakers, even going to bat for them with another famous politician they wanted to interview. On election day 1996, the *New York Times* ran what some consider to be the greatest crossword ever made. The main answer running across the middle is "headline in tomorrow's newspaper," two words, seven letters each. The most obvious answer is "Clinton Elected." According to Creadon, the *Times* "got flooded with phone calls: 'How dare you run that?' 'Who are you to assume that he's going to win?'" The less obvious answer was "BobDole Elected"—an answer that would be obvious to people, like Bill Clinton, who know that Dole is given to referring to himself in the third person as "Bobdole," as if it were one word.

Creadon and O'Malley had contacted Dole earlier about appearing in the film, but his people said no, explaining that Dole is not a particular fan of crosswords.

Clinton then called Dole and persuaded him to give the interview. When Creadon walked into Dole's office, he didn't even say hello: "Boy, you have quite an advance man on your team!"[57]

People who are into crosswords call Clinton—the only president living or dead who is a fan of the puzzle[58]—solver in chief.[59]

Clinton has "the kind of brain that we like in the puzzle business," says Reagle. "We call it a sponge head. . . . He . . . sops up useless and useful knowledge and he can . . . talk on virtually any subject you mention. He retains most of, if not all of, what he reads."[60]

As a boy of ten or twelve, Clinton was inspired by the fact that a justice of the Arkansas Supreme Court, George Rose Smith, made puzzles, some of which were published in the Sunday *New York Times*.[61]

When Victor Fleming would go to the Governor's Mansion on weekend mornings to pick up his daughter, who had spent the night with Chelsea, "Bill would be working the crossword puzzle," Fleming says, "and I'd sit down and participate with him." He once had the Saturday puzzle finished except for one word. Fleming looked at it and immediately got it. "The clue was 'early summers' and . . . he had all but two letters filled in and the answer was 'abacus.'" In November 1995, Fleming, his wife, and daughter were spending the day and night at the White House. Just after lunch, Bill, Victor, and his wife, Susan, were solving the Saturday *New York Times* puzzle while watching a college football game. Hillary, not a puzzle or football fan, was elsewhere, working on her book *It Takes a Village*. The phone rang and the person on the other end informed the president that Israeli prime minister Yitzhak Rabin had been shot. Clinton began to tell the Flemings how much Rabin meant to him and to the world. About thirty minutes later a second call came and he said, "I understand." And this time he said, "Yep, that was just to confirm that Rabin has died." He put the puzzle down, got up, and said, "I'm going to have to go to work now."[62]

GEORGE MCGOVERN asked Bill Clinton to be the speaker for the dedication, in early October 2006, of the George and Eleanor McGovern

Library and Center for Leadership and Public Service at Dakota Wes-
leyan University in the former senator's hometown of Mitchell, South
Dakota. McGovern describes the school as "a little Methodist college"
where McGovern met his wife, earned his undergraduate degree, and
taught history for a few years. Clinton declined because Victor Fleming's
daughter was getting married that day in Little Rock and Chelsea was
her maid of honor.

But McGovern, eighty-four, whose ties to Clinton date to 1972, really
wanted him. "I called him directly at his New York office and told him
how much it would mean to me." Clinton thought some more about it
and called him back to say he'd do it if they could provide him with a
private plane to fly him there and from there to Little Rock. Clinton did
the speech pro bono.

In introducing the former president, McGovern quipped to the audience of more than five thousand seated on a lawn under gorgeous blue
skies: "I understood that being Methodist doesn't save you from sin, but
it does take the fun out of it." Clinton responded with an earnest tribute:
"I've been married to a Methodist for thirty-one years; I know every move
that John Wesley ever made." He spoke of Wesley's concern for the poor
and the coal miners and the factory workers in London and his antislav-
ery role in Europe, and then he said, "I've read a lot about John Wesley
and I think John Wesley would be proud of George McGovern."

"He couldn't have said anything that would have struck a better response with that audience," says McGovern. "Just being familiar with
John Wesley's life and embroidering that to tie it in with my battles
against human hunger and so on—it brought down the house."

After Clinton and McGovern unveiled a life-sized standing bronze of
George and Eleanor McGovern, Clinton saw the crowd that was behind
the restraining ropes, and, says McGovern, "he just reached across the
ropes and grabbed as many hands as he could. . . . Once we got him inside the library where there were probably a couple of hundred other
people, he didn't want to leave. The Secret Service and his staff were
trying to pull him to Little Rock, and he was still chatting with the
people."[63]

Eleanor McGovern, suffering from heart disease, was not there and died soon after.

When Clinton arrived at Elizabeth Fleming's wedding back in Little Rock and saw the father of the bride, he walked over to him, put his arms around him, gave him a big hug, and said, "Boy, we were pretty good in that crossword puzzle movie, weren't we?"[64]

Chapter 9

PHILANDERER
IN CHIEF

ON APRIL 26, 2006, THE NELSON SHANKS PORTRAIT of Bill Clinton was unveiled during a private ceremony at the National Portrait Gallery. It is a big painting—including the frame, more than eight and a half feet high—depicting the former president standing in a jaunty pose, with his hand on his hip. "I tried to get sort of the timbre of the way he moves," Shanks says. "He's not stiff and rigid, yet he's not utterly relaxed, either. It's a little bit self-conscious."

Reporters quickly noticed that Shanks painted Clinton without his wedding band. "He was wearing it," Shanks says. "To be honest with you, I forgot it. I was so busy getting the gesture of the hand." When he showed Hillary a photograph of the painting, she also didn't notice, even though she studied the hands "very, very carefully."

She insisted he do justice to the hands. "And there's no doubt, he has very long fingers, very attractive hands." Hillary complained that Bill's fingers are slimmer than Shanks painted them. "I changed them very minimally just in respect for her thoughts. But I think I got it right the first time."[1]

More than eight years after the fact of Clinton's tryst with Lewinsky, reporters turned an innocent omission into a laugh line. "The artist who painted Bill Clinton's . . . portrait managed to do what Monica Lewinsky could not: make Bubba's wedding ring disappear."[2]

At the unveiling, he was wearing his wedding band. Asked by reporters if Senator Clinton wanted the painting corrected, her spokesman, Philippe Reines, replied, "Can you just quote me giving you a different finger?"[3]

Shanks found the former president looking "pretty good, . . . maybe a little thinner than when I painted him. He seemed . . . pretty moved. A few people said he got tears in his eyes."[4]

Hillary referred to the missing wedding band as "a little tempest in a teapot."[5]

COMPARED WITH the real tempests in her marriage, the missing wedding band was "little." In her memoir, Hillary attempted to preempt potential stories so that they would be old news by the time of a presidential campaign. She revealed, for instance, that she and Bill had had marriage counseling. The president had also confirmed that in the fall of 1999 when *Newsweek*'s Jonathan Alter had attempted to deflect the president's anger from the question of whether he was seeking psychiatric help. "I understand you're in pastoral counseling." "Well, why don't you ask me about that?" Clinton responded. "Well, how's your pastoral counseling going?" "If you ask it that way," Clinton responded, "I'll answer it. It's going very well."[6]

One of those pastors was Tony Campolo, who first met Clinton in October 1993, when he and other Evangelicals were invited for breakfast with the Clintons and Gores. Subsequently, Campolo met Clinton every four or five weeks, usually in the Oval Office, occasionally "upstairs in his private apartment." Campolo describes their conversations as reflecting "on the meaning of scripture in his own life and in his work as president." Clinton would often telephone Campolo "and ask for some of my reflections on how the Bible should guide him in what he was about to say to the American people."[7]

Campolo would not respond to questions about meetings related specifically to the Lewinsky affair, writing instead, "President Clinton is very committed to maintaining his family. . . . I believe he is committed to making his family life successful and his marriage meaningful and loving."

Postpresidency, Campolo has seen Clinton "several times," less than before because "he is constantly traveling."[8] In 2002, Campolo was quoted (by Jonathan Alter) as saying of Clinton, "Any rumors of affairs are erroneous."[9]

Another pastoral counselor—a man who has had his own sexual scandals—was the Reverend Jesse Jackson, who was often at the White House during the Lewinsky crisis and, according to Alter, "prayed with them, talked to Chelsea."[10] Former Clinton military aide Robert Patterson who sometimes screened the president's calls—and always screened them at Camp David—recalled that Clinton would often refuse to take calls from Jackson, who, Patterson claims, "was always calling in favors."[11]

THE AFTERMATH of Lewinsky and impeachment matured Clinton, says Mark Thomann, who was Clinton's Midwest finance chairman. Thomann suggests that today Bill Clinton is a faithful husband. "I think his new passion is . . . his legacy, and I think he understands that . . . if he was involved in another type of scandal like that, it would take away from his second chance, his redemption."[12]

Much more common is the belief that Bill Clinton is simply missing the faithfulness gene, that somehow a dysfunctional childhood and a hedonistic mother caused him not really to understand the concept of fidelity. Anson Beard, who calls the former president "an amazing human being" and supports his CGI, nonetheless says of him: "When you say Bill Clinton, you say a lot of things in superlatives—leader, persuasive, genuine, etc., but personal integrity would not be one of the first words out of my mouth." He compares Clinton with George H. W. Bush, whose upbringing gave him "a tremendous moral compass. That guy knows where north is." The good news about Clinton," Beard adds, "is he is actively dedicating his postpresidential career to doing positive good around the world. He is clearly energized to restore his legacy behind the unfortunate misjudgments and lost opportunities of the last [three] years of his presidency. He is by far this country's best ex-president—to the world's benefit."[13]

One woman who knows Clinton well describes him as almost pathological in that he doesn't recognize lapses in his behavior, just does not see them. "He has never seen his own bad behavior as being a liability; he has always managed in his own mind to rearrange it in some way. . . . I don't think he ever fears the consequences of his behavior. I think it's like a missing piece of his brain."[14]

It's almost a given among people who follow politics that Clinton continues to chase women. "I travel in political circles and I hear things constantly," says University of Virginia political scientist Larry Sabato, who has written much about the underbelly of campaigns and politicians. "Given his history, would anybody be surprised if there were things going on? I mean, let's get real."[15]

One moderate Republican, a well-connected veteran campaign strategist, says, "He's dating!" He recalls a story in which Clinton was in a restaurant and he introduced a beautiful woman as his chief of staff. "He leaves to go to the bathroom and my friend's talking to her: 'Oh, you're chief of staff?' and she's like, 'What the hell are you talking about? I'm not his chief of staff.'"[16]

A Democrat who has been a close and sympathetic friend, before, during, and after his presidency, says of Bill Clinton: "I don't think somebody like him changes much. If he was doing this when he was governor, if he did what he did when he was president, now that he's wealthy and he's free, obviously he's still going to be the same person."[17]

One person who has traveled with Clinton describes him as surrounded by yes men and enablers, pointing particularly to his traveling companion Doug Band. "His whole identity has been completely annihilated. He identifies totally with the guy. . . . He spends something like three hundred nights a year with the president and plays cards with him until four and five in the morning. And sees the world exactly as Clinton does. Clinton never sees himself as making mistakes . . . and Doug is the kind of guy who will sit there with a very straight face and looks at you and says, 'Bill Clinton is sleeping with no one but his wife.'" This person thinks that Clinton has the equivalent of a woman in every port.[18]

"A man is only as moral as his options," a Clinton staffer has been known to say. One woman who has traveled with him postpresidency says, "No less than five hundred women will all make it clear that they will sleep with him that night."[19]

Irena Medavoy sees Clinton as a man who has so many temptations that how could one expect any normal male to resist them all? "I think a lot of . . . girls get crushes on him. . . . Have you ever been around a movie star?"[20]

For all of Clinton's regrets about leaving the White House, there was one aspect, friends say, that he savored—his freedom to have more of a private life. One woman who had seen him around Hollywood for years says, "There probably was a part of him that couldn't wait to get out and be free. . . . I don't think he can help himself. . . . He's a flirt." She describes his technique as, "I got the holding your hand just a little too long, putting the hand on your back, ah, just a little too long."[21]

In an interview in the debut issue of Tina Brown's short-lived *Talk* magazine, Hillary attributed Bill's philandering to a troubled childhood.[22]

John Schmidt, another Democrat and longtime Bill Clinton supporter, says that Clinton has always had "a taste for a certain kind of personality. . . . There's a Hot Springs side of Clinton. . . . Hot Springs is gambling and who knows what else." Schmidt says that meeting Clinton's mother, who lived outside of Hot Springs at the time of her death—she and Schmidt were on the same plane going to the Kentucky Derby—"I thought once you met her you knew there was a side of Clinton that had come from her. She was having a very good time. . . . It's a style that you get . . . in . . . resort communities with gambling and horse racing and a little bit of other things. . . . And Clinton obviously likes that."[23]

The twenty-first-century version of Hot Springs for Clinton and his friend Ron Burkle, says one woman, is "Vegas." She recalls a business meeting that was being arranged involving the Clinton Foundation and Burkle's Yucaipa Capital, and Clinton and Burkle themselves. The two men insisted that the group meet in Las Vegas. "He's still the son of a . . . mother [who] wore tube tops and went to Hot Springs to gamble; there's that part of him, very much," she says.[24] Betty Sheinbaum, who, with her husband, Stanley, was a Hollywood supporter of Bill Clinton's when he was still governor of Arkansas, also speaks contemptuously of Clinton's taste for Las Vegas, claiming that he and Burkle "spend a lot of time" there. When asked what's in Las Vegas, she answers, "Fun."[25]

As for other enablers, often mentioned is Vernon Jordan, former head of the National Urban League, now a partner at Lazard Frères, to whom Clinton remains extremely close.[26] It was Jordan, then a director of Revlon, who called Revlon chief Ronald Perelman and asked him to give Monica Lewinsky a job in New York as a way of getting her out of Washington.[27]

The biggest enabler of all, say many, is Hillary. When the subject of Bill's continued philandering was raised with Hillary, she responded, says one man who knows both Clintons well, "Screw 'em. If they want to go vote for a pro-life Republican, let 'em."[28]

Friends speculate that she likely cared very much about Bill's infidelities at the start of the marriage, but then she gave up, knew she could not control them, and just insisted he be discreet.

Both friends and foes talk about the Clinton marriage as a partnership. Don Hewitt calls them "a team."[29] The more cynical say it's a business deal. She helped him and put up with him despite the humiliation of Gennifer and Monica and likely many others whose names are not known to the public. But the deal is that now it's her turn and he is to behave himself—this doesn't mean that he can't have affairs; it does mean he can't have them with chatty twenty-one-year-old interns—and help her get elected president. Nothing he does between now and November 2008 is to distract from the image or viability of Hillary's candidacy.

"I think early on it was a situation where they were attracted to each other both physically and mentally," says one man who is a longtime friend and financial supporter of both Clintons, "and that they both felt that they could do great things together for the world. . . . He's looking at Hillary in her twenties and saying, 'Boy oh boy, she's brilliant and has a lot of skills and, boy, think of what we could do together.' . . . Then as time went on, she came to understand certain things about his lifestyle, but she came to the conclusion that most of their time together was wonderful. She loved him. She believed he loved her and couldn't stop himself, and this stuff kind of got excused along the way. As the years passed they kept . . . moving on this odyssey. . . . I think she . . . persuaded herself . . . this is a great skill that this man has; every woman loves him, . . . and unfortunately he is not able to turn it off. . . . And so I think she came to accept it over time."[30]

In his recent biography of Hillary, Carl Bernstein reports that two of her Rose Law Firm partners were hired to make certain that women with whom Clinton allegedly—they were named in a lawsuit—had flings while governor would be quiet. The Rose lawyers, Bernstein contends, managed to coax signed statements from the women denying they had had sex with Clinton. Bernstein alleges that Hillary attended one of the meetings at which the women were questioned.[31]

Not only was Bill Clinton unfaithful, he was insultingly indiscreet, but, at key times, Hillary still came to the rescue. At a certain point, she must have calculated that she had put too much time, sweat, and tears into the relationship to end it; that without it she would never reach her political goals, so she did what was necessary to keep him viable. The first time the public watched this dynamic was during the 1992 run for the nomination, when Gennifer Flowers, a receptionist at the Arkansas Unemployment Appeals Board and a part-time nightclub singer, produced audiotapes of telephone conversations to back up charges that she and Bill Clinton had a twelve-year affair. Hillary went on *60 Minutes* then; she went on the *Today* show after the Monica Lewinsky scandal broke; she likely saved his 1992 campaign and made him president the first time and saved his presidency the second.

Don Hewitt got an inside look at the marriage, and at the vulnerabilities of both partners, on Super Bowl Sunday, January 26, 1992, in a room at Boston's Ritz-Carlton when Bill's campaign was imploding over the Gennifer Flowers allegations. For a segment to air on 60 Minutes, they were questioned by Steve Kroft, who, Hewitt later wrote, was unable to get any real answers. They "weaved and bobbed and ducked and left the ring, I thought, unbloodied."[32]

"That night in that hotel room," says Hewitt, "when I knew he was lying and she knew he was lying and he knew she was lying and I knew they were both lying, and yet that's the night they got the nomination, when she said, . . . 'I'm no Tammy Wynette standing by my man,' and somehow that resonated with the American public. I think that was the one line that came out of that thing that people remember the most."[33]

The Clintons' performance was so brilliant that instead of derailing the campaign as the Donna Rice episode did Gary Hart's—a photograph surfaced of the young model on Hart's lap aboard a yacht sailing off the island of Bimini and unfortunately named Monkey Business—they were able to survive and bask in Bill's second-place finish (behind New Englander Paul Tsongas) in New Hampshire, which he turned into a victory—he made second place the new first by declaring himself "The Comeback Kid."

Bill's real challenge that night, Hewitt later wrote, was not Kroft but Hillary after they left the hotel.

Oddly, Hillary seemed to channel her anger to Don Hewitt, the man who could be credited with rescuing Bill's political future, and hers, by giving them this important national forum. "I had gone to White House dinners going back as far as Dwight Eisenhower," Hewitt says, "and I was locked out of there and it was her and not him." In 1999, Hewitt accompanied his correspondents, Wallace, Safer, Bradley, Kroft, and Stahl, to discuss Bosnia with the president. "I said to [Clinton's press secretary] Mike McCurry, . . . 'I know why we're here . . . because she's out of town.' He said, 'You happen to be right.'"[34]

Hewitt recalls that Tim Russert, moderator of Meet the Press, "used to say to me all the time, 'What's the matter with her? You guys made him president. He got the nomination, the night he did that.'"[35]

Hewitt and Hillary "kissed and made up," he says, in July 2001 at the funeral of *Washington Post* owner Katharine Graham. Hewitt had just published a memoir. "She . . . came up to me said, 'Hey, congratulations on your book.' I said, 'Gee, that's awful nice of you to say that because I think I say some things in the book that aren't all that flattering. . . . But, you know something, I'm glad you're my senator.' And she threw her arms around me and said, 'Well, I'm glad you're my constituent.' From that day on the feud was over."[36]

Cynics might suggest that Hillary was shrewd enough, now that she was senator and contemplating a run for president, not to want to keep Don Hewitt an enemy. Could she have also figured that who knew what Bill-related scandal might break on her way back to the White House? Would they need another airing on *60 Minutes*?

THE WOMAN'S name repeatedly linked to the former president's is Belinda Stronach, a forty-one-year-old blonde—twenty years younger than Bill Clinton—twice divorced, mother of two, Canadian heiress and member of Parliament, representing a riding just north of Toronto. She was seen as an up-and-comer—on *Time* magazine's 100 most powerful people list—both in business and in politics.

In the *New York Times*' deconstruction of the Clinton marriage—including an analysis of how much time they spend together pre–presidential race*—Stronach was the only alleged paramour mentioned by name. "Several prominent New York Democrats, in interviews," Patrick Healy wrote, "volunteered that they became concerned last year over a tabloid photograph showing Mr. Clinton leaving B.L.T. Steak in Midtown Manhattan

*"Since the start of 2005, the Clintons have been together about 14 days a month on average. . . . Sometimes it is a full day of relaxing at home in Chappaqua; sometimes it is meeting up late at night. At their busiest, they saw each other on a single day, Valentine's Day, in February 2005—a month when each was traveling a great deal. . . . Out of the last 73 weekends, they spent 51 together."[38]

late one night after dining with a group that included Belinda Stronach, a Canadian politician. The two were among roughly a dozen people at a dinner, but it still was enough to fuel coverage in the gossip pages."[37]

Toronto Life mentioned it in a story headlined "Bubba's Got a Brand New Blonde."[39]

Some describe Stronach as a younger, prettier version of Hillary; others, such as Eric Reguly, a business reporter for the *Globe and Mail* in Toronto, as a younger version of Martha Stewart.[40]

Don Martin, a *National Post* and *Calgary Herald* columnist, and Stronach's biographer, described her, in an interview in December 2006, as five foot eight with a "hard body," a "workout fiend" who's up every morning at five. "She has the proverbial buns of steel and the big breasts. Some say artificially big. . . . For forty years old, she's still a 10."[41]

"She's not the kind you'd want to ask for her favorite muffin recipe," Martin said. "She tends to ooze sexuality and when she puts her mind on a guy I have a feeling he's pretty much going to be taken over and smitten by her." She has, he added, "a pretty vigorous sex appetite; I think in some way she likes to command men and control them."[42] In Martin's biography he quoted her as saying that sex is "great. Better than golf. . . . What better thing is there? Let's face it. I don't sit at home and knit on Friday nights."[43]

She was not known for her brains.[44] One writer called her "Canada's own version of Paris Hilton."[45] A high-profile businessman with Canadian roots who counts himself a friend of Stronach's father says of her, "I never heard her give a public speech that I thought indicated that she had any intelligence. I'm told that while she's not a world beater, she's adequately bright. I've never seen any evidence of it."[46]

Don Martin is more generous, but the bottom line is about the same: "Belinda's got a very strong compassionate streak. She wants to help the hungry and the starving in Africa." But, he added, if you sat down with her and tried to talk about history or political philosophy, you'd "probably draw a blank." She had less than a year of university before dropping out.[47]

She was certainly no intellectual soul mate for Bill Clinton. "I watched Clinton give a speech here a couple of months ago," says Martin. "You just watch the guy talk off the cuff and you go, What does he see in Belinda? This is a guy who could call any intellectual powerhouse in the world and yet he seems to fixate on our billionairist babe. . . . He's going on about the genome and all these other things. We're sitting there going, Huh?"[48]

"Billionairist" and "babe"—and perhaps a fleet of private planes—could have been enough to explain the attraction.

In 2001, at age thirty-five, she became CEO of her father's auto parts empire, Magna International.[49] Frank Stronach, an Austrian tool-and-die maker who came to Canada in 1954 at the age of twenty-two, is a multibillionaire. His empire, according to the *Globe and Mail*, includes much more than auto parts—he has a "Magna air force of executive jets at his disposal; 800 race horses stabled in Ontario, Florida and Kentucky; racetracks from Aqueduct to Woodbine, and all the assets that his massive paycheques—usually the largest in Canada—have enabled him to amass."[50]

The Canadian heiress and the former American president met at her family's compound in Aurora in 2002. At the time, she was married to former Norwegian speed skater Johann Olav Koss. Frank Stronach was hosting a charity golf tournament to inaugurate his private golf course on the corporate land in Aurora. "He wanted Clinton there," says Don Martin, "so I know that the presidential library donation was dangled as the carrot to get him there." Martin says that Frank Stronach told him that "Clinton was pushing hard to get a bigger contribution for the presidential library. . . . They gave a million dollars. . . . And I think Frank thought that was enough for his purposes."

Martin explains "his purposes" as: "Frank loves to be a man who can call up presidents and former presidents and leaders of foreign countries, and he has the business clout to be able to do that."

According to Martin, who interviewed Belinda Stronach for the biography, "She talks in very eloquent and glowing terms about [Clinton] and she seems to basically be enraptured by the fact that he's a man of great intellect and doing a lot of humanitarian work."[51]

"Just connect the dots," says the Canadian newspaper columnist, "and consider the probabilities and possibilities and you've got to think that this is something more than an intellectual connection. . . . But every time you bring up the speculation on other aspects, she clams up and says nothing happens, we're just friends."[52]

Martin had arranged to interview one of her security guards, but the guard seemed to be "gagged . . . days before I was going to interview him and . . . it's not like the woman had a cocaine habit or something. . . . So the only thing I could wonder is if this guy knew more about [their relationship]."[53]

He recalls a tribute to Belinda Stronach on a night when Clinton was in China, "and in the middle of the night . . . [Clinton] found the motivation to pick up the phone and call directly in to the tribute and send greetings. I'm not sure he does that for many people." Another time, she mentioned to Martin, as if in passing, that she had been in New York the weekend before and saw the president.[54]

She went to Clinton's first CGI in September 2005, but she did not go in 2006. Don Martin claims that she did not go because "Hillary didn't want her there."[55]

Stronach has also seen Bill Clinton in Los Angeles. One Hollywood wife who is an active political fund-raiser remembers meeting Belinda in Steve Bing's private box when the Rolling Stones played for global warming activist Laurie David's Natural Resources Defense Council. Bill Clinton was also there. After the concert, this woman says, they all went back to Ron Burkle's house.[56]

"She was in the audience when Clinton went to do *Larry King Live*," says Don Martin, "and after that they went out and had dinner."[57]

Eric Reguly, who has written about Belinda Stronach but never interviewed her, alleges that "Bill Clinton was very much a part of her life." Reguly reasons that she was "safe for him. She's not married; she's very discreet." He adds that he assumes that "anything that happens happens at thirty thousand feet." He also surmises that it would not be difficult for them to find "hideaways" because "the Stronach family has resorts and hotels and cottages all over the place and golf courses. There are probably fifty places around the world they could meet and no one would know about it."[58]

The same Hollywood fund-raiser wonders if Belinda's biggest attraction to Bill is the private plane. "I was just trying to figure it out, is it a plane thing?" She decides that it probably is.[59]

Belinda Stronach has recently returned to the family company, but she received much press, some of it smirking, for leaving Magna International and her $9.1 million salary in January 2004 to run for a Tory seat in Parliament.

Don Martin says that Stronach saw Bill Clinton as "a mentor," but accepts her denial that she consulted with Clinton on her improbable political career. "She was asked that question at a news conference," says Martin, "and she said no and I tend to believe her." It all happened so fast that she had time to consult only with the people who live and breathe Canadian politics.[60]

She created headlines, many angry, in May 2005, when she "crossed the floor," moving from the Tories to the Liberals, after only eleven months as a Tory. By doing so, she temporarily propped up Liberal Paul Martin's government, helping to delay an election the Conservatives were likely to lose until a time a few months later when they could win. Don Martin calls her the "Liberal godmother of today's Conservative government."[61]

Belinda then became a powerless backbencher, and, at the time, Martin describes her as "Sit[ting] on the opposition benches and ask[ing] questions about the status of women."[62]

She became something of joke. "Sellout Barbie" was one new name.[63]

Her betrayal of the Conservatives ended her relationship with Peter MacKay, who would later become foreign minister in Stephen Harper's Tory government. One politician joked that "the only Conservative bone Ms. Stronach had in her body was that of her former boyfriend, Peter MacKay."[64]

"She took a lot of heat for crossing the floor," says Eric Reguly, "because it was considered opportunistic and sleazy." Her constituents voted for a Conservative and ended up with a Liberal. "That was distasteful."[65]

By May 2007, the Canadian press had pronounced the alleged affair over: "They looked hot a year ago, with the charisma of power, but Belinda has since quit Canadian politics to return to the family firm selling car parts to Detroit," and is involved "with a 'tough guy' from the Maple Leafs ice hockey team."[66]

The next month, the Canadian press reported that Stronach had breast cancer and had had a mastectomy and reconstruction.[67]

Before the news of her illness surfaced, Eric Reguly had also pronounced the supposed affair with Clinton likely over. He noted that while she was "rich and attractive," she was no longer "rich, attractive and politically ambitious. One third of the three crucial elements has just disappeared. And maybe Bill is going, 'Well, I could find rich and beautiful anywhere.'" Reguly argues that one of Belinda's attractions to Bill was that she "potentially was the next prime minister of Canada. . . . His girlfriend is prime minister; his wife is president. Where do I go this weekend for a little fun—Ottawa or Washington, D.C.?"[68]

The answer would almost certainly have been Ottawa.

Closer to home, rumors persisted about a married woman, a neighbor in a woodsy, hilly village north of Chappaqua.[69] The tabloids identified her as another Canadian heiress. The two reportedly met at a Christmas party thrown by an investment banker, according to an item in Canada's *Globe and Mail*, which dubbed Clinton "America's First Flirt."[70] One friend of the woman's now ex-husband confirms the story, although she says she has no idea whether Clinton was the cause for the breakup of the couple's marriage.[71]

Mark Updegrove, who has written a book on postpresidencies, describes Clinton's reckless side. "I think he feels entitled to a certain extent." He mentions a conversation that Clinton has had with people in which he ruminates about the tradition of southern governors keeping mistresses and that was just the way it was and nobody investigated it or worried about it.[72]

"Of course Clinton's still screwing around," says a Democrat who has worked diligently for him and mixed often with him socially. "He's never paid a price for his transgressions. . . . I think he's running around like crazy. . . . There are a lot of people who were angry at him then who aren't angry anymore. . . . I would say that in his heart of hearts when he puts his head on the pillow at night, he probably has a little wry smile and says to himself, 'You know, considering everything, I kind of got off okay.' "[73]

To some extent when they were in the White House—but definitely now—Bill and Hillary led separate lives. "They're rarely side by side," says one prominent journalist. Even when they are at the same event, "they're rarely together."[74]

Vartan Gregorian, a fan of both Clintons, says that this separateness is by design. "What you have there is his trying to give . . . room to her. . . . I think he created room for her in Washington and even New York City by moving to Harlem. . . . The two of them are never together in places." He describes a recent event, a dinner at the Four Seasons in New York for the twentieth anniversary of Harvard's Joan Shorenstein Center on the Press, Politics and Public Policy: "Hillary left as the president was coming in."[75]

Hillary did not respond to invitations to attend the Hofstra conference on her husband's presidency. Eric Schmertz, who directed the conference, seems somewhat sensitive on the subject, saying first that she was not invited but, when pressed, saying, "I'd rather put it another way. Of course she was invited, but we received no reply from her office to the invitation." He says the assistants to the president of the university also followed up on the invitation but "she neither responded nor came."[76]

"I was actually at Hillary's house for an event recently," says Mark Thomann. As usual, the former president was not there.[77]

In December 2000, Hillary had settled on the six-bedroom, seven-and-one-half-bath house, built in 1951, in a cul-de-sac in Washington's fashionable Embassy Row. At first she was going to rent but decided to buy—$2.85 million, down from the $3.5 million asking price—after she received the $8 million advance for her memoir. Sandy Berger's wife, Susan, a Washington Realtor, helped Hillary find the neo-Georgian, which has a formal garden, a terrace, a pool, and an elevator, and so did Kathy Sloan, the New York agent who found them their Chappaqua house.[78]

Her mother, Dorothy Rodham, eighty-seven, moved in with her in the fall of 2006. (While campaigning for president in Iowa in December 2007, in an apparent attempt to warm up her image, Hillary brought her mother along and certainly exaggerated—lied, really—when she told potential voters that her mother "lives with Bill and me.")[79] Hillary holds political strategy meetings there, and, according to Jeff Gerth and Don Van Natta in their recent biography of her, "visitors are asked to check their bags, cameras and cell phones at the door, pictures are taken by an authorized photographer."[80]

Hillary supporter Melvin Gitler describes going to the senator's home in Washington for a dinner. Bill Clinton was not there. "Very seldom do they come together to events. He's very overpowering," Gitler says, and in the room of twenty-five at that dinner, had he attended, she would have been diminished.[81]

Before Hillary announced her run for the White House, when the former president came to Washington, it was what Chris Jennings called a quick "pit stop," and he didn't do too many of those. He didn't want to be "a big distraction," Jennings added. When the Clintons got together, it was generally in Chappaqua.[82]

"I have to believe that he is smart enough to make sure that there is no more bimbo gossip," says Don Hewitt of 60 Minutes, "because if Hillary has to put up with that, in addition to putting up with a Republican challenger to her candidacy, that's the kiss of death."[83]

"I hear and everyone hears," says another top Democrat, "rumors that they live separate lives and that the president has friends. It could blow up in her face."[84]

One close friend of both Clintons says that at the point Hillary concludes that his lack of discipline is going to torpedo her chance to be the country's first woman president, that's when she divorces him. Hillary will not put up with him ruining her opportunity.[85]

This same man, shortly after the Lewinsky scandal broke, overheard Hillary's end of a midnight telephone conversation with Bill. "They talked forever that night on the phone." Her words and her tone were "adoring," he says. Inadvertently hearing that conversation "kind of told me that it became acceptable, but it would be unacceptable if it interfered with her great vision of her personal political future."[86]

David Schulte, who knew both Clintons at Yale Law School, assesses Hillary as the embodiment of ambition. "Look how she stayed with this guy no matter what. . . . If Hillary had divorced Bill, would we be talking about her as a candidate? I think not. We might not be talking about her as a senator. . . . She put up with even this final indignity for her own ambitions."[87]

In a column that appeared while Bill Clinton was campaigning in Iowa with Hillary over the Fourth of July weekend in 2007, trying to boost her numbers in the state with the first caucus, Maureen Dowd posited an imaginary conversation between the two. Hillary reminded Bill, "You promised me two terms after your two terms, and I'm not going to get that if you're caught Burkling or Binging."[88] A month later, *New York* magazine reported that the former president "ventured to Paris with playboy pals Ron Burkle and Steve Bing."[89] By the fall of 2007 one national magazine was rumored to be readying a story on Clinton's "mistress."

Others maintain that the Clintons will stay together until one of them dies. A television network executive who knows both well says, "My gut tells me that if she didn't divorce him before, she's not going to divorce him now."[90]

"Nobody who's close to them thinks she's going to divorce him," says Jonathan Alter. "That sort of reminds me of this line from Billy Graham's wife: 'Divorce, never; murder, maybe.' "[91]

And then there are the friends who insist that this is a real love affair—tested, yes; stressed, yes; but genuine. One woman who knows them well and was a guest at the White House during Bill's presidency (pre-Monica, she specifies) says that people, knowing her relationship with the Clintons, would say, " 'Oh, it's got to be a deal; it's like an arrangement.' . . . My impression is that on a certain level . . . she is mad about him, . . . and he couldn't do it without her. They were joined at the hip. . . . People would say, 'She's going to divorce him.' I said, 'No way, you're crazy.' I don't see how they could not be together."[92]

The panoply of affairs from Gennifer to Monica made some women pity her, says former DNC chief Don Fowler, and some "took umbrage at her because she stayed there and took it. Why should she stay with a dog like that? I think she loved him."[93]

Susie Tompkins Buell threw a fund-raiser for Hillary in September 2000 in an old theater in New York. The entertainment was Elton John. Bill and Chelsea were there, along with Barbra Streisand, her husband, James Brolin, Mary Steenburgen, and her husband, Ted Danson. In order "to spread out the celebrities," says Mark Buell, Chelsea was at one table, Bill at another, and Hillary at a third. "When Elton started to play, [Bill] came over and sat next to Hillary and I was at that table and underneath the table, they're holding hands, not for public view, just the two of them, and Chelsea came over and sat on her father's lap. . . . Forget about the psychology of horsing around that went on in his life; they have an enormously close connection and it's really a very tender one."

Buell speculates that growing up, Bill Clinton was lonely. "I think that he has always suffered from being the smartest kid in the class and that's a lonely life." He suggests that one of the reasons that Bill is so bonded to Hillary is that "she's one of the smartest people as well and that they can communicate on a certain level."

When Buell plays golf with Bill Clinton in San Francisco at the Olympic Club, Hillary sometimes calls, and, says Buell, he'll step aside to talk to her. "Every conversation ends with 'I love you, too.'"

Six weeks after Bill Clinton's surgery, Buell saw the former president and Hillary and Chelsea together. "They were standing together the three of them and I realized that they are a very tight-knit little group and that this really scared them. They could have lost him."[94]

People were so fascinated by the Clintons' marriage, says Jake Siewert, that he was often asked, What is it really like? "I've been around my parents for forty years," he would answer, "and I don't really understand their relationship. I've spent a hell of a lot more time with them than I have with President Clinton and Hillary, so don't ask me to explain their relationship. . . . They get along like any married couple. They talked to each other; they talked past each other. . . . There are plenty of times when, at least in our presence, they acted like any . . . couple that had been married for a long time. They have an awful lot in common . . . and there's some real affection between them."[95]

Chapter 10

HILLARY'S (AND BILL'S) RUN FOR THE WHITE HOUSE

AT A WASHINGTON RECEPTION ON JANUARY 4, 2007, after Hillary was sworn in for a second term as senator, the public abuzz with the probability that she would run for the Democratic nomination for president, Hillary was the in-demand half of the couple. A long line of people waited to see her and a short line waited to see her husband. Simon Rosenberg had never seen that before. "It was easy for me to get up to talk to him. I couldn't get near her. I hope he's going to get used to that. . . . He was clearly an afterthought in that room."[1]

IN THE summer of 2006, Bill Clinton was romancing a couple whom he would soon start soliciting for financial support for CGI. The wife asked: "Is Hillary going to run in 2008?" "No," the former president answered, "because she can't win. . . . Do you realize that 51 percent of the people in this country who vote are women? Women don't want Hillary. So I doubt if she's going to run." But he added, "She'd love to be the majority leader in the Senate."

The former president has been heard to say that he doesn't think the country is ready to elect a woman president, and that the first woman to reach that office will likely be a Margaret Thatcher type (i.e., a Republican).[2]

Clinton had also been heard to say that Harold Ford Jr. and Barack Obama "are the two guys with the juice to go all the way some time in the future." In late 2006 and even in very early 2007, Hillary's advisers did not see Obama as a threat. Bill Clinton knew better and advised them to attack Obama before he reached iconic status. They dismissed his advice, for the time being anyway.[3]

PEOPLE CLOSE to the Clintons were not surprised when Hillary announced in January 2007 that she was "in to win." Whatever Bill Clinton's reservations, she wanted to run and he owed it to her to help. "He feels like she made a lot of sacrifices throughout her career for him," says Chris Jennings, "and . . . I could never conceive of him saying, 'Hillary don't run.' "[4]

Out of fear or guilt, Bill Clinton has delivered on his debt to Hillary before, sometimes to the detriment of his presidency. Payback soon after he took office was giving her national health-care reform to run, even when he knew that health care was better handled incrementally, not in the blunderbuss fashion Hillary advocated. She got what she wanted because she held the moral high ground—think Gennifer Flowers et al—and he had to accede to her demands.

In his recent book, former senator and presidential candidate Bill Bradley, who was one of those whom Hillary threatened to "demonize" if he did not support her plan, describes Bill Clinton's tenure in the White House as a "lost opportunity," and he argues that the administration's health-care initiative failed because "Hillary Clinton's political skills were not well honed" and "mistakes of conception, consultation, pace, and strategy" were made.[5]

Bill paid his debt to Hillary again when he acceded to her demand that he appoint a woman as attorney general no matter what. When it turned out that the first two picks, Zoe Baird and Kimba Woods, hadn't paid taxes on their nannies' salaries, Hillary continued to insist on a woman and that's how the unmarried, childless Janet Reno got the job. Some said it was Reno's mishandling of the special prosecutor that resulted in Ken Starr and impeachment.

Once Hillary was in the race, Bill Clinton embraced it wholeheartedly and, as is typical, the race became as much about him as about her. It was his chance to redeem his legacy, to show that running on the Bill Clinton record is a winning strategy—take that, Al Gore!—to prove that he is so loved by the American people that they'll vote for Hillary just to keep Bill in public life and, best of all, to return him to the White House.[6]

At first, she seemed determined to keep her distance from Bill. In the carefully calibrated lead-up to her announcement, when Hillary appeared on *Today*, ostensibly to promote a new edition of *It Takes a Village*, anchor Meredith Vieira kept pushing her to admit that she was set to run. Hillary talked about how important her family was but never mentioned Bill by name, dropping in Chelsea's name twice.[7]

One had the sense that if she could have reverted to being Hillary Rodham she would have. But it was too late for that, and when she announced, she became—oddly for the first woman to be a serious candidate for the presidency—simply "Hillary!" Her website is "Hillary for President."

Through the winter of 2007, the Clintons made a conscious decision not to share the same stage. "I mean unfortunately, as good a speaker, sincere, and wonderful as Hillary Clinton is," says one man who has volunteered for both Clintons since 1992, "someone once said when you look at a 150-watt bulb right in your face, it looks really bright; put it next to the sun, it doesn't look so bright anymore."[8]

They wanted to avoid any repeat of the Coretta Scott King funeral in February 2006, when Bill Clinton left his wife, not yet announced but planning to, in his shadow. His euphoric, pulsating eulogy compared with her stiff, off-key effort became the headline.[9] "This is Bill Clinton in his element," says historian Douglas Brinkley. "He's essentially mastered the African American church pulpit. . . . And that was her at her kind of puritanical worst. . . . Nobody does a better job at catching the cadence and the rhythms of the southern black experience than Bill Clinton."[10]

His natural warmth seemed to capture just about everyone. The Reverend Robert H. Schuller, senior pastor and founder of the Crystal Cathedral in Garden Grove, California, and host of *The Hour of Power* television program, gave the benediction. As the other former presidents came onstage they shook the clergyman's hand—all except Bill Clinton. "He opened his arms and gave me a big hug with his cheek against my cheek and tears in his eyes."[11]

At that service for Mrs. King, Bill Clinton's moral lapses seemed inconsequential. The Reverend Schuller's embrace of Clinton showed how far the former president had moved beyond Monica. Schuller had denounced Clinton publicly in 1998 for "open[ing] a gaping breach of trust with his family and with the nation. . . . We all share part of the shame for . . . high public approval ratings that have enabled President Clinton so far to avoid confronting the problem of his sexual behavior."[12]

Once Hillary was in the race, Bill Clinton was dispatched for solo appearances in which he would sing Hillary's praises, especially as Barack Obama seemed increasingly to be stealing her thunder and Bill's supporters. The former president was attending every fund-raiser for Hillary he could squeeze into his packed speaking schedule; he was deconstructing Obama's position on Iraq and lecturing potential donors that Obama did not deserve to be the progressives' pet, that there's next to no difference between Obama's views on the Iraq War and Hillary's. (She voted in 2002 to authorize military action in Iraq. Obama, then a state senator in Illinois, with no legislative authority on the war, issued a strong antiwar statement.)[13] Mark Buell was at an event starring Bill Clinton at which someone "made a comment about Hillary and her position on the war and implied [something] negative about her. He just jumped all over the person."[14]

Obama was then the man of the hour, and the idea of the first African American president took on a romance that the first woman president, especially one who had grown so stale in the public imagination, did not.

The edict against Bill and Hillary sharing the same stage was soon relaxed.

When both Hillary and Obama were scheduled to preach on March 4, 2007, in African American churches in Selma to mark the forty-second anniversary of "Bloody Sunday," Hillary's strategists decided they needed Bill. They worried about their candidate having to ply her trade in the proximity of Barack Obama.

Hillary's people announced that Bill Clinton would attend with her. The plan had been for Hillary to accept on Bill's behalf the honor of his induction into the Voting Rights Hall of Fame. The change in plans would have the former president accept his honor at the foot of the Edmund Pettus Bridge where, in 1965, mounted state troopers attacked marchers with bullwhips, billy clubs, and tear gas.

That morning, Hillary and Obama preached in black churches on the same street, three blocks apart—her speech at Selma's First Baptist Church came off as condescending and phony; his at Brown Chapel AME Church came off strong and genuine—although later fact-checking of his pitch-perfect stem-winder discovered the exaggeration in his saying that Selma is what brought his parents together to produce him. (He was born four years before Selma.)

Bill Clinton told friends that he had worked with Hillary on her speech until one that morning. Not only did her tone deafness overwhelm the message, but the content even came into question. Syndicated columnist Robert Novak, a conservative, let her have it. "She claimed to have been inspired by being taken by the youth minister to hear [Martin Luther King] speak in Chicago in 1963, a time when she was an active [Barry] 'Goldwater Girl.'" Her hero, Barry Goldwater, was opposed to the 1964 Voting Rights Act—"one of only six Republican senators who joined southern Democratic segregationists opposing the historic Voting Rights Act of 1964 inspired by King."[15]

The Chicago suburban girl, her accent as flat as the terrain of her home city, had slipped into a weird southern cadence dropping her g's. Months later she explained to a group of African American columnists, "I lived all those years in Arkansas, and, you know, I'm in this interracial marriage."[16]

After the church services, Obama was to cross the infamous bridge and, by decree of Hillary's staffers, the Clintons were to cross arm in arm, but the reenactment march was delayed. "A crowd swarmed around Mr. Clinton, who smiled and hugged his admirers, a few of whom were even wearing Obama buttons," reported the *New York Times*. Earlier Clinton had jumped out of his car to greet crowds gathered across from the church in which Obama was speaking.[17]

Although other appearances on Hillary's behalf did not get as dramatic as the one in Selma, Bill Clinton dropped her name into the public airways whenever he could. In May 2007, delivering a joint commencement speech with former president Bush at the University of New Hampshire, he thanked the university's first female president: "Madame President Newman, that has a nice ring to it. . . . I've decided women should run everything; George and I can spend more time playing golf."[18] Once he found a good line, he didn't mind recycling it. Speaking to the NAACP in South Carolina around the same time, he said the same thing, minus the reference to "George."[19]

And Hillary returned the favor, dropping his name in front of the right kind of audience (i.e., African Americans whom she was trying to pry away from Obama).[20] At a candidates' forum in Nevada, she said, instead of answering the question put to her, "And, you know, I believe Bill Clinton was a good president. I'm very proud of the record of his two terms."[21] When she made her first foray to New Hampshire in February 2007, the same weekend Obama announced that he was running, a *New York Times* reporter counted "at least eight times" when she brought up Bill's name."[22]

Still, early in 2007, Hillary was losing some support to Obama. In Chicago, for example, where both senators had strong ties, Obama seemed the favorite. Abandoning a long tradition of not involving himself in primaries, Chicago mayor Richard Daley endorsed Obama. And the mayor's brother, Bill Clinton's friend and cabinet secretary Bill Daley, did likewise.[23] David Schulte, the Clintons' friend from law school days, signed on with Obama. Schulte was recruited by Chicagoan Lou Manilow, another Bill Clinton backer.[24] Lou Susman and trial lawyer Bob Clifford also declared their support for Obama.[25]

Months before Clifford embraced Obama, his mixed feelings about Bill Clinton were evident in an interview. He said he was "turned off" by Clinton's behavior with Lewinsky. "I felt . . . disappointment in the fact that here's a man who we made extraordinary efforts to help elect and he's now shifted the whole debate away from the things that matter most to the whole marital indiscretion. . . . I was always bothered by just the whole vision of the president of the United States having inappropriate sexual . . . activity in the White House." There's no doubt, he concludes, that Clinton's behavior put Bush in the White House.[26]

And in Hollywood, Obama was at least temporarily definitely the "it boy." David Geffen's remarks, in a February 2007 interview with Maureen Dowd, in which he described Obama as "inspirational" and Hillary as "overproduced and overscripted," not to mention a liar, got things rolling: "Everybody in politics lies, but they [Bill and Hillary] do it with such ease, it's troubling."[27] (That was the same interview in which he said, "I don't think anybody believes that in the last six years, all of a sudden Bill Clinton has become a different person.")[28]

The *Wall Street Journal* reported the new Hollywood "catchphrase": "Don't tell Mama, I'm with Obama."[29] A phone interview with Irena Medavoy is interrupted by another call: "That was John Emerson about Obama coming out on Friday. We're very, very excited. He's our star. . . . Barack is black, how revolutionary is that?"[30]

Obama was the next new thing as Bill Clinton had been in an earlier election cycle. Darius Anderson, once a close aide to Ron Burkle, puts it in perspective. "The Hollywood crowd is about the flavor of the week and that's how they run. They loved Clinton. He was interesting, . . . he was fresh; he was exciting. It's the same thing as Barack is. The problem is, if you sit down . . . and ask them ten minutes of questions . . . they don't know anything about him."[31]

Bill Clinton was not happy when everyone from former senator Tom Daschle—who was so close to Bill Clinton that he was one of the people Clinton called during the darkest days of impeachment—to Ted Sorensen to George Clooney, started to compare Obama to Jack and/or Bobby Kennedy and to go public with their Obama endorsements.[32]

And there was something about Obama that made him seem an irresistible alternative to the Clintons. On *The Tonight Show* in December 2006, Jay Leno asked Obama, who admitted in his memoir to having smoked marijuana while in high school: "Did you inhale?" "That was the point," Obama answered.[33]

Determined not to let Obama grab the nomination from Hillary, Bill Clinton pursued the smallest lead in a manner one might expect of a first-time candidate for the state legislature. Melvin Gitler, owner of a sports bar in New Jersey and, as Gitler puts it, "into real estate in Arizona and Louisiana," first communicated with Bill Clinton—with the help of his neighbor Congressman Jerrold Nadler—when he was assigned by his daughter's public school, P.S. 199 on the Upper West Side of New York, to find some "interesting gifts" for the PTA's auction. To Gitler's surprise, the former president called him to tell him that an auction item was on its way. A signed photocopy of a Clinton speech arrived with an invitation to have a "photo opportunity" with the president in his Harlem office.

Gitler next received a call from someone at "Friends of Hillary," asking for his help raising money for her Senate reelection campaign. "I have a big customer base; it was easy to hit up my customers." Gitler's wife is the daughter of Herbert Fisher, the founder of Jamesway, the now defunct chain of discount department stores. Soon Gitler was invited to events, including an invitation to Hillary's house in Washington.

Hillary was to appear at an event at a house in suburban New York. Gitler and his wife were met at the door by the host and hostess who explained that the senator could not make it—she was held up in Washington—so she sent her "B Team." They moved away from the door, "and guess who's standing there?—Bill Clinton."

"I know the senator quite well already," says Gitler. "In fact, I'm going to have cocktails with her this evening." Gitler is now building houses in Louisiana in areas devastated by Katrina and has talked to Bill Clinton at various cocktail parties and fund-raisers about the false, "sugarcoated" view of the devastation. "So all of a sudden you'll get the access"—a meeting in Harlem with Clinton's people. Soon Gitler is licensed to build tract homes in Louisiana.[34]

FIGURING OUT how to use Bill Clinton was tricky. "He has the ability to destabilize the campaign," says New Democratic Network president Simon Rosenberg, who worried that Clinton's presence could "overshadow and downgrade" the other staffers who, out of his shadow, would naturally assume positions of authority and expertise.[35]

Don Fowler calls Bill Clinton "certainly an icon and approaching a god. . . . There is a danger that he could overstep and appear to be casting a shadow over her."[36]

Pollster Peter Hart recalls a conference at which both Bill and Hillary appeared. Bill spoke one night, Hillary the next. When she spoke he was seated in the front row. "She answered one question in a way that he thought was incorrect and he called the moderator down . . . and said, 'I think my wife's got the formulation wrong. Why don't you call on me and I'll clarify it?'" The moderator declined to do so.[37]

Hillary, Leon Panetta predicted, would not repeat Gore's mistake of running away from the accomplishments of the Clinton/Gore terms. And, added Panetta, she would also anoint her husband as strategist in chief, even though he would carry no title. "She knows that she's got probably one of the best political advisers in the business, and she'll make use of him."[38]

"She respects his political sagacity more than her own," said former pollster/adviser Dick Morris.[39] Even someone as cool to the Clintons as Paul Greenberg saw Bill's assets: "If Miss Hillary is as wise and practical as I think she's become, she will listen very closely to his political advice, . . . use him very strategically like a bishop on the board."[40]

THE DOWNSIDE for Hillary was if people wondered who would actually be president. That, some said, was a bigger problem for her than any or all of Clinton's sexual indiscretions. What role would he play in her administration? Would he be her top adviser? And if so, would he really be the president? "If there's a feeling that he's an undue force on her politically and on her decision making," said Tony Coelho, "she'll never get elected president. And I think that's true of a man with an overly forceful woman."[41]

For every Hank Sheinkopf, who saw an enormous plus in Bill Clinton's presence because "when he shows up he reminds people of the way things were when he was president,"[42] there was another pundit who saw the downside. The *Nation*'s Bill Greider calls Bill "a big handicap for Hillary's ambitions. The notion we would have to listen to more of him if she got elected."[43]

Still, when Hillary's fund-raising for two quarters looked anemic compared with that of her rookie rival, Barack Obama, Hillary called a meeting in Chappaqua, with Bill in attendance, to discuss how to respond. Obama had raised more, had more donors, and had raised more on the Internet. In a rare misstep, Bill Clinton had described the deadline for the first quarter of fund-raising as "the first primary of the 2008 race."[44]

Added to that was a national poll in late June 2007 that found 52 percent of Americans saying they wouldn't consider voting for Hillary for president if she captured the Democratic nomination.[45]

That was enough. Hillary's handlers asked Bill to campaign with her.

The first outing, over the Fourth of July weekend 2007, was in Iowa, where Bill Clinton enjoyed huge popularity, and where Hillary was then trailing in the polls for the Iowa caucuses behind John Edwards. Bill's marching orders were to hold Hillary's hand as they walked, exude his warmth and charm along the parade routes, tell voters why Hillary should be the nominee and, come November 2008, the president.

Her campaign staffers had to fine-tune the act as they went. At a rally in Des Moines, Bill introduced Hillary and then retired to a stool onstage while she spoke. He didn't have the Nancy Reagan total-adoration act down and appeared on the verge of drifting off into deep boredom or light sleep.

Both their performances got mixed reviews. Hillary's speech was

boring. In Davenport, Iowa, Bill criticized George W. Bush for com-
muting the sentence of Scooter Libby, which left an opening for a
comeback and Bush's then press secretary, Tony Snow, took it—and
managed to change the subject to Clinton's pardon of Marc Rich: "I
don't know what Arkansan is for chutzpah, but this is a gigantic case
of it."[46]

The Clintons' next outing was to the equally important state of New
Hampshire where Bill earned the name "Comeback Kid" for his second-
place finish after the seemingly devastating stories about his draft record
and his affair with Gennifer Flowers. This time, on the football field at
Keene High School, the biggest cheers were for Bill. As the Clintons
made their way about the state, Bill was kept to ten minutes of introduction and relegated to the stool, perhaps seen as a better bet than a chair
on which the ever sleep-deprived sixty-year-old might do the unthinkable
and doze off. Clinton continued to struggle in New Hampshire as he had
in Iowa with the proper stool posture, sometimes slouching or resting his
head in his hand.[47]

Some of the Clintons' most loyal supporters thought Bill's performance
was an unalloyed advantage. "There'd be none of the dismay over two for
one that there was in '92," says Lynn Cutler, "this time it would just be a total
plus."[48] John Catsimatidis even evoked the name of Dick Cheney: "I think
that if Hillary ever became president, he . . . would be . . . as influential as
Cheney is to George Bush. . . . I think the chances for her to be elected get
amplified tremendously if people think he's going to be behind her."[49]

HE HAD once been the most powerful man in the world, but, as the
campaign proceeded, Bill Clinton embraced the grueling, groveling
work of lining up the all-important endorsements from state legislators
and congressmen and governors. In March 2007, *Newsweek* reported that
Clinton was on a private plane with Malcolm Smith, the Democratic
minority leader of New York's State Senate, who had, a few days before,
been publicly critical of Hillary's campaign. Hillary needed Smith to

help her capture the black vote in the New York primary. "During the two-hour trip, Smith was treated to a full course of Southern-fried charm, courtesy of Bubba himself." Two months later, Smith endorsed Hillary, explaining that the airplane ride with the president was one factor that influenced his decision. "You would get two [presidents] for one, and that's a good thing."[50]

In late May, Bill delivered to Hillary the endorsement of Los Angeles mayor Antonio R. Villaraigosa who was being courted by all the front-runners. Some bet that the influential Hispanic mayor would endorse the half-Hispanic Bill Richardson, but Bill Clinton bagged Villaraigosa. A couple of weeks before, Clinton, accompanied by Ron Burkle, wined and dined Villaraigosa at the Kobe Club, a steakhouse in Manhattan. The news of that endorsement was a tad tarnished when, while at the restaurant, they saw Rush Limbaugh, who, the next day on his radio show, recounted that while he talked to Villaraigosa, Clinton flirted with Limbaugh's date.[51]

In October 2007, African American Georgia congressman John Lewis, a heroic voice in the civil rights arena, gave Barack Obama some kind words and Hillary his endorsement. Obama's spokesman noted the congressman's "long relationship with Bill Clinton."[52]

If the biggest threat to Hillary's quest for the Democratic nomination seemed to be Barack Obama, then the first "black" president was, for a while at least, a huge help. He was dispatched to speak before African American and Hispanic groups. When he keynoted Jesse Jackson's Operation Push annual conference, before he did more than wave to the audience, he got a standing ovation. (Jesse Jackson is supporting Obama for the Democratic nomination; his son Yusef, Ron Burkle's business associate, is supporting Hillary.)[53]

According to a report in *New York* magazine, Bill Clinton called the Reverend Al Sharpton of Tawana Brawley infamy to build a bridge to an endorsement from Sharpton. Clinton's task would not be easy—Sharpton had his own presidential ambitions and was said to be threatened by Obama—so the former president had to think of anything he could to win the reverend's good feelings. He offered his condolences on the death of singer James Brown.[54] He also addressed Sharpton's group, the National Action Network, in New York.[55]

HILLARY BEGAN to surge in the polls, and conventional wisdom had it that she had the nomination sewn up. Still, the road to the nomination was full of potholes, among the deepest the constant allusions to her husband's infidelity, the cheap double entendres, the smirks that even her supporters could not suppress. In Davenport, Iowa, at a town hall meeting of about five hundred, a man asked Hillary, "Do you have what it takes to stand up to evil men like Osama Bin Laden and the dictators of North Korea and Iran?" She paraphrased and amplified the question for those in the audience who might not have heard it: "What in my background equips me to deal with evil and bad men?" The audience laughed out loud, very loud.

Several months later, when the editors of the *New York Times Magazine,* planning a baby-boomer issue, asked the world's most famous baby boomer to contribute to a crossword puzzle, it seemed a perfectly benign activity. Clinton was presented with a completed grid, all the answers filled in, and his job was to create the clues.[56] The baby-boomer-themed puzzle, "Clues by President Bill Clinton," proved good material for his enemies. Clinton's clue for 4 down, seven spaces, was an impolitic one: "It's nice to be on the receiving end of one." The first thought of some people was "blowjob" or "handjob." The answer is a word perhaps more on Clinton's mind these days: "endower."

"Can you imagine the challenge of creating an entrance into the White House so he could sneak in without being noticed?" asks David Schulte. "The Corps of Engineers is probably working on it already."[57]

And the jokes about cigars and putting the former president in charge of the intern program droned on, because, unlike every other former president in history, Bill Clinton had a wife who was running for president. "A lot of people don't want to go back to the Clinton era, don't want to go back to opening up stories about their marriage," says Douglas Brinkley. "People are . . . sick of it and bored and annoyed."[58]

In August 2007, Michelle Obama, in Iowa, introduced her husband: "Our view is that if you can't run your own house, you certainly can't run the White House." Mrs. Obama claimed that she was not referring to Hillary.[59]

STILL, BY the fall of 2007, Hillary had begun to look stronger as some of Obama's magic fizzled.[60] The untested candidate—Obama walked into his U.S. Senate seat without a scratch, because the candidacies of his primary and general election opponents imploded—seemed incapable of punching back.

In late September 2007, on the last day of Bill Clinton's CGI, he gave an interview to Al Hunt for Bloomberg Television's *Political Capital.* Clinton described Obama's experience as about equal to his in 1988 when he decided not to run for president because "I really didn't think I knew enough, and had served enough and done enough to run." People who know Bill Clinton know that inexperience had nothing to do with his decision. He probably considered himself ready to run for president at about the time he graduated from law school. He decided not to run in 1988 because of problems in his marriage and the possibility of a bimbo erupting before he and Hillary were sufficiently primed to shove the bimbo back in her box.

That same weekend Bill Clinton gave interviews to Tim Russert on *Meet the Press* and George Stephanopoulos on *This Week.* Neither interviewer challenged his assertion.

Chris Matthews, host of MSNBC's *Hardball,* speculated in November 2007 that Bill Clinton might be deliberately trying to derail his wife's campaign. Matthews pointed to a speech the former president gave in which he suggested that when her male opponents seized on Hillary's inept performance in a debate—she came off as calculating the political impact of every answer instead of saying what she thought—they were stooping to the level of critics of Al Gore in 2000 who said the vice president was too stiff, or to critics of John Kerry in 2004 who questioned the decorated veteran's war record. Clinton said, in effect, that these men

CLINTON IN EXILE

were "Swift-Boating" his wife. Hillary's campaign advisers disassociated her from her husband's remarks. Matthews blurted out without a trace of doubt that what lost Al Gore the race in 2000 was Bill Clinton.

Again in Iowa, later that month, he gave a 50-minute speech that AP reporter Ron Fournier described as "long-winded, misleading and self-absorbed." The former president larded his speech with "I"—mentioning where he bought coffee that morning, where he ate breakfast, seeming to forget to bring Hillary into the folksy talk—and used his time onstage to polish and even misrepresent his legacy. In a state in which Hillary's vote in 2002 for the Senate resolution authorizing President Bush to go to war against Iraq loses her votes, her husband boasted of having opposed the war from the start; a claim quickly questioned by her opponents. One might have thought he was stumping for Obama, who did oppose the war from the start.

When Bill blasted Obama on PBS's *Charlie Rose Show* in December 2007, he sounded more like a pit bull than a former president. Rose mentioned twice that Clinton's aides had asked his producers to stop the interview. Were they afraid he was hurting Hillary? Or himself?

That same month, Oprah Winfrey drew record crowds for Obama in Iowa, New Hampshire, and South Carolina. The following Monday Bill Clinton hit the hustings in Iowa for a panicked Hillary. "I thought she was the most gifted person of our generation," he rhapsodized. But given the pain and humiliation he caused her, his comments did not ring true. Was a return to the White House more about him than her?

His campaign lines grew to sound almost desperate as Obama eradicated Hillary's lead in early primary states. Campaigning in New Hampshire in late December on the heels of the assassination of former Pakistani prime minister Benazir Bhutto, the former president argued that the future of the world in an age of terrorism and global warming—"whether our grandchildren will even be here fifty years from now"—depended on Hillary winning the nomination.

The first contest—the Iowa caucuses on January 3, 2008—ended dreadfully for the Clintons. Not only did Obama beat Hillary by nine points, John Edwards also beat her, narrowly, but nonetheless relegated

Hillary to third place. Some of Hillary's supporters blamed Bill, for hogging the limelight, for straying off message in weird, sometimes dishonest asides and angry outbursts, for reminding voters that Hillary was not the candidate of change—a mantle then monopolized by Obama—but rather the candidate of the fractious, scandal-scarred 1990s.

Bill's golden rock star glow turned gray. At Hillary's Iowa concession speech he bit his nails as he surveyed the crowd. Although he stood beside Hillary, she never acknowledged him. An AP report described him as a "relic" and pundits noted that while Obama rode a wave of adulation from young people, the faces surrounding Hillary as she conceded were old—Bill's, Madeleine Albright's, General Wesley Clark's.

The day after Iowa and five days before the New Hampshire primary, Bill Clinton addressed a rally at the University of New Hampshire. Writing in the *New York Times*, Mark Leibovich described only "polite applause" as the former president entered and "rows of empty seats." Leibovich acknowledged that the university was on winter break, but then described a rally the next day at a two-thirds empty high school gymnasium.

The Clintons stayed true to their roller-coaster, death-defying style when Hillary, against all media expectations and polls—several of which showed Obama winning by as many as thirteen points—eked out a win in New Hampshire. Although Bill had seemed at his finger-wagging, crimson-faced worst in his bitter attacks on Obama, he was credited by some with helping Hillary pull off a comeback in New Hampshire, a resurrection even more impressive than his own in 1992. Still, Hillary's advisers weren't completely persuaded, and he was off camera during her victory speech.

On to the next contests in Nevada and South Carolina: Bill's putdown of Obama's anti-Iraq war claims as "the biggest fairy tale" offended African Americans and risked that an important South Carolinian, House Majority Whip Jim Clyburn, would break his pledge to remain neutral and endorse Obama. (He didn't, but advised Bill Clinton "to chill a little bit.") A key Clinton supporter pointed out that African Americans had saved Clinton's presidency in the wake of Monica Lewinsky. CNN's Jack Cafferty characterized Bill Clinton's claim, "I did not have sex with that woman, Ms. Lewinsky," as the biggest fairy tale of all. The atmosphere grew so toxic that the former president found it necessary to call in to Al Sharpton's radio show to explain what he meant. (Sharpton would later counsel Clinton to "shut up.") The Reverend Jeremiah Wright, the pastor of Obama's Chicago church, preached that contrary to conventional wisdom, Bill Clinton was "good" for the African American community. "He did the same thing to us that he did to Monica Lewinsky."

Campaigning in Nevada, Bill claimed that he had personally witnessed members of the Culinary Workers Union, which had endorsed Obama, engaging in suppression of voters supporting his wife. Again, Hillary beat expectations and won the Nevada caucus.

Prominent Democrats fretted that Bill Clinton was splitting the party by introducing race into his wife's battle with Obama. Ted Kennedy and Rahm Emanuel advised Clinton to curb his Obama bashing. Jonathan Alter wrote that Kennedy was so offended by Clinton's tactics that he was flirting with endorsing Obama. Former Senate Majority Leader Tom Daschle denounced Clinton's tactics as "not in keeping with the image of a former president" and warned that they could "destroy the party." Senate Judiciary Chairman Patrick J. Leahy endorsed Obama and slammed the former president's "glib cheap shots" as "beneath the dignity of a former president." John Kerry called Clinton's criticisms of Obama an "abuse of the truth" and also endorsed Obama. Later, Chris Dodd, one of the senators whom Bill Clinton called for comfort during the endless nights of impeachment, also endorsed Obama.

On ABC's *Good Morning America* on January 21, Martin Luther King Day, Obama complained that he felt like he was running against both Clintons. The former president "has taken his advocacy on behalf of his wife to a level that I think is pretty troubling. He continues to make statements that are not supported by the facts."

Obama's senior adviser, David Axelrod, who had worked for Bill Clinton, accused the Clintons of employing "a good cop, bad cop" routine in which Bill "slashe[s] and burn[s]" Obama, and Hillary "stays positive." Axelrod described the former president's behavior as "crass" and "disappointing," and urged him to stop "truncat[ing] quotes to make your case."

Bill Clinton was unmoved by the senators and newspaper editorialists

who warned that by playing the ugliest kind of racial politics he was di-
minishing his stature as a world statesman. He paid no attention when
Dick Harpootlian, the former chairman of the South Carolina Democratic Party, compared him to the late Lee Atwater, an infamous Republican dirty trickster.

When the former president came out swinging, when he boiled over with
indignation, waxed disingenuously, and waved that famous index finger, his
wife won two primaries in a row. He believed that his strategy worked, and
so, apparently, did Hillary. Aides to Obama, including one who had worked
for Bill Clinton, raised the possibility that Hillary and her people simply
could not control Bill, and if they could not control him during the campaign, how would they ever control him should she make it to the Oval Office. ABC's George Stephanopoulos, who knew Bill Clinton at his smartest
and most unhinged, said that Hillary had signed on to Bill's approach. If she
hadn't, she would have ordered him to stop and he would have.

Bill Clinton had rehabilitated his reputation many times; most impres-
sively in those early years out of the White House. He figured he would
do so again, this time from 1600 Pennsylvania Avenue in the historic
role as husband of the president.

In the days before the South Carolina primary on January 26, with
Obama widely perceived as the likely winner on the strength of the large
African American vote, Hillary tended to the big states holding primaries
on Super Tuesday, February 5, while Bill and Chelsea remained in South
Carolina, Bill hitting every rally and rope line he could find. If Obama
won, so what? She didn't campaign much there in the final days, while
Obama devoted himself to the state. The Clintons' sub rosa message was:
Obama was the black candidate.

Bill continued to misrepresent Obama's statements. His musing that
Ronald Reagan was a "transformative figure" who managed to attract
conservative Democrats became Obama arguing that Reagan had better
ideas than the Democrats. Fearing that he had gone too far, the former
president let loose a whopper: "I like this election because I haven't had
to be against anybody. I like these people who are running."

He continued to talk too much about how wonderful a president he was, forgetting to mention Hillary, and seeming to be running for a third term. Hillary might have rolled her eyes at his excesses, but she understood, and polls—such as one showing 44 percent of Democrats naming Bill as the reason they would be more likely to support Hillary—supported her belief that significant numbers of primary voters would check her name on the ballot, but they really wanted Bill back.

Both Clintons left South Carolina as the polls closed—Hillary to campaign in Tennessee and Bill in Missouri—because they knew Obama was going to win in a landslide. He captured 55 percent of the vote to 27 for Hillary, and also won a respectable chunk, 24 percent, of the white vote, far exceeding pollsters' predictions.

Analysis of the South Carolina race from exit polling showed that Bill's manic, mean campaigning had hurt Hillary. Six in ten voters cited him as important in their voting decision, but more of them voted for Obama (48 percent) than for Hillary (37 percent). Among those who made up their minds in the final three days, 51 percent went for Obama; only 21 percent for Hillary.

Obama won four of every five black voters in South Carolina; and did particularly well among the black women whom Hillary had courted. The polls there had not yet closed when Bill stuck another knife into Obama, reminding reporters, without being asked—the question on the table was what does it say about Obama that it took two Clintons to try to beat him—that Jesse Jackson won South Carolina in 1984 and 1988. Bill's point was clear: Jackson did not go on to win the nomination and neither would Obama. Further, both Jackson and Obama are black and 53 percent of the state's voters are black, so what did anyone expect? Rep. James Clyburn said he "recoiled" from Bill Clinton's remark. At his victory celebration, Obama warned, "We are up against the idea that it's acceptable to say anything and do anything to win an election."

Two days after South Carolina, in a packed rally at American University in Washington, Ted Kennedy endorsed Obama, comparing him to John Kennedy, and promising that Obama would end "the old politics of race against race . . ." The Massachusetts senator had taken a telephone call from Bill himself, pleading with him to stay neutral. Instead Kennedy seconded his niece, JFK's daughter, Caroline, who, the day before, had endorsed Obama, whom, she wrote, reminded her of her father. She applauded his "dignified and honest campaign." Ted Kennedy was less polite, praising Obama for having the character not to "demonize" people who hold different views—a verb familiar to anyone who watched Hillary's nasty campaign for universal health care in 1993. He openly mocked the Clintons when he described Obama as ready to be president on "day one," a Bill and Hillary staple.

Next came Ethel Kennedy's Obama endorsement. She explained that he reminded her of her late husband, Bobby. JFK speechwriter Ted Sorensen also entered the arena, taking credit in an interview on ABC News for the trend of comparing Obama to JFK. He called Bill Clinton "a great communicator," but added, "The one sentence best remembered is, 'I did not have sexual relations with that woman.'"

Next, Nobel laureate Toni Morrison rebuked the man she had dubbed "the first black president" and endorsed Obama.

Bill Clinton called Jimmy Carter, presumably to head off the possibility that he too would endorse Obama. According to *Wall Street Journal* reporter Douglas Blackmon, the former president said he did not plan to make a formal endorsement, but sang the praises of Obama, and noted that all but one of the members of his extended family were supporting Obama, whom, Carter added, they found "titillating."

Hillary promised that her husband would keep up the wonderful work he was doing, but her advisers hinted that Bill would dial down the intensity and resume a more conventional role as "supportive spouse." He hop scotched among the Super Tuesday states—fifteen primaries, seven caucuses, 1,681 Democratic delegates at stake, 52 percent of the total of 2,025 needed to win the nomination—and for the most part he adhered to scripted speeches, but not always. "We just have to slow down our economy" to fight global warming, he said in a speech in Denver, "'cause we have to save the planet for our grandchildren." He was still prone to speaking off the top of his head, especially if he could hit someone who had betrayed him. He denounced George W. Bush's "No Child Left Behind" law, mentioning Ted Kennedy as a key supporter and adding that

Kennedy and other legislators who backed it obviously did not bother to talk to teachers. NBC's Tim Russert pointed out that among the bill's backers was Senator Hillary Clinton. "Passing this landmark legislation," she said in 2001, "sends a clear message that all American children deserve a world class education."

Bill was no longer the crowd magnet; Obama was. (Michelle Obama and Chelsea Clinton also sometimes attracted bigger audiences.) The former president's speech at the University of Denver basketball stadium was sparsely attended. Earlier in the day Obama spoke in the same stadium and required overflow spaces to contain the crowd.

The Super Tuesday states had smaller black populations and larger Latino ones. Hillary, who won two-thirds of the Latino vote in Nevada, had an edge because, historically, Latinos are reluctant to vote for African Americans. Some Democrats worried that the Clintons—whose advisers reportedly refer to the Latino vote as Hillary's "firewall"—were capable of unleashing a variation on their South Carolina race baiting: pitting Latinos against blacks.

On Super Bowl Sunday, two days before Super Tuesday, Bill Clinton toured four African American churches in Los Angeles, presumably to mend fences that he damaged by his remarks in South Carolina. His reception was polite but muted. A *Washington Post*–ABC News poll found that 50 percent of Americans would be comfortable with Bill back in the White House, down ten points from September.

The former president arranged to watch the Super Bowl with Bill Richardson in the governor's mansion in Santa Fe. Richardson had dropped out of the race for the nomination, but his endorsement was sought by both Obama and Hillary. The next morning, Richardson told reporters that the two old friends had fun watching the game—they smoked cigars and ate heart unhealthy foods—but he was not ready to endorse.

Bill returned to California where he served as Hillary's Super Tuesday "closer," while she campaigned on the other coast and appeared in New York on CBS's *Late Show with David Letterman*. Asked how she'd control Bill, she joked, "In my White House, we'll know who wears the pant suits."

Super Tuesday was a let down for the Clinton camp. They had expected to claim the nomination that night and instead ended in a draw with Obama, each winning just over 7.3 million votes and roughly splitting the delegates. In the two weeks preceding Super Tuesday, polls showed Hillary trouncing Obama.

While each campaign spinned itself as the Super Tuesday winner, Obama's claim seemed stronger. For months, Hillary had been designated the inevitable nominee. When Katie Couric asked Hillary how disappointed she would be if she was not the nominee. "Well, it will be me," Clinton replied. Hillary's campaign chairman, Terry McAuliffe, had been quoted as saying in January, "This thing will be over by February fifth."

Hillary won eight states, including California, pocketing seven in ten Latino votes there—exit polls showed Hillary taking two-thirds of the Latino vote across sixteen states—while Obama won eight of ten African American voters. She also took New York and New Jersey and her "home" state of Arkansas and neighboring Tennessee, also Arizona and Oklahoma and Massachusetts. (In late January, Clinton had led there by thirty points; she ended up winning by about half that.) Obama took thirteen states—including his home state of Illinois (by twice the margin that Hillary took her current "home" state of New York)—and the bellwether state of Missouri.

Obama won Georgia, and carried the black vote by about eight to one. Bill Clinton had campaigned there for Hillary, and she had the support of Bill's friend Andrew Young. The former Atlanta mayor and United Nations ambassador did Hillary no favors when he suggested that "Bill is every bit as black as Barack. He's probably gone with more black women than Barack."

Into the next week, New Mexico was still counting, and Bill Clinton was reportedly seething at Bill Richardson for not having the guts to actually endorse when it mattered. The AP's Ron Fournier reported that Richardson declined to endorse her even after an angry call from the former president, who had appointed Richardson UN secretary and energy secretary: "Isn't two cabinet posts enough?" Richardson's spokesman denied that exchange ever occurred. (Hillary eventually won the state by two thousand votes.)

Obama and Billary—the media's shorthand for the Clintons—pivoted to a primary the next weekend in Louisiana, where African Americans accounted for nearly half of those voting; caucuses in Nebraska and Washington state; and a caucus the next day, Sunday, February 10, in Maine. Hillary campaigned in Washington state and in Maine, leaving Louisiana and Nebraska to Bill and Chelsea.

Obama won every contest, and by huge margins, roughly two-thirds of the vote in Washington state and Nebraska. In Louisiana, 90 percent of black voters who cited race as a factor in the campaign, voted for Obama. On Sunday, Obama won the Maine caucus. Hillary had campaigned hard there and so had Bill and Chelsea. Obama's 59 to 40 percent victory was a shocker because the state's demographics seemed to favor her— white, working class, and support from the state's governor.

To add to the pain of that Sunday, Obama won a Grammy Award for the best spoken word album for the audio book version of his bestseller, *The Audacity of Hope*. He bested Bill Clinton, whose *Giving* had also been nominated.

Of the states in the Potomac primary on February 12—Maryland, the District of Columbia, and Virginia—Hillary considered Virginia to be her best shot: it had the smallest population of African Americans of the three, less than 20 percent. She campaigned there on her own, and Bill campaigned there for her as well. Former Virginia governor L. Douglas Wilder— Virginia was the first state in America to elect an African American governor—endorsed Obama, and said that he had less respect for the former president because of his offensive remarks during earlier primaries. "A time comes and a time goes," Wilder, currently mayor of Richmond, said. "The president has had his time."

Still attempting to make amends with the African American community, Bill campaigned in Maryland at an African America church in Prince George's County and at the Temple of Praise in Southeast Washington. A *Washington Post* reporter described the latter service, usually "filled with singing and clapping," as "subdued." Referring to the uproar over his comments in South Carolina, Bill Clinton insisted, "I didn't say anything negative about Senator Obama."

Obama scored triple landslides—64 to 35 percent in Virginia (this time Bill knew better than to mention that Jesse Jackson had won the Virginia primary in 1988); 60 to 37 in Maryland; and 75 to 24 in Washington, D.C.

Obama won close to 90 percent of the black vote in both Virginia and Maryland, and exit polls showed Obama winning, in Virginia and Maryland, almost 60 percent of female Democrats. Two-thirds of men in both states chose Obama, and Latinos chose Obama over Clinton by six points. Clinton won in Virginia and Maryland among white women, but her margin of victory among that group was significantly smaller than it had been on Super Tuesday. In Virginia and Maryland, Obama even carried the demographic that had previously gone heavily to Clinton, those earning less than $50,000 a year—by twenty-six points in Virginia and twenty-four in Maryland.

Wisconsin and Hawaii voted a week later on February 19. Obama had the advantage in Hawaii, where he was born and reared. In Wisconsin, with its small African American and large working-class population, Hillary would have seemed to have had the edge. Playing the expectations game, she ceded it to Obama, but not really. She campaigned there hoping for an upset, and so did her husband and daughter.

Obama won decisively, 58 to 41 percent. He did better among white men, voters who did not go to college, blue-collar workers, union members, and older voters. Hillary maintained her advantage among older white women, especially those over 60, but again that cohort was shrinking. NAFTA, Bill Clinton's trade agreement with Canada and Mexico that he pushed through Congress in 1993, helped Obama. Seventy percent of Wisconsin Democrats said it cost them their state jobs.

With his win in Hawaii, Obama could claim that Hillary hadn't won a contest since Super Tuesday, while he won ten straight. He had a lead of 154 in pledged delegates.

Bill Clinton intensified his lobbying of super delegates—the 796 elected and party officials, 20 percent of the votes at the convention, who are free to vote for whomever they like, not bound to their states' caucus or primary results—to cast their votes with Hillary. He called in favors extended over decades, jobs and appointments dispensed, campaign appearances made. (Chelsea had her own call list.) The system, exclusive to the Democrats, was created in 1982 to boost the influence of party insiders and deflate the influence of party activists. Super delegates decided the nomination in 1984, when the upstart Gary Hart was battling party warhorse Walter Mondale. (Clinton was then ahead in the super delegate race 238 to 173, but that changed by the hour as Obama added super delegates and Hillary lost them.)

The AP's Ron Fournier predicted that super delegates would abandon the Clintons if they perceived Obama as winning. Members of this elite group, Fournier wrote, "are not all super fans of the Clintons"—some are angry over loss of jobs from NAFTA; some haven't forgiven Clinton for welfare reform; some for the failed health care reform; some for the resulting loss of Congress in 1994; some for the Monica Lewinsky scandal; some for Gore's loss of the presidency in 2000; and some for George W. Bush's two terms.

Georgia congressman John Lewis, who had noted that his district had gone three to one for Obama, and that Obama reminded him of Bobby Kennedy, formally switched his super delegate status from Clinton to Obama. Al Gore was rumored to be staying neutral so he could be an honest broker should the Hillary/Barack battle go all the way to the convention. Two days after Obama's Wisconsin win, a 21-year-old super delegate, a junior at Marquette University in Milwaukee, announced that he was going with Obama. He had been courted by Chelsea, who had taken him to breakfast. He received phone calls from Bill Clinton and Madeleine Albright urging him to go with Hillary.

Speculation persisted that Obama could come to the convention in Denver in August with more delegates, but Hillary could win the nomination by capturing more of the super delegates. And if Bill Clinton helped her capture them, by whatever smoke-filled-room tactics necessary, she would, in the end, owe him her presidency. Sending a message at odds with his wife's vow "to go the distance," Bill told a rally in Beaumont, Texas, that if Hillary won Texas and Ohio, which had primaries on March 4, she would win the nomination. "If you don't deliver for her, I don't think she can be. It's all on you."

Hillary seemed to step on her advantage in Texas, which is 36 percent Hispanic, when she ousted as her campaign manager, Patti Solis Doyle, daughter of Mexican immigrants and the only Hispanic to ever manage a presidential campaign, and replaced her with an old Clinton hand, African American Maggie Williams. Mary Mitchell, an African American columnist for the *Chicago Sun-Times*, quoted New York State senator Ruben Diaz as saying that Solis Doyle was made a scapegoat for Hillary's losses, and that if any of Hillary's top advisers should have been fired, it should have been Bill, who "has made statements that were embarrassing, and he is the one that caused his wife to lose."

The former president continued to serve as the celebrity for cocktail party fund-raisers. For as little as $1,000, supporters could buy a seat at the table with Bill. But would they even want one? *Wall Street Journal* columnist Peggy Noonan described him as having lost his "political acumen," having become a "flat-footed . . . oaf lurching from local radio interview to finger-pointing lecture. Where did the golden gut go?"

Campaigning in eastern Texas, Bill revealed his irritation with the huge crowds that Obama attracted. Although he seconded his wife's declaration that being president was more about finding solutions than giving a good speech, he added, "I've been told I give a pretty good speech." As evidence, he boasted that more than a million people heard him speak in Africa, and more than one hundred thousand heard him speak at the Brandenburg Gate in Berlin.

During a debate with Obama in Austin, Texas, on February 21, Hillary reduced her husband, who was not in attendance, to a laugh line. Asked to describe how she had handled a crisis in her life, she spoke of "crises . . . and . . . challenging moments," and watching her it was clear that she was referring to Monica Lewinsky and impeachment. The line provoked friendly laugher and applause, but it came at her husband's expense. Other than that, she never mentioned him.[61]

IT'S THE general election, stupid!

Should Hillary win the nomination, could she win the general election? At the center of the argument that she can't win the general election is Bill Clinton.

Hillary Clinton has argued that she is the best bet to run against a Republican in November 2008 because she has been "fully vetted," investigated so relentlessly that nothing could possibly turn up to harm her in the general election. The comment raises eyebrows and guffaws because not only is there likely more to uncover about Hillary, but she's married to Bill, whose post–White House activities constitute a Pandora's box.

"I think they're going to kill her," says one woman with close ties to the former president, expressing a fear common among Democrats that Hillary would lose to the Republican nominee, John McCain. They predict that the Republican opposition researchers are developing a dossier of Bill Clinton's postpresidential sexual dalliances that will derail her campaign. "They probably have video," this woman says.[62]

Elaine Kamarck says she has no doubt that the Republicans will dredge up some kind of personal scandal. As to what the former president is actually doing, she says, "Nobody knows; everybody worries."[63]

If Hillary thought the 1992 campaign was humiliating and demoralizing, says Larry Sabato, she hasn't seen anything yet. "My feeling is that nothing will remain private this time. Lots of things were kept out of the press in '92 for various reasons, a lot of it a desire by the press for change after twelve years of Republican administrations. They really did try to give Clinton the benefit of the doubt. I remember myself arguing that his private life should be left alone. . . . I had no clue what he had really done and how many times he'd done it. . . . This time we all have a clue, and it's going to be very different and I just don't think they have an understanding of what they're facing. They think they do but they really don't."

Sabato also says that Hillary should forget about getting the kind of sympathy afforded her after Lewinsky. By now, Sabato says, "I think people realize this is . . . a neurotic relationship and I'm trying to be kind. . . . It cannot possibly be based on the normal marital romantic love. What it's based on is anybody's guess. Many have suggested power. . . . Remember, if she's elected, he moves back into the White House, with less to do. What does that say to most people? I don't know what he's going to do, but my guess is he's not going to be inactive."

For the Democrats, Sabato argues, this is a minefield. "They could very quickly get saddled with her as a nominee and then have to go through all of this Clinton mess all over again for months."[64] Jim Hornstein, a liberal Los Angeles lawyer, calls Hillary "the Republicans' best hope. . . . She'd take California in the primary and in the general election, but I don't think she'll take a single state in the South, and I think she will do a lot worse than Al Gore did the last time around."[65]

Lou Susman, who ran John Kerry's finance operation in 2004, says that the standard line is that Hillary is the best fund-raiser for Republicans. "I know people in Lake Forest [Illinois] that literally will give $2,000 to the Republican nominee and if it's Hillary they'll go out and raise $20,000."[66]

Others think that no matter how much Bill Clinton has been philandering, it will no longer hurt Hillary. "Voters have pretty much discounted it," says Michael Barone. "That's the behavior they expect of him. . . . It's what they say in the financial community—it's built into the price."[67]

Clinton supporter Ray Lesniak argues the scandals won't matter and uses a George W. Bush bit of bluster: "Bring it on!" "The guy was impeached and he had close to 70 percent approval rating when he was impeached. I think their position is . . . 'Gone through it, didn't even scratch us on the surface.'"[68]

Others speculate that the sixty-one-year-old Bill Clinton will be calmer this time just because his age and health require it. The former editorial writer for the *Arkansas Democrat-Gazette*, Kane Webb, says, "He's an old man with two heart operations, right? Surely he's just going to be hobbling through."[69]

And if Americans no longer care about Bill Clinton's sex life, there's always his financial/business/philanthropic life to make headlines.

On January 31, 2008—that night, with John Edwards having just left the race, Hillary and Obama would debate head-to-head for the first time—the *New York Times* ran a front-pager on Frank Giustra, another massively wealthy FOB, an outsized contributor to Bill's causes, and owner of a lavish private jet on which Bill Clinton has traveled the world.

In early September 2005, Clinton accompanied Giustra—a Canadian of Italian roots, son of a nickel miner—on his MD-87, the size of a commercial airliner, complete with a stateroom, to Almaty, Kazakhstan. Giustra's purpose was to make a deal to mine the country's deposits of uranium, a material necessary to fuel nuclear reactors. On arrival, according to *Times* reporters Jo Becker and Don Van Natta, Giustra and Clinton partook of a "sumptuous midnight banquet" with the country's president, Nursultan A. Nazarbayev. Clinton heaped praise on him for "opening up the social and political life of your country." With those words, according to the reporters, Clinton "undercut both American foreign policy and sharp criticism of Kazakhstan's poor human rights record" by none other than Senator Hillary Clinton. She had previously cosigned a letter to the State Department noting that Kazakhstan under Nazarbayev had "serious corruption," including canceled elections. (In December 2005, Nazarbayev won reelection with 91 percent of the vote, allegedly achieved by "intimidation" and "ballot-box stuffing," and suppression of the news media.)

Two days later, according to the *Times*, Giustra, a novice in uranium mining, shocked the industry by signing a deal worth "tens of millions of dollars." In the months following, Giustra gave Clinton $31.3 million for his foundation, on top of $100 million that Giustra had already given, along with a promise of half his future earnings from "natural resource business ventures."

When questioned about the uranium deal, Clinton's spokesman said the former president had "no discussion of the deal with President Nazarbayev, but others disputed that, implying that Giustra's friendship with Clinton was a factor in winning him the deal. Bill Clinton later invited Nazarbayev to attend CGI.

In 2006, Giustra "co-produced" a sixtieth birthday party in Toronto for Clinton. The event, which raised $21 million (Canadian) for the Clinton Foundation to fight AIDS in Africa, featured stars such as Billy Crystal, Kevin Spacey, James Taylor, and Jon Bon Jovi. (A movie buff, Giustra founded and later sold Lions Gate Entertainment, a film production company in Santa Monica.)

In February 2007, Giustra reportedly arranged for the chief of the

Kazakhstan-owned uranium agency to meet with Clinton in Chappaqua. Giustra was present at the meeting. According to the *Times* reporters, both Clinton and Giustra initially denied such a meeting had occurred. Giustra later acknowledged it. The Kazakhstan official came away with the best evidence of all: a photo of him with the former president.

In a stinging editorial titled, "Clinton's Filthy Lucre," *Investor's Business Daily* called it "a bribery racket," claimed that the deal made Giustra a billionaire, and that the potential for President Hillary Clinton granting favors to her husband's donors raises "Marcos-like corruption and a sell-out of American interests on a scale unknown in the U.S." The paper also raised a subject that Bill Clinton hates almost as much as Monica—the Marc Rich pardon: a fat donation to the library followed by a pardon for a fugitive from American justice.

The Giustra relationship, like the relationship with Ron Burkle and Vinod Gupta and others, is surely a gift that would keep on giving to Hillary's general election opponent were she to win the nomination. Recognizing the danger that his tangled postpresidency poses to his and Hillary's return to the White House, Bill promised, should she be elected president, that he would release the names of all future donors to his library and his foundation, only heightening the suspicion that he is hiding something. Is there another Frank Giustra lurking in those donor rolls? He insisted that past donors should remain private, "unless there is some conflict of which I am aware, and there is not." Journalists certainly would not trust him to be the arbiter of what constitutes a conflict.

A look at the library donors—by law their identity and the amount given does not have to be disclosed; a bill to require disclosure passed the House but is stalled in the Senate—who ponied up in the final years of the Clinton administration shows, the *New York Times* reported, that some of them were seeking government policy changes, some were under investigation by the Justice Department, and some were enmeshed in campaign finance scandal. In addition, once Hillary started to run for the Senate and then the presidential nomination, she successfully tapped for her campaigns many of the same donors who had given to the Clinton Foundation and through it to the library.

Presidential foundations can accept as much as donors care to give, and donors can be anyone, including foreigners. They can contribute anonymously and the foundation does not have to disclose their identities. The *Times* discovered donations from the Saudi royal family, the ruler of Dubai, the governments of Kuwait and Qatar, and others.

And then there are the Clinton White House papers. If Hillary is the candidate of experience—she claims thirty-five years, which includes her time as first lady in both Little Rock and Washington—and if a key part of that experience touted by both Clintons is her service to the country and the world as first lady, then why is Bill Clinton refusing to sign off on the release of the White House papers that document that service?

The former president requested in 2002 that the National Archives withhold until 2012 White House papers that contain direct communications between him and Hillary. By law he's entitled, but should Hillary win the nomination, that decision will certainly be questioned by the Republicans, and speculation as to what's in those papers will not be limited only to the imagination of the most rabid Hillary haters. When asked by Tim Russert about release of the papers, Hillary demurred, "Well, that's not my decision to make." Obama had earlier infuriated Hillary and Bill by, in an interview with *Newsweek*'s Howard Fineman and Richard Wolffe, calling Hillary "disingenuous" for claiming that the release of those papers is up to her husband. "She can release these papers," Obama said.

A *Wall Street Journal* editorial headlined "Who Was Hillary Clinton" noted that when the Clinton library, partly supported by public funds, opened in 2004, Hillary promised, "Everything's going to be available." More than three years later, two million pages covering Hillary's days as first lady are still unavailable. The *Journal* speculated that the White House papers might even contain information on a possible role by Hillary in the Marc Rich pardon.

Hillary's campaign released a stunning piece of news on the day after Super Tuesday. She had loaned her campaign $5 million. She claimed that the funds were "my money"; her spokesman said the loan came from her "share of their joint resources," but the assumption was that the money was coming from Bill's postpresidential earnings. What precisely was the source of the money? Ron Burkle? Donors to the library? Donors to the foundation? Organizations and corporations that paid the former president fat speaking fees? What would these people expect in return?

Obama, who had released his tax returns, in addition to his Senate disclosure forms, called on her to do likewise. She refused, arguing that her Senate disclosure forms sufficed and that she would release her tax returns once she wins the nomination. She knew that the tax forms would reveal more about the source of her husband's income for consulting and advisory services to Ron Burkle and Vinod Gupta, for example, beyond the payment is "over $1,000" category that appears on her Senate disclosure forms. It would also give a picture to the American people of whether the Clintons—Bill has said often that he ought to pay more in taxes—employ loopholes or shelters to lower their tax bill.

On February 11, the day before the "Potomac Primary," Hillary Clinton gave an interview to a local television station and to *The Politico*. A reader of the latter asked Hillary if she could offer assurances that "no new business or personal scandal involving Bill Clinton" would erupt were she to be the nominee. She assured the questioner, "that is not going to happen," but added, "You know, none of us can predict the future . . . but I am very confident that that will not happen."

It took three days for another Bill-related story, characteristically complex, to break. On February 14, the *Wall Street Journal* headlined more news about Frank Giustra. According to reporters John Emshwiller and Jose De Cordoba, at the first CGI in 2005 an aide to Bill Clinton introduced Giustra to Colombian President Alvaro Uribe. In February 2007, Clinton and Uribe and Giustra met at Clinton's home in Chappaqua. In March, the three met in Colombia. In June, Giustra, Clinton, and Uribe attended a dinner party in New York. It coincided, the *Journal* reported, with "increasing criticism in Congress due to allegations that Colombian officials had been working with paramilitary death squads."

Giustra eventually profited handsomely from deals involving Colombian oil fields. President Uribe denied that Giustra received special treatment because of his ties to President Clinton.

Other news organizations began to look into this relationship and others.

A detailed story by Bloomberg News's Elliot Blair Smith ran thirteen days before the Texas and Ohio primaries and raised questions about whether the Clinton/Giustra relationship could affect the tax-exempt status of the Clinton Foundation. Smith quoted the executive director of the National Committee for Responsive Philanthropy: "If former President Clinton is making decisions about where to put the charitable efforts of the Clinton Foundation based even partly on where he's likely to benefit personally, or see his friends benefit, then that clearly is a classic conflict of interest."

A Freedom of Information request for FAA flights logs yielded information on where Giustra's plane went, but not on who was onboard. By matching the dates against Clinton's schedule, Smith reports that on the day Giustra hosted the sixtieth birthday party for Clinton in Toronto, his plane made a New York/Toronto round trip. "On May 20, 2007, Giustra's plane flew to Tromso, Norway, on the same day Clinton gave a speech there for which he was paid $290,000. He made five speeches over four days, with two more stops in Norway, one in Denmark and one in Sweden, netting a combined $1.485 million in personal income."

In February 2008, Hillary mounted an aggressive campaign against Obama in Ohio and Texas, after, in Obama's words, throwing "everything but the kitchen sink," at him, questioning his readiness to handle a 3 A.M. crisis and whether he meant it when he promised Ohio voters that he'd do something about NAFTA. Hillary also charged that an Obama adviser had pulled a "wink wink" by promising the Canadians that his anti-NAFTA talk was just posturing—she then pulled off a big win in Ohio and a narrow win in Texas on March 4, and vowed to take the fight to Pennsylvania on April 22. Bill, in addition to warning voters that if Hillary did not win both states she was finished—a brilliant ultimatum as it turned out—had campaigned tirelessly for her in Texas.

The Clintons had staged another stunning comeback. The lesson Obama's advisers took from Ohio and Texas was that he had to hit back hard and focus on tax returns, on donors to the Clinton library and foundation, on post–White House business deals; on the baggage that Bill Clinton dragged behind him.[70]

Chapter 11

FIRST GENT: A DOLLEY MADISON FOR THE TWENTY-FIRST CENTURY?

SHOULD HILLARY WIN THE NOMINATION, HOW WOULD Bill Clinton handle the traditional role of "first lady"?

One thing is certain: A woman as president and her husband, a former president, as first gentleman is, as Melanne Verveer puts it, "a brave new world."[1]

In a July 2007 interview on *Nightline,* Clinton said that he would keep an office in the East Wing, the traditional location of offices of the first lady—Hillary broke that tradition and insisted that hers be where the president and the power was, in the West Wing. He would also keep his office in Harlem.[2] (In subsequent interviews he seemed to backtrack a bit, saying he'd keep an office in whichever wing Hillary wanted him, or even in the White House basement.)[3]

People close to him politically—pollster Peter Hart, for example—say that Clinton would need an "exceptionally well-defined" issue or cause, in the sense that Lady Bird Johnson had wildflowers and Laura Bush has literacy. "Obviously it's her [Hillary's] presidency and the last thing that you would choose is to have his fingerprints all over the Oval Office," says Hart, adding that he doubts it would be a "groundbreaking" issue, such as national health care, because that would put him in a role akin to Hillary's in 1993.[4]

The work he would do from that East Wing office is most often described as a kind of ambassador without portfolio or "goodwill ambassador," which sounds a little like a UNICEF greeting card, or a more high-profile version of Karen Hughes's work for George W. Bush. Sarah Wilson describes the Clinton take on this role as roaming the world practicing "cultural diplomacy," with the goal "for people not to hate America."[5] Leon Panetta sees Clinton as a "very high-level ambassador . . . trying to repair some of the damage that has been done with our allies."[6]

On Labor Day 2007, campaigning with her husband in Iowa, Hillary promised, as Jackie Calmes reported in the *Wall Street Journal*, that Bill would be among the "distinguished Americans from both parties" whom she would send abroad immediately after her election to explain to the world her bipartisan foreign policy. She would charge Bill with telling people, "America is back." In his short but sweet introduction of his wife, the former president asked, "You want to restore America's standing in the world overnight? Elect Hillary Clinton."[7]

Friends say he would certainly serve as one, if not the most important, of Hillary's advisers, shaping policy at the top, what one political strategist calls "high politics and policy."[8] During Clinton's White House years, recalls Alan Solomont, there were "meetings in the residence every week on political strategy," which he assumes would happen in a Hillary White House. "He will not be absent from those meetings."[9] (Clinton told Barbara Walters in December 2007 that he would sit in on cabinet meetings, but "only if asked." He added that he thinks it "better for me to give her my advice privately most of the time.")

Others insist that Hillary would want him to deliver his advice long distance, out of the White House, out of the country, out of her way, and out of the news.[10]

But always engaged in good works and exploiting his network of contacts worldwide: "He would be capable of a considerable amount," says Bob Kerrey. "A United States president has to make those phone calls to the prime minister of Turkey: 'Will you let us put U.S. military forces in Turkey as a staging area for an invasion of Iraq?'" He also sees Bill Clinton being able to work magic on trade agreements and on Capitol Hill. "I would not want former president Clinton to come out and campaign for my opponent, so my guess is that [he] would be enormously helpful on the Hill to President Clinton."[11]

Clinton has implied that he would drop off the speaking circuit if his wife becomes president. He explains that he hopes to have saved enough not to have to work.[12] "I don't think they're people who are looking to amass a fortune," says Alan Solomont. "They don't need to amass a fortune; they have friends who have fortunes enough."[13]

"We'd get all those speeches for nothing," says Bob Kerrey happily.[14]

Most of the people close to him agree that Bill Clinton would continue to devote much of his time—he has quantified it as two to three days a week—to his foundation and the offshoot CGI.[15] "I think he would be smart enough to say that his work in his foundation is his priority," says Mark Buell.[16]

WITH THE exception of his initiative on childhood obesity, Clinton has focused his attentions abroad, and, says Tony Coelho, that would remain the case. "He would stay on the international stage and be very helpful to her. I think he'd be a counselor in effect but stay out of everything domestically." He could not be perceived as being the one who was really running the show.[17]

The key to his role as "First Gentleman," says Chris Jennings, is transparency. The American people must know exactly what he's doing and where he's doing it. There cannot be "an air of mystery or intrigue surrounding him." People would have to be comfortable that "he wasn't president from behind." Jennings argues that Bill Clinton "would be the first to say, 'I'm not president; I'm not copresident; I'm not vice president.'"[18] Appearing on David Letterman's show in September 2007, Clinton said that the Constitution would prohibit him from serving as Hillary's vice president: ". . . that's just not in the cards."[19]

But others, such as Howard Tullman, see the inevitability of Bill as "a partner in the process," indeed a kind of copresident. And that raises the question: in such an arrangement, the role of the vice president becomes something even less tempting than the "bucket of warm piss," as the office was described by John Nance Garner, FDR's vice president. "What would be left for the vice president to do if you had the first husband be a combination secretary of state/everything else?" asks Tullman. Campaigning in Iowa for Hillary in November 2007, Clinton received a standing ovation for a speech that made it sound like he would indeed be running things with Hillary: "We've got to restore the economy, deal with health care, deal with education," Clinton thundered. "Make this country a modern, vibrant, innovative, successful country again." Clinton closed, according to a report on Iowa Radio News, by warning that the ovation meant nothing if his wife didn't win the Iowa caucuses. A month later, campaigning in New Hampshire, the former president was fifteen minutes into an hour-long speech enumerating the challenges that will face the next president before he remembered to add, "Everything I'm saying here is my wife's position, not just mine."[20]

Biographer Carl S. Anthony, who writes about first ladies, sees the prospect of Clinton 42 and Clinton 44 setting up housekeeping at 1600 Pennsylvania Avenue as endlessly fascinating. "I can't imagine a more powerful couple in world history since William and Mary."[21] To Chicago attorney and political player Gery Chico, the unique aspect of this 42/44 White House would be that when the former president gets done advising the current president, instead of returning to his home and family, he "just walks upstairs to the residence," where he might tell her, "I need an appropriation of $10 billion to stand behind me in Africa."[22]

Once Hillary had decided, probably on the advice of her husband, that Bill Clinton was an asset, not an embarrassment to be sidelined, she began, sometimes without even being asked, to suggest roles Bill might play in a Hillary White House.

At the fund-raiser at Ron Burkle's mansion in March 2007—which yielded her campaign $2.6 million—she pronounced him "probably the most popular person in the world."[23] At another event she boasted that her husband's feel for international policy and relations was "a lot better than what we've recently seen."[24]

When Bill Clinton boosters began to ask her at campaign stops if she would name him secretary of state, she cited an antinepotism law passed after John Kennedy named his brother Robert attorney general that, she explained, would preclude family members of presidents from serving in the cabinet or on the West Wing staff. (The law, passed in 1967, also prohibits appointment as an ambassador.) She touted him instead as "an ambassador around the world dealing with problems." (Barack Obama promised, according to the *Chicago Tribune*, that, if elected, he would offer Bill Clinton a cabinet position "in a second.")[25]

The most intriguing role for Bill Clinton, suggested often by his admirers, is Mideast envoy, one who could actually get the process moving again.[26]

"If Bush was a bigger man," says Jonathan Alter, "he would appoint Clinton to go to Syria and start working on this stuff." He'll never do it, Alter says, because his presidency is too often a "built-in reaction to Clinton. . . . Anything Clinton did was wrong and he'd do the opposite. It's moronic." If asked, Alter says, Clinton would "do it in a heartbeat."

Shortly after Clinton left the White House, Alter saw him at the Manhattan restaurant Le Cirque, and they started to talk about the Middle East. After a while they repaired to the bar and "he talked and talked and talked about the Middle East. I said, 'Why doesn't Bush send you over there and get it straightened out?' and he just said he'd love it, but Bush would never do it."[27]

As much as Sandy Berger thinks Bill Clinton would have been the man for the job during the George W. Bush years, he understands why Bush never asked. "It's very tricky when you ask a president to be your envoy. Jimmy Carter did some things for us and you have less control over a former president who is acting as an envoy than you do over someone else."[28] A Hillary Clinton administration would be another story.

People close to Bill Clinton have also suggested in the years since he left the White House that he could fill two specific positions: secretary-general of the United Nations and president of the World Bank.

Clinton has never jumped at the suggestion that he head the United Nations, but he has also never dismissed it—even though it was easily dismissible; in the UN's history there has never been an American secretary-general, and Ban Ki-moon of Korea recently got the job. (The unwritten rule is that none of the Security Council's five permanent members can produce a secretary-general.)[29]

Others argue that Bill Clinton is an exception to almost every rule and that he "ought to be the secretary-general," as Tim Wirth, president of the United Nations Foundation and Better World Fund, says. In mid-2005, before Ban's election, Wirth was at a reception, chatting with the French ambassador. "'What you guys ought to do,' I said, 'is to select Bill Clinton as the next secretary-general,' and he looked at me with some surprise, and he said, 'Well, that's not possible, can't do that.'" About ten minutes later, Wirth and the French ambassador were waiting in a receiving line, "and he turned to me and said, 'We could give him French lessons.'" (Bill Clinton, surprisingly, speaks only English, and high positions at the UN require English and French.)[30]

Some of his friends tried to persuade him that he should let it be known that he'd be interested. "I think you'd be a wonderful secretary-general," Sandy Berger told him, "and . . . it's exactly what the organization needs at this point to revitalize it and to ignite a spark of energy."[31]

Ted Sorensen calls an American, particularly one who had been president, leading the UN a bad idea for the institution and the countries that it serves. "It would distort the whole idea of the United Nations, introduce all kinds of suspicions and tensions."[32] If Clinton ran the UN and Hillary the United States, imagine the conspiracy theories waiting to be hatched. "I don't think you can have a secretary-general," says Alan Solomont, "who's either sleeping with or married to the president of the United States." But if Hillary doesn't make it to the White House, Solomont says, he thinks Bill Clinton would "consider" it.[33]

Rahm Emanuel has a blunt response to the possibility of Clinton leading the UN: "That's fucking bullshit, in my view. . . . I think it's just that people have too much time on their hands."[34]

As for the presidency of the World Bank, Nobel laureate Joseph Stiglitz, who worked in the Clinton administration as chairman of the Council of Economic Advisers before moving to the World Bank in 1997 as chief economist, says that Clinton, with whom he sometimes disagreed, would be "wonderful" in that job because "he has a commitment to the problems of the poorest countries . . . and the kind of . . . magnetism that you need to generate support. . . . It's a very grueling job. I wouldn't be surprised if he'd be interested under the right environment."[35]

After World Bank president Paul Wolfowitz was forced out of that job in May 2007, many names came up as replacements—for example, British prime minister Tony Blair, who had just announced his retirement, and Yale president Richard Levin. But Clinton's name was not among them. (Robert B. Zoellick, who was Bush's U.S. trade representative, got the job.)[36]

Still, Rabbi David Saperstein, a friend of both Clintons, suggests a scenario in which it helps Hillary to install Bill as head of the World Bank. Should she win the nomination, she will have to persuade voters that she, not he, will be president. "If I am president, she could announce, I will appoint President Clinton to head the World Bank." That way voters could be assured, Saperstein explains, "that they both have major things they're doing; full-time things, . . . a very defined role for him that's separate from the White House." Asked if he has discussed this plan with Bill Clinton, Saperstein won't comment, leaving the impression that he has.[37]

Clinton friend Robert Torricelli, former New Jersey senator, says he thinks Clinton would want the position. "No one could marshal international attention and resources on a common agenda like Bill Clinton."[38]

One prominent political strategist who knows Clinton well sees the idea as totally fanciful. "Having been president of the United States, why do you want to manage far-flung employees of the World Bank?"[39]

SOME WHO have lived in the White House found it to be a prison and could not wait to escape. Nobody puts Bill Clinton in that group. To a person, his friends agree that he would love to move back in and would enjoy revisiting a role he played as president: first host.[40]

All those Lincoln Bedroom guests know how much Bill Clinton loved and became a student of the White House and its history. They also know just how warm a host he could be, and he was that good when he was president and presumably busy; and Hillary, who did not seem to enjoy entertaining sleepover guests, was first lady, and presumably less busy.

When Patricia Duff spent the night in the Lincoln Bedroom with her husband at the time, Mike Medavoy, she famously called Clinton "a full-service President."[41] Aiming to please his Hollywood friends, the president knocked on their door very early one Sunday morning in 1993 to deliver a mug of coffee to Mike, who was leaving Washington that morning to fly home to Los Angeles.[42]

That sleepover was a particularly juicy one for gossips because Hillary was not home and across the hall in the Queen's Bedroom was Barbra Streisand. One woman who knows Streisand well says, "He was a total flirt. Whether he went beyond that, . . . she was certainly taken with him."[43] Hillary was said to be furious about the innuendos and the president appeared with a scratch on his face, about which he offered various explanations.

President Clinton seemed happiest when he had a full White House, especially when things were uncomfortable with Hillary. In April 1998—the weekend of the White House Correspondents Association Dinner—he had Mark and Susie Buell in the Lincoln Bedroom and the golfer Greg Norman and his wife in the Queen's Bedroom. Hillary was home that weekend—she had been deposed that day by Ken Starr in the basement of the White House—and she was accompanying Bill to the dinner knowing that one of the guests would be Paula Jones, whose lawsuit against her husband would eventually lead to the discovery of the Monica Lewinsky affair.[44]

Bill Clinton presumably preferred not to be alone with Hillary that night. (The presence of both Hillary and Paula at that dinner was the headline worldwide.) When the Clintons returned, Susie recalls, "they asked us to come up and we joined them in the private quarters." In addition to the Buells and Normans, Erskine Bowles and his wife were there, and so was one of the president's classmates from Oxford.[45]

Clinton suggested they have a drink, although, friends say, they never saw him drink alcohol while he was president. (For toasts at official dinners his wineglass usually contained water.)[46] Clinton didn't have the private quarters "very well stocked," says Mark Buell, so when the butler, Buddy, came around to take drink orders and the men all wanted beers, Buddy had to run out to the 7-Eleven and buy some.[47]

The next morning, the president gave the Buells a comprehensive tour of the Oval Office.[48]

Tom Vilsack, when he was governor of Iowa, recalls "an extraordinary opportunity," in February 1999, when Bill Clinton gave him and his wife, Christie, "a personal tour," two and a half hours long, of the second floor of the White House. After the tour of the private quarters and the lessons about the artifacts in each room ended around midnight, the exhausted Vilsacks retired to the Lincoln Bedroom.

It was Hillary who had invited the Vilsacks to sleep over that Monday night. Consumed by the Monica scandal—the impeachment trial in the Senate had ended in acquittal less than two weeks before—and contemplating her own run for the Senate, Hillary, recalls Vilsack, "was very tired that night and had actually forgotten that we were going to stop by." It was, after all, Bill Clinton who had been the subject of the impeachment trial, yet he was not too tired to play host.

The next morning, the Vilsacks awakened early, before seven, to return to Iowa. "As we tiptoed out of the bedroom [Bill] was in the president's study on the second floor. . . . We didn't know what to do because he was in a sort of a jogging outfit and his hair was kind of messed up. It was obvious he had just . . . gotten up, he hadn't showered, maybe he had worked out. . . . It wasn't the kind of attire you'd expect to see the president in and so we just walked by the office, we didn't stop in and say, 'We're leaving.'" If they had, they would have missed their flight because he would have found some other lesson to give them.[49]

Carl Anthony describes Bill Clinton as "an ideal first gent—more heart and soul and power and activism than any prince consort. . . . He might very well prove to be as hospitable a host of the executive mansion in a manner not seen since Dolley Madison—he possesses her depth and gregariousness."[50] (She was first lady from 1809 to 1817.)

"I don't think he's going to be planning menus and selecting the flowers," jokes Lynn Cutler. "He could even say 'I don't want to bake cookies' and get away with it."[51]

In late September 2007, on *The Daily Show with Jon Stewart*, plugging his new book *Giving*, Bill Clinton joked that being "first husband" might not be so great after all. "No, I may slit my throat," he said, before reverting to his usual pledge to do anything Hillary asked him to do to help.[52]

TRADITIONALISTS WHO fret about how, in the absence of a first lady, the official social activities of the White House would be discharged suggested that Chelsea Clinton fill that role. Her father, appearing on *Larry King Live*, said absolutely not. "There is no way she should stop doing what she's doing and try to assume that role."[53]

If Chelsea were to interrupt her career to serve as her mother's hostess—a nineteenth-century notion that seems outlandishly outdated—she would be giving up a big income.

By agreement between her parents and the press, when Chelsea lived in the White House, she was largely left alone. Snippets leaked out—it was reported, repeatedly, for example, that she wanted to be a pediatric cardiologist[54]—but not many. Having decided not to pursue medical school, she graduated from Stanford in 2001 with a degree in history.

Admirers of her parents, such as Susan Davis, imagine Chelsea doing good works for nonprofits. "She was at a formative age when she got to travel around the world and see firsthand the plight of the poorest," says Davis, chairperson of the Grameen Foundation USA, who has observed Chelsea but doesn't know her personally. "It's a very powerful experience and whenever anybody sees it firsthand they always become champions for life."[55]

In the immediate aftermath of 9/11, Chelsea wrote an essay for the now defunct *Talk* magazine. "For most young Americans I know, 'serving' in the broadest sense now seems like the only thing to do. Is banking what's important right now?"[56]

While at Oxford, Chelsea became what one reporter called the "it girl." She turned up at the Versace show in Paris in January 2002 in a Versace pantsuit, eyes and hair by Donatella Versace herself, seated in the front row next to Madonna and Gwyneth Paltrow. (She later flew to Milan for Versace's ready-to-wear show.) She was seen dancing with Sir Paul McCartney, chatting with Bianca Jagger, dining with her father and U2's Bono, mixing with Kevin Spacey at the London premiere of one of his films, dining and dancing at the priciest restaurants and clubs in London. In June 2002, *Vanity Fair* proclaimed her "the new JFK Jr." and "a sex symbol."[57]

After earning a master's degree in international relations from University College, Oxford, and returning to New York in 2003, she went to work for McKinsey & Co., a management consulting firm. According to a recent profile in the *New York Times*, "She was the youngest in her class, hired at the same rank as those with M.B.A. degrees."[58] Susan Davis explains that decision to join McKinsey as one that would be helpful to Chelsea when she entered the nonprofit world. "I think that this [McKinsey] is about skill building. . . . McKinsey is a firm that has a very good reputation for ethical integrity and as a place where you can hone diagnostic and analytical skills to be able to develop a wider perspective on the economy and the world and on business, which is very important when you go into the nonprofit world."[59] (She took a leave from the hedge fund in early December 2007 to campaign full-time for her mother.)

She left McKinsey to take a job analyzing investments at Avenue Capital, a $12 billion hedge fund run by Marc Lasry, a financial supporter of Democrats and of her parents.[60] The *Times* reported that by moving to Avenue, she might "improve on her low-six-figure McKinsey salary—reportedly $120,000—by hundreds of thousands of dollars . . . because of potential bonuses, according to industry headhunters."[61]

Chelsea is said to be close to her father, which says something about the depth of the relationship given the embarrassment she had to have felt over the Monica Lewinsky revelations. Most painful for the president, friends say, was Chelsea being exposed to the sordid details of the scandal. "He had to be deeply shaken by that," says David Schulte, his friend from law school.[62] Clinton's military aide, Robert Patterson, recalls that one of the things that most angered Hillary about the scandal was "the damage it caused to Chelsea . . . who was caught off guard and obviously hurt by it." Patterson says that the weekend after the story broke Chelsea flew home from Stanford and "Mrs. Clinton sent Chelsea and the president up to Camp David by themselves to hash it out."[63]

When she moved with her parents to Washington in 1993, she was not quite thirteen. Strong roots in Little Rock, and a close friendship maintained with Elizabeth Fleming, helped her to finesse the move. Victor Fleming says that his family has been "a sort of home away from home for Chelsea," who visited them, usually for a couple of days at a time, during her White House years. His impression from talking with Chelsea is that "she has a very strong relationship with both parents still."[64] Bill Clinton, friends say, is often on his cell phone talking to Chelsea.[65] Don Hewitt remembers that when Clinton was in the 60 Minutes studio, "he would excuse himself a lot and go to the phone to talk to Chelsea. . . . He is crazy about that kid and he's probably a very good father."[66]

While Chelsea was at Stanford, after Clinton left the presidency, Mark Buell played golf with him in Palo Alto. Also in their party was John Doerr, the Silicon Valley venture capitalist, and former Clinton friend Vinod Gupta. At dinner afterward at a Cuban restaurant in Palo Alto, with a bunch of Chelsea's friends in tow, Buell and Doerr "conspired" privately to split the bill. "When the president heard about this," Buell recalls, "he said, 'No I'm paying. I have an income now.' It was really kind of sweet. . . . And I thought it was sort of a poignant scene as a father."

On another occasion in San Francisco, Bill Clinton had dinner with the parents of Chelsea's then boyfriend and was obviously pleased with himself. It was the first time he had met them. "And he came back," recalls Buell, "and he said like any father would, 'I think they liked me.' He was wanting to impress his daughter's boyfriend's family. . . . It was so . . . touching, just to see him wanting to make a good impression."[67]

Chelsea's current boyfriend is Marc Mezvinsky, a fellow Stanford graduate whom she has known since their teenage years in Washington. Once an intern in the Clinton White House, now an investment banker at Goldman Sachs in New York—*New York* magazine reported that he bought a $3.8 million apartment—he is the son of Marjorie Margolies-Mezvinsky and Edward M. Mezvinsky, both former Democratic members of Congress.

Edward Mezvinsky is currently in prison for, according to the *New York Times*, "swindling dozens of investors out of $10 million." The Mezvinskys were frequent guests at state dinners during the Clinton years and ABC News reported that prosecutors claim that "Mezvinsky used his connections to the Clintons and his son's social relationship with Chelsea to persuade people to give him money to participate in the scams."

Marjorie Margolies-Mezvinsky lost her seat in the House in 1994 after one term when Bill Clinton strong-armed her to support his deficit-reduction bill and break a deadlock. She ended up casting one of the two decisive votes that resulted in a 218–216 victory for the president. She had promised her wealthy, Republican-leaning constituents to oppose all tax increases.[68]

HILLARY'S RACE for the White House changed everything for Bill Clinton. Instead of the glamour and gratification of elegant speaking venues and four-star dinners, instead of going, as usual, to Davos in late January 2008, he stayed home or mixed it up on the campaign trail. He was applauded, certainly, but he was also ridiculed and denounced for slinging mud and erupting in red-face rages. No one could imagine such behavior from George H. W. Bush or even Jimmy Carter.

During those early primary battles he was working as hard as he had ever worked—for Hillary, but also, more so, for himself. He knew his legacy remained soiled and fragile, and that Hillary's election would do more to clean and enhance it than anything he could do in Africa. The Bill Clinton holding HIV-positive babies and toddlers, that global statesman and philanthropist the world had come to admire was, temporarily, on leave.

Bill Clinton's timing has always been good, and so it seemed to be in late 2007 and early 2008 as he presented himself as helping "the finest mind of their generation," as he took to calling her, become the first woman president. His postpresidency act was thriving in a way, but it was also growing a bit stale. His Africa initiative was losing some steam as other foundations and even George W. Bush won kudos for their work. CGI was brilliantly conceived, but the 2008 meeting would be the fourth and the excitement and novelty was bound to wane. His speaking fees were beginning to attract attention again; a handful of his buddies and funders were in the news for the wrong reasons. Sometimes he still seemed so ridiculously needy; sometimes his behavior was embarrassing.

In fact, until Bill Clinton hit the trail in earnest for his wife's presidential campaign, he was in danger of becoming a bore—so in love with the sound of his own voice as to seem almost comical. His friend Howard Tullman worried out loud that the former president was flirting with becoming "the next Jesse Jackson," who shows up wherever a controversy brews or a spotlight beckons.[69]

Few Clinton observers finish trying to explain what makes him tick without mentioning that he feeds off of public acclaim. "He wants to an inordinate degree to please people," says Arkansas journalist Bill Simmons.[70] He's "a master at understanding how to get people to like him," says Lou Weisbach.[71]

But one woman who has spent time with Clinton and stayed the night at the White House says that Clinton's humiliations have changed him, that he's "a little less sensitive to his environment than he was before, a little more likely to just opine forever," and miss the signals that he has lost his audience. Clinton's need for company is outsized and weird, this woman says. "He is one of the most gregarious human beings, who's just hungry for human contact and interaction all the time," and it's exacerbated now because he essentially lives alone and especially misses Chelsea.[72]

Robert Sam Anson, writing about Clinton's postpresidency in *Vanity Fair* in June 2004, offered a sad view: "One man-about-Manhattan tells of inviting Clinton to a cocktail party that was to run from six to eight. Clinton arrived at seven; an hour and a half later, he was still surrounded by a crowd hanging on every syllable. Join us for dinner, the guest of honor invited. Clinton did—at 9:15. 'I can't stay,' he said. 'Maybe I'll just have dessert.' He sat down and started to talk: about Chelsea ('a serial monogamist,' he has called her); Hillary ('the most interesting, important, worthwhile person' he'd ever met, he has said); his 'work' (the thing he missed most about the White House). At midnight he was still talking (about having been reduced to 'watching movies all the time'), and the rest of the party was looking at watches. 'Bill,' one of them said finally, 'we have to go to work tomorrow.' Clinton's face fell. 'He looked so lost,' says the host. 'Like, Where am I going now?'"[73]

Mel Gitler and his wife attended a fund-raiser for Hillary's Senate race in 2006. She couldn't make it so she sent her husband. It was eleven at night and the former president was still talking and, says Gitler, "the hostess got tired." He was supposed to wrap it up by ten, but he did not want to stop answering questions. "He could have gone on all night," says Gitler. The host, receiving signals from his wife, "got up and said that we'll have a couple more questions and we'll call it an evening."[74]

Sometimes when he gave a speech, especially on a weeknight, he talked so long that some in the audience hoped a hook would drop and drag him off the stage. At the Jewish United Fund (JUF) dinner he keynoted in Chicago in November 2005, many of the eighteen hundred who packed the hotel's grand ballroom lived in the suburbs, had babysitters waiting, and jobs to go to the next morning; they were stealing glances at their watches. Finally one of the evening's hosts took the stage, thanked Clinton for being so generous with his time, and announced that the former president would take one more question.

Conrad Black saw him in a similar circumstance at a paid speech in Toronto. "He was very knowledgeable about the state of public Medicare plans in Canada, . . . but left to his own he sort of garrulously chats on and . . . it's uneven, it's certainly not galvanizing. It's not an address that gathers you up and brings you to a conclusion and that uplifts you at all."[75]

Still, given the right audience and the benefit of an afternoon engagement, he could reliably bring down the house. In June 2006, Bill Clinton spoke, pro bono, to the annual convention of the Association of Alternative Newsweeklies, meeting that year in Little Rock. Patricia Calhoun, then AAN's editorial chair, says the former president's assorted "handlers" insisted that his speech would run twenty minutes, and that there would be no questions, not even the two preapproved questions that Calhoun had in hand. "I can tell you that all bets were very quickly off as he came back to greet the editor and the publisher of the *Arkansas Times*. 'Hey, I'll take questions from the audience,' he said."

Clinton ended up talking for an hour to what Calhoun calls a "rapt and hypnotized" audience of five hundred representing more than a hundred newspapers, people usually skeptical, left leaning, and rude. No one asked about Monica or Rwanda or welfare reform, she says. "In our group for no one to ask about Monica Lewinsky was pretty interesting. . . . Everybody in that room would have thought, 'You are so smart, why were you so stupid?'" But nobody asked that question. "It was as though Elvis were in the room," says Calhoun. "This was a rock star."[76] Another editor later noted the ovations and cheers, and blogged, "You'd have thought he was talking to a room full of supporters at the height of an election campaign."[77]

Calhoun, editor of *Westword* in Denver, joined Clinton onstage to ask him questions and then opened it up to the audience: "I'm getting the sign from the handler that it's time to cut it off. He pats his chest, . . . he holds up two fingers and there are two more questions. I said, 'Well, President Clinton, you've held the most powerful position in the world, but your handler seems to be in charge of your schedule.' . . . President Clinton says, 'No, we'll take some more questions.'"

Forty-five minutes later, as Clinton continued to encourage questions, Calhoun said to him, "President Clinton, it appears that your staffer has collapsed in shock over the timing." He said, "Oh, that's okay, he'll get over it." And he took more questions.[78] After the Q and A, Clinton rushed to the security ropes and chatted and signed autographs for another hour.[79]

Calhoun, who had never before met Clinton, says that he looked great—"really well tailored suit, impeccably groomed white hair," trim, oddly "smooth hands." Like others, she noted that the longer he engaged with the audience, the better he looked; "the people contact is what seems to energize him."

The one jarring note was the toilet paper stuck to his shoe.[80]

ON AUGUST 19, 2006, Bill Clinton turned sixty. He was not happy about it, lamenting that he had more days behind him than ahead of him, that he always used to be the youngest person in the room, but now he was often the oldest. He showed a childlike side by insisting on celebrating his birthday over and over, unlike most aging adults who would rather just blow out the candles once and be done with it.

On his actual birth date, he celebrated in Martha's Vineyard at the home of Mary Steenburgen and Ted Danson. At the Vineyard party, says Susie Tompkins Buell, who was there, "he played the saxophone and Hillary and Chelsea danced and were just so proud of him and having so much fun. Hillary loves to dance." There were, says Buell, about a hundred people, including Maurice Tempelsman, Jackie Onassis's last boyfriend, Meg Ryan, Vernon Jordan, and Walter Cronkite.[81]

That was not a night for Clinton to worry about his heart. He ate his favorite foods—spareribs, chicken, potato salad, coleslaw. Susie Buell recalls him "off in the corner opening his presents, just beaming with pride at having so many nice friends, and getting books . . . trying not to be depressed about getting sixty." The Clintons, who were staying in a guesthouse on Steenburgen's property, partied until the very end.[82]

In Little Rock, at the Clinton Library, there was a party in absentia for the former president.

The next day he celebrated again, this time at Innisfree, the Nantucket summer home of Smith Bagley, heir to a tobacco fortune, and Elizabeth Frawley Bagley, Clinton's former ambassador to Portugal. That night Carly Simon and her two children sang "Happy Birthday" to him.[83] (He celebrated his sixty-first birthday at the Bagleys also, in the midst of a $2,300-a-head fund-raiser for Hillary.)[84]

On September 9, he celebrated in Toronto.[85]

It was during that event that Bill Clinton gave *The American Spectator* founder and editor, R. Emmett Tyrrell, material for his new book, *The Clinton Crack-Up: The Boy President's Life After the White House.* Conrad Black, a friend of Tyrrell's, and an acquaintance of Clinton's—Clinton blurbed Black's biography of FDR—got Tyrrell a ticket to the event and Tyrrell was able to corral Clinton to pose for a photo with him. (Clinton's aides, eventually figuring out who Tyrrell was, refused permission for Tyrrell to use the photo in his belittling book.) Tyrrell described the former president as wandering aimlessly around the event, in and out of the men's room, obviously failing to recognize the man whose magazine printed the first stories about Clinton's sex life while governor and who dispatched reporters to Arkansas to find Paula Jones and thus in a sense initiated the misery of impeachment.[86]

On the weekend of October 27–29, with Chelsea Clinton and Terry McAuliffe as cohosts, twenty-one hundred "friends" were offered birthday packages that ranged from $60,000 at the low end—a thousand a year—to $500,000 and higher. The weekend, according to a report in the *Washington Post,* included a golf tournament, brunch, receptions, and dinner at the American Museum of Natural History. Those who wrote checks for $500,000 or more received the "Birthday Chair Package," which included the "'Backstage Pass' dinner and photo with Clinton, and platinum seating at the Saturday dinner" and the Rolling Stones private concert at the Beacon Theater on upper Broadway. Proceeds went to the Clinton Foundation. He had his friend Ron Burkle seated behind him at the concert, which was packed with celebrities and people whom Clinton was tapping to support his foundation, his CGI, and his wife.[87]

Shortly before his birthday, Clinton addressed a World AIDS Conference in Toronto. "In just a few days, I will be 60 years old. I hate it, but it's true," he said. "For most of my working life, I was the youngest person doing what I was doing. Then one day I woke up and I was the oldest person in every room. Now that I have more days behind me than ahead of me, I try to wake up with a discipline of gratitude every day."

In a column entitled "Clinton's Prostate Turns 60," conservative commentator Ben Shapiro gave his take of that speech: "Turning 60 is certainly a bummer for a man as reliant on his prostate as Clinton is. Nonetheless, Clinton's speech was a stunning testament to his egocentricity. Who whines about a post-midlife crisis while discussing a disease that has pushed Angola's average life span to 39.9 years, Zambia's to 39.7, and Zimbabwe's to 37.9? Who tells a roomful of people worried about the devastation caused by a global plague that he is personally devastated by having another birthday?"[88]

Bill Clinton, that's who. And the audience loved him.

IF THERE was a memorial service for a prominent person, Clinton was often there. He became a kind of mourner in chief: have corpse, he'll travel, and he'll give a eulogy, and the eulogy would occasionally stray into being as much about Bill Clinton as the deceased.

In November 2006, he turned up as a "surprise guest" and eulogist at the funeral, at the Riverside Church in Manhattan, for CBS newsman Ed Bradley. Entertainment included Jimmy Buffett and Wynton Marsalis. It was, said Sony chief executive Howard Stringer, "a full house" of two thousand mourners. "I knew I had arrived in national politics," Clinton said in his eulogy, "when Ed Bradley wanted to interview me."[89]

In February 2007, he attended the memorial service for historian Arthur Schlesinger Jr. in the Great Hall at Cooper Union in Lower Manhattan. In that room in 1860, Abraham Lincoln spoke about his presidential candidacy, reported Adam Clymer in the *New York Times*. Clinton recalled that Schlesinger, who was editing a series of biographies, had asked him to write one of Lincoln. Clinton explained that he was under contract to write his own memoir, to which Schlesinger replied, "Lincoln is a better story, and it's shorter."[90]

He "does" plenty of funerals for the rich and famous, or their dearly departed: Terry McAuliffe's father;[91] Ann Richards, the former governor of Texas. He also delivered the principal eulogy at Senator Lloyd Bentsen's funeral. "Lloyd felt that Clinton was one of the most brilliant people he'd ever met," says Houston mayor Bill White, to whom Clinton signed and sent his original notes for the eulogy. "He really has learned to do a good job at those special occasions."[92]

"He empathizes like no one else I know," says Melanne Verveer.[93] "I happen to know that Bill Clinton is very good at occasions like funerals," says Ted Sorensen, and it doesn't sound like a compliment.[94]

Clinton also delivers eulogies and comforting words at funerals of people not known to the general public. In November 2005, he starred at the funeral of Carl Whillock who had served as a special assistant to Clinton during his second term; but, more important, in 1974, when Clinton was contemplating a race for the U.S. House, Whillock accompanied Clinton through the Third Congressional District, stopping in every town and introducing Clinton to the people he needed to know. Although he lost that race, Clinton has said that, without Whillock, he would not have become president. Whillock's wife, Margaret, also worked in the Clinton White House, as deputy director of the White House Visitors Office. During the funeral, says the *Arkansas Democrat-Gazette's* Phyllis Brandon, the former president "sat with Margaret and held her hand."[95]

In February 2006, Clinton spoke at the funeral of his longtime friend and aide Eli Segal, who died of a rare form of cancer. In March 2006, he delivered one of four eulogies for Steve Gleason, an Iowa physician who committed suicide and who had worked on health-care policy in the Clinton White House. Former Iowa governor Tom Vilsack—Gleason had been his chief of staff—also delivered a eulogy. "He didn't have to come," says Vilsack, "it was a labor of love for him to come. . . . He obviously has a way with people and a way to express sympathy and empathy. . . . He's physically a big man, as I am, and when a big person like that hugs you or puts his arm around you, I think it's a comforting feeling." Vilsack sat next to Clinton during the service: "One thing I found out about the guy; he can't sing worth a lick, and neither can I. The two of us were belting out those church hymns as if we could."[96]

In April 2006, Clinton joined his successor as Arkansas governor, Jim Guy Tucker, at the funeral in Arkansas for Jim Pledger, who had been Clinton's chief of staff when he was governor. Clinton delivered the eulogy.[97]

When Eppie Lederer (aka Ann Landers) lay dying of cancer in her East Lake Shore Drive apartment in Chicago in June 2002, Bill Clinton paid a private visit. No one but the former president and the advice columnist knew about it. She died a month later.

While he was in the White House and after he moved out, he would call people who are not famous who had a death in their family—in December 1999, he called restaurateur Phil Stefani, at midnight; his father's wake was the next morning. "We had a conversation for about fifteen minutes. He told me about how he grew up without his father. He had just come from that fire in Boston where the wall collapsed and firemen died. Here it is one in the morning in D.C. . . . And I'm thinking, the president of the United States takes the time out to make a phone call. . . . And again, I'm not a check writer. . . . [It] wasn't just, 'Hey, I'm sorry your father died, talk to you later.' "[98]

While Clinton was president, he called Tom Kean just after he suffered a heart attack and underwent an angioplasty and insertion of a stent to clear a blocked artery: "Typical Bill Clinton, he talked to me so darned long, the nurses told me to get off the phone. I was sweating." Just out of surgery, Kean also started to doze, but Clinton continued to talk. He was in the heat of budget negotiations with the Republican Congress. "What do you know about this fellow . . . Newt Gingrich?" Clinton asked.[99]

Chapter 12

GETTING THE FULL CLINTON—PRO BONO

TRAVEL AND TIME, FRIENDS SAY, WERE THE TWO "great balms" for Bill Clinton. "To go abroad as former president and be treated with the respect that he thought he was due," says Jonathan Alter, "that brought his spirits back."[1]

Lou Susman, who sits on the Citigroup Advisory Board, hosted a meeting in Paris in March 2004 and paid Clinton $250,000 to speak. Susman was impressed; the dinner audience at the Paris Opera House consisted of "very powerful people. . . . He wowed them. He didn't use a note. . . . They ate up his speech."[2]

Not surprisingly, Clinton drew solace and cheer from how good he looked in retrospect. "People recognized that brains count for something," says Alter. "Part of him wasn't sure whether he could be happy without the power and without public office. He found out that he got to be kind of bigger than public office; people were always [wondering], 'What's he going to be? Is he going to be secretary-general of the UN? Is he going to be this or that?' . . . It's like Jesse Jackson was for a while. He just became Bill Clinton; he became his own brand and it was a huge international brand. And I think he fed off of that. . . . 'You know what? I'm not a has-been. In America there's room for a different kind of former president.'"[3]

As George W. Bush's administration came unhinged by the Iraq War, Clinton's reception in the United States, as well as abroad, became fit for, well, a rock star or a movie star. John Emerson, chairman of the board of the Los Angeles Music Center, invited his old boss to speak two years running, sold-out back-to-back nights each time. "I'm telling you people can't get enough of him."[4] Bud Yorkin was there: "I never heard an audience that raucous. It was like you thought you were in a football game. . . . He got such ovations. . . . The speech stopped every other line almost." When it was over, the Yorkins and Clinton went out: "It's amazing," Clinton told Yorkin. "Everyplace I go, I get this welcome and I guess if people are paying that much money to hear me talk, they really like me."[5]

He was still being paid obscenely fat speaking fees. In June 2005, he pocketed $800,000 from Gold Services International, based in Bogotá, Colombia. For four days running, at $200,000 each, he spoke in Mexico City, Bogotá, and twice in São Paulo. In Canada, for The Power Within, he spoke on consecutive days, one day in Toronto and the next in Calgary, and collected $650,000. He also managed to squeeze in another speech in Toronto before the Calgary speech for a mere $125,000.[6]

Clever planning around the Jewish United Fund booking in Chicago allowed the former president to pull in $400,000 for three speeches—two on November 7. (On November 8 and 9 he was back in New York where he picked up another $400,000.) Clinton was well worth the money that the JUF paid him. Its dinner normally attracts from five hundred to eight hundred people; for the dinner featuring Bill Clinton, the JUF drew eighteen hundred.[7]

Some of Clinton's friends fear that his moneymaking approaches moneygrubbing and that he is pricing himself out of the market. He's "getting to the point," says Howard Tullman, at which he is "embarrassingly expensive."[8]

And at least twice, he has accepted invitations to speak to groups under federal investigation. In December 2001, he took a fee of $125,000 from International Profits Associates, a management consulting firm for small businesses, to speak in suburban Chicago. Charges against it included, according to a report in the *Washington Post,* allegations of "widespread sexual harassment."[9]

Clinton supporter Mike Cherry represents the company's founder and managing director, John Burgess. Burgess's press coverage has been awful, including allegations of criminal conduct. IPA was reportedly extremely generous to Hillary whose campaign and PAC collected nearly $150,000 in donations from IPA executives. She also flew on the company's corporate jet.[10]

Vinod Gupta proclaimed himself close friends with Bill Clinton when responding to a request for an interview. The sixty-one-year-old Gupta, based in Omaha but calling from Scotland, asked if Clinton had authorized the book, and, when told no, stopped returning calls. After meeting President Clinton at a dinner in Washington in 1994, Gupta began to raise money for Clinton's reelection and became a presidential golfing buddy at the famous St. Andrews course in Edinburgh and a sometimes vacation companion. He also scored an overnight in the Lincoln Bedroom and offers of ambassadorships and appointment to the board of the Kennedy Center for the Performing Arts.

Gupta is the immigrant success story. Born to poverty in rural India, he arrived in Omaha in 1967. He is chairman of the publicly traded infoUSA, a provider of database processing services. Speaking in Aspen in 2004, Clinton gave the company a priceless plug when he said that companies like Gupta's could have prevented 9/11 because "Vin has all these terrorists in the computer—legally." Gupta is Clinton's financial supporter, employer—Gupta has paid Clinton more than $3 million in consulting fees—and also the host of the conference to which Clinton was speaking for a fee of $200,000. Gupta also appointed Clinton's moneyman, Terry McAuliffe, to the board of one of his companies. In addition, Bill Clinton got six figures from Gupta for his presidential library, and another million for the Clinton Foundation.

The arrangement attracted little public attention until Gupta made front-page news in the *New York Times* and the *Washington Post* in late May 2007 and again the front page of the *New York Times* in July 2007. The news stories reported $900,000 worth of travel—charged to the company as "business development"—by Bill and Hillary (also by Terry McAuliffe) on Gupta's corporate plane. They flew to such places as Switzerland, Hawaii, Jamaica, and Mexico, some of them vacation destinations, another, in New Mexico, a campaign fund-raiser for Hillary.

A shareholder lawsuit charged that hiring Clinton was a "waste of corporate assets." The lawsuit described the "extremely vague purpose" of Clinton's hiring to provide "strategic growth and business judgment." (As required by federal law, the Clintons reimbursed Gupta for some of Hillary's travel, but they paid the cost of a first-class ticket, which does not come close to covering private air travel.)

The investors who sued questioned Gupta's need for the corporate jet and for an eighty-foot yacht anchored in the Virgin Islands that boasts an all-female crew.

The suit also focused unwanted attention on a *New York Times* report the week before that infoUSA allegedly "sold consumer data several years ago to telemarketing criminals who used it to steal money from elderly Americans. It advertised call lists with titles such as 'Suffering Seniors,' a compilation of people with cancer or Alzheimer's disease."[11]

With a shove from the Clintons, Gupta no longer boasts his ties to them on his website; he helped to plan a fund-raiser in New York for Hillary in June 2007 but did not attend it. In November 2004, the company informed shareholders that the SEC had begun an "informal investigation," although the allegation that hiring Bill Clinton was "a waste of corporate assets" was dismissed, the court noting company claims that Clinton might have been responsible for as much as $40 million in sales.[12]

CLINTON COULD not have been happy with another zinger from columnist Maureen Dowd in 2007: "When you rake in $10 million a year from speeches, do you really need that $150,000 for speaking to the Boys and Girls Club of L.A.?"[13]

He was giving more speeches pro bono, however, especially when the people asking were old friends and/or financial supporters. Bob Kerrey got him pro bono for his university's School of Urban Planning and Management. S. Daniel Abraham, founder of SlimFast, says that when he asked Clinton to speak at an event and tried to pay him, he wouldn't take any money for it. (On the other hand, Abraham, a billionaire, is a major supporter of Hillary's campaigns, of Bill's library, and of his CGI; on the latter he paid for the interreligious dialogue panel.)[14]

When he spoke at the Kids in Distressed Situations dinner in New York, the group's president, Janice Weinman Shorenstein, the daughter-in-law of real estate mogul and Clinton friend Walter Shorenstein, says nothing went to him personally, but the organization gave him $1 million worth of new children's clothes and shoes and toys for distribution through the Clinton Foundation. The Bush/Clinton tsunami relief effort also received $250,000 in cash. Clinton's speech was a knockout, Weinman says. "People were just overtaken with his conviction and with his energy and with his articulateness; he never looked at a word, he spoke from his heart. . . . He was absolutely electric."[15]

When he spoke to the National Council of La Raza in Los Angeles, he did it pro bono as a favor to Mickey Ibarra whose lobbying firm represents La Raza. "We created a special session that started at nine in the morning at the LA convention center," says Ibarra. "Our worst fear was that nobody would show up. . . . As it turns out, at eight in the morning, the place was packed," and the speech sparked "ovations, over and over."

Clinton flew in on a private jet from Aspen that morning and, says Ibarra, didn't even charge them for his transportation. "The president of LULAC (League of United Latin American Citizens) called it a $250,000 gift." (The year before he spoke pro bono in Little Rock to LULAC's convention.)[16]

Persuading Bill Clinton to commit to be the pro bono speaker at the Sargent Shriver National Center on Poverty Law dinner required the help of Clinton friends Rahm Emanuel and former Commerce secretary Mickey Kantor. It also helped that the dinner's honoree was R. Sargent Shriver Jr., first director of the Peace Corps and, says the organization's then executive director Rita McLennon, the visionary who "totally revolutionized the delivery of legal aid to poor people in this country." Clinton is a big fan of Shriver's.

Luckily for McLennon, she was friends with Kantor, who suggested Rahm Emanuel as the person to call Clinton and ask him to say yes and to do it for free. McLennon says the organization could not afford even a fraction of his fee. Clinton said he'd do anything for Shriver, but he insisted that the dinner be held in Los Angeles; she would have preferred Chicago where the organization is headquartered. He also insisted on a private plane to fly him to Los Angeles. McLennon recalls that she "panicked and I called Mickey who didn't even blink."

"Yeah, I'll get it for him. Don't worry about that."

The dinner, at the Beverly Hilton, attracted Shriver's son-in-law, Arnold Schwarzenegger, and other movie stars who would not have shown up in Chicago. One of them, Melanie Griffith, approached McLennon's teenage daughter and said, "Gee, I really love your dress. Who's it by?" "We bought it at Target," McLennon says, "so nothing could have made my daughter happier."[17]

In his speech, Clinton paid tribute to Shriver, suffering from Alzheimer's disease, as the "quintessential example of someone who just through the force of his own personality was able to change the world." Clinton got a standing ovation.[18]

Georgette Bennett worked almost a year to persuade Clinton to give the Rabbi Marc H. Tannenbaum Memorial Lecture, named for her late husband. He did it, not for free, but at a reduced rate. Because she knows him—she and the organization she heads participate in CGI—she was able to lobby him face-to-face. She also had an important ally. "Billy Graham was very helpful to us . . . very close to my late husband." And then there were the Clintons' next-door neighbors in Chappaqua. He sits on her board and plays golf with the former president.

Bennett still sounds moved when she recalls his speech. "He had a text but I never felt he was using it. His eye contact was wonderful, he has charming modesty about him. After he finished his remarks and we finished our Q and A and I escorted him down from the stage, he said, 'Well, I guess that went all right, didn't it?' It was extraordinary. . . . People were just riveted . . . a standing ovation."

Walking with Clinton to his car, she explained that her first and only child with Rabbi Tannenbaum was born in 1992, seven weeks after the rabbi died. "I told him the story of how I went to the polls on that November day, very cold day, with my infant, bundled up and held in my arms because I wanted my child to be part of . . . electing Bill Clinton. . . . I gave him the visual, this little baby who had just been born, whose father wasn't there for his birth; . . . and how important to have him there to vote for Bill Clinton."

She says that "his eyes started tearing up and he gave me this wonderful hug. He's this wonderful bear of a person, very physical in a good way. I'm not at all alluding to Monica Lewinsky and Gennifer Flowers; I'm just talking about a wonderful natural warmth that he has."[19]

RECENTLY, WHEN rankings of senatorial wealth were published, Senator Hillary Clinton was listed as the twenty-fifth richest member of Congress. In 2007, the *Washington Post* estimated the Clintons' worth at between $10 and $50 million, basing it on Hillary's most recent disclosure form, which does not include details on the money Bill is getting from Ron Burkle but does include the millions he's making on speeches.[20]

Jimmy Carter still disapproves, but once Clinton launched CGI, the relationship between him and Jimmy Carter warmed up. Clinton invited Carter to speak at CGI.

If Carter is envious of the puffy front-page *New York Times* stories glorifying Bill Clinton's work in Africa, he doesn't show it. "There are parts of Jimmy Carter that are very big," says journalist and biographer Christopher Ogden, "and parts of him that are very small, and I think that in this case because he's regained a lot of confidence, . . . he has been acknowledged, he's a Nobel laureate, . . . I think he'd say there's room enough for everybody in this pool to help our fellow man, and if Clinton's spending more time on that instead of chasing women, then isn't that great."[21] Chris Jennings says that the new relationship between the men has them viewing their work as "complementary." He also sees Jimmy Carter as "comfortable with who he is. He's a spiritual man. . . . I don't see that jealousy at all."[22]

One close aide to Bill Clinton in the White House suggests not getting too carried away with the new, warmer relationship. "The relationship of Clinton and Carter has never improved, and never will," he says. And he goes way back, saying that Clinton will never get over the "Mariel boatlift."[23]

Douglas Brinkley agrees. He calls Clinton's famous friendship with George H. W. Bush just Clinton being Clinton—"stealing a page" from Jimmy Carter's friendship with Gerald Ford. Clinton took what Carter did in his postpresidency and tried to one-up him. He calls the Carter/Ford friendship "a less Day-Glo version of Clinton and Bush, and the reason why [they] get so much more attention is because he's the father of the sitting president and Bill Clinton's like an international rock superstar."

Brinkley judges Carter as a man who "walks the walk and talks the talk," while Clinton, whose work is "straight from Jimmy Carter," is more of a spokesman, even a showman—"the Bono of American politics." Carter, on the other hand, has this "Baptist missionary streak in him where he wants to endure suffering himself."[24]

Kevin De Cock has seen Jimmy Carter in Kenya and says "he doesn't grab the crowds quite as much" as Clinton does. Clinton "comes across as a famous person." Clinton so relishes crowds, relishes human contact, that it would be difficult for him, if he saw a crowd, "not to go up to it and shake hands." Carter is more cerebral, more analytic, "dryer than Clinton. . . . Clinton sort of gushes."[25] Chris Ogden puts it more bluntly: Clinton is "gregarious"; Carter, "constipated."[26]

Sandy Berger, who worked in the State Department during the Carter years, sees Carter as "more narrowly focused"—attacking guinea worm in the Sudan, river blindness in Ethiopia, monitoring an election in Paraguay, increasing agricultural productivity in drought-stricken Eritrea. Bill Clinton, he says, is more "macro" in his focus; Carter is putting his attention to "neglected" diseases and Clinton to diseases such as AIDS that are very much in the public eye.[27]

Trained as an engineer, ridiculed for monitoring who used the White House tennis courts, Jimmy Carter approaches his work like the engineer he is, says Vartan Gregorian—"structure, organization," methodical, not a multitasker.[28]

On a more basic level, Clinton, determined to keep Hillary's prospects viable, is an accommodator who will do or say whatever is necessary. Jimmy Carter has nothing to lose, says Susan Davis, so he's a "sharp critic and a truth teller. . . . He doesn't have anybody that he needs to worry about, except his country."[29]

If Jimmy Carter had to confine his lust for women to his heart, so Bill Clinton has to confine his lust for the Nobel Peace Prize to his heart. The fact that Jimmy Carter received the prize in 2002 made Bill Clinton want one all the more; and when Al Gore won his in October 2007 for, according to the Nobel Committee citation, "disseminat[ing] information about manmade climate change," sharing the $1.5 million prize with the United Nations Intergovernmental Panel on Climate Change, Clinton's need for one grew exponentially.[30] Gore had morphed from an often ridiculed loser to the "Goreacle," a kind of prophet in his own time.

Clinton had hoped to win the Nobel Peace Prize while still president for achieving peace in the Middle East.[31] (Theodore Roosevelt won the prize in 1906, during his first full term in office; Woodrow Wilson won the Nobel Peace Prize in 1919 during his second term.) Asked if Clinton deserves one, Nobel laureate Joseph Stiglitz says, "I think he certainly has made a very important contribution, and . . . some of his efforts came within a hairsbreadth of really being successful while he was president. . . . It's sad that things didn't turn out."[32]

People who are more obviously in Clinton's corner, Tom Downey, for instance, think he will ultimately get the prize. "CGI is going to win him a Nobel Peace Prize one of these days." And if it's not for CGI, Downey imagines that the next president, he hopes a Democrat, perhaps Hillary, will give Clinton more responsibility to deal with issues like the Middle East and other matters "where his enormous talents and persuasive abilities are put to some use."[33]

Some who are more skeptical of Clinton—Hofstra history professor Stanislao Pugliese, for example—think Clinton's entire "Africa initiative" is all about "angling for the Nobel Peace Prize."[34] To writer Mark Updegrove it is obvious that the postpresidency plan is designed to reap that prize. "He is extraordinarily ambitious and obsessed with his legacy, so I can't think of anything that would make him appear to historians to be more venerable as a former president than receiving a Nobel Peace Prize." It's a way for this damaged man to "strive for respectability."[35]

One favorable sign for Clinton winning the Nobel, says Michael Barone, is "If the . . . Norwegians think that they could give a poke in the eye to a Republican administration by giving Bill Clinton a prize, I'm sure they'd be happy to do it. That's why Carter got his."[36]

PERHAPS IT'S Bill Clinton's insecurity, perhaps his restless intelligence, but he does want to get the book thing right. The disappointment and criticism that greeted his memoir—he so wanted it to be judged among the great ones and instead it was dismissed as, at best, average—made him want to try again.

He loved to talk to writers; he toyed with taking on a big subject himself; he told people he was most interested in writing about Abraham Lincoln. According to a report by the *Washington Post*'s Al Kamen, Bill Clinton was at a book party in June 2006 for former *New Republic* editor Peter Beinart, at the home of Mark Penn, Clinton's pollster and also Hillary's pollster and chief strategist. Clinton approached writer Jay Winik, who had recently published *April 1865: The Month That Saved America*. He asked Winik what he thought of Joshua Wolf Shenk's *Lincoln's Melancholy*. Kamen quotes Clinton as saying, "I wanted to write that book, but he beat me to the punch. I was going to write it next year. I love Lincoln—for all of his problems, he grows larger with history."[37]

Kamen's source for the exchange was *Washington Post* reporter Laura

Blumenfeld who was at the party. President Clinton had read and ad-mired Blumenfeld's book, *Revenge: A Story of Hope*, published four years before, about her search and eventual reconciliation with a Palestinian terrorist who had shot and slightly wounded her father in 1986 while he was visiting Israel.

When Clinton asked Blumenfeld what she was writing next, it was not their first conversation. Clinton had telephoned her in early 2002, sparked by a conversation with Jonathan Alter in Clinton's car en route to his Harlem office. Alter told the former president that he had just finished reading *Revenge*. "Oh, I'm really interested in that," Clinton said, ex-plaining that he too had read the book and "thought it was fantastic."

"Do you think I could get in touch with her? . . . Do you know her?" Alter did and gave Clinton Blumenfeld's number. Clinton called her and became so absorbed in the conversation that he kept his lunch date, Wil-lie Mays, waiting for twenty minutes.[38]

In his quest to cleanse his legacy, Clinton might, like Richard Nixon, see writing as a path back to respectability. Jimmy Carter has also proven to be a prolific and successful writer, with twenty-four books, fourteen of them bestsellers.[39] Jonathan Alter sees Clinton's strength, not as a writer, but as a speaker and convener.[40]

Ultimately, Clinton was stuck with his own, unfinished story.

If he were to follow Douglas Brinkley's advice, he would waste no time in selecting an official presidential biographer, a serious historian, to make sense of Clinton's two tumultuous terms. "Maybe a left-center kind of scholar," Brinkley suggests, "who could really do a nice job of explain-ing the president to people. But nobody would want to enter that if Presi-dent Clinton is going to whitewash all the warts out of his biography."[41]

A book about Clinton by his close friend Taylor Branch, the Pulitzer Prize–winning writer best known for the three-volume *America in the King Years, 1954–1968*, definitely does not fill that bill. In 1998, Branch, who worked on both of Clinton's inaugural addresses, told the *New York Times* that he and Clinton had discussed a collaboration on Clinton's memoir but dropped the plan. "After a while, I told him I wouldn't be taken seriously because I'm not objective about him."[42] (In the summer and fall of 1972, while organizing Texas for George McGovern, Clinton roomed with Taylor Branch.)

In a letter to this writer of August 18, 2006, Branch refused to be interviewed because "I have just undertaken to write a memoir about him myself," based on eighty secret sessions, across both terms, during which Branch taped conversations with the president. Most of the time they met in a second-floor office in the family quarters of the White House—and once at Camp David—often talking as late as 2 A.M. (After each session, Branch told the *Times*, Clinton would hide the tapes in his sock drawer.) As he drove home, Branch would record his memories of their conversations.[43]

A spokesman for Simon & Schuster said that the former president has no input on the project, but Branch has also been quoted as saying he doesn't know whether he'll let the president read the draft before publication. Branch did tell the AP that he spoke to Clinton the night the Monica scandal broke, but that the focus will be more about "Yeltsin, China and Osama."[44]

In the summer of 2006, Clinton signed another contract with Knopf, this one to focus on what he has been doing since he left the White House. *Giving: How Each of Us Can Change the World*, mostly about his work in Africa, was advertised as a compilation of the inspiring stories he has heard as he traveled the world.[45] Knopf published the book to coincide roughly with Clinton's September 2007 CGI. With a first printing of 750,000, the book's launch also gave Bill Clinton a reason to combine book promotion—an appearance, for example, on *The Oprah Winfrey Show*—with Hillary promotion.[46]

The early *Publishers Weekly* review was a reminder that writing is not this president's forte. The reviewer described the book as a "homily" and complained that it "uncritically surveys a vast philanthropic landscape." The profiles that comprise its heart are "formulaic"; the book's stories are "often as eye-glazing as Clinton's memoir could be."[47] The *Washington Post*'s Peter Baker, who wrote a book about Clinton's impeachment, called it "an extended public service announcement masquerading as a book," and he pointed out that Clinton's claim that since leaving office he has switched the focus of his life from "getting" (votes, contributions, endorsements) to "giving" skips "the fact that he has spent a good part of the last six years getting $46 million in speaking fees."[48] *New York* magazine also took up the giving versus getting theme, pointing out that in the book Clinton pushes ethanol and pays tribute to the people, such as billionaire Sir Richard Branson, who invest in ethanol plants, while not revealing his ties to Ron Burkle's Yucaipa fund, which invests in ethanol plants. "So long as the fund does well, [Clinton's] given a cut of the profits." (In December 2007, Clinton promised to ease out of his ties—one report used the word "sever," another "reduce"; Hillary spokesman Jay Carson characterized Clinton's intention as "taking steps to ensure . . . an appropriate transition" to Yucaipa should Hillary win the nomination. In late January 2008, the *Wall Street Journal* reported that Clinton would be receiving approximately $20 million from two of Yucaipa's domestic funds, apparently a step on the way to the again mentioned "appropriate transition.")[49]

As before, the crowds were huge and adoring. Outside Borders in Chicago, hundreds waited as long as twelve hours for Clinton to sign their books. So many fans showed up that Borders began to turn them away.[50] After hitting the number one spot on the *New York Times* bestseller list, it dropped down, behind the new book by conservative Clinton basher Laura Ingraham. Six weeks after its publication date, the AP reported that the book was not selling well.[51]

WHEN TONY COELHO talked to Bill Clinton about how to conduct his postpresidency, Jimmy Carter's name never came up. If there was anyone whom Clinton wanted to emulate, Coelho says, it was John F. Kennedy. "He was the only political hero he ever had," says Coelho. That Kennedy did not accomplish much as president, that, as Coelho argues, he "brought about the civil rights revolution because he died," seems not to have mattered to Clinton, who was attracted to Kennedy's sex appeal and charisma. Coelho argues that Kennedy was in "serious trouble" at the time of his death and might not have won a second term.[52]

The most widely acclaimed postpresidencies of the twentieth century are not ones likely to appeal to Bill Clinton—besides Jimmy Carter, the name that comes up most frequently as an impressive postpresident is that of Herbert Hoover. Seventy-five years after he left the White House and forty-four years after his death, when most people hear the name "Hoover," they think of the Great Depression and the miserable "Hoovervilles" that resulted. "Of all the ex-presidencies in my lifetime," says Ted Sorensen, "Hoover had a very constructive [one]"—made possible, Sorensen adds, by President Harry Truman who named Hoover head of the Hoover Commission to make government more efficient.[53]

FDR never had a postpresidency, so his legacy rests on his terms in office, and, because he led the country in a different era, certainly not on relationships he had with Lucy Mercer or other women thought to have been his White House intimates. Had he outlived his last term, says his biographer, Conrad Black, he would have spent his retirement pursuing hobbies—deep-sea fishing, coastal sailing—and he would have built a house in Key West, Florida, from which to pursue them. He would have continued to try to reverse the ravages of polio; during the last five years in office he rarely walked with his braces alone. He would have written a memoir. "He strangely was not a particularly talented writer," says Black. And because he lacked the discipline to write a book, he would have told it to others who would have written it and he would have edited the typescript. He described to a friend his plans for what would become the United Nations and the friend wrote in her diary that FDR would like, postpresidency, to be "chairman" (i.e., secretary-general).[54]

Harry Truman did not play an active role postpresidency; Eisenhower stuck to his farm in Gettysburg, Pennsylvania, just as Lyndon Johnson stuck to his ranch outside Austin, Texas.

Bill Clinton never met LBJ and certainly gave no thought to emulating him. In the spring of 1968, shortly before Clinton graduated from college, LBJ announced that he would not run again. Had he run, he might have been defeated, so bitter were the arguments over Vietnam. "I think that Vietnam took a lot of life out of him," says his older daughter, Lynda Robb. "No question, he was a casualty."

He shared heart disease with Bill Clinton and the sense that he would die young. "He had said to everybody over and over and over again," says his daughter, "that none of the men in his family lived past sixty, or much past."

Johnson's postpresidency could not have been more different from Bill Clinton's. He made amends with people whose feelings he hurt during the heat of political battle. He went to University of Texas and Dallas Cowboy football games, happy to be surrounded by his family. He bought gifts for his wife and children and grandchildren. He doted on his grandson, Lyndon, and on Lucinda, his firstborn granddaughter. Much to Lady Bird's distress, he took to micromanaging the ranch. "His sphere was not quite as large as it had been," explains Lynda Robb. "He was organizing everybody around the ranch, . . . trying to raise chickens and gather their eggs and . . . try to make that part of the world pay for itself. . . . That didn't work out for too long." He took vacations, to Florida, to Mexico. "It was something he hadn't done before."

He also worked on his memoir, which didn't turn out the way his daughter would have liked. "I wish somebody had just gotten a tape recorder and gotten him to start talking. Because he was so good in small groups, one-on-one. . . . I think he believed that it wouldn't be presidential to write a kind of a folksy book. . . . The presidency was very special to him. . . . I think he felt that he wanted to be very respectful of the office, so I think his book was a little too textbook. . . .

"He let his hair grow long and scraggly," says Lynda Robb. "He thought that was funny. He laughed because he said that's what all the young people were doing."[55]

Johnson also worried about his legacy. He mostly stayed clear of Washington, but in 1970 Katharine Graham, owner and publisher of the *Washington Post*, invited LBJ to the paper's dining room to meet with top editors Ben Bradlee and Phil Geyelin—the men's criticism of Vietnam had made Johnson's life in the White House miserable. Another *Post* editor who was there, Eugene Patterson, recalled, "It was really a fascinating sidelight on history to sit and listen to this bird." He was accompanied by his assistant, Tom Johnson, a White House fellow and Johnson's deputy press secretary who had followed his boss to Texas. Johnson—who later ran CNN—supplied the backup data, the documents LBJ needed to vindicate himself. Patterson recalled that the former president "brought a whole file drawer full of paper, so LBJ would simply hold his hand out over his shoulder and Tom would whisk out a paper. . . . He was trying to get his spin on history before we got around to writing it." The lunch started at noon, and four hours later, Johnson was still holding forth. As the editors were wondering if they were going to get out the next day's paper, Lady Bird called and ordered him across the street to the Madison Hotel, where they were staying. "Come home for your nap, Lyndon."[56]

Johnson did not have a public role in the Nixon administration. "President Nixon very graciously would have somebody come down and brief Daddy on what was going on," says Lynda Robb. "He really did try to keep Daddy in the loop."

Johnson went on only one board, that of the Mayo Clinic. He gave some speeches, but Lynda Robb thinks he was not paid for them. "He just didn't do that."[57] In 1971, some two-plus years after he left office, he dedicated his Lyndon Baines Johnson Library and Museum, on the University of Texas campus in Austin. It adjoins the LBJ School of Public Affairs.

There's obviously a bit of sensitivity on Lynda's part when it comes to Bill Clinton. Probably the most famous photograph of Clinton—next to that of him greeting the beret-topped Monica on a rope line as if she were just another rallygoer—is the one of the sixteen-year-old Arkansan shaking hands with JFK. Lynda Robb opened her home to Bill Clinton, but, friends say, she's a bit put off that the supposedly voraciously curious Clinton has showed so little curiosity about her father.[58]

Sometime in the mid-1980s when Chuck Robb was governor of Virginia and Bill Clinton governor of Arkansas, the men and their wives traveled on a trade mission to Taiwan. "I would have to tell you that my father-in-law's older daughter never thought he was as vocal in praising her father as he could have been," recalls Chuck Robb. "She would have liked for him to have been more visibly supportive of some of the programs and policies that were developed by her father but . . . the charismatic young leader was JFK, not LBJ."[59]

He died on January 22, 1973, at Gillespie County, Texas.

Nixon's circumstances were as peculiar as the man. Having left the presidency in disgrace, says Ted Sorensen, "obviously he didn't have the same stature and influence that the others did."[60]

Although the parallels between Lyndon Johnson and Bill Clinton, both such enormously talented politicians who left the White House under a cloud, are striking, some see a closer parallel between Nixon and Clinton. Paul Orfalea notes a similar resilience in both men—Nixon's losing the governorship in 1962 after losing the presidency by a squeaker two years earlier, perhaps stolen from him by the partnership of JFK's father, Joseph Kennedy, and Chicago mayor Richard J. Daley, brooding, but organizing himself to come back. "Nixon managed in spite of himself. . . . Clinton is the same way," says Orfalea.[61]

To writer Mark Updegrove, Clinton's postpresidency is a combination of Carter's and Nixon's: "Nixon's because he left the White House under a cloud of controversy and pursued an activist postpresidency seeking rehabilitation for the sins that he committed in the White House and did so with great success, being celebrated against all odds . . . more as a venerable elder statesman than as a disgraced former president, the first to resign the presidency. The Nixon postpresidency is a model [for Clinton]," Updegrove argues, "because of the rehabilitation he was able to achieve."[62]

Nixon became a wise man who invited other wise men or would-be wise men to his home in Saddle River, New Jersey, where he fussed over the wine and pontificated off the record on great international issues. If the rest of the world saw the Monica Lewinsky scandal as incomprehensibly minor, so did much of the world find Watergate much ado about next to nothing. Larry Sabato, who sees a clear tie between Nixon and Clinton, says that Nixon "was able to pursue his career abroad if not at home, mainly because most of the other countries didn't regard Watergate as being serious. . . . They didn't even understand it. . . . Nixon had an excellent opportunity to rehabilitate himself because of his encyclopedic knowledge of foreign policy."[63]

Jonathan Alter also recognizes the parallel, although he sees the insecurities of the two men as being much different. Clinton, whom

Alter calls "a damaged soul in other ways," was not insecure in the way Nixon was. "They set about restoring their reputations in different ways. Nixon didn't really go off and try to help people; he wrote books. Clinton might write some more books, but he's not going to try to make his way back as a writer, but as a speaker and a convener. . . . He has always seen his role as bringing people together, like he did with Arafat and Rabin."[64]

President Clinton did communicate with Nixon and, says Jake Siewert, read and appreciated the long memos about specific world trouble spots that Nixon sent him. Nixon went about his memo writing in a classy manner. "Say what you want about Nixon," says Siewert, "and in my family he was the devil, but that was a very constructive way for an ex-president to act. You write a very thoughtful memo, that's really an eyes-only memo; you send it in quietly and you don't brag to the press that you're giving advice. Clinton would read it and he'd say, 'Hey, this guy grappled with this issue; he was as serious as anyone about figuring out how to deal with Russia.' . . . He'd read it, absorb it, and take something from it." Unlike Carter, says Siewert, who would pop up on CNN boasting about giving advice to Clinton, Nixon would do so without the need to take credit or publicize his contribution.[65] Clinton would later say publicly that Nixon, in the final weeks of his life, gave him his "wise counsel, especially with regard to Russia." At Nixon's funeral, Clinton also mentioned a telephone conversation and a letter received "just a month ago."[66]

For most "name" Democrats, any comparison of Clinton to Nixon is blasphemy. To Lynn Cutler, Nixon was "a crook" who "tried to take the country down."[67]

"I don't see any parallel," says Ted Sorensen. "Not only was Nixon a crook, but he was forced out of the White House, forced to resign in the middle of his term, and Clinton . . . wasn't forced out. . . . Those so-called sessions Nixon had, inviting people to see him, may have boosted his ego, but they didn't do anything for his reputation. They were so private that I know nothing about them."[68]

Yet, there was something about Nixon that struck a chord with Bill

Clinton; it wasn't only that they had both, at times, faced hideous demons within the walls of the White House. There was something more.

When Richard Nixon died on April 22, 1994, President Clinton immediately announced a state funeral. "[There was] not going to be any suggestion that Nixon was entitled to anything less," says Nixon's most recent biographer, Conrad Black. "He basically drew a line through Watergate and said, 'twice our president, twice our vice president; the nation officially mourns him.'"[69]

All four former presidents—Reagan, Bush, Ford, Carter—sat in the same row, making Clinton look boyish by comparison. The main eulogy was delivered by former secretary of state Henry A. Kissinger: "He stood on pinnacles that dissolved into precipices. He achieved greatly, and he suffered deeply, but he never gave up."[70]

Clinton's words that day were not as vivid as Kissinger's—the *Washington Post*'s television critic, Tom Shales, declared Clinton's eulogy "flat and uninspired."[71] But there is poignancy in what 42 said about 37, four years before 42 would come perilously close himself to losing his presidency.

"As a public man," Clinton said, "he always seemed to believe the greatest sin was remaining passive in the face of challenges, and he never stopped living by that creed. . . . Oh, yes, he knew great controversy amid defeat as well as victory. He made mistakes, and they, like his accomplishments, are part of his life and record. . . . But the enduring lesson of Richard Nixon is that he never gave up being part of the action and passion of his times. He said many times that unless a person has a goal, a new mountain to climb, his spirit will die. . . . May the day of judging President Nixon on anything less than his entire life and career come to a close."[72]

BILL CLINTON'S friends cannot get out of their minds how close they came to attending his funeral in the late summer of 2004, that even a short delay in his bypass surgery could have meant a fatal heart attack. While some say he's the same old Bill Clinton, that he did not seem to take much in the way of life lessons away from his illness, others say he's fundamentally changed. Hank Sheinkopf sees "a different air about him, a much more thoughtful look . . . less glib."[73] Tony Coelho says that Clinton, postsurgeries, "doesn't look as healthy, but he looks much more relaxed. . . . He really looks at peace with himself now."[74]

He is also noticeably older and slighter looking. Ray Lesniak says that when the two embraced recently, "he felt a little frail."[75] Clinton is in better shape than he was "when he was eating those cheeseburgers," says Larry King, "but the older you get, you get a little hunched over. You lose an inch in height."[76] To one journalist who has extensive one-on-one time with Clinton, he looks shorter, less commanding. "There's something about his gravitas that has sort of gone away a little."[77]

Others say they like the new look: the white hair, the lean physique. Nelson Shanks, who painted his portrait, calls him "pudgy" when he was in the White House; later "much better looking . . . not as pudgy in the face and a little more wizened perhaps; the whiter hair was much more interesting than the salt and pepper."[78]

Clinton is more disciplined about his eating, although he still can't resist a bowl of Doritos or Fritos and granola bars when he finds them waiting on a private plane.[79] When he eats at Phil Stefani's restaurants, he eats pasta, lamb—Stefani says he particularly loves lamb—chicken, even steak. He would not order a pasta with a cream sauce but would order one with marinara sauce.[80]

He drinks little alcohol, wine occasionally, but remains addicted to Diet Coke. He chews on rather than smokes cigars and plays incessantly with the clipper.[81]

He is proud of his exercise regimen—he no longer runs, but he walks four miles a day.[82] He described his routine to former Iowa governor Tom Vilsack: "It's a German-based training system that involves balance and light weights; it's pretty intricate. Like everything else, he has an understanding of the detail of it. . . . Most of us are just thankful if we can lace the shoes and get on the treadmill."[83]

Clinton's friends worry about his pace and his seeming inability to keep any sort of normal sleep schedule. "I would like to know that he rested more," says Susie Tompkins Buell, "but . . . he's the man who doesn't rest."[84]*

John Emerson traces Clinton's driven nature to his boyhood. "When someone has a parent . . . who died young, you feel like you better hurry up because you never know, is this day going to be your last? Now he's the most optimistic guy I've ever met, . . . so he's not someone who's sitting there, 'Oh, my gosh I might die tomorrow,' but I think in part the drive and the energy . . . that's sort of his mind-set . . . I wish he'd slow down and take care of himself more." But, says Emerson, Bill Clinton says to himself, "I've got a lot I want to do and I just have to keep pushing at it.' "[86]

IN 2007, as Clinton campaigned for his wife, he was looking and feeling good. Don Hewitt calls Clinton "about as attractive a male as anybody's ever seen. When you marry that with former president of the United States, you get an animal who's one of a kind."[87]

When Simon Rosenberg saw him in January 2007 at a reception in Washington marking Hillary's reelection to the Senate, "he looked amazing. . . . He looked better physically than I've seen him in a couple of years."[88]

Yet as the campaign heated up and Hillary took the humiliating loss in Iowa, he looked exhausted; some days he looked seventy, not sixty-one. His hair seemed as unhinged as his speeches; he no longer looked elegant. He seemed bloated; his jackets didn't fall right and they pulled at the button. On the Sunday before Martin Luther King Day 2008, he was the guest of honor at services to mark the holiday at the Covenant Avenue Baptist Church in Harlem. Seated in a comfortable chair behind the preacher, he fell asleep. His futile struggle to keep awake was on

---

*While appearing on *The Daily Show with Jon Stewart,* in late September 2007, Clinton suggested that presidential candidates get more sleep and diagnosed what was wrong with the Congress: "I do believe sleep deprivation has a lot to do with some of the edginess of Washington today," he said.[85]

video for the world to view. The *New York Post* headlined its story, complete with photos and video, "Bill Has a 'Dream.'"

Bill Clinton still predicts that he won't live a long life. At first, when he left the White House and was preparing to hit the lecture circuit, he would say, according to Jake Siewert, "I need to provide for my family because no one in my family lives very long."[89]

His quadruple bypass focused his attention on the fragility of life. "He had a second chance and most people don't even have a first chance," says Chris Stamos.[90] Two surgeries later, his friends worry about him because they don't know what fixes are left should he relapse. "I do believe that the president is pushing himself far too hard," writes Tony Campolo. "His health has failed him at times, and I sometimes think that he is not aware of his own physical vulnerabilities."[91]

Alan Solomont sits on a board with Ira Magaziner who is always saying that they worry about Clinton's intensity and pace—always running around the world.[92] Lou Weisbach has the same concern, which he mentioned to Hillary. She said that she and his doctors think he's doing more than he should be doing.[93]

Leon Panetta describes the transformative nature of Clinton's illness: it forced him to "think about what life is all about and what you want life to be." On the other hand, Panetta admits, Clinton is falling back into his old habits. "He seems to be getting back into that pretty quickly. . . . He's got a campaign schedule now that won't stop. . . . I was just listening to him speak. . . . You could hear it in his voice; he's reached a point where it's starting to wear."[94]

Chapter 13

IT'S MONICA, STUPID!

WILL BILL CLINTON, LIKE JIMMY CARTER, NOT BE able to fix his presidential legacy, and, in the end, have to settle for being judged a better postpresident than president?

"I think Bill Clinton is following in the footsteps of Jimmy Carter," says Susan Davis, "in being probably a more important leader and figure in his postpresidency than even while he's president." She does not blame the scandals for weakening his presidential legacy—those scandals were "amplified," she says, "because you had full-time forces working to try to generate scandal, his personal failings notwithstanding"—but the very nature of politics that keeps a leader, no matter how talented, from achieving significant change. She admires Clinton's postpresidency, she says, because "he could be just making lots of money and playing golf." Instead, "he has displayed great leadership and been a convener and mobilizer for citizen action . . . and social entrepreneurs."[1]

Tim Wirth sees Bill Clinton as having finally, in a sense, grown up, having finally come to accept that the appellation "rock star" is just silly. When asked if he thinks that it annoys Jimmy Carter that Clinton is always referred to as a rock star, Wirth says, "Jimmy Carter wouldn't want to be a rock star. . . . When you think about Jimmy Carter, you think of a great humanitarian, and Bill Clinton's learning how to do that, too."[2]

When, at the dedication of his library, George McGovern introduced Clinton, he said that the former president, "very possibly will do more in the years ahead to reduce disease and poverty and hunger than any other person on the planet."[3]

And while some scoff at Clinton's celebrity, seeing it as an affectation that impedes accomplishment, others see it as a positive in a world in which communication is global and celebrity can move millions. Tony Coelho sees Clinton as "the most recognized person in the world today since the previous pope's death"—bigger even than Nelson Mandela.[4]

Some see Clinton as a man who is simply better suited to the postpresidency than to the presidency. It's as if the missteps and the pain of his presidency were necessary to forge this enormously impressive postpresidential product. Peter Hart characterizes Clinton's postpresidency as "miraculous."[5]

Clinton's personal charisma and his popularity are keys to this larger-than-life, okay, rock star, quality that clings to him through illness and time. Yes, he now looks his age, and then some. Yes, the boyish quality is gone. But what remains is a character that Patrick Creadon relished after filming Bill Clinton for his movie *Wordplay*. He and his wife and an assistant "played a little game. How could we top this? Who on earth would we be able to interview who would be better than Bill Clinton? We thought about it for a long time. We threw out a couple of names and they paled by comparison and we realized of all the people on the planet there's really nobody else that we would rather have interviewed for our film. . . . If you had 125 world leaders . . . , and Bill Clinton was in the room, I would say most people would be really excited to go meet Bill Clinton."

Clinton would even walk away with the honors, Creadon says, if the room were full of the hottest stars in Hollywood. "It doesn't matter if Bono and Brad Pitt and Angelina Jolie and Tony Blair, even Nelson

Mandela. . . . There is a glow around Bill Clinton. . . . I've seen it first-hand and I've experienced it and I think that's why I say that I think history will be very good to him."[6]

SOME MIGHT say that the boyhood struggles Clinton faced and, for the most part, overcame, explain the later lapses. Still, the disturbing parts of the Clinton legacy cannot be wished away or excused away. To some extent, what's behind today's celebration of the Clinton presidency is the shrinking of the George W. Bush presidency because of the fiasco in Iraq.

It is surprising how many people who know and like Bill Clinton come to the same sad conclusion: Monica Lewinsky and impeachment are an implacable part of Clinton's White House legacy, and all the wondrous works in the years ahead may enhance his reputation as an ex-president, but not as a president.

In the end, Bill Clinton was old enough to be her father; he was the one with all the authority, and he took advantage of her because he thought he could. His friends may blame Monica for flashing her thong, or Tipper Gore for being such a bluenose, or even Hillary for looking the other way or for not being much fun as a companion, but no one says it with much conviction.

"I was thinking about something the other day," says Don Hewitt. "Do you know there's not one kid who has died in Iraq who wouldn't be alive today if there never was a Monica Lewinsky. Monica Lewinsky changed the world. Had there been no Monica Lewinsky, Tipper Gore wouldn't have insisted that she didn't want her husband campaigning with Bill Clinton; they would have won two more states if they had allowed him to campaign with them in the South. . . . I think [Monica] did more to change the world than Cleopatra."[7]

One friend and former supporter of Bill Clinton's—he's now in the Obama camp—says with some bitterness, "I hope it was a really good blow job. But you think about what he gave up for that. If he had not been morally compromised, publicly, . . . Al Gore would not have run from him but toward him and Gore would have been elected and we'd be finishing the second term of the Gore presidency and the world would be a different place."[8]

When Peggy Noonan, who has composed some important speeches for Republicans, wrote a tribute in the *Wall Street Journal* to Gerald Ford on his death in December 2006, every word seemed a rebuke to the legacy-obsessed Bill Clinton. "One of the greatest things about Gerald Ford as a former president was that he didn't say much. He had no need for the spotlight. . . . There is no evidence that he was obsessed with his legacy. He didn't worry and fret about whether history would fully capture and proclaim his excellence, and because of this he didn't always have to run around proving he was right. . . . The legacy of a man who spends his time worrying about his legacy is always: He worried about his legacy. . . . Gerald Ford fought for his country. He didn't indulge his angers and appetites. He seems to have thought, in the end, that such indulgence was for sissies—it wasn't manly."[9]

Larry King, who loves Bill Clinton, recalls the days when Clinton was governor of Arkansas and King had a radio show: "He called up my old radio show at two in the morning about an issue we were discussing and I said, 'What are you doing up at two in the morning, Governor?' And he said, 'Never mind.' I think people regard him as a guy with a weakness who happens to be a tremendous person, who if he didn't have this weakness would be up there with Jefferson and Washington and Lincoln." King is one of many who promises, "History will be very good to Bill Clinton."

Especially if the historians can somehow sit across from him, have a conversation with him. "Not doing it quietly like Carter," says King, who probably has it just about right when he says, "You could take his strongest critic. Put him alone in a room for five minutes and he likes Bill Clinton. I've never met a political figure like that."[10]

To one important Democrat, Lou Susman, who ran the finance end of the Kerry campaign and has aligned himself this time with Obama, in the end what Clinton does postpresidency is irrelevant. The history books that generations to come will read will focus on Clinton's presidency; it won't matter how many trips to Africa he makes, how many babies he holds, how many billions he raises at CGI conferences. What matters is what he did or didn't do as president. "His legacy will be his morals," says Susman, adding as his frustration rises, "How do you have an affair with an intern in the White House? You don't have to let that happen. That shows total lack of judgment and discipline."[11]

Hillary, again, pays the price for her husband's sins: "I think Hillary's a very bright woman," says one man who works at the top of the Democratic Party, "but . . . I'll kill myself if she's the nominee."[12]

Bob Clifford, another of Bill Clinton's supporters, who has switched to Barack Obama, says about the former president, "He's just a unique human being, as unique in politics as Muhammad Ali or Barry Bonds are in sports."[13]

The operative name is Barry Bonds, whose home run record will carry, if not a literal, then a figurative asterisk for alleged steroid use. Bill Clinton's legacy will also always carry an asterisk, although there is nothing "alleged" about the fact that he was impeached. (Andrew Johnson and Bill Clinton are the only presidents in American history to be impeached; both were impeached by the House and acquitted by the Senate.)

"I don't think it's any great mystery," says Leon Panetta, "that what happened in the second term obviously created the shadow [over] a lot of the good things that I think President Clinton did, . . . would have made him one of the great presidents but for what happened in that second term."[14] Elaine Kamarck calls Clinton's "an interrupted presidency." Coming off his big reelection win in 1996, he had the political capital to revamp the entitlement programs, Social Security and Medicare, pension reform, which only a Democrat could do, just as it took a Republican to open up China. Clinton "squandered his chance to be Franklin Roosevelt's true successor" and instead "had to use every bit of his political capital to save his presidency in the impeachment vote." The consequence was that he took "a very promising second term and basically threw it away."[15]

When historian Douglas Brinkley is asked whether Lewinsky and impeachment will appear in the first sentence of Clinton's obituary, he responds that if it's not in the first sentence, it will be in the first paragraph—no matter what Bill Clinton accomplishes in the years to come.[16]

ACKNOWLEDGMENTS

My husband has always had much more confidence in me than I have in myself, and this time most of all. He wanted me to write this book, and helped me in every way he could, including sacrificing time together and vacations. He expressed impatience only once, when he suggested that we needed to take a vacation together right away, and that even Baghdad was beginning to sound good to him.

My children were my mainstay, my support, and my sounding board. If they missed spending time with me, and I like to think that they did, they always made me feel that I was embarked on something worthy, and that the anecdotes I was pulling from interviews—167 of them, almost all done within six months—were interesting to them and would be interesting to readers as well.

The idea for a postpresidency book on Bill Clinton came to me one sleepless night while I read Patricia O'Toole's *When Trumpets Call: Theodore Roosevelt After the White House* (2005). I had written a biography of TR's firstborn, Alice, published in 1988, and Joseph Gardner's *Departing Glory: Theodore Roosevelt as Ex-president* (1973) had been a source for that book.

I am a compulsive follower of politics and of selected American presidents, and my collection of books on Teddy Roosevelt was out-numbered only by my collection of books on Bill (and Hillary) Clinton. It seemed that every square inch of Bill Clinton's life had been examined, but I knew that one segment had not yet been covered in a book—the years after he left the White House on January 20, 2001, trailing controversy, scandal, misunderstanding, and, typically, drama, both high and low.

Before dawn, I e-mailed my agent, Flip Brophy, and I was soon working under the guidance of Henry Ferris—this is our first book together—a passionate editor who knows what he wants and did not want the thematic approach to biography that I presented him with in my first draft. "Chronology, chronology, chronology," he lectured me, suggesting that I remember the real estate adage "location, location, location" whenever I felt the urge to drift. He also insisted that I stick to the postpresidency years, not allowing me too often to wander back into the White House years, or, worse yet, the Georgetown, Oxford, Yale Law, and Little Rock years. Henry kept me to the point, and, probably to the reader's benefit, insisted that I cut 50,000-plus words. He was not shy about telling me which words would not be missed.

Henry's assistant, Peter Hubbard, has been attentive, helpful, and cheerful. I look forward to working more with him as the book moves toward publication.

Flip Brophy has been my friend and agent for twenty-four years. I value her advice, her ability to cut to the main point, a profanity or two usually dropped along the way, and her special sensitivity to people like me who write about politics and media. She seems to know everyone in the business and everyone seems to know (and respect) her.

I also want to thank my editor at *Chicago* magazine, Chris Newman. We have worked together since the early 1980s. She is a close friend and an editor of enormous talent and insight. She called me regularly to make certain I was keeping my head above the piles of news clips, books, and untranscribed tapes. (We both wondered why I felt I had to transcribe the tapes myself.)

Chicago magazine photo editor Brittney Blair, whom I came to know and admire for her work on the profiles I write for *Chicago* magazine, agreed to take on the freelance job of picture research. As always, she is the best at translating into a visual the story I am trying to tell. Her boss, *Chicago* editor in chief Richard Babcock, told me what I already knew about Brittney, that she is "first-rate." He also told me more than once—and lifted my sometimes sagging spirits—that he and his staff missed the profiles I had been writing for them, every one of which benefited enormously from his editorial vision and skill.

The author photo was shot by Randi Shepard. I'd rather transcribe tapes than be photographed, as Randi already knew; still her talent and patience produced—well, you can see for yourself—and imagine what she might have done with a better subject. Cid Nowosad expertly designed, improved, and enhanced my website, and it too you can see for yourself, at carolfelsenthal.com.

Also thanks to Laurie McGee, the meticulous and smart copy editor who left her mark on almost every line of the manuscript, and to Kathryn Erickson for her able assistance with legal matters.

Finally, thanks to all my sources who agreed to talk to me on the record, and also to those who talked but did not want to be named, in most cases concerned about the reaction of Bill and Hillary, a powerful pair whether or not they return this time to the White House. Bill Clinton will continue to be, as he is so often called, "the most popular man in the world," and Hillary will never abandon her plan, this time or next, to become the first woman president.

NOTES

The following abbreviations are used throughout:
A D-G Arkansas Democrat-Gazette
AP Associated Press
BG The Boston Globe
C S-T Chicago Sun-Times
CT The Chicago Tribune
LAT The Los Angeles Times
NYDN The New York Daily News
NY mag New York magazine
NYob New York Observer
NYP The New York Post
NYT The New York Times
NYT mag The New York Times Magazine
NYer The New Yorker
NW Newsweek
VF Vanity Fair
WSJ The Wall Street Journal
WP The Washington Post

Chapter 1 OH, FOR JUST ONE MORE TERM

1. Donna Shalala, Interview with author, September 25, 2006; David Schulte, Interview with author, September 8, 2006; Neil Hartigan, Interview with author, November 28, 2006.

2. Terry McAuliffe, with Steve Kettmann, *What a Party: My Life Among Democrats, Presidents, Candidates, Donors, Activists, Alligators, and Other Wild Animals*, St. Martin's Press, Thomas Dunne Books, 2007, p. 262.

3. Jim Guy Tucker, Interview with author, November 13, 2006.

4. Mark Buell, Interview with author, August 22, 2006.

5. Transcript of Democratic National Committee dinner remarks, June 30, 1999, Chicago.

6. Melanne Verveer, Interview with author, January 27, 2007.

7. Noemie Emery, "Days of Their Lives: The Hillary and Bill Show, America's Longest-Running Soap Opera," *Weekly Standard*, June 4, 2007.

8. Burt and Carol Stringfellow, "Hatch Helped Our Son," *Salt Lake Tribune*, July 26, 2006; Rocky Anderson, Interview with author, October 20, 2006.

9. Rocky Anderson, Interview with author, October 20, 2006.

10. Jack Quinn, Interviews with author, February 1, 2007, February 13, 2007, March 1, 2007.

11. Editorial, "Geffen and Clinton," *New York Sun*, February 22, 2007.

12. Jack Quinn, Interviews with author, February 1, 2007, February 13, 2007, March 1, 2007; Stephen Braun and Dan Morain, "Famous Allies Were Often at Odds; David Geffen Shocked Many by Speaking Out Against Hillary Clinton. But He and Bill Clinton Had a Rocky Friendship," *LAT*, March 4, 2007; Editorial, "The Democratic Field," *WSJ*, January 20, 2007; Alison Leigh Cowan, "Panel Says Top Justice Dept. Aide Held Information on Rich's Pardon," *NYT*, March 13, 2002; Amy Goldstein and Susan Schmidt, "Clinton's Last-Day Clemency Benefits 176; List Includes Pardons for Cisneros, McDougal, Deutch and Roger Clinton," *WP*, January 21, 2001.

13. Jack Quinn, Interviews with author, February 1, 2007, February 13, 2007, March 1, 2007.

14. Ibid.

15. Ibid; Sally Bedell Smith, *For Love of Politics: Bill and Hillary Clinton: The White House Years*, Random House, 2007, p. 448.

16. Terry McAuliffe, with Steve Kettmann, *What a Party: My Life Among Democrats, Presidents, Candidates, Donors, Activists, Alligators, and Other Wild Animals*, St. Martin's Press, Thomas Dunne Books, 2007, p. 271; Larry King, Interview with author, October 28, 2006.

17. Interview; source wishes to remain anonymous.

18. Bill Miller, "Clinton Administration Delays in Issuing Pardons; Debate Over McDougal Holds Up Announcement," *WP*, January 20, 2001.

19. Chris Jennings, Interview with author, August 2, 2006.

20. John F. Harris, "'We Did a Lot of Good'; The Clintons Depart for a Radically New Life in New York," *WP*, January 21, 2001; Sally Bedell Smith, *For Love of Politics: Bill and Hillary Clinton: The White House Years*, Random House, 2007, p. 449.

21. Amy Goldstein and Susan Schmidt, "Clinton's Last-Day Clemency Benefits 176; List Includes Pardons for Cisneros, McDougal, Deutch and Roger Clinton," *WP*, January 21, 2001.

22. Interview; source wishes to remain anonymous.

23. Marjorie Williams, "Scenes from a Marriage (Bill Clinton and Al Gore)," in *The Woman at the Washington Zoo: Writings on Politics, Family, and Fate*, edited by Timothy Noah, Public Affairs, 2005, p. 134.

24. Melanne Verveer, Interview with author, January 27, 2007.

25. Tony Coelho, Interview with author, September 5, 2006; Tom Downey, Interview with author, January 9, 2007.

26. Tom Downey, Interview with author, January 9, 2007; Lynn Cutler, Interviews with author, June 22, 2006, June 29, 2006.

27. Leon Panetta, Interview with author, October 17, 2006; Tom Downey, Interview with author, January 9, 2007; Michael Barone, Interview with author, September 19, 2006; Joe Power, Interview with author, August 14, 2006; Larry King, Interview with author, October 28, 2006.

28. Mark Buell, Interview with author, August 22, 2006.

29. Tony Coelho, Interview with author, September 5, 2006; *Tim Russert Conversations* (with Sally Bedell Smith), MSNBC, October 28, 2007.

30. Jake Siewert, Interview with author, January 15, 2007; Sally Bedell Smith, *For Love of Politics: Bill and Hillary Clinton: The White House Years*, Random House, 2007.

31. Leon Panetta, Interview with author, October 17, 2006.

32. Don Fowler, Interview with author, February 14, 2007.

33. Douglas Brinkley, Interview with author, September 14, 2006.

34. Larry Sabato, Interview with author, July 31, 2006.

35. Lynn Cutler, Interview with author, June 29, 2006.

36. Howard Tullman, Interview with author, June 26, 2006.

37. Joe Power, Interview with author, August 14, 2006.

38. Tony Coelho, Interview with author, September 5, 2006.

39. Larry Sabato, Interview with author, July 31, 2006.

40. Anson Beard Jr., Interview with author, September 27, 2006.

41. Chris Jennings, Interview with author, August 2, 2006.

42. Jake Siewert, Interview with author, January 15, 2007.

43. Ibid.

44. Richard L. Berke and Katharine Q. Seelye, "The 2000 Campaign: The Vice President; In Latest Shift, Gore's Campaign Names New Chief," NYT, June 16, 2000.

45. Tony Coelho, Interview with author, September 5, 2006.

46. Howard Tullman, Interview with author, June 26, 2006; David Plotz, "Larry Summers," *Slate*, June 30, 2001.

47. Leon Panetta, Interview with author, October 17, 2006.

48. Interview; source wishes to remain anonymous.

49. John Catsimatidis, Interview with author, October 9, 2006.

50. Lee Hockstader, "Clinton Bids Farewell to Israelis and Palestinians; Letters Ask Each to Push for Peace," WP, January 20, 2001; Sally Bedell Smith, *For Love of Politics: Bill and Hillary Clinton: The White House Years*, Random House, 2007.

51. John F. Harris, "'We Did a Lot of Good'; The Clintons Depart for a Radically

New Life in New York," WP, January 21, 2001; Dan Morgan and Amy Goldstein, "Racing the Clock with New Regulations; Clinton Administration Scrambles in Final Hours to Get Rules into Register," WP, January 20, 2001.

52. Jake Siewert, Interview with author, January 15, 2007.

53. Richard W. Stevenson, "The Inauguration: The Agenda; To Do: 1. Undo Most Recent Actions of My Predecessor," NYT, January 21, 2001.

54. Bill Daley (earlier interview for Chicago magazine profile, February 2005).

55. Phil Ross, Interview with author, October 9, 2006; Mark Evans, Interview with author, October 16, 2006.

56. George McGovern, Interview with author, November 1, 2006.

57. Gina Piccalo, "A Glamorous Drug, an Illness, a Very Public Battle; In the Strange Trial of Irena Medavoy Versus Botox, Nobody Is Left Looking Perfect," LAT, September 22, 2004; Irena Medavoy, Interviews with author, October 23, 2006, October 25, 2006; Bud Yorkin, Interview with author, October 9, 2006.

58. Lou Weisbach, Interview with author, July 11, 2006.

59. Phil Stefani, Interview with author, August 15, 2006.

60. Ibid.

61. "President's Visit," C S-T, January 9, 2001; Eric Holder, Interview with author, December 5, 2006.

62. Sabrina L. Miller, "Clinton Last Hurrah Roaring in Chicago; In the Waning Days of His Presidency, Bill Clinton Returns to His Kind of Town for a Love Fest," CT, January 10, 2001.

63. Paul McGrath, Interview with author, July 31, 2006.

64. Scott Fornek and Abdon M. Pallasch, "Thank You from the Bottom of Our Hearts," C S-T, January 10, 2001.

65. Rick Kogan, Interview with author, May 26, 2006.

66. Richard Roeper, "President Makes Time to Talk Running Times," C S-T, January 11, 2001.

67. Robert Torricelli, Interview with author, October 6, 2006.

68. Anne-Marie O'Connor, "Hollywood Patrons Beset by Politicians; Finance: Candidates from Throughout the Nation Seek Out Celebrities' Star Power to Raise Campaign Funds," LAT, February 24, 2002.

69. Sally Bedell Smith, For Love of Politics: Bill and Hillary Clinton: The White House Years, Random House, 2007, p. 446.

70. Terry McAuliffe, with Steve Kettmann, What a Party: My Life Among Democrats, Presidents, Candidates, Donors, Activists, Alligators, and Other Wild Animals, St. Martin's Press, Thomas Dunne Books, 2007, p. 254; John F. Harris and Bill Miller, "In a Deal, Clinton Avoids Indictment; President Admits False Testimony," WP, January 20, 2001; Peter Baker, "Clinton Settles Paula Jones Lawsuit for $850,000," WP, November 14, 1998.

Chapter 2 THE BEST HOUSE

1. John F. Harris and Bill Miller, "In a Deal, Clinton Avoids Indictment; President Admits False Testimony," *WP*, January 20, 2001.

2. "The Inauguration; Excerpt from Clinton Radio Address. Following Are Excerpts from President Clinton's Radio Address Yesterday, His Last as President, as Released by the White House," *NYT*, January 21, 2001; John F. Harris, "'We Did a Lot of Good'; The Clintons Depart for a Radically New Life in New York," *WP*, January 21, 2001; Tom Shales, "Commander in Chief of the Small Screen," *WP*, January 20, 2001; Mike Allen and Edward Walsh, "Bush Calls for Unity, Civility; Texan Sworn in as the Nation's 43rd President," *WP*, January 21, 2001; Sally Bedell Smith, *For Love of Politics: Bill and Hillary Clinton: The White House Years*, Random House, 2007, p. 450.

3. Jake Siewert, Interview with author, January 15, 2007.

4. Katharine Q. Seelye, "The Inauguration: The Departure; Gore Takes a Last Bow with Grace and Relief," *NYT*, January 21, 2001; Sally Bedell Smith, *For Love of Politics: Bill and Hillary Clinton: The White House Years*, Random House, 2007, p. 450.

5. Melinda A. Henneberger, "The Inauguration: The Speech; In His Address, Bush Lingers on a Promise to Care," *NYT*, January 21, 2001.

6. Sarah Wilson, Interview with author, February 16, 2007.

7. Ibid.; Jake Siewert, Interview with author, January 15, 2007.

8. Jake Siewert, Interview with author, January 15, 2007.

9. Adam Nagourney, "The Inauguration: The Departing President; After 'Ride of My Life,' Clinton Is Sentimental," *NYT*, January 21, 2001.

10. Terry McAuliffe, with Steve Kettmann, *What a Party: My Life Among Democrats, Presidents, Candidates, Donors, Activists, Alligators, and Other Wild Animals*, St. Martin's Press, Thomas Dunne Books, 2007, p. 256; Adam Nagourney, "The Inauguration: The Departing President; After 'Ride of My Life,' Clinton Is Sentimental," *NYT*, January 21, 2001; John F. Harris, "'We Did a Lot of Good'; The Clintons Depart for a Radically New Life in New York," *WP*, January 21, 2001.

11. Charles Robb, Interview with author, October 23, 2006.

12. Jake Siewert, Interview with author, January 15, 2007.

13. Ibid.

14. Jonathan Alter, Interview with author, August 10, 2006.

15. Tom Shales, "Misty Eyes Through TV's Misty Lens," *WP*, January 21, 2001.

16. Mickey Ibarra, Interview with author, November 7, 2006.

17. Charles Robb, Interview with author, October 23, 2006.

18. Ibid.; Sarah Wilson, Interview with author, February 16, 2007.

19. Sarah Wilson, Interview with author, February 16, 2007.

20. Rocky Anderson, Interview with author, October 20, 2006; Mickey Ibarra, Interview with author, November 7, 2006.

21. Stan Brand, Interview with author, September 13, 2006; Amy Goldstein and Susan Schmidt, "Clinton's Last-Day Clemency Benefits 176; List Includes Pardons for

Cisneros, McDougal, Deutch and Roger Clinton," *WP*, January 21, 2001; Jim Guy Tucker, Interview with author, November 13, 2006.

22. Susan Schmidt, "White House Ordered to Surrender Lawyers' Notes; Appeal Planned of Ruling That Whitewater Discussions with First Lady Are Not Privileged," *WP*, May 3, 1997; Sharon LaFraniere, "Records List Hubbell White House Visits; Former Official Saw Clintons Four Times After Resigning Justice Post," *WP*, May 3, 1997.

23. Ron Kaufman, Interview with author, December 11, 2006; "Bush Bows Out; 'Mr. and Mrs. Citizen' Fly Home to Houston," *Seattle Post-Intelligencer*, January 21, 1993; William E. Clayton Jr., Jo Ann Zuniga, and Stefanie Asin, "The Clinton Inauguration; 'This Is Our Time,' Clinton Says; Bush: 'It's Been One Helluva Ride'; Ex-President Says Goodbye to D.C., Hello to Houston," *Houston Chronicle*, January 21, 1993.

24. Melanne Verveer, Interview with author, January 27, 2007.

25. Terry McAuliffe, with Steve Kettmann, *What a Party: My Life Among Democrats, Presidents, Candidates, Donors, Activists, Alligators, and Other Wild Animals*, St. Martin's Press, Thomas Dunne Books, 2007, p. 259; Dana Milbank, "An Orderly—and Uncomfortable—Power Transfer," *WP*, January 21, 2001; Tom Shales, "Misty Eyes Through TV's Misty Lens," *WP*, January 21, 2001; John F. Harris, "'We Did a Lot of Good'; The Clintons Depart for a Radically New Life in New York," *WP*, January 21, 2001.

26. Sandy Berger, Interview with author, October 3, 2006.

27. Jake Siewert, Interview with author, January 15, 2007; Adam Nagourney, "His Perks and Power Gone, Clinton Faces Storm Alone," *NYT*, March 1, 2001; Susan Baer, "Hillary's World," *Washingtonian*, April 2007; AP, "Clintons' Neighbors Shot Near Home, Disbarred Lawyer, Teacher Are Forced Off Road and Shot En Route from NYC," November 20, 2006.

28. Interview; source wishes to remain anonymous.

29. Howard Tullman, Interview with author, June 26, 2006.

30. Interview; source wishes to remain anonymous.

31. Larry Sabato, Interview with author, July 31, 2006.

32. Joanna Coles, "Private Life, Public Fiasco," *Times* (London), February 21, 2001.

33. Mark Buell, Interview with author, August 22, 2006.

34. Joanna Coles, "Private Life, Public Fiasco," *Times* (London), February 21, 2001.

35. Jake Siewert, Interview with author, January 15, 2007; Sally Bedell Smith, *For Love of Politics: Bill and Hillary Clinton: The White House Years*, Random House, 2007, p. 452.

36. Susie Tompkins Buell, Interview with author, September 5, 2006.

37. Chris Jennings, Interview with author, August 2, 2006.

38. Jonathan Alter, Interview with author, August 10, 2006.

39. Sarah Wilson, Interview with author, February 16, 2007.

40. Lynn Cutler, Interview with author, June 29, 2006.

41. Larry Sabato, Interview with author, July 31, 2006.

42. Jake Siewert, Interview with author, January 15, 2007.

43. Ibid.

44. Ibid.

45. Mary McGrory, "Bush's Inadvertent Benefactors," WP, January 25, 2001.

46. Larry Sabato, Interview with author, July 31, 2006.

47. Transcript, *The Tonight Show with Jay Leno*, NBC, January 25, 2001.

48. Jake Siewert, Interview with author, January 15, 2007.

49. Melanne Verveer, Interview with author, January 27, 2007.

50. Terry McAuliffe, with Steve Kettmann, *What a Party: My Life Among Democrats, Presidents, Candidates, Donors, Activists, Alligators, and Other Wild Animals*, St. Martin's Press, Thomas Dunne Books, 2007, p.269.

51. Jake Siewert, Interview with author, January 15, 2007.

52. Mark Buell, Interview with author, August 22, 2006.

53. Jake Siewert, Interview with author, January 15, 2007; Sally Bedell Smith, *For Love of Politics: Bill and Hillary Clinton: The White House Years*, Random House, 2007, pp. 53, 352.

54. Amy Goldstein and Susan Schmidt, "Clinton's Last-Day Clemency Benefits 176; List Includes Pardons for Cisneros, McDougal, Deutch and Roger Clinton," WP, January 21, 2001; Christopher Spencer, "Starr Expresses Regret Clinton Inquiry Grew; Harding Lecture Focuses on Presidential Election," A D-G, April 21, 2001.

55. Ibid.

56. Melanne Verveer, Interview with author, January 27, 2007.

57. Jonathan Alter, Interview with author, August 10, 2006.

58. Mary Leonard, Susan Milligan, and Wayne Washington, "Clinton Exit Gives Party Shudders," BG, January 31, 2001.

59. Peter Slevin and George Lardner Jr., "Rush of Clinton Pardons Unusual in Scope, Lack of Scrutiny," WP, as reprinted in *South Bend Tribune*, March 11, 2001.

60. Robert Sam Anson, "Bill and His Shadow," VF, June 2004; Editorial, "Between Two Eras," NYT, February 11, 2001; Sally Bedell Smith, *For Love of Politics: Bill and Hillary Clinton: The White House Years*, Random House, 2007, p. 437.

61. Jack Quinn, Interview with author, February 1, 2007.

62. Eric Holder, Interview with author, December 5, 2006.

63. Scott Shane, "As Trial Begins, Cheney's Ex-Aide Is Still a Puzzle," NYT, January 17, 2007.

64. Jack Quinn, Interviews with author, February 1, 2007, February 13, 2007, March 1, 2007.

65. Interview; source wishes to remain anonymous.

66. Peter Slevin and George Lardner Jr., "Rush of Clinton Pardons Unusual in Scope, Lack of Scrutiny," WP, as reprinted in *South Bend Tribune*, March 11, 2001.

67. Alison Leigh Cowan, "Panel Says Top Justice Dept. Aide Held Information on Rich's Pardon," NYT, March 13, 2002; Mike Dorning, "Obama's Policy Team Loaded with All-Stars," CT, September 17, 2007.

68. Alison Leigh Cowan, "Panel Says Top Justice Dept. Aide Held Information on Rich's Pardon," NYT, March 13, 2002.

69. Eric Holder, Interview with author, December 5, 2006.

70. Interview; source wishes to remain anonymous; Don Fowler, Interview with author, February 14, 2007.

71. John Catsimatidis, Interview with author, October 9, 2006.

72. Jack Quinn, Interviews with author, February 1, 2007, February 13, 2007, March 1, 2007.

73. Leon Panetta, Interview with author, October 17, 2006.

74. Jim Guy Tucker, Interview with author, November 13, 2006.

75. Jake Siewert, Interview with author, January 15, 2007.

76. Al Kamen, "One Uninsured Group Can Now Exhale," WP, January 31, 2007.

77. Bill Clinton, *My Life*, Knopf, 2004, pp. 941–942.

78. Jake Siewert, Interview with author, January 15, 2007.

79. Ibid.

80. Ibid.

81. Ibid.

82. Ibid.

83. Ibid.

84. Ibid.

85. Editorial, "Between Two Eras," NYT, February 11, 2001.

86. Transcript, Lester Holt, MSNBC, February 16, 2001.

87. Interview; source wishes to remain anonymous; Terry McAuliffe, with Steve Kettmann, *What a Party: My Life Among Democrats, Presidents, Candidates, Donors, Activists, Alligators, and Other Wild Animals*, St. Martin's Press, Thomas Dunne Books, 2007, p. 262.

88. Janis Kearney, Interview with author, September 15, 2006.

89. Melanne Verveer, Interview with author, January 27, 2007.

90. Douglas Brinkley, Interview with author, September 14, 2006.

91. Larry Sabato, Interview with author, July 31, 2006.

92. Ibid.

93. Scott Jacobs, "Unchecked Baggage; Too Many Anonymous Sources and Little Insight Make for Weak Clinton-Bashing Attempt," C S-T, April 15, 2007.

94. Larry Sabato, Interview with author, July 31, 2006.

95. Joe Power, Interview with author, August 14, 2006.

96. Jake Siewert, Interview with author, January 15, 2007.

97. Anthony Campolo, e-mail to author, October 27, 2006.

98. Irena Medavoy, Interview with author, October 23, 2006.

99. Interview; source wishes to remain anonymous.

100. Hank Sheinkopf, Interview with author, August 21, 2006.

101. Mary Voboril, "Will NY Always Love Him?; Ex-Prez' Affection for City Is Mutual," *Newsday*, February 12, 2001.

102. Jake Siewert, Interview with author, January 15, 2007.

103. Adam Nagourney, "His Perks and Power Gone, Clinton Faces Storm Alone," NYT, March 1, 2001.

104. Bob Kerrey, Interviews with author, July 5, 2006, July 24, 2006.

105. Jonathan Alter, Interview with author, August 10, 2006; Sally Bedell Smith, *For Love of Politics: Bill and Hillary Clinton: The White House Years*, Random House, 2007, p. 355.

106. Bob Kerrey, Interview with author, July 24, 2006.

107. Ibid.; John E. Harris, *The Survivor*, Random House, 2005, pp. 90–92.

108. Jonathan Alter, Interview with author, August 10, 2006.

109. Bob Kerrey, Interview with author, July 24, 2006.

110. Lloyd Grove, "The Reliable Source," *WP*, February 6, 2001.

111. Elizabeth Kolbert, "Senator Bob Kerrey Brings His Enigmatic Ways to New York," *NYer*, March 5, 2001; Dana Kennedy, "Bob Kerrey, New New Yorker," *NYT*, May 5, 2002; e-mail to the author from Elizabeth Kolbert, July 16, 2006; Bob Kerrey, Interviews with author, July 5, 2006, July 24, 2006.

112. Theodore Sorensen, Interview with author, August 16, 2006.

113. Ibid.

114. Howard Tullman, Interview with author, June 26, 2006.

115. Larry King, Interview with author, October 28, 2006.

116. Nelson Shanks, Interview with author, September 14, 2006.

117. Ibid.

118. Ibid.

119. Michael Kranish, "Clinton, Act Two; The Former President's Speech at Salem State Tomorrow Is Part of a Campaign to Repair His Image, Raise Millions of Dollars, and Establish a Legacy," *BG*, March 25, 2001.

120. Larry Sabato, Interview with author, July 31, 2006.

121. Melanne Verveer, Interview with author, January 27, 2007.

122. John Emerson, Interview with author, September 20, 2006.

123. John Balzar, "Victory Seen But Not Inspiration; Democrats Opting for Prosaic Competence," *LAT*, July 21, 1988; Hamilton Jordan, *No Such Thing as a Bad Day: A Memoir*, Pocketbooks, 2001, pp. 193–194.

124. Don Fowler, Interview with author, February 14, 2007.

125. Tom Shales, "The Numb and the Restless," *WP*, July 21, 1988; Hamilton Jordan, *No Such Thing as a Bad Day: A Memoir*, Pocketbooks, 2001.

126. Interview; source wishes to remain anonymous.

127. "From Doghouse to White House?" AP, July 31, 1988.

128. Charles Robb, Interview with author, October 23, 2006.

129. John Emerson, Interviews with author, September 20, 2006, September 22, 2006.

130. Jake Siewert, Interview with author, January 15, 2007.

131. Bill Simmons, Interview with author, August 24, 2006.

132. Hank Sheinkopf, Interview with author, August 21, 2006.

133. From news services, "Republicans Seek New Probes of Clinton," *WP*, February 2, 2001; Charles Krauthammer, "The Presidential Corruption Index," *WP*, February 2, 2001.

134. Charles V. Bagli with Marc Lacey, "Criticized on Office Rent, Clinton Looks to Harlem," *NYT*, February 13, 2001.

135. Mary Voboril, "Will NY Always Love Him?; Ex-Prez' Affection for City Is Mutual," *Newsday*, February 12, 2001.

136. From news services, "Republicans Seek New Probes of Clinton," *WP*, February 2, 2001.

137. Elisabeth Bumiller, "Deal Allows Clinton to Lease Space He Wants in Harlem," *NYT*, February 17, 2001.

138. Joanna Coles, "Private Life, Public Fiasco," *Times* (London), February 21, 2001.

139. Patrick Healy, "Clinton's Talks with Democrats May Signal '08 Bid," *NYT*, December 3, 2006.

140. Jake Siewert, Interview with author, January 15, 2007.

141. Vartan Gregorian, Interview with author, December 14, 2006.

142. Joe Power, Interview with author, August 14, 2006.

143. Interview; source wishes to remain anonymous.

144. Elisabeth Bumiller, "Deal Allows Clinton to Lease Space He Wants in Harlem," *NYT*, February 17, 2001.

145. Ibid.

146. Elisabeth Bumiller and Dexter Filkins, "Snag in Clinton's Office Plan: Giuliani Stakes Claim to Space," *NYT*, February 14, 2001.

147. Jake Siewert, Interview with author, January 15, 2007.

148. Jonathan Alter, "Citizen Clinton Up Close," *NW*, April 8, 2002.

149. Charles V. Bagli with Marc Lacey, "Criticized on Office Rent, Clinton Looks to Harlem," *NYT*, February 13, 2001.

150. Elisabeth Bumiller and Dexter Filkins, "Snag in Clinton's Office Plan: Giuliani Stakes Claim to Space," *NYT*, February 14, 2001.

151. Ibid.

152. Ibid.

153. Joanna Coles, "Private Life, Public Fiasco," *Times* (London), February 21, 2001.

154. Don Hewitt, Interview with author, September 7, 2006.

155. Jonathan Alter, "Citizen Clinton Up Close," *NW*, April 8, 2002.

156. Bill Clinton, "A Man Called Hope," *VF*, July 2007.

157. Robert Sam Anson, "Bill and His Shadow," *VF*, June 2004.

158. Jake Siewert, Interview with author, January 15, 2007.

159. Adam Nagourney, "His Perks and Power Gone, Clinton Faces Storm Alone," *NYT*, March 1, 2001; David D. Kirkpatrick, "Publisher Will Pay Clinton Over $10 Million for Book," *NYT*, August 7, 2001.

160. "Earthquake Strikes India, Killing Thousands," *NYT*, January 28, 2001; Celia W. Dugger, "A Faint Voice in the Rubble, and a 5-Day Ordeal Is Ended," *NYT*, February 1, 2001; John F. Burns, "In Quake, Unity Overcame Diversity," *NYT*, February 10, 2001.

161. Richard Feachem, Interview with author, November 5, 2006; Michael Kranish, "Clinton, Act Two; The Former President's Speech at Salem State Tomorrow Is

Part of a Campaign to Repair His Image, Raise Millions of Dollars, and Establish a Legacy," *BG*, March 25, 2001.

162. Raymond C. Offenheiser Jr., Interview with author, December 20, 2006; Karen Tumulty, cover story, "The Incredible Shrinking Ex-President: How Can We Miss You If You Never Go Away?; Smelly Pardons, Expensive Gifts, Deluxe Offices—Is This Any Way for a Former President to Behave?" *Time*, February 26, 2001.

163. Melanne Verveer, Interview with author, January 27, 2007; Bill Clinton, "A Man Called Hope," *VF*, July 2007.

164. Melanne Verveer, Interview with author, January 27, 2007.

165. Rob Karwath and Daniel Egler, "14.5% State Pay Hike Proposed; Governor Would Make $106,839," *CT*, April 26, 1990.

166. John Solomon and Matthew Mosk, "For Clinton, New Wealth in Speeches; Fees in 6 Years Total Nearly $40 Million," *WP*, February 23, 2007.

167. "In a Deal, Clinton Avoids Indictment; President Admits False Testimony," *WP*, January 20, 2001.

168. Jake Siewert, Interview with author, January 15, 2007.

169. Terry McAuliffe, with Steve Kettmann, *What a Party: My Life Among Democrats, Presidents, Candidates, Donors, Activists, Alligators, and Other Wild Animals*, St. Martin's Press, Thomas Dunne Books, 2007, pp. 180, 187.

170. Bud Yorkin, Interview with author, October 9, 2006.

171. Jake Siewert, Interview with author, January 15, 2007.

172. Amy Archerd, "Just for Variety," *Daily Variety*, February 15, 2001.

173. John E. Harris, *The Survivor*, Random House, 2005, p. 223.

174. Robert Torricelli, Interview with author, October 6, 2006.

175. From news services, "Republicans Seek New Probes of Clinton," *WP*, February 2, 2001.

176. Melanne Verveer, Interview with author, January 27, 2007.

177. Michael Kranish, "Clinton, Act Two; The Former President's Speech at Salem State Tomorrow Is Part of a Campaign to Repair His Image, Raise Millions of Dollars, and Establish a Legacy," *BG*, March 25, 2001.

178. Don Hewitt, Interview with author, September 7, 2006.

179. Bud Yorkin, Interview with author, October 9, 2006.

180. Interview; source wishes to remain anonymous.

181. Jonathan Alter, Interview with author, August 10, 2006.

182. Scott Reed, Interview with author, December 1, 2006.

183. John R. Emshwiller, "Burkle v. Follieri Offers a Window on Ugly Breakup," *WSJ*, June 14, 2007.

184. John Solomon and Matthew Mosk, "For Clinton, New Wealth in Speeches; Fees in 6 Years Total Nearly $40 Million," *WP*, February 23, 2007; Devlin Barrett, "Bill Clinton Made $10 Million for Talks," AP, June 14, 2007; "United States Senate Financial Disclosure Report for Annual and Termination Reports," 2000, 2001, 2002, 2003, 2004, 2005, 2006.

185. John Solomon and Matthew Mosk, "For Clinton, New Wealth in Speeches; Fees in 6 Years Total Nearly $40 Million," WP, February 23, 2007.

186. Michael Kranish, "Clinton, Act Two; The Former President's Speech at Salem State Tomorrow Is Part of a Campaign to Repair His Image, Raise Millions of Dollars, and Establish a Legacy," BG, March 25, 2001.

187. Mike Cherry, Interview with author, May 14, 2006.

188. Alan Solomont, Interview with author, August 9, 2006.

189. Tony Coelho, Interview with author, September 5, 2006.

190. John Solomon and Matthew Mosk, "For Clinton, New Wealth in Speeches; Fees in 6 Years Total Nearly $40 Million," WP, February 23, 2007.

191. Tony Coelho, Interview with author, September 5, 2006.

192. David Saperstein, Interview with author, September 26, 2006.

193. John Solomon and Matthew Mosk, "For Clinton, New Wealth in Speeches; Fees in 6 Years Total Nearly $40 Million," WP, February 23, 2007.

194. Larry Sabato, Interview with author, July 31, 2006.

195. Al Kamen, "A Red Light, a Peephole and a Whisper," WP, March 26, 2001.

196. David Abel, "Clinton, Eyeing Legacy, Basks in Salem Spotlight," BG, March 27, 2001.

197. Michael Kranish, "Clinton, Act Two; The Former President's Speech at Salem State Tomorrow Is Part of a Campaign to Repair His Image, Raise Millions of Dollars, and Establish a Legacy," BG, March 25, 2001.

198. Joe Fitzgerald, "Three Integrity-Touting Figures Are Just Big Fakes," Boston Herald, March 28, 2001.

199. David R. Guarino and Joe Battenfeld, "Clinton Casts Spell on Salem State Crowd," Boston Herald, March 27, 2001.

200. Ellen Warren and Terry Armour, "INC: Fundraiser Takes Off While Travel Agency's Up in Air," CT, June 15, 2001.

201. Roger Ebert (earlier interview for Chicago magazine profile, December 2005).

202. Phil Stefani, Interview with author, August 15, 2006; Lou Weisbach, Interview with author, July 11, 2006.

Chapter 3 GETTING SERIOUS, STUDYING THE LEGACY OF JIMMY CARTER

1. Don Fowler, Interview with author, February 14, 2007; Michael Barone, Interview with author, September 19, 2006; Christopher Ogden, Interview with author, August 29, 2006; Scott Reed, Interview with author, December 1, 2006.

2. Lynn Cutler, Interview with author, June 29, 2006.

3. Bob Kerrey, Interview with author, July 24, 2006.

4. Elaine Kamarck, Interview with author, October 10, 2006.

5. Jake Siewert, Interview with author, January 15, 2007.

6. Mark Updegrove, Interview with author, October 22, 2006.

7. Jody Powell, Interview with author, December 7, 2006.

8. Douglas Brinkley, *The Unfinished Presidency: Jimmy Carter's Journey to the Nobel Peace Prize*, Viking/Penguin, 1998, p. 354; Terry McAuliffe, with Steve Kettmann, *What a Party: My Life Among Democrats, Presidents, Candidates, Donors, Activists, Alligators, and Other Wild Animals*, St. Martin's Press, Thomas Dunne Books, 2007, p. 35.

9. Don Fowler, Interview with author, February 14, 2007.

10. Bill Simmons, Interview with author, August 24, 2006.

11. Hamilton Jordan, *No Such Thing as a Bad Day: A Memoir*, Pocketbooks, 2001, p. 191.

12. Bill Simmons, Interview with author, August 24, 2006.

13. Jody Powell, Interview with author, December 7, 2006.

14. Hamilton Jordan, *No Such Thing as a Bad Day: A Memoir*, Pocketbooks, 2001.

15. Alessandra Stanley, "On Tour with Jimmy Carter; Worlds of Advice, Bittersweet," *NYT*, January 14, 1993; Anne E. Kornblut and John M. Broder, "The Ex-Presidents' Club Bids a Member Goodbye," *NYT*, January 3, 2007.

16. Hamilton Jordan, *No Such Thing as a Bad Day: A Memoir*, Pocketbooks, 2001, p. 199.

17. Douglas Brinkley, *The Unfinished Presidency: Jimmy Carter's Journey to the Nobel Peace Prize*, Viking/Penguin, 1998, p. 369.

18. Interview; source wishes to remain anonymous; Hamilton Jordan, *No Such Thing as a Bad Day: A Memoir*, Pocketbooks, 2001, pp. 199–200.

19. Jody Powell, Interview with author, December 7, 2006.

20. Larry King, Interview with author, October 28, 2006.

21. Jake Siewert, Interview with author, January 15, 2007.

22. Larry Sabato, Interview with author, July 31, 2006; *Playboy*, November 1976.

23. Douglas Brinkley, Interview with author, September 14, 2006.

24. Douglas Brinkley, *The Unfinished Presidency: Jimmy Carter's Journey to the Nobel Peace Prize*, Viking/Penguin, 1998.

25. Mark Updegrove, Interview with author, October 22, 2006; Thomas M. DeFrank, *Write It When I'm Gone*, Putnam, 2007, pp. 132, 138–139.

26. Anne E. Kornblut and John M. Broder, "The Ex-Presidents' Club Bids a Member Goodbye," *NYT*, January 3, 2007.

27. Douglas Brinkley, *The Unfinished Presidency: Jimmy Carter's Journey to the Nobel Peace Prize*, Viking/Penguin, 1998, p. 497.

28. Douglas Brinkley, Interview with author, September 14, 2006; Jody Powell, Interview with author, December 7, 2006; Douglas Brinkley, *The Unfinished Presidency: Jimmy Carter's Journey to the Nobel Peace Prize*, Viking/Penguin, 1998, p. 364.

29. Interview; source wishes to remain anonymous.

30. Conrad Black, Interview with author, December 14, 2006.

31. Interview; source wishes to remain anonymous.

32. Bob Douglas, "Democrats in Trouble, and the Pardons Are Just the Half of It," editorial, *A D-G*, February 25, 2001.

33. Douglas Brinkley, Interview with author, September 14, 2006.

34. Peter Osnos, The Century Foundation.

35. Douglas Brinkley, *The Unfinished Presidency: Jimmy Carter's Journey to the Nobel Peace Prize*, Viking/Penguin, 1998, p. 476; Jody Powell, Interview with author, December 7, 2006.

36. Nick Paumgarten, "Here to There Jimmy Carter Aloft," "Talk of the Town," *NYer*, December 11, 2006; Jody Powell, Interview with author, December 7, 2006.

37. Bob Thompson, "Peace Provocateur Jimmy Carter's New Hammer? It Looks an Awful Lot Like a Book," WP, December 10, 2006; Douglas Brinkley, *The Unfinished Presidency: Jimmy Carter's Journey to the Nobel Peace Prize*, Viking/Penguin, 1998, pp. 475–476.

38. Christopher Ogden, Interview with author, August 29, 2006.

39. Interview; source wishes to remain anonymous.

40. Interview; source wishes to remain anonymous.

41. Alexander Chancellor, "Footnote," *Daily Telegraph* (London), August 8, 2001.

42. Jim Rutenberg and David D. Kirkpatrick, "Timing of Clinton Memoir Is Everything, for Kerry," NYT, April 13, 2004; Virginia Kelley, with James Morgan, *Leading With My Heart*, Simon & Schuster, 1994, p. 208.

43. Mark Sauer, "Reading Hillary Between the Lines," *San Diego Union-Tribune*, January 2, 2001.

44. David D. Kirkpatrick, "Publisher Will Pay Clinton Over $10 Million for Book," NYT, August 7, 2001; David D. Kirkpatrick, "Authors Clinton: One's Early, One Needs Extension," NYT, June 24, 2002; Jonathan Alter, "Citizen Clinton Up Close," NW, April 8, 2002; "Will Ted Tell Mary Jo Truth?" NYP, November 28, 2007.

45. Maureen Dowd, "Liberties; A Very Personal History," NYT, August 8, 2001.

46. David D. Kirkpatrick, "Publisher Will Pay Clinton Over $10 Million for Book," NYT, August 7, 2001.

47. Jonathan Alter, "Writing the Book of Bill," NW, August 20, 2001.

48. Ibid.; Clarence Fanto, "A New View of Our 18th President," *Berkshire Eagle*, July 11, 2007; Bob Jamieson, "Grant's Memoirs Kick Off Civil War Lecture Series," *Eagle Star-Gazette* (Elmira, New York), May 3, 2007.

49. Jonathan Alter, "Writing the Book of Bill," NW, August 20, 2001.

50. Ibid.

51. Interview; source wishes to remain anonymous.

52. Marjorie Williams, "Scenes from a Marriage (Bill Clinton and Al Gore)," *The Woman at the Washington Zoo: Writings on Politics, Family, and Fate*, edited by Timothy Noah, Public Affairs, 2005, pp. 133, 152.

53. Ron Fournier, "Clinton Says, 'Rally Behind the President' in Aftermath of Attacks; Gore Offers Support," AP, September 11, 2001.

54. Elaine Kamarck, Interview with author, October 10, 2006.

55. Susie Tompkins Buell, Interview with author, September 5, 2006; Jonathan Alter, Interview with author, August 10, 2006; Tom Downey, Interview with author, January 9, 2007; Katharine Q. Seelye, "After the Attacks: The Former Administration; Tragedy Reunites Clinton and Gore," NYT, September 15, 2001.

56. Elaine Kamarck, Interview with author, October 10, 2006.

57. Katharine Q. Seelye, "After the Attacks: The Former Administration; Tragedy Reunites Clinton and Gore," *NYT*, September 15, 2001.

58. Jonathan Alter, Interview with author, August 10, 2006.

59. Tom Downey, Interview with author, January 9, 2007.

60. Elaine Kamarck, Interview with author, October 10, 2006.

61. Ray Lesniak, Interview with author, September 16, 2006.

62. Natalie Datlof, Interview with author, September 8, 2006; Eric Schmertz, Interview with author, September 1, 2006; Herman Berliner, Interview with author, October 5, 2006.

63. Steve Grossman, Interview with author, August 24, 2006.

64. Ibid.

65. Eric Holder, Interview with author, December 5, 2006.

66. Mark Buell, Interview with author, August 22, 2006.

67. Paul Bedard and Mark Mazzetti, "Washington Whispers," *U.S. News & World Report*, October 15, 2001.

68. Jim Houlihan, Interview with author, July 18, 2006.

69. Ray Lesniak, Interview with author, September 16, 2006.

70. Donna Shalala, Interview with author, September 25, 2006.

71. Sandy Berger, Interview with author, October 3, 2006.

72. Beryl Anthony, Interview with author, October 3, 2006.

73. John Emerson, Interview with author, September 20, 2006.

74. Mark Buell, Interview with author, August 22, 2006.

75. Jim Houlihan, Interview with author, July 18, 2006.

76. Leon Panetta, Interview with author, October 17, 2006.

77. Donna Shalala, Interview with author, September 25, 2006.

78. Leon Panetta, Interview with author, October 17, 2006.

79. Bud Yorkin, Interview with author, October 9, 2006.

80. Mark Buell, Interview with author, August 22, 2006.

81. Robert Patterson, Interview with author, January 4, 2007.

82. Don Hewitt, Interview with author, September 7, 2006.

83. Ray Lesniak, Interview with author, September 16, 2006.

84. Matthew Mosk and John Solomon, "Largess to Clintons Lands CEO in Lawsuit; Case Is a Window on Couple's Ties," *WP*, May 26, 2007; Mike McIntire, "Suit Sheds Light on Clintons' Ties to a Benefactor," *NYT*, May 26, 2007.

85. AP photo by J. Scott Applewhite; Ann Gerhart, "Sad News About Buddy; A Democratic Dog That Was Everyone's Buddy; Clintons' Lab Killed by Car in New York," *WP*, January 4, 2002.

86. Terry McAuliffe, with Steve Kettmann, *What a Party: My Life Among Democrats, Presidents, Candidates, Donors, Activists, Alligators, and Other Wild Animals*, St. Martin's Press, Thomas Dunne Books, 2007, p. 162.

87. "Famous Cuban Photographer Alberto Corda Buried in Havana," *RIA Novosti*, May 30, 2001. (His name is sometimes spelled Alberto Korda Diaz or Alberto "Korda" Diaz Gutierrez.)

88. Mark Buell, Interview with author, August 22, 2006; "Near and Far," *San Francisco Chronicle*, September 3, 2002.

89. William O'Rourke, "Bill Clinton for N.J. Senator?" *C S-T*, October 8, 2002.

90. Robert Sam Anson, "Bill and His Shadow," *VF*, June 2004.

91. Elaine Kamarck, Interview with author, October 10, 2006; Elaine Kamarck, "Future Tense: The Toughest Campaign of All; The Former President Fights to Leave a Legacy Behind That Will Restore His Time in Office," *Newsday*, June 22, 2004.

92. Robert Sam Anson, "Bill and His Shadow," *VF*, June 2004.

93. Janet Reno, Interview with author, November 2, 2006.

94. Robert Torricelli, Interview with author, October 6, 2006.

95. "Alabama Gov. Don Siegelman," *WP*, November 7, 2002.

96. Mike Allen and Manuel Roig-Franzia, "Presidents Clash Over Florida Governor's Race; Bush, Clinton in Last-Minute Pushes for Jeb Bush, McBride," *WP*, November 3, 2002.

97. R. Emmett Tyrrell Jr., *The Clinton Crack-up: The Boy President's Life After the White House*, Thomas Nelson, 2007, p. 142.

98. "Rev. Al Blasts 'Beige' Clinton," *NYP*, December 6, 2002.

99. Andrew DeMillo, "Clinton Library Spans a Presidency," *A D-G*, November 14, 2004.

100. Vartan Gregorian, Interview with author, December 14, 2006; Sally Bedell Smith, *For Love of Politics: Bill and Hillary Clinton: The White House Years*, Random House, 2007; John Solomon and Jeffrey H. Birnbaum, "Clinton Library Got Funds From Abroad: Saudis Said to Have Given $10 Million," *WP*, December 15, 2007; Don van Natta Jr., Joe Becker, and Mike McIntire, "In Charity and Politics, Clinton Donors Overlap," *NYT*, December 20, 2007.

101. Karoun Demirjian, "House Approves Bill to Divulge Funding of Presidential Libraries," *CT*, March 15, 2007.

102. Terry McAuliffe, with Steve Kettmann, *What a Party: My Life Among Democrats, Presidents, Candidates, Donors, Activists, Alligators, and Other Wild Animals*, St. Martin's Press, Thomas Dunne Books, 2007, p. 379.

103. Leon Panetta, Interview with author, October 17, 2006.

104. Donna Shalala, Interview with author, September 25, 2006.

105. Interview; source wishes to remain anonymous.

106. Conrad Black, Interview with author, December 14, 2006.

107. John Emerson, Interview with author, September 20, 2006.

108. Interview; source wishes to remain anonymous.

109. David Schulte, Interview with author, December 8, 2006.

110. Rick Kogan, Interview with author, May 26, 2006.

111. Anson Beard Jr., Interview with author, September 27, 2006.

112. Interview; source wishes to remain anonymous.

113. Steve Grossman, Interview with author, August 4, 2006.

114. R. Emmett Tyrrell Jr., *The Clinton Crack-up: The Boy President's Life After the White House*, Thomas Nelson, 2007.

115. Mark Buell, Interview with author, August 22, 2006.

116. Ibid.

117. Tony Coelho, Interview with author, September 5, 2006.

118. Melanne Verveer, Interview with author, January 27, 2007.

119. Richard Marlink, Interviews with author, October 16, 2006, October 30, 2006.

120. Alison Mitchell, "Critics Skeptical of Clinton's AIDS Goal," *Austin American-Statesman*, May 19, 1997.

121. Michael Specter, "The Vaccine; Has the Race to Save Africa from AIDS Put Western Science at Odds with Western Ethics?" *NYer*, February 3, 2003.

122. Kevin De Cock, Interview with author, December 6, 2006; Robert Fogel, Interview with author, May 26, 2006; Lauran Neergaard, "Critical Clinton AIDS Advisers Demand Needle Exchanges," AP, March 16, 1998; Lauran Neergaard, "Members of AIDS Panel May Resign," AP, October 8, 1997.

123. *Harvard Crimson* via University Wire, March 15, 2000.

124. Richard Marlink, Interview with author, October 16, 2006.

125. Donna Shalala, Interview with author, September 25, 2006.

126. Tony Lake, Interview with author, November 1, 2006.

127. Sandy Berger, Interview with author, July 27, 2006.

128. Eric Goosby, Interview with author, December 11, 2006.

129. Kevin De Cock, Interview with author, December 6, 2006; Bethany McLean, "The Power of Philanthropy," *Fortune*, September 7, 2006.

130. Eric Goosby, Interview with author, December 11, 2006.

131. Ibid.

132. Richard Marlink, Interview with author, October 16, 2006.

133. Richard Feachem, Interview with author, November 5, 2006.

134. Richard Marlink, Interview with author, October 16, 2006.

135. Bill Bicknell, Interview with author, December 28, 2006.

136. Richard Feachem, Interview with author, November 5, 2006.

137. Richard Marlink, Interviews with author, October 16, 2006, October 30, 2006.

Chapter 4 NOT QUITE READY FOR PRIME TIME

1. Don Hewitt, Interview with author, September 7, 2006.

2. Ibid.

3. Larry King, Interview with author, October 28, 2006.

4. Don Hewitt, Interview with author, September 7, 2006.

5. Jonathan Alter, "The Bill and Bob Show," NW, March 17, 2003.

6. Leon Panetta, Interview with author, October 17, 2006.

7. Don Hewitt, Interview with author, September 7, 2006.

8. Larry King, Interview with author, October 28, 2006.

9. Tony Coelho, Interview with author, September 5, 2006.

10. Scott Reed, Interview with author, December 1, 2006; Carl M. Cannon, "Dole Honored in Emotional White House Ceremony; Clinton Presents Medal of Freedom to Former Competitor," *Baltimore Sun*, January 18, 1997.

11. Sholto Byrnes, "Pandora," *Independent* (London), September 6, 2002.

12. Scott Reed, Interview with author, December 1, 2006.

13. Don Hewitt, Interview with author, September 7, 2006.

14. Tony Coelho, Interview with author, September 5, 2006.

15. Jonathan Alter, "The Bill and Bob Show," NW, March 17, 2003.

16. Don Hewitt, Interview with author, September 7, 2006.

17. Ibid.

18. David Carr, Interview with author, December 8, 2006.

19. Joe Sharkey, "'Enabling' Is Now a Political Disease," NYT, September 27, 1998.

20. Interview; source wishes to remain anonymous.

21. Irena Medavoy, Interview with author, October 23, 2006.

22. Anthony Campolo, e-mail to author, October 27, 2006.

23. Leon Panetta, Interview with author, October 17, 2006.

24. Jim Rutenberg and David D. Kirkpatrick, "Timing of Clinton Memoir Is Everything, for Kerry," NYT, April 13, 2004.

25. Douglas Brinkley, Interview with author, September 14, 2006; Jake Siewert, Interview with author, January 15, 2007; Janis Kearney, Interviews with author, June 2, 2006, September 15, 2006; Eric Schmertz, Interview with author, September 1, 2006.

26. John Emerson, Interview with author, September 20, 2006; Jake Siewert, Interview with author, January 15, 2007; Stephen Kinzer, "Clinton, on the Road Again, Stumps for a Book, Not a Seat," NYT, June 4, 2004.

27. Martin Peretz, "Village People," "Cambridge Diarist," *The New Republic*, January 15, 2007.

28. Lou Weisbach, Interview with author, July 11, 2006.

29. Bud Yorkin, Interview with author, October 9, 2006.

30. Anne-Marie O'Connor, "Stars Have Kerry in Their Eyes; The Front-runner's Bandwagon Is Pulling into Town with Many of Hollywood's Democrats Ready to Pull Out Their Checkbooks," *LAT*, February 28, 2004.

31. Stanley Sheinbaum, Interview with author, October 12, 2006; Anne-Marie O'Connor, "Hollywood Patrons Beset by Politicians; Finance: Candidates from Throughout the Nation Seek Out Celebrities' Star Power to Raise Campaign Funds," *LAT*, February 24, 2002.

32. "Kerry: Keeping Hollywood Abuzz," *The Hotline*, January 3, 2003.

33. Anne-Marie O'Connor, "Reviving Salons as Hotbeds of New Ideas; Writers, Filmmakers and Others Are Drawn to Diverse Gatherings That Provide 'A Place to Share the Life of the Mind' in Far-Flung L.A.," *LAT*, January 24, 2001.

34. Stanley Sheinbaum, Interview with author, October 12, 2006.

35. Betty Sheinbaum, Interview with author, October 12, 2006.

36. Stanley Sheinbaum, Interview with author, October 12, 2006.

37. Interview; source wishes to remain anonymous.

38. Interview; source wishes to remain anonymous.

39. Don Hewitt, Interview with author, September 7, 2006.

40. Dick Morris, e-mail responses to author's questions, August 29, 2006.

41. Harry Shearer, *Slate* magazine, August 27, 1996.

42. Hank Sheinkopf, Interview with author, August 21, 2006.

43. Interview; source wishes to remain anonymous.

44. Interview; source wishes to remain anonymous.

45. Sarah Ellison and Rhonda L. Rundle, "L.A. Billionaires Join in Bidding for Tribune Co.," *WSJ*, November 9, 2006.

46. John M. Broder and Patrick Healy, "How a Billionaire Friend of Bill Helps Him Do Good, and Well," *NYT*, April 23, 2006; Vanessa Grigoriadis, "Billionaires Are Free; And, These Days, a Dime a Dozen. But Even for Today's B Boys, There Are Some Things Money Can't Buy," *NY mag*, November 6, 2006.

47. Matthew Miller, "The Rise of Ron Burkle," *Forbes*, December 11, 2006; Deborah Solomon, "Friend of Bill and Hill," *NYT mag*, March 18, 2007; Thomas S. Mulligan and James Rainey, "3 of L.A.'s Billionaires Have Eyes on Times; Tribune Rebuffs Broad, Geffen and Burkle, For Now, After They Inquire About Buying the Paper," *LAT*, July 29, 2006.

48. John M. Broder and Patrick Healy, "How a Billionaire Friend of Bill Helps Him Do Good, and Well," *NYT*, April 23, 2006.

49. Darius Anderson, Interview with author, December 21, 2006.

50. Ibid.

51. Ibid.

52. Ibid.

53. Ibid.

54. Ibid.

55. Robert Sam Anson, "Bill and His Shadow," *VF*, June 2004; Vanessa Grigoriadis, "Billionaires Are Free; And, These Days, a Dime a Dozen. But Even for Today's B Boys, There Are Some Things Money Can't Buy," *NY mag*, November 6, 2006; John M. Broder and Patrick Healy, "How a Billionaire Friend of Bill Helps Him Do Good, and Well," *NYT*, April 23, 2006; John R. Emshwiller and Merissa Marr, "Return to Treasure Island: Hollywood's Moguls Compete to Raise Cash for Democratic Candidates. Whose House Is Better?" *WSJ*, March 17, 2007; James Sterngold, "Enmeshed in Scandal; Billionaire Ron Burkle Claims to Eschew the Spotlight But Finds Himself the Center of Attention," *San Francisco Chronicle*, May 2, 2006.

56. Darius Anderson, Interview with author, December 21, 2006; John R. Emshwiller and Merissa Marr, "Return to Treasure Island: Hollywood's Moguls Compete to Raise Cash for Democratic Candidates. Whose House is Better?" *WSJ*, March 17, 2007; "The New Establishment 2007," *VF*, October 2007.

57. Robert Sam Anson, "Bill and His Shadow," *VF*, June 2004; John R. Emshwiller and Merissa Marr, "Return to Treasure Island: Hollywood's Moguls Compete to Raise Cash for Democratic Candidates. Whose House Is Better?" *WSJ*, March 17, 2007.

58. Matthew Miller, "The Rise of Ron Burkle," *Forbes*, December 11, 2006.

59. John R. Emshwiller, "Controversy, by the Truckload Battle for Car Hauler Puts Spotlight on Burkle's Dealings," *WSJ*, May 2, 2007.

60. James Ylisela Jr., "Under the Radar: 'Radar Is a Work in Progress,' Says Yusef Jackson. 'I Think We're Still Finding Our Editorial Voice,'" *Chicago* magazine, July 2007; John Kass, "If You Ask Obama, Then Ask All of Them," *CT*, March 4, 2007;

Robert Sam Anson, "Bill and His Shadow," *VF*, June 2004; "Friend of Rev. Jackson Lobbied A-B for Distributorship," *Modern Brewery Age*, April 16, 2001; Phil Rosenthal, "Yusef Jackson Lands on Media Map with Radar," *CT*, June 30, 2006.

61. James Ylisela Jr., "Under the Radar: 'Radar Is a Work in Progress,' Says Yusef Jackson. 'I Think We're Still Finding Our Editorial Voice,'" *Chicago* magazine, July 2007; Keith Kelly, "New Blip on Radar—Roshan's Resurrected Magazine Hits Newsstands," *NYP*, February 9, 2007; Phil Rosenthal, "Yusef Jackson Lands on Media Map with Radar," *CT*, June 30, 2006; Matthew Karnitschnig, "Radar Returns for a Third Try in the Buzz Business Blog and Big Backers Help Give Latest Launch Shot at Success; Editor Is Still a Favorite Target," *WSJ*, February 26, 2007.

62. Deborah Solomon, "Friend of Bill and Hill," *NYT mag*, March 18, 2007.

63. Irena Medavoy, Interview with author, October 23, 2006.

64. Ibid.

65. Maureen Dowd, "Obama's Big Screen Test: Hillary Is Not David Geffen's Dreamgirl," *NYT*, February 21, 2007.

66. Jennifer Steinhauer and David M. Halbfinger, "Et Tu, David? A Lucrative Friendship Sours," *NYT*, February 23, 2007.

67. Darius Anderson, Interview with author, December 21, 2006; Eric Alterman, "The Hollywood Campaign: Want Big Money to Get Elected to National Office? If You're a Democrat, You Need to Head for the Hills—Beverly Hills. A Miner's Map, for the Liberal Gold Rush," *Atlantic Monthly*, September 2004; John R. Emshwiller and Merissa Marr, "Return to Treasure Island: Hollywood's Moguls Compete to Raise Cash for Democratic Candidates. Whose House Is Better?" *WSJ*, March 17, 2007; Stephen Braun and Dan Morain, "Famous Allies Were Often at Odds; David Geffen Shocked Many by Speaking Out Against Hillary Clinton. But He and Bill Clinton Had a Rocky Friendship," *LAT*, March 4, 2007; James Rainey, "2 Southland Billionaires Make Case to Buy Tribune; Eli Broad, Ron Burkle Meet with Panel Also Reviewing Offer by The Times' Founding Family," *LAT*, January 21, 2007; Ben Casselman and Christina S. N. Lewis, "'Underpriced' at $100 Million," *WSJ*, August 24, 2007.

68. John M. Broder and Patrick Healy, "How a Billionaire Friend of Bill Helps Him Do Good, and Well," *NYT*, April 23, 2006; James Sterngold, "Enmeshed in Scandal; Billionaire Ron Burkle Claims to Eschew the Spotlight but Finds Himself the Center of Attention," *San Francisco Chronicle*, May 2, 2006.

69. Darius Anderson, Interview with author, December 21, 2006; Jared Paul Stern, Interview with author, July 18, 2006; Geraldine Fabrikant and Laura Holson, "Odd Couple Ponder Bid for Tribune," *NYT*, January 16, 2007; Bill Toland, "Reclusive Penguins Investor Now Makes Headlines," *Pittsburgh Post-Gazette*, April 11, 2006; William Sherman, "The Billionaire, the Post and the $220G Shakedown; Page Six Writer Wanted $$$ to Stop Inaccurate Coverage," *NYDN*, April 7, 2006; Matthew Miller, "The Rise of Ron Burkle," *Forbes*, December 11, 2006; Vanessa Grigoriadis, "Billionaires Are Free; and, These Days, a Dime a Dozen. But Even for Today's B Boys, There Are Some Things Money Can't Buy," *NY mag*, November 6, 2006.

70. "LAT 100 Most Powerful," *LAT*, August 13, 2006; James Rainey, "2 Southland Billionaires Make Case to Buy Tribune; Eli Broad, Ron Burkle Meet with Panel Also

Reviewing Offer by The Times' Founding Family," *LAT*, January 21, 2007; Sarah Ellison, "Dow Jones Hears Alternative Proposals; Burkle and Greenspan Present Plans to Vie with News Corp," *WSJ*, July 11, 2007.

71. Deborah Solomon, "Friend of Bill and Hill," *NYT mag*, March 18, 2007; Jeremy W. Peters, "Radar Magazine Rises from the Ashes Again," *NYT*, June 29, 2006; James Ylisela Jr., "Under the Radar: 'Radar Is a Work in Progress,' Says Yusef Jackson. 'I Think We're Still Finding Our Editorial Voice,'" *Chicago* magazine, July 2007; John Kass, "If You Ask Obama, Then Ask All of Them," *CT*, March 4, 2007.

72. Patrick Healy, "For Clintons, Delicate Dance of Married and Public Lives," *NYT*, May 23, 2006.

73. Interview; source wishes to remain anonymous.

74. Interview; source wishes to remain anonymous.

75. Darius Anderson, Interview with author, December 21, 2006; Interview; source wishes to remain anonymous.

76. John R. Emshwiller, "Controversy, by the Truckload Battle for Car Hauler Puts Spotlight on Burkle's Dealings," *WSJ*, May 2, 2007.

77. Interview; source wishes to remain anonymous.

78. Patrick Creadon, Interview with author, October 31, 2006.

79. Jared Paul Stern, Interview with author, July 18, 2006; Deborah Solomon, "Friend of Bill and Hill," *NYT mag*, March 18, 2007; James Sterngold, "Enmeshed in Scandal; Billionaire Ron Burkle Claims to Eschew the Spotlight but Finds Himself the Center of Attention," *San Francisco Chronicle*, May 2, 2006; Campbell Robertson, "Billionaire and Post Writer in a Dance of Tips and Turns," *NYT*, April 12, 2006.

80. Choire Sicha, "Jared Paul Stern Is Slouching Back with Book, Lawsuit," *NYob*, October 23, 2006; Robert Lee Hotz, "Cleared Gossip Writer Says He'll Sue; A Page Six Contributor Says Extortion Claims by Ron Burkle Ruined Him," *LAT*, January 25, 2007.

81. James Barron, "Contributor to Gossip Column Won't Be Charged," *NYT*, January 24, 2007; Maureen Dowd, "Can He Crush Hillary?" *NYT*, June 17, 2007; Robert Lee Hotz, "Cleared Gossip Writer Says He'll Sue; A Page Six Contributor Says Extortion Claims by Ron Burkle Ruined Him," *LAT*, January 25, 2007.

82. Jared Paul Stern, Interview with author, July 18, 2006, e-mail to author, November 6, 2007; James Barron and Campbell Robertson, "Page Six, Staple of Gossip, Reports on Its Own Tale," *NYT*, May 19, 2007; Michael Calderone, David Foxley, and Felix Gillette, "Did Page Six Kill 'Numerous' Items on the Clintons?" *NYob*, May 22, 2007.

83. Mike Medavoy, Interview with author, October 19, 2006; Fox News, March 25, 2007.

84. Anne-Marie O'Connor, "He's Giving Himself Quite a Name; Politics: Haim Saban's $7-million Donation to Democrats Cements the L.A. Rainmaker's Clout," *LAT*, March 23, 2002; Sharon Waxman and Bill McAllister, "Clinton Draws Comfort and Cash on Trip; Ignoring Protests and Silent on Scandal, President Raises Millions in Major States," *WP*, September 28, 1998.

85. Anne-Marie O'Connor, "He's Giving Himself Quite a Name; Politics: Haim Saban's $7-million Donation to Democrats Cements the L.A. Rainmaker's Clout," *LAT*, March 23, 2002.

86. Alan Solomont, Interview with author, August 14, 2006.

87. Ibid.; Tovah Lazaroff, "TAU Opens New US Policy Institute," *Jerusalem Post*, January 18, 2002; Federal News Service, "Remarks by Former President William J. Clinton and Others at Inauguration of the Saban Institute for the Study of the American Political System," January 20, 2002.

88. Alan Solomont, Interview with author, August 14, 2006.

89. Corky Hale, Interview with author, October 12, 2006.

90. Landon Thomas Jr., "Jeffrey Epstein: International Moneyman of Mystery," NY *mag*, October 28, 2002.

91. "Murky World of Clinton Pal," NYP, October 20, 2002; Landon Thomas Jr., "Jeffrey Epstein: International Moneyman of Mystery," NY *mag*, October 28, 2002; Robert Sam Anson, "Bill and His Shadow," VF, June 2004; Nicole Janok, "Mystery Money Man Faces Soliciting Charge," *Palm Beach Post*, July 24, 2005.

92. Landon Thomas Jr., "Jeffrey Epstein: International Moneyman of Mystery," NY *mag*, October 28, 2002.

93. Ibid.; "Murky World of Clinton Pal," NYP, October 20, 2002.

94. Palm Beach police documents; *Gawker*, July 27, 2006; Nicole Janok, "Mystery Money Man Faces Soliciting Charge," *Palm Beach Post*, July 24, 2005.

95. Vanessa Grigoriadis, "Billionaires Are Free; And, These Days, a Dime a Dozen. But Even for Today's B Boys, There Are Some Things Money Can't Buy," NY *mag*, November 6, 2006.

96. Interview; source wishes to remain anonymous.

97. Joan Fleischman, "Face Cards: Two S. Florida Fugitives in 'Wanted' Deck," *Miami Herald*, May 22, 2004; "Gore Returns to S. Florida, Political Arena," *Miami Herald*, February 27, 2002.

98. Robert Sam Anson, "Bill and His Shadow," VF, June 2004.

99. Interview; source wishes to remain anonymous.

100. David M. Halbfinger and Allison Hope Weiner, "Hollywood Evidence Raises Questions," NYT, April 12, 2007; "The New Establishment 2007," VF, October 2007.

101. John R. Emshwiller and Merissa Marr, "Return to Treasure Island: Hollywood's Moguls Compete to Raise Cash for Democratic Candidates. Whose House Is Better?" WSJ, March 17, 2007; Philip Sherwell, "Hollywood's Glitterati Line Up for Obama," *Sunday Telegraph*, February 19, 2007; David M. Halbfinger, "Politicians Are Doing Hollywood Star Turns," NYT, February 6, 2007.

102. Terry McAuliffe, with Steve Kettmann, *What a Party: My Life Among Democrats, Presidents, Candidates, Donors, Activists, Alligators, and Other Wild Animals*, St. Martin's Press, Thomas Dunne Books, 2007, p. 225.

103. Interview; source wishes to remain anonymous.

104. Irena Medavoy, Interview with author, October 23, 2006.

105. Robert Sam Anson, "Bill and His Shadow," VF, June 2004.

106. Interview; source wishes to remain anonymous.

107. Don Fowler, Interview with author, February 14, 2007.

108. Charles Manatt, Interview with author, November 27, 2006.

109. Conrad Black, Interview with author, December 14, 2006; Robin Givhan, "Hillary Clinton's Tentative Dip into New Neckline Territory," WP, July 20, 2007.

110. Interview; source wishes to remain anonymous.

111. David Schulte, Interview with author, December 8, 2006.

112. Interview; source wishes to remain anonymous.

113. Interview; source wishes to remain anonymous.

114. Ron Fournier, "Clinton at Ease: Cutthroat Card Games," AP, October 27, 1996.

115. Michael Kobold, Interview with author, October 27, 2006.

116. Ibid.; Patrick Creadon, Interview with author, October 31, 2006.

117. Mark Buell, Interview with author, August 22, 2006.

118. Lou Susman, Interview with author, May 30, 2006; John Schmidt, Interview with author, August 9, 2006; Robert Sam Anson, "Bill and His Shadow," VF, June 2004; editorial, BG, November 7, 2004; Elizabeth Fulk and Peter Savodnik, "Some Red-State Democrats Facing Balancing Act with Dean at DNC," The Hill, February 10, 2005.

119. Robert Sam Anson, "Bill and His Shadow," VF, June 2004.

120. Hank Sheinkopf, Interview with author, August 21, 2006.

121. Lou Weisbach, Interview with author, July 11, 2006.

122. Simmie Knox, Interview with author, September 18, 2006.

123. Bridgette Bartlett, "Making History," Essence, December 2004.

124. Simmie Knox, Interview with author, September 18, 2006.

125. Lucy Howard, Bret Begun, and Susannah Meadows, "Periscope," NW, February 26, 2001; Simmie Knox, Interview with author, September 18, 2006.

126. Simmie Knox, Interview with author, September 18, 2006.

127. Kevin Freking, "Ceremony Introduces Portraits of Clintons," A D-G, June 15, 2004; AP, "Bill Clinton's Stepfather," February 1, 2007; Delia M. Rios, "Bushes, Clintons Forge Surprising Bond; Familial Rivalry Transforms into a Friendship," Newhouse News Service, June 19, 2005.

128. Gary Hart, Interview with author, November 15, 2006; George McGovern, Interview with author, November 1, 2006.

129. Larry King, Interview with author, October 28, 2006.

130. Douglas Brinkley, Interview with author, September 14, 2006.

131. Janis Kearney, Interviews with author, June 2, 2006, September 15, 2006.

132. Christopher Ogden, Interview with author, August 29, 2006.

133. Jonathan Alter, Interview with author, August 10, 2006.

134. Jonathan Alter, Interviews with author, July 7, 2006, August 10, 2006.

135. Ibid.

136. Donna Shalala, Interview with author, September 25, 2006.

137. Leon Panetta, Interview with author, October 17, 2006.

138. Interview; source wishes to remain anonymous.

139. Leon Panetta, Interview with author, October 17, 2006.

140. Douglas Brinkley, Interview with author, September 14, 2006.

141. Jake Siewert, Interview with author, January 15, 2007.

142. Vartan Gregorian, Interview with author, December 14, 2006.

143. Douglas Brinkley, Interview with author, September 14, 2006.

144. Theodore Sorensen, Interview with author, August 16, 2006.

145. Larry Sabato, Interview with author, July 31, 2006.

146. Christopher Ogden, Interview with author, August 29, 2006.

147. Elaine Kamarck, Interview with author, October 10, 2006.

148. Paul Greenberg, Interview with author, October 4, 2006.

149. Kane Webb, Interview with author, February 6, 2007.

150. Bob Minzesheimer, "Clinton's Hefty Memoir Flies Off Shelves," *USA Today*, June 24, 2004.

151. Ibid.; Jeffrey A. Trachtenberg, "Clinton's 'Giving' Book Is Slated for Fall Season," *WSJ*, July 11, 2007; "Correction," *NYT*, June 13, 2004; Amy Argetsinger and Roxanne Roberts, "At the Moonlite Bunny Ranch, Politics and Strange Bedfellows," *WP*, November 28, 2007 (reports sales of 2.5 million and advance of $10 million).

152. Bob Minzesheimer, "Clinton's Hefty Memoir Flies Off Shelves," *USA Today*, June 24, 2004; Amy Argetsinger and Roxanne Roberts, "At the Moonlite Bunny Ranch, Politics and Strange Bedfellows," *WP*, November 28, 2007 (claims 1.5 million sold).

153. Ibid.; Christine Simmons, AP, August 20, 2007.

154. Irena Medavoy, Interview with author, October 23, 2006.

155. Robert Sam Anson, "Bill and His Shadow," *VF*, June 2004.

156. Interview; source wishes to remain anonymous; Alan Solomont, Interview with author, August 14, 2006.

157. Lou Susman, Interview with author, May 30, 2006.

158. Irena Medavoy, Interview with author, October 23, 2006.

159. Interview; source wishes to remain anonymous.

160. Jonathan Alter, "Writing the Book of Bill," *NW*, August 20, 2001.

161. Jennifer Senior, "Bill Clinton's Plan for World Domination; Clear Your Schedule for His Third Inauguration, Here in New York in September," *NY mag*, August 22, 2005.

162. Conor Feehan, "Bill Swings into Action After His Marathon Book Signing Session," *Irish Independent*, August 26, 2004.

163. Robert Torricelli, Interview with author, October 6, 2006.

164. Jennifer Senior, "Bill Clinton's Plan for World Domination; Clear Your Schedule for His Third Inauguration, Here in New York in September," *NY mag*, August 22, 2005.

165. Robert D. McFadden, "Clinton Suffers Pains in Chest; Surgery Is Set," *NYT*, September 4, 2004; Lawrence K. Altman, "Clinton Operation Aims to Restore Blood Flow," *NYT*, September 4, 2004; Susan Schindehette, Sharon Cotliar, Diane Herbst, Marianne V. Stochmal, Macon Morehouse, and Linda Kramer, "Midlife Crisis; Recovering Well from Quadruple Heart Bypass, Junk-Food-Loving Former President Bill Clinton Now Must Stick to a New Economic Plan—Low Fat, All the Time," *People*, September 20, 2004.

166. Melanne Verveer, Interview with author, January 27, 2007.

167. Jake Siewert, Interview with author, January 15, 2007.

168. Robert D. McFadden, "Clinton Suffers Pains in Chest; Surgery Is Set," NYT, September 4, 2004.

169. Terry McAuliffe, with Steve Kettmann, What a Party: My Life Among Democrats, Presidents, Candidates, Donors, Activists, Alligators, and Other Wild Animals, St. Martin's Press, Thomas Dunne Books, 2007, p. 359.

170. Leon Panetta, Interview with author, October 17, 2006; Susan Schindehette, Sharon Cotliar, Diane Herbst, Marianne V. Stochmal, Macon Morehouse, and Linda Kramer, "Midlife Crisis; Recovering Well from Quadruple Heart Bypass, Junk-Food-Loving Former President Bill Clinton Now Must Stick to a New Economic Plan—Low Fat, All the Time," People, September 20, 2004.

171. Thomas Kean, Interview with author, January 22, 2007.

172. Anthony Campolo, e-mail to author, October 27, 2006; Susan Schindehette, Sharon Cotliar, Diane Herbst, Marianne V. Stochmal, Macon Morehouse, and Linda Kramer, "Midlife Crisis; Recovering Well from Quadruple Heart Bypass, Junk-Food-Loving Former President Bill Clinton Now Must Stick to a New Economic Plan—Low Fat, All the Time," People, September 20, 2004.

173. Larry King, Interview with author, October 28, 2006.

174. Victor Fleming, Interview with author, November 2, 2006.

175. Phil Ross, Interview with author, October 19, 2006.

176. Bill Clinton, interview by Sanjay Gupta, Anderson Cooper 360 Degrees, CNN, August 24, 2005; Susan Schindehette, Sharon Cotliar, Diane Herbst, Marianne V. Stochmal, Macon Morehouse, and Linda Kramer, "Midlife Crisis; Recovering Well from Quadruple Heart Bypass, Junk-Food-Loving Former President Bill Clinton Now Must Stick to a New Economic Plan—Low Fat, All the Time," People, September 20, 2004.

177. Jim Schachter, Interview with author, May 3, 2007.

178. Bill Clinton, interview by Sanjay Gupta, Anderson Cooper 360 Degrees, CNN, August 24, 2005.

179. Beryl Anthony, Interview with author, October 3, 2006.

180. Susie Tompkins Buell, Interview with author, September 5, 2006.

181. Jim Guy Tucker, Interview with author, November 13, 2006.

182. Donna Shalala, Interview with author, September 25, 2006.

183. Jonathan Alter, Interview with author, August 10, 2006.

184. George McGovern, Interview with author, November 1, 2006.

185. Adam Nagourney and David M. Halbfinger, "The Democratic Nominee: Kerry Enlisting Clinton Aides in Effort to Refocus Campaign," NYT, September 6, 2004.

186. AP, January 5, 2007, from Terry McAuliffe, with Steve Kettmann, What a Party: My Life Among Democrats, Presidents, Candidates, Donors, Activists, Alligators, and Other Wild Animals, St. Martin's Press, Thomas Dunne Books, 2007.

187. Susie Tompkins Buell, Interview with author, September 5, 2006.

188. Interview; source wishes to remain anonymous.

189. Corky Hale, Interview with author, October 12, 2006.

190. Lou Susman, Interview with author, May 30, 2006; Interview—source wishes to remain anonymous; Noam Scheiber, "Over-Billed," *The New Republic*, February 13, 2008.

191. R. Emmett Tyrrell Jr., *The Clinton Crack-up: The Boy President's Life After the White House*, Thomas Nelson, 2007, p. 189.

192. Elaine Kamarck, Interview with author, October 10, 2006.

193. Tony Coelho, Interview with author, September 5, 2006.

194. Stan Brand, Interview with author, September 13, 2006.

195. Interview; source wishes to remain anonymous.

196. Greg Norman with Donald T. Phillips, *The Way of the Shark: Lessons on Golf, Business, and Life*, Atria, 2006, p. 311.

Chapter 5 CLINTON OPENS HIS LIBRARY IN A DOWNPOUR

1. Lynn Cutler, Interview with author, June 29, 2006.

2. Phil Stefani, Interview with author, August 15, 2006.

3. Janis Kearney, Interviews with author, June 2, 2006, September 15, 2006.

4. Howard Tullman, Interview with author, June 26, 2006.

5. Kane Webb, Interview with author, February 6, 2007.

6. Jim Dailey, Interview with author, December 20, 2006.

7. Ibid.

8. Kane Webb, Interview with author, February 6, 2007.

9. Jim Dailey, Interview with author, December 20, 2006.

10. Leon Panetta, Interview with author, October 17, 2006.

11. Susie Tompkins Buell, Interview with author, September 5, 2006.

12. Sarah Wilson, Interview with author, February 16, 2007.

13. Kane Webb, Interview with author, February 6, 2007.

14. John Emerson, Interview with author, September 20, 2006.

15. Susie Tompkins Buell, Interview with author, September 5, 2006.

16. *The Arkansas Traveler*, vol. 3, no. 3, July 2005.

17. Mickey Ibarra, Interview with author, November 7, 2006.

18. Mark Buell, Interview with author, August 22, 2006.

19. Lynn Cutler, Interview with author, June 29, 2006.

20. Karoun Demirjian, "House Approves Bill to Divulge Funding of Presidential Libraries," *CT*, March 15, 2007; http://kakihockersmith.com; Anne E. Kornblut, "In His Wife's Campaign, Bill Clinton Is a Free Agent," *WP*, October 30, 2007; Andrew De-Millo, "Clinton Library Gets a Green Penthouse View," *CS-T*, November 11, 2007.

21. Phyllis Brandon, Interview with author, June 27, 2006; Maureen Dowd, "Hillary Rodham Clinton Strikes a New Pose and Multiplies Her Images," *NYT*, December 12, 1993.

22. Paul Greenberg, Interview with author, October 4, 2006.

23. Kane Webb, Interview with author, February 6, 2007; Kim Coryat, Archives Technician, Clinton Presidential Library, e-mail, June 2, 2007.

24. Jim Dailey, Interview with author, December 20, 2006.

25. Ibid.

26. Kane Webb, Interview with author, February 6, 2007.

27. Ron Kaufman, Interview with author, December 11, 2006.

28. Mark Silva, "Praise for One-Time Foe; Bushes Celebrate Clinton's Skills," *CT*, November 19, 2004.

29. Ron Kaufman, Interview with author, December 11, 2006; John Emerson, Interview with author, September 22, 2006; Chris Jennings, Interview with author, August 2, 2006; Bud Yorkin, Interview with author, October 9, 2006.

30. John Emerson, Interview with author, September 22, 2006.

31. Kane Webb, Interview with author, February 6, 2007.

32. Terry McAuliffe, with Steve Kettmann, *What a Party: My Life Among Democrats, Presidents, Candidates, Donors, Activists, Alligators, and Other Wild Animals*, St. Martin's Press, Thomas Dunne Books, 2007, pp. 380–382.

33. Mark Silva, "Praise for One-Time Foe; Bushes Celebrate Clinton's Skills," *CT*, November 19, 2004.

34. States News Service, May 6, 2005.

35. John Emerson, Interview with author, September 20, 2006.

36. William Brantley, "Too Much Scar Tissue Is Not a Good Thing," *Edmonton Journal* (Alberta), March 21, 2005; *Facts on File World News Digest*, March 17, 2005; Adam Lisberg, "Clinton's 'Glad to Be Home': Full Recovery Expected," *NYDN*, March 15, 2005; Andrew DeMillo, "Clinton Surgery Goes Well; Doctors Expect Full Recovery," *A D-G*, March 11, 2005; Lawrence K. Altman, "Clinton's 4-Hour Surgery Went Well, Doctors Say," March 11, 2005.

37. Mark Ward, Interview with author, September 1, 2006; Stephen Fitzpatrick, "Tsunami Refugee Reborn Behind Picket Fence," *The Australian*, December 8, 2006.

38. Mark Ward, Interview with author, September 1, 2006.

39. Ibid.; Matthew Miller, "The Rise of Ron Burkle," *Forbes*, December 11, 2006.

40. Mark Ward, Interview with author, September 1, 2006.

41. Tony Freemantle, "'41' and '42'—No Baggage; The Not-Really-So-Odd Couple; Two Former Presidents Have Overcome Differences and Formed a Friendship, as Shown in Tsunami Tour," *Houston Chronicle*, March 7, 2005.

42. Mark Ward, Interview with author, September 1, 2006.

43. Raymond Offenheiser Jr., Interview with author, December 20, 2006.

44. Mark Ward, Interview with author, September 1, 2006.

45. Raymond Offenheiser Jr., Interview with author, December 20, 2006.

46. Peggy Harris, "Clinton Speaks Against 'Demonizing' Political Leaders," AP, June 17, 2006; States News Service, May 6, 2005.

47. Mark Ward, Interview with author, September 1, 2006; Michael Duffy, "When Opposites Attract; Actually, Bush and Clinton Discovered They Were Not So Different After All While on the Road Raising Relief Money. Inside an Improbable Friendship," *Time*, December 26, 2005.

48. Greg Norman, with Donald T. Phillips, *The Way of the Shark: Lessons on Golf, Business, and Life*, Atria, 2006, p. 302.

49. Mark Ward, Interview with author, September 1, 2006.

50. States News Service, May 6, 2005.

51. Mark Ward, Interview with author, September 1, 2006; States News Service, May 6, 2005.

52. Mark Ward, Interview with author, September 1, 2006.

53. Ibid.

54. William Brantley, "Too Much Scar Tissue Is Not a Good Thing," *Edmonton Journal* (Alberta), March 21, 2005; *Facts on File World News Digest*, March 17, 2005; Adam Lisberg, "Clinton's 'Glad to Be Home': Full Recovery Expected," *NYDN*, March 15, 2005; Andrew DeMillo, "Clinton Surgery Goes Well; Doctors Expect Full Recovery," A *D-G*, March 11, 2005; Lawrence K. Altman, "Clinton's 4-Hour Surgery Went Well, Doctors Say," March 11, 2005.

55. *The Late, Late Show*, CBS, March 14, 2005; *The Hotline*, March 15, 2005.

56. Thomas Kean, Interview with author, January 22, 2007.

57. Ibid.; Alvin S. Felzenberg, *Governor Tom Kean: From the New Jersey Statehouse to the 9-11 Commission*, Rivergate Books/Rutgers University Press, 2006, pp. 395, 398.

58. Thomas Kean, Interview with author, January 22, 2007.

59. Mark Ward, Interview with author, September 1, 2006.

60. Ibid.

61. Ron Kaufman, Interview with author, December 11, 2006; Delia M. Rios, "Bushes, Clintons Forge Surprising Bond; Familial Rivalry Transforms into a Friendship," Newhouse News Service, June 19, 2005.

62. Anson Beard Jr., Interview with author, September 27, 2006.

63. Mark Ward, Interview with author, September 1, 2006.

64. Jake Siewert, Interview with author, January 15, 2007.

65. Peggy Harris, "Clinton Speaks Against 'Demonizing' Political Leaders," AP, June 17, 2006; Mary Anna Towler, "Missing (Bill) Clinton," June 28, 2006, post.

66. Beryl Anthony, Interview with author, October 3, 2006.

67. Mark Updegrove, Interview with author, October 22, 2006; Thomas Beaumont, "Stumping for Wife, Clinton Can Help, or Hurt, Anybody," *Des Moines Register*, November 25, 2007; Peter Hamby, "Bill Clinton: George H. W. Bush Will Help President Hillary," CNN, December 18, 2007; Rebecca Sinderbrand, "Elder Bush Nixes Clinton Trip Idea," CNN, December 18, 2007.

68. Tony Freemantle, "'41' and '42'—No Baggage; The Not-Really-So-Odd Couple; Two Former Presidents Have Overcome Differences and Formed a Friendship, as Shown in Tsunami Tour," *Houston Chronicle*, March 7, 2005.

69. Mark Ward, Interview with author, September 1, 2006; Michael Duffy, "Bill Clinton and George H. W. Bush; Proving the Power of Two," *Time*, May 8, 2006.

70. Raymond C. Offenheiser Jr., Interview with author, December 20, 2006.

71. Mark Ward, Interview with author, September 1, 2006.

72. Chris Stamos, Interview with author, November 2, 2006.

73. John Emerson, Interview with author, September 22, 2006.

74. Mark Updegrove, Interview with author, October 22, 2006.

75. Larry King, Interview with author, October 28, 2006.

76. Delia M. Rios, "Bushes, Clintons Forge Surprising Bond; Familial Rivalry Transforms into a Friendship," Newhouse News Service, June 19, 2005.

77. Michael Duffy, "Bill Clinton and George H. W. Bush; Proving the Power of Two," *Time*, May 8, 2006.

78. Tony Coelho, Interview with author, September 5, 2006.

79. Mark Ward, Interview with author, September 1, 2006.

80. Thomas Kean, Interview with author, January 22, 2007.

81. Scott Reed, Interview with author, December 1, 2006.

82. Ron Kaufman, Interview with author, December 11, 2006.

83. "Former President Bush Sobs While Talking of Son's Leadership as Florida Governor," AP, December 5, 2006.

84. "Bill Clinton One-on-One; Is There a Clinton Dynasty?" *Good Morning America*, ABC, September 27, 2007.

85. Thomas Kean, Interview with author, January 22, 2007.

86. Paul Orfalea, Interview with author, February 28, 2007.

87. Joe Conason, "The Third Term," *Esquire*, December 2005.

88. ABC News, May 19, 2007.

89. Douglas Brinkley, Interview with author, September 14, 2006.

90. Mark Ward, Interview with author, September 1, 2006.

91. Bill White, Interview with author, September 26, 2006.

92. Ron Kaufman, Interview with author, December 11, 2006.

93. Steve Grossman, Interview with author, August 4, 2006.

94. *Leadership for the Global Future, a Conversation Between Bill Clinton and Paul Orfalea*, DVD, The Orfalea Center for Global and International Studies, University of California, Santa Barbara, October 13, 2006.

95. Theodore Sorensen, Interview with author, August 16, 2006.

96. Interview; source wishes to remain anonymous.

97. Tony Coelho, Interview with author, September 5, 2006.

98. Jim Wallis, Interview with author, December 14, 2006.

99. Ibid.

100. Francis X. Clines, "Morality Mission Faces Capital Reality," *NYT*, June 7, 1998.

101. Jim Wallis, Interview with author, December 14, 2006.

102. Jake Siewert, Interview with author, January 15, 2007.

103. Vartan Gregorian, Interview with author, December 14, 2006.

104. Jake Siewert, Interview with author, January 15, 2007.

105. Interview; source wishes to remain anonymous.

106. Susan Davis, Interview with author, November 22, 2006.

107. Tim Wirth, Interview with author, November 7, 2006.

108. Susan Davis, Interview with author, November 22, 2006.

109. Chris Jennings, Interview with author, August 2, 2006.

110. Vartan Gregorian, Interview with author, December 14, 2006.

111. Richard Feachem, Interview with author, November 5, 2006.

112. Melanne Verveer, Interview with author, January 27, 2007.

113. Susan Davis, Interview with author, November 22, 2006.

114. Sandy Berger, Interview with author, October 3, 2006.

115. Susan Davis, Interview with author, November 22, 2006.

116. Chris Stamos, Interview with author, November 2, 2006.

117. Ibid.

118. Joseph Stiglitz, Interview with author, February 12, 2007.

119. Georgette Bennett, Interview with author, October 18, 2006.

120. Anson Beard Jr., Interview with author, September 27, 2006.

121. Steve Grossman, Interview with author, August 4, 2006.

122. Julian H. Robertson Jr., Interview with author, October 4, 2006.

123. Susan Davis, Interview with author, November 22, 2006.

124. Anson Beard Jr., Interview with author, September 27, 2006.

125. Raymond Offenheiser Jr., Interview with author, December 30, 2006; Melanne Verveer, Interview with author, January 27, 2007; Sandy Berger, Interviews with author, July 27, 2006, October 3, 2006; Oliver Burkeman, "Bill Clinton: Hillary Wants Me to Restore Image of US," *Guardian*, October 5, 2007.

126. Scott Reed, Interview with author, December 1, 2006.

127. Anthony Campolo, e-mail to author, October 27, 2006.

128. Georgette Bennett, Interview with author, October 18, 2006.

129. Leon Panetta, Interview with author, October 17, 2006.

130. Nara Schoenberg, "Bill Clinton's Global Reach Embraces Chicagoan," *CT*, April 27, 2007.

131. *Larry King Live*, CNN, April 19, 2007.

132. John R. Emshwiller, "Burkle v. Follieri Offers a Window on Ugly Breakup," *WSJ*, June 14, 2007; John R. Emshwiller and Gabriel Kahn, "Presidential Connection: How Bill Clinton's Aide Facilitated a Messy Deal; Mr. Band Introduced Italian to Ron Burkle; Lawsuit over Spending," *WSJ*, September 26, 2007.

Chapter 6   BILL CLINTON FIXES AFRICA

1. Nara Schoenberg, "Bill Clinton's Global Reach Embraces Chicagoan," *CT*, April 27, 2007.

2. Victor Davis Hanson, "Kerry Turning into the Ugly American," Tribune Media Services, February 2, 2007; Sheryl Gay Stolberg, "Bush Requests $30 Billion to Fight AIDS," *NYT*, May 31, 2007; Brendan Miniter, interview with Laura Bush, *WSJ*, July 14, 2007; Kevin De Cock, Interview with author, December 6, 2006.

3. Richard Feachem, Interview with author, November 5, 2006.

4. Ibid.

5. Kevin De Cock, Interview with author, December 6, 2006.

6. *Leadership for the Global Future, a Conversation Between Bill Clinton and Paul Orfalea*, DVD, The Orfalea Center for Global and International Studies, University of California, Santa Barbara, October 13, 2006.

7. Sandy Berger, Interview with author, July 27, 2006.

8. Melanne Verveer, Interview with author, January 27, 2007.

9. Richard Marlink, Interview with author, October 30, 2006.

10. Bill Clinton, "A Man Called Hope," VF, July 2007.

11. Alan Solomont, Interview with author, August 9, 2006.

12. Eric Goosby, Interview with author, December 11, 2006.

13. Chris Stamos, Interview with author, November 2, 2006.

14. Interview; source wishes to remain anonymous.

15. Bill Bicknell, Interview with author, December 28, 2006.

16. Eric Goosby, Interview with author, December 11, 2006.

17. Tunku Varadarajan, "Desmond Tutu, The Archbishop," WSJ, December 30, 2006; Sarah Boseley, "World Aids Day: Living with HIV/Aids: Searching for a Way Forward: Technological Advances, Cultural Adjustments and Education All Have a Role in Combating This Pandemic," Guardian Weekly, December 1, 2006.

18. Eric Goosby, Interview with author, December 11, 2006.

19. Chris Stamos, Interview with author, November 2, 2006.

20. Melanne Verveer, Interview with author, January 27, 2007; Bill Clinton, "A Man Called Hope," VF, July 2007.

21. Chris Stamos, Interview with author, November 2, 2006.

22. Richard Feachem, Interview with author, November 5, 2006.

23. Chris Stamos, Interview with author, November 2, 2006.

24. Bill Bicknell, Interview with author, December 28, 2006.

25. Celia W. Dugger, "Clinton Helps Broker Deal for Medicine to Treat AIDS," NYT, December 1, 2006.

26. Elisabeth Rosenthal, "African Children Often Lack Available AIDS Treatment," NYT, November 15, 2006.

27. Kevin De Cock, Interview with author, December 6, 2006.

28. Richard Marlink, Interview with author, October 16, 2006.

29. Ibid.

30. Kevin De Cock, Interview with author, December 6, 2006.

31. Chris Stamos, Interview with author, November 2, 2006.

32. Sabin Russell, "China Finally Taking Steps to Fight Its HIV Problem; Methadone Clinics, Condoms in Hotels, Free Testing Offered," San Francisco Chronicle, July 30, 2006.

33. Bill Bicknell, Interview with author, December 28, 2006.

34. Richard Marlink, Interview with author, October 16, 2006.

35. Kevin De Cock, Interview with author, December 6, 2006.

36. Richard Feachem, Interview with author, November 5, 2006.

37. Richard Marlink, Interview with author, October 30, 2006.

38. Eric Goosby, Interview with author, December 11, 2006.

39. Kevin De Cock, Interview with author, December 6, 2006.

40. Nicholas D. Kristof, "Ten Suggestions for Rescuing the Bush Legacy," NYT, December 31, 2006; Raymond Offenheiser Jr., Interview with author, December 20, 2006.

41. Chris Stamos, Interview with author, November 2, 2006.

42. Richard Marlink, Interview with author, October 30, 2006.

43. Chris Stamos, Interview with author, November 2, 2006.

44. Michael Woyton, "FDR's Ideals Are Guiding Light for Clinton, Honorees," *Poughkeepsie Journal*, October 23, 2005; John Davis, "Freedoms Medal Is Clinton's," *Poughkeepsie Journal*, October 19, 2005.

45. Thomas Kean, Interview with author, January 22, 2007.

46. Douglas Brinkley, Interview with author, September 14, 2006.

47. Eric Schmertz, Interview with author, September 1, 2006.

48. Carolyn Eisenberg, Interview with author, October 23, 2006.

49. Douglas Brinkley, Interview with author, September 14, 2006.

50. Carolyn Eisenberg, Interview with author, October 23, 2006.

51. Eric Schmertz, Interview with author, September 1, 2006; Eric Schmertz, e-mail to author, September 9, 2006.

52. Natalie Datlof, Interview with author, September 8, 2006.

53. Slade Gorton, Interview with author, October 5, 2006; Elaine Kamarck, Interview with author, October 10, 2006.

54. Douglas Brinkley, Interview with author, September 14, 2006.

55. Natalie Datlof, Interview with author, September 8, 2006.

56. Douglas Brinkley, Interview with author, September 14, 2006.

57. Stanislao Pugliese, Interview with author, September 21, 2006.

58. Douglas Brinkley, Interview with author, September 14, 2006.

59. Carolyn Eisenberg, Interview with author, October 23, 2006.

60. Ibid.; Daniel Geiger, "Harry Macklowe Honored," *Real Estate Weekly*, November 16, 2005.

61. Natalie Datlof, Interview with author, September 8, 2006.

62. Stanislao Pugliese, Interview with author, September 21, 2006.

63. Ibid.; Carolyn Eisenberg, Interview with author, October 23, 2006.

64. Natalie Datlof, Interview with author, September 8, 2006.

65. Olivia Winslow, "Deconstructing Clinton's Presidency at Hofstra," *Newsday*, November 10, 2005.

66. Douglas Brinkley, Interview with author, September 14, 2006.

67. Stuart Rabinowitz, Interview with author, September 20, 2006.

68. Douglas Brinkley, Interview with author, September 14, 2006.

69. Leon Panetta, Interview with author, October 17, 2006.

70. Elaine Kamarck, Interview with author, October 10, 2006.

71. Interview; source wishes to remain anonymous.

72. Slade Gorton, Interview with author, October 5, 2006; William Booth, "All's Quiet in the Other Washington," *WP*, February 22, 1999; Jo Becker, "The Long Run: G.O.P. Hopeful Took Own Path in the Senate," *NYT*, September 30, 2007.

73. Michael Barone, Interview with author, September 19, 2006.

74. Carolyn Eisenberg, Interview with author, October 23, 2006.

75. Eric Schmertz, Interview with author, September 1, 2006.

76. Herman Berliner, Interview with author, October 5, 2006.

77. Stuart Rabinowitz, Interview with author, September 20, 2006.

Chapter 7 THE PATH TO 9/11

1. Thomas Kean, Interview with author, January 22, 2007; Dan Eggen, "9/11 Panel to Have Rare Glimpse of Presidential Briefings," WP, November 16, 2003.

2. Thomas Kean, Interview with author, January 22, 2007.

3. Sandy Berger, Interviews with author, July 27, 2006, October 3, 2006.

4. Don Fowler, Interview with author, February 14, 2007.

5. Larry King, Interview with author, October 28, 2006.

6. Mickey Ibarra, Interview with author, November 7, 2006.

7. Robert Torricelli, Interview with author, October 6, 2006.

8. Terry McAuliffe, with Steve Kettmann, *What a Party: My Life Among Democrats, Presidents, Candidates, Donors, Activists, Alligators, and Other Wild Animals*, St. Martin's Press, Thomas Dunne Books, 2007, pp. 162, 163, 171.

9. Bob Kerrey, Interviews with author, July 5, 2006, July 24, 2006.

10. Thomas Kean, Interview with author, January 22, 2007; Alvin S. Felzenberg, *Governor Tom Kean: From the New Jersey Statehouse to the 9-11 Commission*, Rivergate Books/Rutgers University Press, 2006, p. 433.

11. Slade Gorton, Interview with author, October 5, 2006.

12. Bob Kerrey, Interview with author, July 24, 2006.

13. R. Jeffrey Smith, "Berger Case Still Roils Archives, Justice Dept.," WP, February 21, 2007; "The Berger Files," WSJ, February 21, 2007.

14. Steve Emerson, Interview with author, January 8, 2007.

15. Michael Barone, "Berger and Libby: A Tale of Two Crimes," Creators Syndicate, March 12, 2007.

16. Lanny Breuer, Interview with author, October 30, 2006.

17. Slade Gorton, Interview with author, October 5, 2006.

18. Thomas Kean, Interview with author, January 22, 2007.

19. Bill Sammon, "He's Back: Sandy Berger Now Advising Hillary Clinton," *Examiner*, October 8, 2007; Andrew Sullivan, "Berger and Clinton," The Daily Dish, theAtlantic.com, October 9, 2007.

20. Scott Collins and Tina Daunt, "Five Years After; ABC Stands by Its 9/11 Story—Almost; After Minor Edits in Response to Democratic Critics, the Miniseries Will Air as Scheduled. It's Already Set Off a Bitter Election-Year Dispute," LAT, September 9, 2006; Tim Rutten, "Five Years After; Regarding Media: ABC Follows a Path to Shame," LAT, September 9, 2006; Samantha Bonar, "Television Review: On Dangerous Ground," LAT, September 9, 2007.

21. Cyrus Nowrasteh, Interview with author, September 17, 2006.

22. Cyrus Nowrasteh, Interview with author, September 14, 2006.

23. Ibid.

24. Michael Barone, Interview with author, September 19, 2006.

25. Cyrus Nowrasteh, Interview with author, September 14, 2006.

26. Cyrus Nowrasteh, e-mail to author, January 8, 2007.

27. Thomas Kean, Interview with author, January 22, 2006.

28. Sandy Berger, Interview with author, October 3, 2006.

29. Thomas Kean, Interview with author, January 22, 2007.

30. Cyrus Nowrasteh, Interviews with author, September 14, 2006, September 15, 2006, September 17, 2006, February 23, 2007, June 1, 2007; Cyrus Nowrasteh, "The Path to 9/11: Committing the Truth," *The Magazine of the Writers Guild of America, West,* December 2006; Tim Rutten, "Five Years After; Regarding Media: ABC Follows a Path to Shame," *LAT,* September 9, 2006.

31. Cyrus Nowrasteh, "Remembering 9/11: The Path to Hysteria," *WSJ,* September 18, 2006; Howard Kurtz, "Clinton Administration Officials Assail ABC's 'The Path to 9/11,' " *WP,* September 9, 2006; Maureen Dowd, "The Unslammed Phone," *NYT,* September 9, 2006; Samantha Bonar, "Television Review: On Dangerous Ground," *LAT,* September 9, 2007; Mike Medavoy, Interview with author, October 19, 2006.

32. John Ziegler, Interview with author, September 22, 2006.

33. Cyrus Nowrasteh, Interview with author, September 14, 2006; Cyrus Nowrasteh, "The Path to 9/11: Committing the Truth," *The Magazine of the Writers Guild of America, West,* December 2006.

34. Sandy Berger, Interview with author, October 3, 2006; Barbara Bodine, Interview with author, September 27, 2006.

35. Sandy Berger, Interview with author, October 3, 2006.

36. Thomas Kean, Interview with author, January 22, 2007.

37. John Ziegler, Interview with author, September 22, 2006; Edward Wyatt, "More Questions of Accuracy Raised About ABC Mini-Series on 9/11 Prelude," *NYT,* September 12, 2006.

38. Jesse McKinley, "Three from Clinton Administration Urge Disney to Cancel or Revise 9/11 Mini-Series," *NYT,* September 7, 2006.

39. Sandy Berger, Interview with author, October 3, 2006.

40. Edward Wyatt, "More Questions of Accuracy Raised About ABC Mini-Series on 9/11 Prelude," *NYT,* September 12, 2006.

41. Sandy Berger, Interview with author, October 3, 2006.

42. Jane Mayer, "Whatever It Takes; The Politics of the Man Behind '24,' " *NYer,* February 19, 2007.

43. Maureen Dowd, "The Unslammed Phone," *NYT,* September 9, 2006.

44. Cyrus Nowrasteh, Interview with author, September 14, 2006.

45. John Ziegler, Interview with author, September 22, 2006.

46. Cyrus Nowrasteh, Interviews with author, September 14, 2006, September 15, 2006, September 17, 2006, February 23, 2007, June 1, 2007.

47. Thomas Kean, Interview with author, January 22, 2007.

48. Cyrus Nowrasteh, Interview with author, June 1, 2007; Cyrus Nowrasteh, e-mails to author, July 20, 2007, July 26, 2007.

49. Interview; source wishes to remain anonymous.

50. Jane Hamsher, Interview with author, September 28, 2006.

51. Cyrus Nowrasteh, Interviews with author, September 14, 2006, September 15, 2006, September 17, 2006, February 23, 2007, June 1, 2007.

52. Cyrus Nowrasteh, e-mail to author, March 15, 2007.

53. Cyrus Nowrasteh, e-mail to author, February 7, 2007; Anne E. Kornblut, "In His Wife's Campaign, Bill Clinton Is a Free Agent," WP, October 30, 2007. (Carson is now working for Hillary's campaign but remains close to the former president.) Contacted by this writer on November 8, 2007, Paramount PR man, Michael Vollman, e-mailed, "We have no comment."

54. Cyrus Nowrasteh, Interviews with author, June 1, 2007, November 8, 2007; Cyrus Nowrasteh, e-mail to author, July 10, 2007.

55. Cyrus Nowrasteh, Interviews with author, September 14, 2006, February 23, 2007; Max Blumenthal, Interview with author, November 8, 2007; author's e-mail and telephone call to Jay Carson, November 7, 2007: no response to either.

56. Cyrus Nowrasteh, Interviews with author, September 14, 2006, September 17, 2006.

57. Thomas Kean, Interview with author, January 22, 2007.

58. Cyrus Nowrasteh, Interview with author, September 14, 2006.

59. John Ziegler, Interview with author, September 22, 2006.

60. Robert Patterson, Interview with author, January 4, 2007; Cyrus Nowrasteh, Interview with author, September 14, 2006; Edward Wyatt, "More Questions of Accuracy Raised About ABC Mini-Series on 9/11 Prelude," NYT, September 12, 2006.

61. Cyrus Nowrasteh, Interview with author, September 14, 2006.

62. Steve Emerson, Interview with author, January 8, 2007.

63. Sandy Berger, Interview with author, October 3, 2006.

64. Edward Wyatt, "More Questions of Accuracy Raised About ABC Mini-Series on 9/11 Prelude," NYT, September 12, 2006; Patrick Healy and Jesse McKinley, "Passions Flare as Broadcast of 9/11 Mini-Series Nears," NYT, September 8, 2006.

65. Thomas Kean, Interview with author, January 22, 2007.

66. Cyrus Nowrasteh, Interview with author, September 14, 2006.

67. Thomas Kean, Interview with author, January 22, 2007.

68. Sandy Berger, Interview with author, October 3, 2006.

69. Barbara Bodine, Interview with author, September 27, 2006.

70. Sandy Berger, Interview with author, October 3, 2006.

Chapter 8 A LUDDITE MEETS THE BLOGGERS

1. Rick Boxer, Interview with author, July 20, 2006.

2. Howard Tullman, Interview with author, June 26, 2006; "President Clinton Remarks at DNC Dinner, Corcoran Gallery of Art," Federal News Service, January 2, 1998.

3. Simon Rosenberg, Interview with author, January 26, 2007.

4. Dave Johnson, Interview with author, September 26, 2006; Jeralyn Merritt, Interview with author, September 27, 2006; Leon Panetta, Interview with author, October 17, 2006; Howard Kurtz, "Loneliness, Lies and Videotape," WP, September 18, 2006.

5. *Countdown with Keith Olbermann*, MSNBC, September 20, 2006; Dave Johnson, Interview with author, September 26, 2006; Jeralyn Merritt, Interview with author, September 27, 2006.

6. Dave Johnson, Interview with author, September 26, 2006; Jeralyn Merritt, Interview with author, September 27, 2006.

7. Jane Hamsher, Interview with author, September 28, 2006.

8. Interview; source wishes to remain anonymous.

9. Jeralyn Merritt, Interview with author, September 27, 2006.

10. Interview; source wishes to remain anonymous.

11. Jeralyn Merritt, Interview with author, September 27, 2006.

12. Jane Hamsher, Interview with author, September 28, 2006; *Countdown with Keith Olbermann*, MSNBC, September 20, 2006.

13. John Ziegler, Interview with author, September 22, 2006.

14. Jane Hamsher, Interview with author, September 28, 2006.

15. Jeralyn Merritt, Interview with author, September 27, 2006.

16. Jane Hamsher, Interview with author, September 28, 2006.

17. Jeralyn Merritt, Interview with author, September 27, 2006; Interview—source wishes to remain anonymous.

18. Jeralyn Merritt, Interview with author, September 27, 2006.

19. Interview—source wishes to remain anonymous; Paul Orfalea, Interview with author, February 28, 2007.

20. Janis Kearney, Interviews with author, June 2, 2006, September 15, 2006.

21. Elaine Kamarck, Interview with author, October 10, 2006; Leon Panetta, Interview with author, October 17, 2006.

22. Leon Panetta, Interview with author, October 17, 2006.

23. John Emerson, Interview with author, September 20, 2006.

24. Interview with Bill Clinton, *Fox News Sunday with Chris Wallace*, September 24, 2006.

25. Interview; source wishes to remain anonymous.

26. Leon Panetta, Interview with author, October 17, 2006.

27. Sandy Berger, Interview with author, October 3, 2006; Jake Siewert, Interview with author, January 15, 2007.

28. Stephen Rodrick, "Limbaugh for Lefties," NY mag, April 16, 2007.

29. Mark Silva, "Mr. November? Democrats Count on Clinton for Late-Inning Campaign Magic," CT, September 28, 2006.

30. Slade Gorton, Interview with author, October 5, 2006.

31. Robert Torricelli, Interview with author, October 6, 2006.

32. Scott Reed, Interview with author, December 1, 2006.

33. Elaine Kamarck, Interview with author, October 10, 2006.

34. Conrad Black, Interview with author, December 14, 2006.

35. Thomas Kean, Interview with author, January 22, 2007.

36. Paul Greenberg, Interview with author, October 4, 2006.

37. Don Fowler, Interview with author, February 14, 2007; Interview—source wishes to remain anonymous.

38. Rahm Emanuel, Interview with author, July 21, 2006.

39. Naftali Bendavid, "The House That Rahm Built," *CT*, November 12, 2006.

40. Elaine Kamarck, Interview with author, October 10, 2006.

41. John M. Broder and Anne E. Kornblut, "A Rescue Bid for His Party and His Reputation, Too," *NYT*, October 6, 2006.

42. Lou Weisbach, Interview with author, July 11, 2006.

43. Bob Kerrey, Interview with author, July 24, 2006; Edward Walsh, "Pragmatic Centrist in Debt to JFK; Living Religion, Honing Ambition," *WP*, June 15, 2003.

44. Steve Grossman, Interview with author, August 4, 2006.

45. Jonathan Alter, Interview with author, August 10, 2006.

46. Interview—source wishes to remain anonymous; Peter Hart, Interview with author, September 7, 2006.

47. Tony Coelho, Interview with author, September 5, 2006.

48. Interview; source wishes to remain anonymous.

49. Interview; source wishes to remain anonymous.

50. Rod Blagojevich (earlier interview for *Chicago* magazine profile, November 2003).

51. Bethany McLean, "The Power of Philanthropy," *Fortune*, September 18, 2006.

52. Howard Kurtz, "Falling Apart?" *WP*, November 30, 2006; Paul Mirengoff, "Paul Mirengoff Provides a Quick History Lesson on the Virginian," *Daily Press*, October 20, 2006.

53. Charles Robb, Interview with author, October 23, 2006.

54. Lanny Breuer, Interview with author, October 30, 2006.

55. Charles Robb, Interview with author, October 23, 2006.

56. Jonathan Alter, Interviews with author, July 7, 2006, August 10, 2006.

57. Patrick Creadon, Interview with author, October 31, 2006.

58. Will Shortz, Interview with author, October 30, 2006.

59. Merl Reagle, Interview with author, October 31, 2006.

60. Ibid.

61. Victor Fleming, Interview with author, November 2, 2006.

62. Ibid.

63. George McGovern, Interview with author, November 1, 2006.

64. Victor Fleming, Interview with author, November 2, 2006.

Chapter 9 PHILANDERER IN CHIEF

1. Nelson Shanks, Interview with author, September 14, 2006; "Bill's Naked Finger," *NYP*, April 26, 2006.

2. "Bill's Naked Finger," *NYP*, April 26, 2006.

3. Ibid.

4. Nelson Shanks, Interview with author, September 14, 2006.

5. Ibid.

6. Hillary Rodham Clinton, *Living History*, Scribner, 2004; Jonathan Alter, Interview with author, August 10, 2006.

7. Anthony Campolo, e-mail to author, October 27, 2006; Gustav Niebuhr, "Not All Presidential Advisers Talk Politics," *NYT*, March 18, 1997.

8. Anthony Campolo, e-mail to author, October 27, 2006.

9. Jonathan Alter, "Citizen Clinton Up Close," *NW*, April 8, 2002.

10. Jonathan Alter, Interview with author, August 10, 2006; Irena Medavoy, Interview with author, October 23, 2006.

11. Robert Patterson, Interview with author, January 4, 2007.

12. Mark Thomann, Interview with author, December 14, 2006.

13. Anson Beard Jr., Interview with author, September 27, 2006.

14. Interview; source wishes to remain anonymous.

15. Larry Sabato, Interview with author, July 31, 2006.

16. Interview; source wishes to remain anonymous.

17. Interview; source wishes to remain anonymous.

18. Interview; source wishes to remain anonymous.

19. Interview; source wishes to remain anonymous.

20. Irena Medavoy, Interview with author, October 23, 2006.

21. Interview; source wishes to remain anonymous.

22. Howard Kurtz, "Tina Brown's Talk Magazine Suddenly Silenced," *WP*, January 19, 2002.

23. John Schmidt, Interview with author, August 9, 2006.

24. Interview; source wishes to remain anonymous.

25. Betty Sheinbaum, Interview with author, October 12, 2006.

26. Robert Novak, "Democratic Front-Runners May Find Richardson Is Running Close at Their Heels," *C S-T*, March 11, 2007.

27. Geoffrey Gray, "Hillary Hampton '07; A Weekend in the Country That'll Cost You," *NY mag*, July 30, 2007.

28. Interview; source wishes to remain anonymous.

29. Don Hewitt, Interview with author, September 7, 2006.

30. Interview; source wishes to remain anonymous.

31. As quoted in Peter Baker and John Solomon, "Books Paint Critical Portraits of Clinton; 2 Biographies Detail Marital Strife and Driving Ambition," *WP*, May 25, 2007; Carl Bernstein, *A Woman in Charge*, Knopf, 2007.

32. Don Hewitt, Interview with author, September 7, 2006; Don Hewitt, *Tell Me a Story: Fifty Years and 60 Minutes in Television*, Public Affairs, 2001, pp. 175–177; Diane Haithman, "Hollywood's Party Politics; Clinton, Kerrey Front-Runners on Democratic Circuit," *LAT*, January 31, 1992.

33. Don Hewitt, Interview with author, September 7, 2006.

34. Ibid.; Don Hewitt, *Tell Me a Story: Fifty Years and 60 Minutes in Television*, Public Affairs, 2001, p. 177.

35. Don Hewitt, Interview with author, September 7, 2006.

36. Ibid.; Don Hewitt, *Tell Me a Story: Fifty Years and 60 Minutes in Television*, Public Affairs, 2001, p. 177.

37. Patrick Healy, "For Clintons, Delicate Dance of Married and Public Lives," *NYT*, May 23, 2006.

38. Ibid.

39. "The Year That Was: An Uncensored Look At Our Year of Living Dangerously," "Bubba's Got a Brand New Blonde," *Toronto Life*, January 2004.

40. Eric Reguly, Interview with author, August 9, 2006.

41. Don Martin, Interview with author, December 18, 2006.

42. Ibid.

43. Andrew Allentuck, "Tales of Two Stronachs," *Globe and Mail*, October 28, 2006.

44. Ibid.

45. Ibid.

46. Interview; source wishes to remain anonymous.

47. Don Martin, Interview with author, December 18, 2006.

48. Ibid.

49. Andrew Allentuck, "Tales of Two Stronachs," *Globe and Mail*, October 28, 2006; Michael Valpy, "Belinda: 'I Don't Sit at Home and Knit on Friday Nights,'" *Globe and Mail*, September 30, 2006.

50. Ibid.

51. Don Martin, Interview with author, December 18, 2006.

52. Ibid.

53. Ibid.

54. Ibid.

55. Ibid.

56. Interview; source wishes to remain anonymous.

57. Don Martin, Interview with author, December 18, 2006.

58. Eric Reguly, Interview with author, August 9, 2006.

59. Interview; source wishes to remain anonymous.

60. Don Martin, Interview with author, December 18, 2006.

61. Andrew Allentuck, "Tales of Two Stronachs," *Globe and Mail*, October 28, 2006.

62. Don Martin, Interview with author, December 18, 2006.

63. Lynn Crosbie, "After Bill: What Belinda Did Next," *The First Post*, October 10, 2006.

64. Jane Taber, "Ignatieff Team All About Being Convention Ready," Ottawa Notebook, *Globe and Mail*, November 11, 2006.

65. Eric Reguly, Interview with author, August 9, 2006.

66. Charles Laurence, "Bill's Been Told: No More Embarrassments," *The First Post*, May 28, 2007.

67. CTV, ca. June 23, 2007.

68. Eric Reguly, Interview with author, August 9, 2006.

69. Interview; source wishes to remain anonymous.

70. Janis MacKey Frayer, "A House Divided, and Then a Presidential 'Pardon Me,'" *Globe and Mail*, October 5, 2002.

71. Interview; source wishes to remain anonymous; Robert Sam Anson, "Bill and His Shadow," *VF*, June 2004; George Rush and Joanna Molloy, "Stylish Power Struggle on 42nd St.," *NYDN*, November 3, 2002; Mark Coleman, "Clinton Seen with New Blonde," *The Scotsman*, September 18, 2002; Blair Golson, "Seagram's Heir to Sell Townhouse for $27 m," Manhattan Transfers, *NYO*, August 5, 2002; "Next Chapter," *NYP*, June 12, 2002; "Tabloid Tale of Bill and Babe," *NYP*, April 19, 2002.

72. Mark Updegrove, Interview with author, October 22, 2006.

73. Interview; source wishes to remain anonymous.

74. Interview; source wishes to remain anonymous.

75. Vartan Gregorian, Interview with author, December 14, 2006.

76. Eric Schmertz, Interview with author, September 1, 2006; Natalie Datlof, Interview with author, September 15, 2006.

77. Mark Thomann, Interview with author, December 14, 2006.

78. Michael Crowley, "The Real Reason She Won't Apologize, Hillary's War," *New Republic*, April 2, 2007; Susan Baer, "Hillary's World," *Washingtonian*, April 2007; Daniela Deane, "Dream House II: "How the Clintons Found Their New Home—Fast—in D.C.," *WP*, January 20, 2001; Sally Bedell Smith, *For Love of Politics: Bill and Hillary Clinton: The White House Years*, Random House, 2007, p. 436.

79. Susan Baer, "Hillary's World," *Washingtonian*, April 2007; R. Emmett Tyrrell Jr., *The Clinton Crack-up: The Boy President's Life After the White House*, Thomas Nelson, 2007, p. 37; Mike Glover, "Clinton Makes Campaign a Family Business," AP, December 8, 2007.

80. As quoted in Peter Baker and John Solomon, "Books Paint Critical Portraits of Clinton; 2 Biographies Detail Marital Strife and Driving Ambition," *WP*, May 25, 2007.

81. Melvin Gitler, Interview with author, September 29, 2006.

82. Chris Jennings, Interview with author, August 2, 2006.

83. Don Hewitt, Interview with author, September 7, 2006.

84. Interview; source wishes to remain anonymous.

85. Interview; source wishes to remain anonymous.

86. Interview; source wishes to remain anonymous.

87 David Schulte, Interview with author, December 8, 2006.

88. Maureen Dowd, "Fireworks for Former First Lady and Future First Lad," *NYT*, July 4, 2007.

89. Mark Adams, "It Happened Last Week," *NY mag*, August 27, 2007.

90. Interview; source wishes to remain anonymous.

91. Jonathan Alter, Interview with author, August 10, 2006.

92. Interview; source wishes to remain anonymous.

93. Don Fowler, Interview with author, February 14, 2007.

94. Mark Buell, Interview with author, August 22, 2006.

95. Jake Siewert, Interview with author, January 15, 2007.

Chapter 10 HILLARY'S (AND BILL'S) RUN FOR THE WHITE HOUSE

1. Simon Rosenberg, Interview with author, January 26, 2007.

2. Interview—source wishes to remain anonymous; Scott Reed, Interview with author, December 1, 2006.

3. Interview—source wishes to remain anonymous; Lynn Sweet, "Did Hillary Underestimate Obama? Book Says Clinton Team Didn't View Obama as a Huge Political Threat Late Last Year," C S-T, June 8, 2007.

4. Chris Jennings, Interview with author, August 2, 2006.

5. As quoted in Michiko Kakutani, "From the Sidelines, a View of the Middle as the Loser," NYT, April 3, 2007.

6. E-mail responses to author's questions from Dick Morris, August 29, 2006.

7. Federal News Service, December 18, 2006.

8. Interview; source wishes to remain anonymous.

9. Patrick Healy, "For Clintons, Delicate Dance of Married and Public Lives," NYT, May 23, 2006; Darryl Fears, "Coretta Scott King's Legacy Celebrated in Final Farewell," WP, February 8, 2006; Robert Schuller, Interview with author, December 1, 2006.

10. Douglas Brinkley, Interview with author, September 14, 2006.

11. Darryl Fears, "Coretta Scott King's Legacy Celebrated in Final Farewell," WP, February 8, 2006; Robert Schuller, Interview with author, December 1, 2006.

12. Joe Sharkey, "'Enabling' Is Now a Political Disease," NYT, September 27, 1998; David S. Broder, "Troubles for the Democrats," WP, September 11, 1998; Richard Morin and David S. Broder, "Worries About Nation's Morals Test a Reluctance to Judge," WP, September 11, 1998.

13. Patrick Healy, "Clinton Camp Turns to a Star in Money Race," NYT, March 31, 2007; Patrick Healy, "Obama Disputes Claim of Sharing Clinton's Stance on War," NYT, May 18, 2007.

14. Mark Buell, Interview with author, August 22, 2006.

15. Robert Novak, "Former 'Goldwater Girl' Tripped Up," C S-T, March 12, 2007.

16. Les Payne, "Could Hillary Clinton Also Be a 'Black' Leader?" Newsday.com, August 12, 2007.

17. Patrick Healy and Jeff Zeleny, "Clinton and Obama Unite in Pleas to Blacks," March 5, 2007; Mary Mitchell, "Bill Clinton Is Hillary's Best Bet to Bridging Her Racial Divide," C S-T, March 4, 2007; Nedra Pickler, "Obama, the Clintons Turn Selma Marches into Campaign Event," AP, March 4, 2007.

18. ABC News, May 19, 2007.

19. Jonathan Darman, "Does Bill Clinton Help or Hurt Hillary? It's Another First: The Spouse of an Ex-President Running for the White House. What Role Is He Playing, and What Would He Do as, Yes, 'First Gentleman'?" NW, May 28, 2007.

20. Patrick Healy, "After a Delicately Worded Pitch, Clinton Draws Cheers," NYT, February 20, 2007; Katharine Q. Seelye, "Clinton-Obama Quandary for Many Black Women," NYT, October 14, 2007.

21. Chris Cillizza and Dan Balz, "Clinton, Obama Camps' Feud Is Out in the Open," WP, February 22, 2007.

22. Patrick Healy, "Political Memo: Clinton Reminds New Hampshire, I'm with Bill," NYT, February 13, 2007; ABC News, "Clinton on Rove, Gingrich, and DeLay: 'I'm the One Person They Are Most Afraid Of,'" February 11, 2007.

23. Fran Spielman, "Rare Daley Move: Endorses Obama for Primary," C S-T, December 20, 2006; Paul Merrion, "What's a Dem Donor to Do? Local Bigwigs Agonize Over Choice Between an Old Pal and a Hometown Hero," Crain's Chicago Business, January 15, 2007.

24. Jill Zuckman, "Democratic Candidates Jockey for Top Fundraisers," CT, February 9, 2007; Mike McIntire and Leslie Wayne, "Democrats Turning Away Money from a Fugitive," NYT, August 31, 2007; Matthew Mosk, "The $75 Million Woman: Barack Obama's Finance Director Helped Transform a Fledgling Campaign into a Fundraising Machine," WP, October 8, 2007.

25. Jill Zuckman, "Democratic Candidates Jockey for Top Fundraisers," CT, February 9, 2007.

26. Robert Clifford, Interview with author, June 6, 2006; Lynn Sweet, "Obama Talking Small Bucks, Thinking Big; 'Ordinary' Donors No Match for Elite 'Bundlers,'" C S-T, April 15, 2007.

27. Maureen Dowd, "Obama's Big Screen Test: Hillary Is Not David Geffen's Dreamgirl," NYT, February 21, 2007. New York Sun, February 22, 2007.

28. Patrick Healy and Jeff Zeleny, "Clinton and Obama Unite in Pleas to Blacks," March 5, 2007; Mary Mitchell, "Bill Clinton Is Hillary's Best Bet to Bridging Her Racial Divide," C S-T, March 4, 2007; Nedra Pickler, "Obama, the Clintons Turn Selma Marches into Campaign Event," AP, March 4, 2007.

29. John R. Emshwiller and Merissa Marr, "Return to Treasure Island: Hollywood's Moguls Compete to Raise Cash for Democratic Candidates. Whose House Is Better?" WSJ, March 17, 2007; David M. Halbfinger, "Politicians Are Doing Hollywood Star Turns," NYT, February 6, 2007.

30. Irena Medavoy, Interview with author, October 23, 2006.

31. Darius Anderson, Interview with author, December 21, 2006.

32. Anne E. Kornblut, "Clinton Fights to Keep Impeachment Taboo: After Spat, Campaigns Know to Expect Swift Reprisal for Any Hint of the Scandal," WP, February 25, 2007; Jeff Zeleny, "Obama's Back Fund-Raising in New York, Not Quietly," NYT, March 10, 2007; Evan Thomas, "Is Hillary Afraid of Being Embarrassed by Bill? Hillary Expected an Attack from the Right. But the Shots Came from an old Hollywood Buddy of Bill's," NW, March 5, 2007.

33. The Tonight Show with Jay Leno, NBC, December 1, 2006.

34. Melvin Gitler, Interview with author, September 29, 2006.

35. Simon Rosenberg, Interview with author, January 26, 2007.

36. Don Fowler, Interview with author, February 14, 2007.

37. Peter Hart, Interview with author, September 7, 2006.

38. Leon Panetta, Interview with author, October 17, 2006.

39. Dick Morris, e-mail responses to author's questions, August 29, 2006.

40. Paul Greenberg, Interview with author, October 4, 2006.

41. Tony Coelho, Interview with author, September 5, 2006.

42. Hank Sheinkopf, Interview with author, August 21, 2006.

43. William Greider, e-mail to author, August 7, 2006.

44. Patrick Healy, "Clinton Holds Strategy—Not Fund-Raising—Session," *NYT*, April 4, 2007; Jeanne Cummings, "It's Official: Obama, Clinton Way Out Front," *Politico*, July 16, 2007.

45. Mason-Dixon Polling and Research, June 29, 2007.

46. Terence Hunt, "Bush Spokesman Says Clintons Have Chutzpah for Criticizing Bush on Libby," AP, July 5, 2007.

47. Michael Luo, "'Comeback Kid' of '92, Now Half of Combo, Returns to New Hampshire," *NYT*, July 14, 2007.

48. Lynn Cutler, Interview with author, June 29, 2006.

49. John Catsimatidis, Interview with author, October 9, 2006.

50. Jonathan Darman, "Does Bill Clinton Help or Hurt Hillary? It's Another First: The Spouse of an Ex-President Running for the White House. What Role Is He Playing, and What Would He Do as, Yes, 'First Gentleman'?" *NW*, May 28, 2007.

51. Transcript, *Rush Limbaugh Show*, May 17, 2007; Patrick Healy, "Clinton Secures Endorsement of the Mayor of Los Angeles," *NYT*, May 30, 2007.

52. Patrick Healy, "Obama and Clinton Clash Over Iran," *NYT*, October 13, 2007; "Civil Rights Leader Backs Clinton," AP, October 13, 2007.

53. Maudlyne Ihejirika, "Bill Clinton Gets Hero's Welcome," *C S-T*, June 3, 2007.

54. "Is Hillary Secret Rev. Al Ally?" *NY mag*, April 9, 2007.

55. Raymond Hernandez, "Obama's Rise Strains Loyalty on Clinton Turf," *NYT*, April 24, 2007.

56. Jim Schachter, Interview with author, May 3, 2007.

57. David Schulte, Interview with author, December 8, 2006.

58. Douglas Brinkley, Interview with author, September 14, 2006.

59. Jeff Zeleny, "Obama Takes Sharper Tone to the Trail," *NYT*, August 17, 2007.

60. Peter Hecht, "Widening Her Lead; New Survey Shows Clinton Dominating the Democratic Field in California—Obama Said to Be Losing His Luster," *Sacramento Bee*, August 17, 2007.

61. Kristin Jensen, "Bill Clinton Says He Was More Experienced Than Obama," Bloomberg.com, September 28, 2007; Patrick Healy, "Bill Clinton Questions Obama's Experience," *NYT*, September 28, 2007; Tom Downey, Interview with author, January 9, 2007; Nedra Pickler, "Hillary Clinton Rivals Take On Bill," AP, November 6, 2007; *Hardball with Chris Matthews*, MSNBC, November 6, 2007; Ron Fournier, "'Good Bill' vs. 'Bad Bill,'" On Deadline, AP, November 28, 2007; Patrick

Healy, "Bill Clinton Flatly Asserts He Opposed War at Start," *NYT*, November 28, 2007; Marc Ambinder, "Bill Clinton . . . Well, He Just Puts Everything On the Table," *NYT*, December 14, 2007; Anne E. Kornblut and Alec MacGillis, "Warning of Threats, Clinton Sells Clinton," December 30, 2007; Mike Glover, "Clinton Says Hillary Was Always the One," AP, December 10, 2007; Howard Kurtz, "The First Laddie Issue Is Out of the Closet," *WP*, December 12, 2007; Glenn Thrush, "Clinton Insiders Question Top Aide's Approach," *Newsday*, December 12, 2007; Patrick Healy and John M. Broder, "A Campaign Retools to Seek Second Clinton Comeback," *NYT*, January 5, 2008; Nancy Benac, "Hillary Clinton Leans on 'Relic' Bill," AP, January 5, 2008; Mark Leibovich, "In New Hampshire, Bill Clinton Is Finding Less Spark," *NYT*, January 7, 2008; Ben Smith, "Racial Tensions Roil Democratic Race," *The Politico*, January 11, 2008; Carl Hulse, "Civil Rights Tone Prompts Talk of an Endorsement," *NYT*, January 11, 2008; Dorothy Rabinowitz, "The Battle Begins," *WSJ*, January 11, 2008; Michael Hill, "Powerhouse Chicago Preacher Draws Attention, and Plenty of Controversy," *Baltimore Sun*, January 16, 2008; Ben Smith, "Bill Clinton Says He Witnessed Voter Supression," January 19, 2008; Jonathan Alter, "Leading Democrats to Bill Clinton: Pipe Down," NW, January 19, 2008; "Barack vs. Bill: Obama Hits Ex-Prez Over 'Troubling' Attacks," ABC News, January 20, 2008; Rebecca Sinderbrand and Alexander Mooney, "Congressman to Bill Clinton: 'Chill a Little Bit,'" CNN, January 21, 2008; Jessica Yellin, "Obama: I feel Like I'm Running Against Both Clintons," CNN, January 21, 2008; Ben Smith, "Clinton Plan: Let Bill Lash Out," *The Politico*, January 22, 2008; Alec MacGillis and Anne E. Kornblut, "Some in Party Bristle at Clintons' Attacks," January 23, 2008; "Kerry Blasts Bill Clinton for 'Abusing Truth,'" CNNpolitics. com, January 25, 2008; Deborah Charles, "Bill Clinton Again Wagging Finger, Raising Eyebrows," Reuters, January 25, 2008; David Espo and Charles Babington, "Obama Runs Away with South Carolina Primary, January 26, 2008; Dan Balz, Anne E. Kornblut, and Shailagh Murray, "Obama Is Big Winner in S.C. Primary: Democratic Race Continues with No Clear Front-Runner," WP, January 27, 2008; Jake Tapper, "Bubba: Obama Is Just Like Jesse Jackson," ABC, January 26, 2008; Alexander Mooney, "Exit Polls: Bill Clinton's Effect," CNN, January 26, 2008; Vaughn Ververs, "Bill Clinton's Lost Legacy," CBS, January 26, 2008; Caroline Kennedy, "A President Like My Father," *NYT*, January 27, 2008; Katharine Q. Seelye, "Ex-President, Back in the Thick of It," *NYT*, January 27, 2008; Robert Novak, *C S-T*, January 27, 2008; Abdon M. Pallasch, "Black Vote Key to Obama Blowout," *C S-T*, January 27, 2008; Mike Allen and Carrie Budoff Brown, "Ted Kennedy Embraces Obama," *The Politico*, January 28, 2008; Rick Klein, "Author Toni Morrison to Endorse Obama," ABC News, January 28, 2008; Patrick Healy, "Clinton Camp Seeks Gentler Role for Ex-President," *NYT*, January 28, 2008; Adam Nagourney, "Races Entering Complex Phase Over Delegates," *NYT*, January 28, 2008; Roger Simon, "Obama: Resident of the New Camelot?" *The Politico*, January 28, 2008; Jeff Zeleny, "Kennedy Backs Obama with 'Old Politics' Attack," *NYT*, January 29, 2008; Jonathan Kaufman and Gerald F. Seib, "Two Plays for Latino Vote," *WSJ*, January 29, 2008. Douglas A. Blackmon, "Carter Stays Neutral in Race, But Praises Obama's Oratory," *WSJ*, January 30, 2008; Jake Tapper, "Bill: 'We Just Have to Slow Down Our Economy' to Fight Global Warming," ABC news, January 31, 2008; Mary Ann Akers, "Clinton's LBJ Comments Infuriated Ted Kennedy," *WP*, January 31, 2008; Peter Baker, "Bill Clinton's Legacy: How Former President Is Viewed Could Affect Vote," *WP*, February 3, 2008; Alexander Mooney, "Poll Suggests Obama, Clinton in Dead Heat in California," CNN, February 3, 2008; Jessica Yellin, "Bill Clinton Tours African American Churches," CNN, February 3, 2008; Tim Russert, *Meet the Press*, NBC-TV, February 3, 2008; Alexander Mooney, "Richardson: No Endorsement Yet," CNN, February 4, 2008; Katharine Q. Seelye, "What About Bill?" *NYT*, February 4, 2008: "Clinton Says Her Campaign is Taking a Page from the New York Giants," AP, February 4, 2008; Geoff Earle, "For Cryin' Out Loud! Hillary Turns on the Tears Again," *NYP*, February 5, 2008; Chris Cillizza, "Obama Beats Clinton in Georgia," *WP*, February 5, 2008; Katharine Q. Seelye, "Live Blogging the Democratic Contests," *NYT*, February 5, 2008; Dan Balz and Anne E. Kornblut, "Clinton and Obama Trade Victories: N.Y. Senator Withstands Push By Surging Rival in Key Battlegrounds," *WP*, February 6, 2008; David Paul Kuhn, "Race, Sex Divide Dems; Ideology Splits GOP," *The Politico*, February 6, 2008; Bill Schneider, "How Trends Played out Nationally," CNN, February 6, 2008; Roger Simon, "Dems Head for Messy Nomination Process," *The Politico*, February 6, 2008; "No Rest for Clinton, Obama; 7 More Contests Fast Approach," CNN, February 6, 2008; Adam Cohen, "Will the Capital of Change Choose Change or Experience?" Editorial Observer, *NYT*, February 5, 2008; "Obama: Super Tuesday 'Big Victory' for His Campaign," CNN, February 6, 2008; Bob Herbert, "Questions For The Clintons," *NYT*, January 26, 2008; Shailagh Murray and Matthew Mosk, "Clinton Lent Her Campaign $5 Million: Delegate Race With Obama Is Nearly Even," *WP*, February 7, 2008; Bill Turque and Anne E. Kornblut, "Va. Is Next Battleground In Democrats' Long Fight," *WP*, February 7, 2008; George F. Will, "Democrats Living Dangerously; Early Voting Insanity and a GOP Gift," *WP*, February 7, 2008; Timothy Noah, "Triumph of the Arithmecrats," Chatterbox, *Slate*, February 6, 2008; Christopher Cooper and Amy Chozick, "Deadlocked Democrats Brace for Long Run: Clinton Seeks Cash, Obama Needs Latinos," *WSJ*, February 7, 2008; June Kronholz, "Democrats' Nightmare: Back to Smoke-Filled Rooms," WSJ, February 7, 2008; Monica Davey, "Razor-Thin Margins in Missouri Reflect Nationwide Split," *NYT*, February 7, 2008; Jennifer Steinhauer, "Unusual Divides in California Benefit McCain and Clinton," *NYT*, February 7, 2008; Marc Ambinder, "A Fine Mess," *NYT*, February 7, 2008; Kenneth R. Bazinet, "Chelsea Clinton Taking an Expanded Role in Hillary's Campaign," *NYDN*, February 8, 2008; Susan Donaldson James, "Passing the Torch: Kennedy's Touch on Obama's Words; Ted Sorensen, Legendary Speechwriter, Lends Support, Eloquence to Democratic Contender," ABC News, February 8, 2008; Stephen Ohlemacher, "Obama Leads Clinton by Only 2 Delegates," AP, February 9, 2008; Michael D. Shear and Anne E. Kornblut, "Obama Handily Wins Nebraska, Louisiana, Washington," *WP*, February 10, 2008; "Democrats Kick off Virginia Campaign," CNN, February 10, 2008; Adam Nagourney and Carl Hulse, "Democrats Woo Superdelegates," *NYT*, February 10, 2008; "Half-Way There," *The Economist*, February 9–15, 2008; Matthew Mosk and Paul Kane, "796 Insiders May Hold Democrats' Key," *WP*, February 10, 2008; Ben Smith, "Obama wins Maine," *The Politico*, February 10, 2008; Hamil R. Harris, "Bill

Clinton Stumps at Area Churches," WP, February 11, 2008; Josh Freedom duLac, "Obama Beats Clinton for Award," WP, February 11, 2008; Katharine Q. Seelye, "Maine to Obama; Clinton Replaces Campaign Leader," NYT, February 11, 2008; Maggie Haberman, "Latino Slams Clinton," NYP, February 12, 2008; Jay Newton-Small, "Can Obama Keep the Momentum?" Time, February 12, 2008; Chris Cillizza, "Obama Defeats Clinton in Virginia Primary," WP, February 12, 2008; Bill Nichols, "Obama Sweeps Potomac Primary," The Politico, February 12, 2008; Alexander Mooney, "Exit Polls: Obama Stealing Clinton's Base," CNN, February 12, 2008; Ben Smith, Avi Zenilman, and Kenneth P. Vogel, "Obama Takes on New Aura of Momentum," The Politico, February 13, 2008; Jonathan Weisman, "Shifting Loyalties: Cracks in Clinton Coalition May Mark a Turning Point," WP, February 13, 2008; Ron Fournier, "On Deadline," "Chickens Come Home to Roost," AP, February 12, 2008; Howard Kurtz, "Hillary Sinks in Potomac," WP, February 13, 2008; Dan Balz and Tim Craig, "Winning Streak Extends To District, Md. and Va," WP, February 13, 2008; Anne E. Kornblut, "Clinton Makes a Play for Wisconsin," WP, February 13, 2008; Mary Mitchell, "Hillary's Move Riles Hispanic Supporters: Dumping Campaign Manager Solis Doyle Possibly Backfiring," C S-T, February 14, 2008; Karen Tumulty, "Is It Too Late for Hillary?" Time, February 14, 2008; Emily Fredrix, "Bill Clinton: Choose Record Not Speeches," AP, February 14, 2008; Mike Allen, "Clinton Pits Herself Against Business," The Politico, February 14, 2008; Peter Hamby, "Valentine's Day with Hillary Clinton," CNN, February 14, 2008; Margaret Carlson, "Clinton, Iron Lady, Needs Another Game Plan," Bloomberg.com, February 15, 2008; "Some Black Superdelegates Reassess Clinton Support," CNN, February 14, 2008; Peggy Noonan, "Confidence or Derangement?" WSJ, February 15, 2008; Abdon M. Pallasch, "Bill Touts Hillary's 'Solutions'," C S-T, February 15, 2008; Jackie Calmes, "Clinton Bets Big on Ohio and Texas," WSJ, February 15, 2008; Domenico Montanaro, "Bill Blames Obama for Ouster of Candidates," MSNBC First Read, February 16, 2008; Robert Novak, "Hillary to Paint Obama as Leftist," C S-T, February 17, 2008; Mary Murray, "Bill Spars with Obama Supporter," MSNBC First Read, February 17, 2008; Mike Dorning, "Wisconsin to Obama Decisively," CT, February 20, 2008; Jackie Calmes, "Obama Holds Off Clinton in Wisconsin," WSJ, February 20, 2008; Patrick Healy and Jeff Zelany, "Wisconsin Hands Obama Victory, Ninth in a Row," NYT, February 20, 2008; John Meachem, "The Editor's Desk," NW, February 25, 2008; Rebecca Sinderbrand, "Superdelegate Schmoozed by Chelsea, Backs Obama," CNN, February 22, 2008; Ronn Fournier, "Race is Obama's to Lose," On Deadline, AP, February 20, 2008; Sarah Wheaton, "Bill Clinton Raises the Stakes of 2 Contests Next Month," NYT, February 22, 2008; Rebecca Sinderbrand, "Clinton Won't Clarify Post-March 4 Plans," CNN, February 22, 2008; Roger Simon, "Dem Tension Hinges on Plagiarism Charges," The Politico, February 22, 2008; Hardball with Chris Matthews, NBC, February 22, 2008; Mark Leibovich, "No Longer in Race, Richardson Is a Man Pursued," NYT, February 23, 2008.

62. Interview; source wishes to remain anonymous.

63. Elaine Kamarck, Interview with author, October 10, 2006.

64. Larry Sabato, Interview with author, July 31, 2006.

65. Jim Hornstein, Interview with author, September 27, 2006.

66. Lou Susman, Interview with author, May 30, 2006.

67. Michael Barone, Interview with author, September 19, 2006.

68. Ray Lesniak, Interview with author, September 16, 2006.

69. Kane Webb, Interview with author, February 6, 2007.

70. Jo Becker and Don Van Natta Jr., "An Ex-President, a Mining Deal and a Big Donor," *NYT*, January 31, 2008; Doug Ward, *Vancouver Sun*, June 21, 2007; Michael Isikoff and Mark Hosenball, "Here An F.O.B., There An F.O.B." *NW*, February 4, 2008; Andy Hoffman, "Giustra, Clinton Host Fete," *The Globe and Mail* (Canada), January 17, 2008; Melissa Leong, "Cupcakes and Stars at Clinton Bash in Toronto: 60th Birthday—Again," *National Post* (Canada), September 11, 2006; Don Van Natta Jr., Jo Becker, and Mike McIntire, "In His Charity and Her Politics, Many Clinton Donors Overlap," *NYT*, December 20, 2007; Frank Rich, "The Billary Road to Republican Victory," *NYT*, January 27, 2008; "Clinton's Filthy Lucre," editorial, *Investor's Business Daily*, February 4, 2008; "Who Was Hillary Clinton," editorial, *WSJ*, February 2, 2008; Josh Gerstein, "Clinton's 'Considered' Reply on Donors: Not Yet," *New York Sun*, September 28, 2007; Peter Baker and Matthew Mosk, "No Names Please: Clintons Mum on Donors," *WP*, September 28, 2007; Peter Baker, "Bill Clinton's Legacy: How Former President Is Viewed Could Affect Vote," *WP*, February 3, 2008; Howard Fineman and Richard Wolffe, "'What She Can't Do Is Have It Both Ways'," *NW*, November 12, 2007; Michael Isikoff, "The Hillary Paper Chase: 3,022,030 Documents To Go," *NW*, November 12, 2007; Jim VandeHei and Mike Allen, "Five Reasons Hillary Should Be Worried," *The Politico*, February 6, 2008; Nedra Pickler, "Analysis: Clinton and Obama Enter Protracted Campaign That May Not End For Weeks," AP, February 6, 2008; Jeanne Cummings, "Obama on Pace to Raise $30 Mil in Feb," February 7, 2008; Shailagh Murray and Matthew Mosk, "Clinton Lent Her Campaign $5 Million: Delegate Race With Obama Is Nearly Even," *WP*, February 7, 2008; Perry Bacon Jr., "The Trail," "Clinton Emphasizes Loan was 'My Money'," *WP*, February 6, 2008; Jim Kuhnhenn, "Clinton Lends Her Campaign $5 Million as Rival Barack Obama Outraised Her," AP, February 6, 2008; Matthew Mosk, "Aggressive Obama TV Spending Prompted Clinton's Loan," *WP*, February 8, 2008; Mike Allen, "Hillary Hits Obama on Transparency, Style," *The Politico*, February 11, 2008; John R. Emshwiller and Jose De Cordoba, "Bill Clinton's Complex Charities: Former President Works Global Ties; Giustra Relations," *WSJ*, February 14, 2008; "Monica Langley and Amy Chozick, "Clinton Team Seeks to Calm Turmoil," *WSJ*, February 14, 2008; Joe Hallet, "The People of Ohio Get Me," *The Columbus Dispatch*, February 14, 2008; Nedra Pickler, "Obama Supports Individual Gun Rights," AP, February 5, 2008; Martina Stewart, "Obama Backers Suggest Clintons Lack Candor, Resist Disclosure," CNN, February 15, 2008; Elliott Blair Smith, "Cloud Over Air Bubba," *NYP*, February 22, 2008; John R. Emshwiller and James Bandler, "Clintons' Tax Returns Would Cast a Wider Light," *WSJ*, February 23, 2008; Jonathan Alter, "Between the Lines," "Hillary Should Get Out Now," *NW*, March 3, 2008.

Chapter 11 FIRST GENT: A DOLLEY MADISON FOR THE TWENTY-FIRST CENTURY?

1. Melanne Verveer, Interview with author, January 27, 2007.

2. Kate Snow, "Bill Clinton as First Gentleman," *Nightline*, ABC News, July 13, 2007; Ryan Lizza, "The Legacy Problem: Hillary and Her Rivals Take On the Clinton Administration," *NYer*, September 17, 2007.

3. *This Week with George Stephanopoulos*, September 30, 2007.

4. Peter Hart, Interview with author, September 7, 2006.

5. Sarah Wilson, Interview with author, February 16, 2007.

6. Leon Panetta, Interview with author, October 17, 2006.

7. Patrick Healy, "Clinton's Altered Iowa Speech," NYT, September 3, 2007; Jackie Calmes, "Two-for-One Deal, Take Two: Hillary Clinton Eases Her Husband into the Campaign Limelight," *WSJ*, September 4, 2007.

8. Lanny Breuer, Interview with author, October 30, 2006; Interview—source wishes to remain anonymous.

9. Alan Solomont, Interview with author, August 9, 2006; "Bill Clinton: I'd Sit in on Hillary's Cabinet Meetings 'Only If Asked,'" ABC News, December 5, 2007.

10. Jonathan Darman, "Does Bill Clinton Help or Hurt Hillary? It's Another First: The Spouse of an Ex-President Running for the White House. What Role Is He Playing, and What Would He Do as, Yes, 'First Gentleman'?" NW, May 28, 2007.

11. Bob Kerrey, Interview with author, July 5, 2005.

12. Patrick Healy, "Clinton as First Spouse," *NYT*, May 9, 2007.

13. Alan Solomont, Interview with author, August 9, 2006.

14. Bob Kerrey, Interview with author, July 5, 2006.

15. Kate Snow, "Bill Clinton as First Gentleman," *Nightline*, ABC News, July 13, 2007.

16. Mark Buell, Interview with author, August 22, 2006; Chris Jennings, Interview with author, August 2, 2006; Alan Solomont, Interview with author, August 9, 2006; *Larry King Live*, CNN, April 19, 2007; Patrick Healy, "Clinton as First Spouse," *NYT*, May 9, 2007.

17. Tony Coelho, Interview with author, September 5, 2006.

18. Chris Jennings, Interview with author, August 2, 2006.

19. *Late Show with David Letterman*, CBS, September 4, 2007.

20. Howard Tullman, Interview with author, June 26, 2006; O. Kay Henderson, "Clinton Predicts His Wife Will Win By 'Good Margin,'" Iowa Radio News, November 8, 2007; Thomas Beaumont, "Stumping For Wife, Clinton Can Help, or Hurt, Anybody," *Des Moines Register*, November 25, 2007; Holly Ramer, "Clinton Says Wife Is a 'World-Class Genius,'" AP, December 21, 2007.

21. Carl S. Anthony, e-mail to author, October 3, 2006.

22. Gery Chico, Interview with author, December 1, 2006.

23. Roger Friedman, "Hillary Clinton's $2.6 Million Hollywood Hit," Fox News, March 25, 2007.

24. Carla Marinucci, "Clinton Sees Role for Husband Campaign 2008: Senator Tells S.F. Crowd the Former President Could Be a Diplomat," *San Francisco Chronicle*, February 24, 2007.

25. Perry Bacon Jr., "Candidate Clinton Praises Ambassador Clinton," WP, May 26, 2007; Carla Marinucci, "Clinton Sees Role for Husband Campaign 2008: Senator Tells S.F. Crowd the Former President Could Be a Diplomat," San Francisco Chronicle, February 24, 2007; Larry King Live, CNN, April 19, 2007; Tim Russert, Meet the Press, NBC, September 30, 2007; Sally Bedell Smith, For Love of Politics: Bill and Hillary Clinton: The White House Years, Random House, 2007, pp. 25–26; "Obama's Dream Cabinet? Bill and Al," The View from the Swamp, CT, November 30, 2007; Sally Bedell Smith, "Two Presidents in the White House?" WSJ, December 11, 2007.

26. Sarah Wilson, Interview with author, February 16, 2007.

27. Jonathan Alter, Interview with author, August 10, 2006.

28. Sandy Berger, Interview with author, July 27, 2006.

29. Tony Lake, Interview with author, November 1, 2006.

30. Tim Wirth, Interview with author, November 7, 2006.

31. Sandy Berger, Interview with author, July 27, 2006.

32. Theodore Sorensen, Interview with author, August 16, 2006.

33. Alan Solomont, Interview with author, August 9, 2006.

34. Rahm Emanuel, Interview with author, July 21, 2006.

35. Joseph Stiglitz, Interview with author, February 12, 2007.

36. James Chapman, "Blair Tipped to Be World Bank President as Disgraced Wolfowitz Resigns," Daily Mail, May 18, 2007.

37. David Saperstein, Interview with author, September 26, 2006.

38. Robert Torricelli, Interview with author, October 6, 2006; Herman Berliner, Interview with author, October 5, 2006.

39. Interview; source wishes to remain anonymous.

40. Alan Solomont, Interview with author, August 9, 2006.

41. Ephraim Hardcastle, Daily Mail, July 2, 1999.

42. Interview; source wishes to remain anonymous.

43. Interview; source wishes to remain anonymous.

44. Mark Buell, Interview with author, August 22, 2006; Susie Tompkins Buell, Interview with author, September 5, 2006.

45. Susie Tompkins Buell, Interview with author, September 5, 2006.

46. Mark Buell, Interview with author, August 22, 2006; Irena Medavoy, Interview with author, October 23, 2006; Sally Bedell Smith, For Love of Politics: Bill and Hillary Clinton: The White House Years, Random House, 2007, p. 63.

47. Mark Buell, Interview with author, August 22, 2006.

48. Susie Tompkins Buell, Interview with author, September 5, 2006.

49. Tom Vilsack, Interview with author, January 29, 2007.

50. Carl S. Anthony, e-mail to author, October 3, 2006.

51. Lynn Cutler, Interview with author, June 29, 2006.

52. The Daily Show with Jon Stewart, Comedy Central, September 20, 2007.

53. Larry King Live, CNN, April 19, 2007.

54. Susan Schindehette, "The Ties That Bind," People, February 15, 1999.

55. Susan Davis, Interview with author, November 22, 2006.

56. Chelsea Clinton, "Being There: Chelsea Clinton in Her Own Words," *Talk*, December 2001/January 2002.

57. Jaimee Rose, "From Awkward Teenager to Savvy Celebrity," *The Times Union*, May 23, 2002; Damian Whitworth, "Chelsea Is Her Father's Daughter: While Her Classmates Are Not Sold on Her Charms, All Are Certain That the Young Clinton Will Enter Politics," *Ottawa Citizen*, May 21, 2002; Sarah Lyall, "Britain Is Becoming, Chelsea Clinton Finds," *NYT*, March 31, 2002.

58. Jodi Kantor, "Chelsea Clinton Is Primed for Another Parent's White House Run," *NYT*, July 31, 2007.

59. Philip Sherwell, "Hillary Clinton Turns to Chelsea in a Bid to Soften Her Image," *Sunday Telegraph*, January 29, 2007; Susan Davis, Interview with author, November 22, 2006.

60. Landon Thomas Jr., "Hedge Fund Chiefs, with Cash, Join Political Fray," *NYT*, January 25, 2007.

61. Jodi Kantor, "Chelsea Clinton Is Primed for Another Parent's White House Run," *NYT*, July 31, 2007; "Who Makes How Much—*New York*'s Salary Guide 2005."

62. David Schulte, Interview with author, December 8, 2006.

63. Robert Patterson, Interview with author, January 4, 2007.

64. Victor Fleming, Interview with author, November 2, 2006.

65. Interview—source wishes to remain anonymous; Donna Shalala, Interview with author, September 25, 2006.

66. Don Hewitt, Interview with author, September 7, 2006.

67. Mark Buell, Interview with author, August 22, 2006.

68. Brian Ross and Joseph Rhee, "Former Congressman Duped by Nigerian Scams," The Blotter, ABC News, December 8, 2006; John E. Harris, *The Survivor*, Random House, 2005; Nigel Hamilton, *Bill Clinton: Mastering the Presidency*, Public Affairs, 2007; Bill Clinton, *My Life*, Knopf, 2004; AP candidate biographies; Lloyd Grove, "Chelsea's Morning," *New York* magazine, march 3, 2008.

69. Howard Tullman, Interview with author, June 26, 2006.

70. Bill Simmons, Interview with author, August 24, 2006.

71. Lou Weisbach, Interview with author, July 11, 2006.

72. Interview; source wishes to remain anonymous.

73. Robert Sam Anson, "Bill and His Shadow," *VF*, June 2004.

74. Melvin Gitler, Interview with author, September 29, 2006.

75. Conrad Black, Interview with author, December 14, 2006.

76. Patricia Calhoun, Interview with author, June 23, 2006.

77. Ibid.; Mary Anna Towler, "Missing (Bill) Clinton," *City Newspaper/Rochester* .*gyrosite.com*, June 28, 2006.

78. Patricia Calhoun, Interview with author, June 23, 2006.

79. http://search.westword.com.

80. Patricia Calhoun, Interview with author, June 23, 2006.

81. Susie Tompkins Buell, Interview with author, September 5, 2006.

82. Ibid.

83. Carol Beggy and Mark Shanahan, "Simon Says Happy Birthday, Mr. President," *BG*, August 22, 2006.

84. David D. Kirkpatrick, "Follow the Money(ed)," *NYT*, August 21, 2007.

85. Dan Balz, "Bill Clinton's 60th Birthday Benefit Blowout," *WP*, September 28, 2006.

86. Robert Novak, "Clinton Ally, a Washington Super-Lawyer, Switches Allegiance to Back Obama," *C S-T*, March 4, 2007; Evan Thomas, "Fragged by an F.O.B.; Hillary Expected an Attack from the Right. But the Shots Came From an Old Hollywood Buddy of Bill's," *NW*, March 5, 2007.

87. Dan Balz, "Bill Clinton's 60th Birthday Benefit Blowout," *WP*, September 28, 2006; Matthew Miller, "The Rise of Ron Burkle," *Forbes*, December 11, 2006; Bob Tyrrell, "Birthday Boy Bubba," August 24, 2006, www.JewishWorldReview.com.

88. Ben Shapiro, "Clinton's Prostate Turns 60," August 23, 2006, http://www.town hall.com/columnists/BenShapiro/2006/08/23/clintons_prostate_turns_60.

89. As quoted in David Bauder, "Dignitaries Remember Bradley at Memorial," AP, November 21, 2006; as quoted in Jacques Steinberg, "Subjects and Colleagues Recall Ed Bradley," *NYT*, November 22, 2006.

90. Adam Clymer, "Scholars and Officials Alike Gather in Schlesinger Tribute," *NYT*, April 24, 2007.

91. Tony Coelho, Interview with author, September 5, 2006.

92. Bill White, Interview with author, September 26, 2006.

93. Melanne Verveer, Interview with author, January 27, 2007.

94. Theodore Sorensen, Interview with author, August 16, 2006.

95. Phyllis Brandon, Interview with author, June 27, 2006; "Carl Whillock; Clinton Adviser, Leader in Arkansas," *WP*, November 23, 2005.

96. Tom Vilsack, Interview with author, January 29, 2007; Tony Leys, "Clinton Joins in Farewell to Gleason," *Des Moines Register*, March 31, 2006; Thomas Beaumont, "Clinton's Tribute to Gleason Is Simple and Personal," *Des Moines Register*, March 31, 2006.

97. Jim Guy Tucker, Interview with author, November 13, 2006; "Ex-Fair Chief, State Official Pledger Dies," *A D-G*, April 1, 2006.

98. Phil Stefani, Interview with author, August 15, 2006.

99. Thomas Kean, Interview with author, January 22, 2007; Alvin S. Felzenberg, *Governor Tom Kean: From the New Jersey Statehouse to the 9-11 Commission*, Rivergate Books/Rutgers University Press, 2006, p. 395.

Chapter 12 GETTING THE FULL CLINTON — PRO BONO

1. Jonathan Alter, Interview with author, August 10, 2006.

2. Lou Susman, Interview with author, May 30, 2006.

3. Jonathan Alter, Interview with author, August 10, 2006.

4. John Emerson, Interview with author, September 20, 2006.

5. Bud Yorkin, Interview with author, October 9, 2006.

6. Devlin Barrett, "Disclosure Forms Show Bill Clinton Made More Than $10 Million

from Speeches Last Year," AP, June 14, 2007; John Solomon and Matthew Mosk, "For Clinton, New Wealth in Speeches; Fees in 6 Years Total Nearly $40 Million," WP, February 23, 2007.

7. Lee Miller, Interview with author, July 24, 2006.

8. Howard Tullman, Interview with author, June 26, 2006.

9. John Solomon and Matthew Mosk, "For Clinton, New Wealth in Speeches; Fees in 6 Years Total Nearly $40 Million," WP, February 23, 2007; Chris Fusco, Dave McKinney, and Lynn Sweet, "Lawyer with Rezko Link Helps Hillary; One 'Chair' of Chicago Fund-raiser Was Referenced in Indictment," C S-T, June 25, 2007; Chris Fusco, "Clinton Hasn't Returned Cash from Firm Under Investigation; Two Governors Decided to Give Up IPA Money," C S-T, June 25, 2007.

10. Mike McIntire, "Rubbing Shoulders with Trouble, and Presidents," NYT, May 7, 2006.

11. Matthew Mosk and John Solomon, "Largess to Clintons Lands CEO in Lawsuit; Case Is a Window on Couple's Ties," WP, May 26, 2007; Mike McIntire, "Suit Sheds Light on Clintons' Ties to a Benefactor," NYT, May 26, 2007; Mike McIntire, "Clinton Backer's Ties to Powerful Cut Both Ways," NYT, July 14, 2007; Sally Bedell Smith, For Love of Politics: Bill and Hillary Clinton: The White House Years, Random House, 2007.

12. Mike McIntire, "Clinton Backer's Ties to Powerful Cut Both Ways," NYT, July 14, 2007; Matthew Mosk, "SEC Opens Investigation of Company Headed by Key Supporter of Clintons," WP, November 22, 2007.

13. Maureen Dowd, "Can He Crush Hillary?" NYT, June 17, 2007.

14. Shannon McCaffrey, "Clinton PAC Raises $662,325 in First 6 Months," AP, July 20, 2001.

15. Janice Weinman Shorenstein, Interview with author, December 12, 2006.

16. Mickey Ibarra, Interview with author, November 7, 2006.

17. Rita McLennon, Interview with author, July 27, 2006.

18. Jim Hornstein, Interview with author, September 27, 2006.

19. Georgette Bennett, Interview with author, October 18, 2006.

20. John Solomon and Matthew Mosk, "For Clinton, New Wealth in Speeches; Fees in 6 Years Total Nearly $40 Million," WP, February 23, 2007; Devlin Barrett, "Disclosure Forms Show Bill Clinton Made More Than $10 Million from Speeches Last Year," AP, June 14, 2007.

21. Christopher Ogden, Interview with author, August 29, 2006.

22. Chris Jennings, Interview with author, August 2, 2006.

23. Interview; source wishes to remain anonymous.

24. Douglas Brinkley, Interview with author, September 14, 2006.

25. Kevin De Cock, Interview with author, December 6, 2006.

26. Christopher Ogden, Interview with author, August 29, 2006.

27. Sandy Berger, Interview with author, July 27, 2006.

28. Vartan Gregorian, Interview with author, December 14, 2006.

29. Susan Davis, Interview with author, November 22, 2006.

30. Douglas Brinkley, Interview with author, September 14, 2006; William Booth,

"Al Gore, Rock Star Oscar Hopeful May Be America's Coolest Ex-Vice President Ever," *WP*, February 25, 2007; Mike Allen, "Gore Nobel Boosts Talk of White House Run," *Politico*, October 12, 2007.

31. Bret Stephens, "Who Killed Palestine?" *WSJ*, June 26, 2007.

32. Joseph Stiglitz, Interview with author, February 12, 2007.

33. Tom Downey, Interview with author, January 9, 2007.

34. Stanislao Pugliese, Interview with author, September 21, 2006.

35. Mark Updegrove, Interview with author, October 22, 2006.

36. Michael Barone, Interview with author, September 19, 2006; Howard Schneider and Debbi Wilgoren, *WP*, October 12, 2007.

37. Al Kamen, "Rudderless Democrats Had Best Not Count On Bill Clinton Returning to the Political Fray Anytime Soon," *WP*, June 16, 2006.

38. Jonathan Alter, Interview with author, August 10, 2006.

39. Peter Osnos, the Century Foundation; Patricia Cohen, "Jimmy Carter the Book Tour (Soon to Be a Major Motion Picture)," *NYT*, October 11, 2007 (his twenty-fifth book, about his mother, will be published Mother's Day 2008).

40. Jonathan Alter, Interview with author, August 10, 2006.

41. Douglas Brinkley, Interview with author, September 14, 2006.

42. Julie Bosman, "Book on Bill Clinton Emerges from Years of Tapes," *NYT*, March 22, 2007.

43. Letter to author from Taylor Branch, August 18, 2006; Julie Bosman, "Book on Bill Clinton Emerges from Years of Tapes," *NYT*, March 22, 2007.

44. Amy Argetsinger and Roxanne Roberts, "A Scorching Response to a Food Critic," *WP*, March 23, 2007; Jonathan Alter, "Citizen Clinton Up Close," *NW*, April 8, 2002.

45. *Publishers Weekly*, July 10, 2006.

46. Sara Nelson, "Send the Bill," *Publishers Weekly*, July 16, 2007; "News Briefs," *Publishers Weekly*, July 16, 2007; Charlotte Abbott, "On Sale Next Week," *Publishers Weekly*, August 27, 2007.

47. "Forecasts," review of *Giving: How Each of Us Can Change the World*, by Bill Clinton, *Publishers Weekly*, September 4, 2007.

48. Peter Baker, "His Changing World; Bill Clinton Says He's Switched from 'Getting' to 'Giving,'" *Washington Post Book World*, September 9, 2007.

49. "'Giving' (And Also Getting)," Intelligencer, *NY mag*, September 17, 2007; Katharine Q. Seelye, "Moving to Avoid a Conflict," *NYT*, December 13, 2007; John R. Emshwiller, "Bill Clinton May Curb Ties to Burkle's Firm," *WSJ*, December 13, 2007; John R. Emshwiller, "Bill Clinton May Get Payout of $20 Million," *WSJ*, January 22, 2008.

50. Karoun Demirjian, "Clinton Draws Fans to Michigan Ave. Some Wait 12 Hours for 'About 5 Seconds,'" *CT*, September 8, 2007.

51. AP, "Sales of Bill Clinton Book Drops," October 16, 2007.

52. Tony Coelho, Interview with author, September 5, 2006.

53. Theodore Sorensen, Interview with author, August 16, 2006; Michael Barone, Interview with author, September 19, 2006.

54. Conrad Black, Interview with author, December 14, 2006; Barbara Ireland, "At the Home of F.D.R.'s Secret Friend," *NYT*, September 7, 2007.

55. Lynda Robb, Interview with author, January 12, 2007.

56. Carol Felsenthal, *Power, Privilege and the* Post: *The Katharine Graham Story,* Putnam, 1993, pp. 285–286.

57. Lynda Robb, Interview with author, January 12, 2007.

58. Ibid.; Charles Robb, Interview with author, October 23, 2006.

59. Charles Robb, Interview with author, October 23, 2006.

60. Theodore Sorensen, Interview with author, August 16, 2006.

61. Paul Orfalea, Interview with author, February 28, 2007.

62. Mark Updegrove, Interview with author, October 22, 2006.

63. Larry Sabato, Interview with author, July 31, 2006.

64. Jonathan Alter, Interview with author, August 10, 2006.

65. Jake Siewert, Interview with author, January 15, 2007.

66. "President Clinton's Eulogy at President Nixon's Funeral," AP, April 28, 1994.

67. Lynn Cutler, Interview with author, June 29, 2006.

68. Theodore Sorensen, Interview with author, August 16, 2006.

69. Conrad Black, Interview with author, December 14, 2006.

70. Ibid.; Harry F. Rosenthal, "Nixon Completes His Journey as Thousands Pay Respects," AP, April 27, 1994; Federal News Service, "Funeral Services for President Richard Milhous Nixon; Officiant: The Reverend Billy Graham; Eulogists: Henry A. Kissinger, Former Secretary of State, Senator Bob Dole (R-KS), Governor Pete Wilson (R-CA), President Clinton; the Richard Nixon Library and Birthplace, Yorba Linda, California," April 27, 1994.

71. Tom Shales, "The Missed Moment," WP, April 29, 1994.

72. "President Clinton's Eulogy at Nixon's Funeral," AP, April 28, 1994.

73. Hank Sheinkopf, Interview with author, August 21, 2006.

74. Tony Coelho, Interview with author, September 5, 2006.

75. Ray Lesniak, Interview with author, September 16, 2006.

76. Larry King, Interview with author, October 28, 2006.

77. Interview; source wishes to remain anonymous.

78. Nelson Shanks, Interview with author, September 14, 2006.

79. Jonathan Darman, "Does Bill Clinton Help or Hurt Hillary? It's Another First: The Spouse of an Ex-President Running for the White House. What Role Is He Playing, and What Would He Do as, Yes, 'First Gentleman'?" NW, May 28, 2007.

80. Phil Stefani, Interview with author, August 15, 2006.

81. Irena Medavoy, Interview with author, October 23, 2006; Interview—source wishes to remain anonymous.

82. Susan Baer, "Hillary's World," *Washingtonian,* April 2007.

83. Tom Vilsack, Interview with author, January 29, 2007.

84. Susie Tompkins Buell, Interview with author, September 5, 2006.

85. *The Daily Show with Jon Stewart,* Comedy Central, September 20, 2007.

86. John Emerson, Interview with author, September 20, 2006.

87. Don Hewitt, Interview with author, September 7, 2006.

88. Simon Rosenberg, Interview with author, January 26, 2007.

89. Jake Siewert, Interview with author, January 15, 2007.

90. Chris Stamos, Interview with author, November 2, 2006.

91. Anthony Campolo, e-mail to author, October 27, 2006.

92. Alan Solomont, Interview with author, August 9, 2006.

93. Lou Weisbach, Interview with author, July 11, 2006.

94. Leon Panetta, Interview with author, October 17, 2006.

Chapter 13 IT'S MONICA, STUPID!

1. Susan Davis, Interview with author, November 22, 2006.

2. Tim Wirth, Interview with author, November 7, 2006.

3. George McGovern, Interview with author, November 1, 2006.

4. Tony Coelho, Interview with author, September 5, 2006.

5. Peter Hart, Interview with author, September 7, 2006.

6. Patrick Creadon, Interview with author, October 31, 2006.

7. Don Hewitt, Interview with author, September 7, 2006; Simon Rosenberg, Interview with author, January 26, 2007; Patricia Calhoun, Interview with author, June 23, 2006; Rocky Anderson, Interview with author, October 20, 2006.

8. Interview; source wishes to remain anonymous.

9. Peggy Noonan, "Ford Without Tears," WSJ, December 30, 2006.

10. Larry King, Interview with author, October 28, 2006.

11. Lou Susman, Interview with author, May 30, 2006.

12. Interview; source wishes to remain anonymous.

13. Bob Clifford, Interview with author, June 6, 2006.

14. Leon Panetta, Interview with author, October 17, 2006.

15. Elaine Kamarck, Interview with author, October 10, 2006.

16. Douglas Brinkley, Interview with author, September 14, 2006.

INDEX